The Way of
Qigong

氣功之道

The Way of

Qigong

THE ART AND SCIENCE OF
CHINESE ENERGY HEALING

Kenneth S. Cohen

WITH A FOREWORD BY LARRY DOSSEY, M.D.

BALLANTINE BOOKS
NEW YORK

http://www.randomhouse.com

Library of Congress Cataloging-in-Publication Data
Cohen, Kenneth S., 1952–
The way of qigong = [Ch'i kung chi tao]: the art and science of
Chinese energy healing / by Kenneth S. Cohen;
with a foreword by Larry Dossey.
          p.   cm.
Parallel title in Chinese.
Includes bibliographical references and index.
ISBN 0-345-39529-8
1. Ch'i kung.   I. Title.
RA781.8.C64   1997
613.7'1—dc21   96–50407
                          CIP

Text design by Holly Johnson
Illustrations by Bonnie J. Curnock

Manufactured in the United States of America

First Edition: April 1997

10 9 8 7 6 5 4 3 2 1

To my teachers and colleagues.
And to my continuing teachers: my students.

The faith in the order of nature which has made possible the growth of science is a particular example of a deeper faith. This faith cannot be justified by any inductive generalisation. It springs from direct inspection of the nature of things as disclosed in our immediate present experience. . . . To experience this faith is to know that in being ourselves we are more than ourselves: to know that our experience, dim and fragmentary as it is, yet sounds the utmost depths of reality. . . .
　　　　　　—ALFRED NORTH WHITEHEAD
　　　SCIENCE AND THE MODERN WORLD

Contents

Acknowledgments

I make a deep bow to the teachers who started me on this path with their careful, patient instruction: Qigong and Daoist Master, Dr. Henry K. S. Wong, and Masters William C. C. Chen and B. P. Chan. I thank Tom Downes, Ph.D., for first introducing me to Taiji Quan in the late '60s and for standing by me as a friend and colleague. I thank Alan Watts, my dear mentor and friend, for his many lessons, his cosmic laughter, and for the confidence he placed in a young student. It was Alan who pointed me in the direction of Chinese studies and who first encouraged me as a writer.

I am also grateful for the opportunity to have studied with the following noted Masters of Qigong or Chinese Martial Arts: Stephen Chang, Adam Hsu, Share K. Lew, Liang Shou-yu, and Tang Ru-kun. Though my course of study with these individuals was brief, their influence was long. I also extend a special *Duo xie lao shi*, "Thank you so much, teacher" to Chen Style Taiji Quan Master and beloved friend, Madame Gao Fu for sharing her art so generously.

Taiji Quan Master T. T. Liang once said, "The best thing about Taiji is Taiji friends." I am so grateful to my Taiji and Qigong friends. I have learned from them, shared with them, as colleagues walking the same trail. Thank you to Masters: Dan Farber, Ken Fish, Paul Gallagher, Nonoy Gallano, S. H. Guan, Ray Hayward, Patricia Leung, Michael Mayer, Tom

McCombs, Harrison Moretz, David Mott, Janet Murphy, L. Shila, Mike Sigman, and Jampa Mackenzie Stewart.

Thank you to my past teachers of movement *as* meditation, who celebrate through the body the holiness of the everyday: Ruthy Alon, Josef Dellagrotte, Richard Freeman, Charlotte Selver and Charles Brooks, and Frank Wildman. And to the shining examples of simplicity and wisdom provided by Sunyata, Swami Venkatesananda, Millie Johnstone, Hisashi Yamada, and instructors from the Urasenke Tea Ceremony Society.

Academically and personally, I am indebted to the fine professors of Chinese language and culture who helped me to keep *wen* (scholarship) and *wu* (practical training) in balance: Professors Wolfram Eberhard, Huai I Juang, Nancy Lay, Irene Liu, Edward Schafer, Bernard Solomon, Michel Strickmann, and other faculty members of Queens College (NYC), the New School for Social Research, and UC Berkeley. I also thank my Chinese-language tutor, Madame Chu Xing-yan, whose brilliance and enthusiasm could inspire even a beginner to think in Chinese.

The more you know, the more you realize what you don't know. I am grateful to those who helped fill in the gaps—first, to my wife, Rebecca, for her critical eye, grammatical expertise, and constant support. She is a counselor in more ways than one. And to the scholars, researchers, and clinicians who contributed insight, data, suggestions and/or critical review: Megan Andersen, R.N., Daniel Benor, M.D., Bob Flaws, DOM, Elmer Green, Ph.D., Steve Fahrion, Ph.D., Robert Fried, Ph.D., Carla Hickey, M.S., Peter Parks, M.S., Carol Schneider, Ph.D., Barry Sears, Ph.D., Mark Seem, Ph.D., Norman Shealy, M.D., Ph.D., Professor Douglas Wile, and my colleagues at ISSSEEM, who continue to build a bridge between science and spirit. I also hope that master builders Rich Tillotson and Joe Buckmaster enjoy the fruit of their generosity in helping to create the elegant office from which these words were written.

How can I thank the many individuals who graced me with the warmth and hospitality of their homes as I, a wandering student, pursued twenty years of learning, training, and teaching? These include several of my Taiji friends listed above as well as Char Cato, Robert Johns, Philippe Leblond, Michele Rinfret, and so many others. I also thank Dr. Sandy Lillie and family for their generous support during a critical period of my research and life. And a special WADO and NYAWEH to Rolling Thunder, Keetoowah, and Twylah Nitsch, Native American elders and treasured friends who helped open my mind and heart to the connections between qigong and indigenous healing.

This work never would have spread far beyond my log cabin had it not been for the confidence, support, and integrity of my agent Ned Leavitt and the soulful business expertise of Tami Simon of Sounds True. My editor, Virginia Faber of Ballantine Books, helped me to speak with a clearer and stronger voice. If the reader reaps a good harvest from this book, it is because of Ginny's tireless, compassionate effort at pruning and nurturing the soul and substance of my work. I feel blessed to have found an editor so dedicated to excellence. I also thank Bonnie Curnock for her beautiful illustrations, Tu Xin-shi for his powerful and qi-full calligraphies, and Larry Dossey for his kind words at the beginning of this book.

Traditionally, a first book is dedicated to one's parents. I felt that they belonged on this page of acknowledgments. I thank my parents, Eleanor and Ronald, whose generosity allowed me to pursue an unusual and unconventional education from an early age. I also commend my daughter for putting up with Dad's frequent bouts of "computeritis" these past years.

And a thankfulness beyond words to the spirit of these high mountains who provided the most constant inspiration throughout the writing of this book.

—Ken Cohen
Indian Peaks Wilderness, Colorado
April 1997

Foreword

Sometimes we learn the lessons we most desperately need in the form of illness. That was my experience, and I know it is the experience of many persons who will read this book. Let me explain why Kenneth S. Cohen's insights could have helped me, and why they will benefit you.

As a first-year student I attempted to drop out of medical school because of chronic, classical migraine headache syndrome—recurrent episodes of blindness, nausea, vomiting, and insufferable headache, followed by periods of incapacitation. I was concerned I might injure someone during surgery if the blindness came on unpredictably, as it always did. My medical school adviser, however, convinced me to endure the problem and remain in school.

I was unaware at the time that my problem was compounded by anxiety, stress, and overwork. I was an excellent student—intelligent enough, and utterly compulsive and driven. I had no insight whatever into the mind-body relationships so commonly discussed today. In fact, I was unaware I *had* a mind-body connection. That came years later—when I discovered biofeedback and meditation, which for the first time allowed relief from the problem that nearly halted my career and made my life miserable.

When I recall my medical school experience, I regret that there were no Kenneth Cohens around. If there had been, I am certain my experience would have been pleasantly different. But at that time we medical students had never heard of qigong. I am delighted that the situation is changing.

Someday soon, the principles of healing you are about to read about will be taught in all our medical schools. In fact, this is already beginning to take place, as an increasing number of institutions develop courses in alternative or complementary medicine, including qigong.

There are two main reasons for the growing acceptance of these methods: They constitute both good science and authentic wisdom. Science and the venerable tradition of qigong are joining hands, as you are about to read. As a consequence, qigong can no longer be considered just a matter of faith or belief, nor as only a body of practical knowledge accumulated across the centuries, although this would be impressive enough. When the methods Cohen describes are subjected to rigorous empirical tests, they repeatedly demonstrate their worthiness. These developments are immensely important. They indicate not only increasing acceptance of qigong, but increasing openness within science and medicine as well.

Modern medicine, as everyone knows by now, can be spectacularly successful and woefully inadequate. It alternately inspires praise and condemnation. Almost every thinking person, both inside and outside the profession, realizes we need more than a mechanical, technical approach to healing. We hunger for a balance between body, mind, and spirit—which is contained in the healing approach of qigong.

In his discussion of qigong, Cohen wears two hats, as all modern healers should. First, he is a scientist. He realizes that science has become the dominant metaphor of our culture, and that we cannot ride roughshod over its methods and messages. Unlike many unorthodox healers who seem to carry a grudge against science, Cohen realizes it has something valuable to offer. Among other things, it remains a valuable way of guarding against certain kinds of delusions. Cohen's other hat is that of a healer and mystic—one who honors the great mysteries of existence, and who feels that a union with the Divine Principle—God, Goddess, Allah, the Dao, the Universe—is possible. I would never trust a healer who does not have respect for both science and spirituality. That is why I trust Cohen. That is why I recommend him to you.

Neither would I trust a healer who does not have a sense of humor. Cohen's lightness of heart comes through on every page. In a time when people are often "dead serious" about their health, humor and levity are needed more than ever.

Reading Cohen's book, I felt a connection that stayed with me from start to finish. One of Cohen's mentors was the late Alan Watts, the great scholar, teacher, and author of books on the wisdom of the Orient, particularly Zen Buddhism. Cohen pays homage to Watts in his acknowledgments; I pay mine here. In the spiritual desert of medical school, Watts's writings and tapes helped me to regrow my spiritual roots, for which I shall always remain grateful, and they remain a tonic with which I periodically refresh myself. His wisdom comes through in Cohen's insights. That is one reason I admire his book so much.

Throughout *The Way of Qigong*, Cohen never trivializes the great mysteries of healing. He is quick to acknowledge our limited understanding about how qigong healing takes place. He implies throughout that *it is acceptable not to know.* This is expressed in many ways—for example, the admonition to go slow in qigong practice; to be content with gradual, not meteoric, increases in wisdom; to occasionally do less ritual instead of more; and to rely on the invisible wisdom of the body and of nature, instead of always trying to *make* things happen.

Cohen's advice to cooperate with the healing power of nature will be a great challenge to many who encounter qigong for the first time. In our typically aggressive, extroverted way, we often try to whip nature into line. We "fight" our disease and try to "conquer" our illnesses. Prepare for a gentle approach. Qigong is not a hammer. In fact, its primary purpose is not to defeat disease at all, "but to become expert at being more fully who you are" (p. 183).

And who is *that?* The answer to the great question of who we are lies at the heart of the greatest healing traditions, including qigong. Gently, wisely, Cohen invites us to discover our Self—that part of us that is beyond illness, disease, and death—to discover, in the end, that we did not need his book to begin with.

Until that realization dawns, enjoy the paradox—and read on.

—Larry Dossey, M.D.
Author of *Healing Words:*
The Power of Prayer and
the Practice of Medicine

The Pronunciation of Chinese Words

The Chinese language consists of pictures, ideograms, rather than letters. Western scholars have devised various methods to represent the sound of these ideograms using roman letters. Until recently, most English-language works about Chinese culture used a system of romanization known as Wade–Giles. In the Wade–Giles system, the word for life energy, pronounced "chee" is spelled ch'i, and the art of cultivating this energy, "chee gung" is written ch'i-kung. Other common words include Tao and Taoism, pronounced "Dao" and "Daoism," referring to China's ancient school of philosophy and religion.

The Wade–Giles system was problematic because it did not set an international standard. Each country, including China, adopted its own method of representing Chinese. For instance, in the French *Dictionnaire Classique de la Langue Chinoise*, the word for martial arts, spelled "wu" in Wade–Giles, is written "ou." The active, masculine principle, commonly spelled "yang" in English, is written "iang." To make matters worse, individual authors, confused by these various conventions, sometimes invented their own systems of romanization. It became impossible for readers to know when different authors were writing about the same subject. Tourists needed to consult a map to be sure that when various travel guides described Canton, Kuangchou, or Guangzhou, they were referring to the same province.

TABLE 1: PRONUNCIATION OF COMMON QIGONG WORDS

Pinyin	Wade–Giles	Pronunciation	Meaning
Dan Tian	Tan T'ien	Dan Tian	Elixir Field
Dao	Tao	Dow	The Way
Dao De Jing	Tao Te Ching	Dow De Jing	Daoist Classic
Jing	Ching	Jing	Sexual Essence
Lao Zi	Lao Tzu	Lao Dze	Daoist Name
Qi	Ch'i	Chee	Life Energy
Qigong	Ch'i Kung	Chee Gung	Energy Work
Taiji Quan	T'ai Chi Ch'uan	Tiejee Chuan	Taiji Martial Art
Xian	Hsien	See-en	Daoist Sage
Zhuang Zi	Chuang Tzu	Juong Dze	Daoist Name

To remedy this situation, in 1958 linguists from the People's Republic of China devised a standard phonetic system to represent the Mandarin (the official Chinese dialect) pronunciation of Chinese characters using Latin letters. It is known as Hanyu Pinyin, or Pinyin for short. Although Pinyin pronunciation does not always conform to English usage, it does provide a uniform way of representing Chinese.

Pinyin is used consistently in translations published in China, and gradually more and more Western scholars are adopting this standard. I have used Pinyin exclusively throughout this text. Thus ch'i and ch'i-kung are spelled qi and qigong. Taoism is spelled Daoism. The ancient Chinese exercise T'ai Chi Ch'uan is now written Taiji Quan. Table 1, above, will help readers cross-reference common qigong terms and learn their pronunciation.

An Important Note from the Author

This book is intended as an educational work on China's great healing treasure, Qigong. It is not meant to take the place of therapy or treatment by a physician, but rather to help you make better, informed choices about health and treatment options.

SECTION I

What Is Qigong?

CHAPTER ONE

What Is Qigong?

*To study and at times practice what one has
learned, is that not a pleasure?*

—CONFUCIUS

QI is the Chinese word for "life energy." According to Chinese medicine, qi is the animating power that flows through all living things. A living being is filled with it. A dead person has no more qi—the warmth, the life energy is gone. A healthy individual has more than one who is ill. However, health is more than an abundance of qi. Health implies that the qi in our bodies is clear, rather than polluted and turbid, and flowing smoothly, like a stream, not blocked or stagnant.

It is also the life energy one senses in nature. The earth itself is moving, transforming, breathing, and alive with qi. Modern scientists speak the same language as ancient poets when they call the Earth *Gaia*, a living being. When we appreciate the beauty of animals, fish, birds, flowers, trees, mountains, the deep ocean, and floating clouds, we are sensing their qi and feeling an intuitive unity with them. Human beings are part of nature and share qi with the rest of the earth.

Gong means "work" or "benefits acquired through perseverance and practice." Thus, *qigong* means working with the life energy, learning how to control the flow and distribution of qi to improve the health and harmony of mind and body.

Qigong is a wholistic system of self-healing exercise and meditation, an ancient, evolving practice that includes healing posture, movement, self-massage, breathing techniques, and meditation. Through these various methods, qi is accumulated and stored in the body, like filling a reservoir. Impure or polluted qi—the essence of disease—can also be cleansed and refined into pure, healing qi. The goal of some qigong practices is to discharge and eliminate the impure qi in a manner analogous to breathing. Breathing is a process of absorbing a pure source of energy, oxygen, and eliminating the impure, carbon dioxide. Like proper breathing, qigong practice can make this exchange more efficient.

Qigong is called a "practice" or "training" because, unlike medication, it is not "prescribed" for a limited period of time, but, rather, practiced daily. This is easy to do because qigong is as enjoyable as any sport, yet does not require a great expenditure of time or money. Students generally practice an average of twenty to forty minutes each day. There is no need for special equipment or a large workout space.

Anyone can practice qigong. There are techniques suitable for every age and physical condition. Qigong includes standing, seated, and supine methods. With only slight adjustments in technique, it is possible to practice most standing exercises from a seated or lying down position. This makes qigong an ideal exercise for the disabled.

QIGONG CATEGORIES

Qigong techniques are divided into two general categories: dynamic or active qigong *(dong gong)* and tranquil or passive qigong *(jing gong)*. Dynamic qigong includes obvious movement. The entire body moves from one posture to another, as though performing a dance, or a posture is held while the arms move through various positions. Dong gong is the most popular kind of qigong in both China and the West. It is *yang*, active, yet it conceals the *yin*, passive. Externally there is movement, but internally, the mind is quiet, peaceful, and at rest.

In tranquil qigong the entire body is still. The qi is controlled by mental concentration, visualization, and precise methods of breathing. Jing gong is externally yin, passive, but internally yang, active. The body is still, yet the breath is moving. The mind is alert and actively paying attention to the qi.

To put it simply, dynamic qigong is exercise, and tranquil qigong is meditation. Yet these categories are not rigid. Stillness and action are relative, not absolute, principles. It is important to find a balance of yin and yang, not just in qigong, but in everyday life. In movement, seek stillness and rest. In rest, be mindful and attentive.

APPLICATIONS OF QIGONG

There are several reasons to practice qigong. Most important, qigong is a way to prevent disease and improve health. *Medical Qigong* (Yi Jia Gong) is the main subject of this book. Medical qigong, learned through books, videos, audiotapes, and from professional qigong teachers, can be practiced as a complete and independent system of self-healing. Many doctors of Chinese medicine also prescribe medical qigong for their patients. Chinese medicine includes acupuncture, herbology, massage, and qigong. Chinese doctors may recommend qigong as an adjunct to other necessary therapies or as a way for patients to maintain optimum health. Patients who practice qigong recover more quickly and gain the skills necessary to take charge of their own health.

External Qi Healing (Wai Qi Zhi Liao) is an ancient Chinese method of healing touch and a branch of medical qigong. When the qigong student is able to control internal qi flow, he or she can attempt to heal others. The healer places his or her hands on or near a client's body, assesses the health of the client's qi, and then transmits healing qi. (See Chapter 15.)

After a few months of self-healing qigong practice, students sometimes remark, "I have so much energy now. What do I do with it?" The answer is, "Share it!" By practicing External Qi Healing, you can share healing energy with friends, loved ones, or clients. You can also share qi with nature by taking a walk in a beautiful and nourishing place. Nature has a wonderful way of creating relaxation and balance, feeding us with energy we need and draining off any excess.

In *Meditative* or *Spiritual Qigong* (Jing Gong) the student's focus is on developing a clear, tranquil state of mind, with deeper self-awareness and harmony with nature. Some authors divide meditative qigong into two categories, Buddhist Fo Jia Gong and Daoist Dao Jia Gong, reflecting the influence of Buddhist and Daoist philosophy. The distinction between these two schools of qigong is, however, often hazy. Throughout Chinese history, Buddhist and Daoist philosophy have influenced each other. The same can be said of their qigong. Practitioners of meditative and medical qigong share a common goal of *xing ming shuang xiu*, "spirit and body both cultivated," the Chinese equivalent of "a sound mind in a sound body." Because mind and body influence each other, it is impossible to have a truly healthy body without a healthy mind and vice versa. Thus, meditative qigong is always practiced as a complement to medical qigong.

Confucian Qigong (Ru Jia Gong) is qigong that improves character. The Chinese philosopher Confucius (551–479 B.C.), taught the importance of ethical behavior and harmonious interpersonal relations. Although there is no evidence that Confucius practiced qigong, many students of his philosophy have also been students of qigong. Confucian qigong stresses the traditional Chinese belief that a healthy individual is more likely to behave with integrity. If you care for yourself, you are more likely to care for others. Conversely, abuse of self leads to abuse of others and unethical behavior. Confucian qigong is not so much a school as an orientation. Practitioners of Confucian qigong work on the same qigong techniques as other qigong students. They differ only in their goal of using qigong to cultivate benevolence, sincerity, respect, and other virtues.

Martial Qigong, Wu Gong, refers to Chinese martial arts (*wu shu*), the most popular sport in China. Although martial qigong implies qigong exercises that improve one's ability to defend and attack, the techniques can also improve performance in other sports. A wu gong student is likely to emphasize dynamic exercises more than meditation. The practice strengthens, stretches, and conditions the body and speeds recovery from sports-related injuries.

Today a new application for qigong is emerging: *Business Qigong*. Qigong practice can help employees feel less stressed, maintain better health, and improve productivity. One of my students, the owner of one of the largest used-car lots in the United States, found that his personnel were more relaxed and in tune with their customers' needs after he required his employees to spend the first twenty minutes of their workday practicing qigong. Sales went up significantly. Another of my students, an adviser to the World Bank and key attorney in international business negotiations, believes that qigong can help negotiators stay centered and make wiser decisions, a difficult task when the stakes are high. Perhaps cultivating qi is like managing money. Success requires competence in accumulating, maintaining, and replenishing your "principal."

According to Andrew Pollack's article "A Business Tool Way Beyond the Balance Sheet," published in *The New York Times* on November 28, 1995, interest in qigong is running high among Japanese businessmen. Kozo Nishino, a sixty-nine-year-old master of *ki* (the Japanese pronunciation of "qi"), teaches qigong breathing exercises to such prominent business executives as Shoichiro Irimajiri of Sega Enterprises, former director of Honda operations in the United States; Yuichi Haneta, a senior vice president of NEC Corporation; and Kazuo Wakasugi, president of the Japan Petroleum Exploration Corporation. Major institutions, including Sony Corporation and Japan's Ministry of International Trade and Industry, are funding research to explore qi.

There is a close, reciprocal relationship among all applications of qigong. For instance, a healthy body creates a healthy spirit and vice versa. Good health creates the stamina and power necessary for martial arts or other sports and may prevent or lessen the severity of injuries. Martial arts training teaches postural alignment, correct breathing, sensitivity, and can improve health. A clear, calm mind and strong body create confidence, self-control, and more ethical behavior. And improved mind-body health can help you achieve financial goals.

Any qigong technique may be used for a variety of purposes, depending on the student's intent. One student might practice a breathing exercise in order to help heal bronchitis. Another student practices the same exercise as a way of developing more power in her tennis serve. A musician practices qigong to improve posture, breath control, and performance. Qigong is the art and science of refining and cultivating internal energy. It develops skills that can have very broad applications.

I continue the Chinese tradition of using the unqualified term "qigong" to refer to the healing and meditative applications of qigong training. It is not necessary to specify "medical qigong" unless the context is ambiguous. Qigong is a jewel that has many facets. In focusing on the facet of healing, it is important to remember that qigong is not limited to healing. Qigong practice can influence every aspect of one's life.

ONE RIVER, MANY TRIBUTARIES

There is not one style or school of qigong, but rather many thousands, all based on common principles of balance, relaxation, healthy breathing, and good posture. Some qigong styles are named after animals whose movements they imitate: Crane Style, Snake Style, Dragon Style, the Five Animal Frolics, etc. Others carry the names of their actual or legendary founders: Li Family Qigong, Eighteen Monk Qigong, Taoist Monk Chen Xi-yi Qigong. Still others sound like schools of philosophy: Undifferentiated (*Wuji*) Qigong, Primal Limit (*Yuanji*) Qigong, Intelligence (*Zhineng*) Qigong. Some qigong style names might simply describe what the qigong exercises do: Iron Body Qigong, Tendon Strengthening Qigong, Reducing Inflammation Qigong, and so on.

How do we choose the style or styles to practice? Always begin with the basics, the fundamentals. This does not mean simplistic or beginner's level.

In qigong basics are the root of one's practice, whether you are just beginning or have practiced for fifty years—the techniques that emphasize good habits of posture, movement, and breathing and that engender relaxed wakefulness. In this book, we will explore qigong techniques that have withstood the test of time and proven their efficacy in improving health and enhancing life. We will build a good root for qigong training. By emphasizing a deep root and strong foundation, the student can reach to the high heavens without fear of toppling over.

Students sometimes inquire, "I've already studied some qigong. Is there more to learn?" I always find this an amusing question, since after twenty-five years of practice and research, the reaches of human potential seem more elusive to me than when I was a beginner! As the Chinese say, "There is always a higher peak to climb." Has any pianist given the best performance of a Mozart concerto of all time? In qigong terms, who ever completely masters relaxation, breathing, or the ability to stand and move with grace, poise, and power?

GO WITH THE FLOW

According to Chinese medical theory, health means a full and flowing supply of qi. Using a modern metaphor, we can regard the body as a battery that can either lose, maintain, or increase its charge. Stress, worry, and poor health habits dissipate qi. Proper self-care helps to maintain or improve health. Moderate and correct practice of qigong can fully "charge" the body, increasing the reservoir of healing energy. This means greater vitality and an improved ability to fight off disease and infection.

Healing energy is only helpful if it can get where it is needed. It is therefore essential that qi flow to all the cells of the body. For this reason, qi has been compared to blood, which in a similar way must reach all parts of the body, bringing oxygen and nutrients and carrying away waste. The Chinese recognize this analogy in their saying, "Where the qi goes, the blood flows."

However, unlike blood, qi is an invisible, subtle force. We know it exists the same way we know sunlight and wind exist. We cannot capture or grasp these forces in the hand, yet we can experience them. Science does not need to prove their existence in order for us to believe in them. Nevertheless, it is wonderful to know that science *can* measure these things. Qi is quantifiable, as research increasingly is proving, but it is more than a quantity! Anyone who takes a walk in nature knows that sunlight is far more than photons and wind far more than changes in atmospheric pressure. So it is with qi.

In acupuncture, fine needles are inserted into parts of the body where the flow of qi is impeded. It is presumed that stagnant qi, like stagnant water, breeds disease. When qi does not flow, certain areas of the body have too much energy (a *yang* condition), other areas are depleted, with too little energy (a *yin* condition). Acupuncture needles open the dams, to drain excesses and fill hollows, restoring health and homeostasis. Qigong practice is like acupuncture without the needles. The patient learns to use physical movements, respiratory techniques, and intent to move the qi. He or she learns to self-regulate the qi flow, to send it to distressed areas so the body can repair itself more quickly and easily.

Qigong is easy to learn, but mastering it requires dedication and perseverance. It is also inexpensive, since it requires neither exercise equipment nor invasive or costly medical procedures, only the God-given components of one's own body and mind. Very importantly, if practiced correctly, qigong has no side effects. These factors plus its emphasis on prevention of disease suggest that qigong offers the possibility of greatly decreasing personal and national medical costs. With a qigong "prescription," physicians do not have to worry about patient compliance. Qigong is fun. It empowers the patient to be self-reliant and responsible rather than shifting all decision-making into the hands of the doctor.[1] According to National Institutes of Health official Dr. Wayne Jonas, if American health care emphasized wellness and self-empowerment in the treatment of most chronic diseases instead of the treatment of specific disease causes, the average savings per U.S. citizen would be approximately $9,000/year.[2]

COMPLEMENTARY MEDICINE

As East and West learn from each other, the labels used to describe various medical systems can become confusing. In China, acupuncture, herbs, and qigong are the "traditional medicine." In the West, these same methods are called "alternative." I prefer not to use this term. Although "alternative" may imply freedom of choice, it too often suggests that the patient must choose between alternatives. This seems unfair. Why should a patient select only one of several helpful forms of therapy, where each might address a different facet of the problem?

The term I prefer is *complementary medicine.*[3] Qigong works well with other healing modalities, complementing them. This fact is recognized in the modern Chinese health-care system, which regularly utilizes techniques of Western medicine. A Chinese practitioner of Western medicine might prescribe surgery, medication, *and* qigong for cancer. Some Chinese hospitals are based on the model of traditional Chinese medicine. Here we would

expect to find qigong clinics. However, in China even hospitals that emphasize Western medicine frequently incorporate qigong departments and
clinics for both inpatient and outpatient care. Qigong can and should be
practiced in addition to rather than instead of any required allopathic interventions.

According to an article published in *The New York Times Magazine*
("The Mainstreaming of Alternative Medicine," October 4, 1992), some
experts believe that within twenty-five years complementary medical techniques will be widely practiced in both primary care and specialized fields
of medicine. Unfortunately, the West is not there yet. Today, students of
qigong may need to educate their physicians about qigong or to at least provide a bibliography for study. If you are seriously ill, it is important to inform
your physician about your qigong training, as it can affect the dosage requirements for medications such as insulin, chemotherapy, or drugs for high
blood pressure. Certain kinds of qigong may be contraindicated for some
conditions.

Medical researchers also need to learn more about qigong and other
complementary modalities. If researchers are unaware that subjects are receiving treatment from complementary healing practitioners, the conclusions they draw from scientific experiments using these subjects may be
flawed. When a nurse at a major hospital brought up this concern with an
oncologist who was testing a new treatment for brain tumors, he replied, "I
never thought of that. I have no idea if the subjects are involved in any kind
of alternative medicine." Was this ignorance, oversight, or perhaps symptomatic of a common assumption that complementary medicine is unscientific
and unlikely to affect treatment outcome? In fact, complementary methods
like qigong can have powerful and measurable effects on patient health. As
we will see in later chapters, qigong has a strong body of clinical and experimental evidence behind it.

FINDING INNER PEACE

Human beings have always been subject to various stresses that cause wear
and tear within the body. Primitive humans had to deal with the challenges
of disease, changing weather, environmental dangers, family and community
relations, fluctuations in food supply, the fear of disability and death. Stress is
a natural part of life. "Yet," says Dr. Kenneth R. Pelletier, "for people living
in sophisticated, postindustrial Western cultures, the degree of stress has become excessive and deleterious."[4] We have a host of new stresses related to
mortgage loans; school achievement; relationships between employer, em-

ployees, and customers; economic concerns; national and world politics; new devastating diseases; anxiety over time and schedules; and the effects of noisy, polluted, and crowded environments.

The fact that we have gotten used to these stressors does not lessen their harmful effects on physical and mental health. Stress causes a general state of physical and mental tension, a condition that Chinese call *wai qiang nei gan*, "the outside strong, the inside rots." When we can't easily change our circumstances, we often internalize our frustrations as muscular tension. Beneath this hard shell, the qi becomes sluggish, unable to flow smoothly either internally or between the body and the environment. This can lead to disease and pain. Scientific research has proven that prolonged stress is a contributing factor in most of the "diseases of civilization": high blood pressure, headaches, digestive disorders, arthritis, cancer, heart disease, and respiratory disorders.

Under continuous stress, the nervous system learns to desensitize itself as a means of coping. We tune out the air conditioners, the drone of passing cars, or the rattling of the subway. We ignore the noxious fumes of automobiles and industry. In an overcrowded city, we may also lose sensitivity to the feelings of others as a way of protecting our own privacy. When we have little physical space, we tend to create mental space, distancing ourselves from others. Many of us try to avoid and escape our worries, dulling our senses with drugs, alcohol, and excessive television.

Many external stresses are, of course, beyond our control. To the extent that we cannot control the outer environment, it is imperative that we seek to control and maintain the health of the internal environment. If we cannot change or remove ourselves from the stressful situation, we can at least control our reactions to it. Qigong, like Western biofeedback therapy, is a systematic training in psychophysiological self-regulation. It teaches us to deal intelligently with stress, to keep the body relaxed and supple and the internal energy strong and healthy, and to develop skills to regulate the health, balance, and movement of healing energy in the mind ("psycho") and body ("physiological"). The world may not be peaceful, but we can do much to create peace within.

CHAPTER TWO

Roots and Branches: The History of Qigong

A journey of a thousand miles begins with the first step.

—CHINESE PROVERB

NATURAL BEGINNINGS

The ancient Chinese were an agrarian people who learned the principles of qigong naturally by observing the cycles of planting and harvesting, life and death.

A farmer cultivates his crops by carefully tending them, making sure they get the proper nourishment from soil and sun, and pruning his field to remove destructive or pathogenic influences. Like farming, qigong requires daily attention, especially during the early hours of the day. The early stages of qigong practice are the most important, in order to ensure that the "seed" of qi germinates and establishes strong, healthy roots. A healthy plant is filled with living, moving sap (qi). It is supple, yet strong. It sways with the breeze, but doesn't break. When the plant is sick, withered, or dead, it is stiff and rigid, easily broken. In a healthy field, several crops are grown, or crops are rotated. This creates a mineral-rich environment, in which no single crop will draw excessively on the balance of nutrients or deplete the soil. Similarly, the vast repertoire of qigong self-healing techniques allows us to deal effectively with different states of health or disease.

12

DAO-YIN: THE ORIGINAL QIGONG

Qigong has been known by many names throughout Chinese history. In ancient times, it was called *tu gu na xin* "expelling the old energy, drawing in the new," *xing qi* "moving the qi," *yang sheng* "nourishing the forces of life," *nei gong* "inner achievement," or most commonly as *dao-yin* "leading and guiding the energy." Dao-yin can also be translated as "guiding the qi and extending the limbs," thus referring to two of the primary components of self-healing: breathing and exercise.

The term "qigong" is actually quite recent. It was first mentioned in a text[1] attributed to Daoist master Xu Sun (died A.D. 374), but probably dating from the Ming Dynasty (1368–1644). The word "qigong" was not used in its present specialized sense—"the art of qi cultivation"—until the twentieth century. According to Daoist scholar and author Catherine Despeux, the word qigong appears in the titles of two works published in 1915 and 1929, where it "designates the force issued by working with the qi and the martial applications [of this force]. The therapeutic [medical] use of the term dates only from 1936: a certain Dong Hao published in Hangzhou a work entitled *Special Therapy for Tuberculosis: Qigong.*"[2] Since that time, "qigong" has been widely used in this medical sense, representing all Chinese self-healing exercise and meditation disciplines from ancient times to the present.

Probably the earliest qigong-like exercises in China are the animal dances of ancient Chinese shamans. During the Zhou Dynasty (1028–221 B.C.), there was a popular New Year's ritual known as the Great Exorcism (*Da No*). A shaman would wear a bearskin over his head, with four golden eyes, as though seeing in the four directions. Dancing through the village, followed by a procession of villagers wearing masks of the zodiacal animals (Dragon, Horse, Tiger, etc.), he drove out pestilence and demons. Similar animal dances are recorded on rock art panels throughout China. Some of these include uniform, preset dance patterns performed by many people at once. Others depict a combination of animal postures and military drills, providing possible evidence of an early link between animal movements, qigong, and the martial arts. We also know that by the third century B.C. there was a popular sport known as *jiao di* "horn butting" in which two unarmed men, each wearing an ox hide and ox horns, tried to wrestle each other to the ground. Animal motifs resurface again and again in qigong history and practice. Individual qigong postures and entire styles are modeled after animals. Typical qigong posture names cited by the Daoist philosopher Huai Nan Zi (d. 122 B.C.) include: Bathing Duck, Leaping Monkey, Glaring Owl, and Turning Tiger. From qigong systems developed within the last few centuries come: Lion's Roar, Monkey Hanging from the Tree, Coiling Snake, Old Bear in the Woods, Flying Crane. The qigong student cultivates *animal skills*: balance, suppleness, grace, and strength. Most important, through qigong practice, we hope to embody the health, hardiness, and vitality of the animals.

Many of today's qigong exercises are sets of linked postures, each flowing into the next, as in a beautiful, slow-motion dance. Inspired by ancient ritual dances designed to alter consciousness, they give both performer and observer a feeling of unity with the omnipresent qi. Some of these dances were believed to confer health and longevity. When the daughter of King Wu (r. 514–495 B.C.) died, he ordered a public performance of the Crane Dance, the symbol of triumph and power over death. Around the same period, Wang Zi-qiao (ca. 550 B.C.) a prince and Daoist sage from the state of Qin, practiced the Crane Dance as a means to immortality. According to Daoist legend, when Prince Wang died, he rode to heaven on the back of a crane. *The Spring and Autumn Annals*, an historical document from the third century B.C., contains an important reference to the antiquity of healing dances. We read that during the reign of mythical Emperor Yao (ca. 2,000 B.C.), great floods caused stagnation and congestion in both the land and people. Catherine Despeux translates a portion of this document in her essay "Gymnastics [Dao-yin]: The Ancient Tradition":

> The ways of water were broken and obstructed, so that the flow was bad from the very sources.
>   For the same reason, when the breath or energy of the individual is congested and stagnant, the muscles and bones are contracted and don't flex well. One therefore prescribes certain dances which guide the breath and ensure that it moves throughout the body in a harmonious fashion.[3]

In the second century A.D., the great physician Hua Tuo expressed the same wisdom when he reminded his student, "The door hinge will rust if it is not used." Or as one of my teachers used to say, "The reason that the teeth fall out instead of the tongue is that the tongue is always moving!"

The earliest documented reference to qigong (called "dao-yin" during this period) as a healing exercise rather than dance is inscribed on twelve pieces of jade, dating to the sixth century B.C., containing advice to collect the breath and allow it to descend in the body, presumably to the lower abdomen. Sinologist Joseph Needham includes a complete translation of the inscription in his monumental *Science and Civilization in China*:

> When it [the qi] goes down it becomes quiet. When it becomes quiet it will solidify. When it becomes solidified it will begin to

sprout. After it has sprouted it will grow. As it grows it will be pulled back again (to the upper regions). When it has been pulled back it will reach the crown of the head. Above, it will press against the crown of the head. Below it will press downwards.

Whoever follows this will live; whoever acts contrary to it will die.[4]

This ancient text could easily be describing present-day qigong techniques. By cultivating quiet, relaxed breathing, qi accumulates and "solidifies," making the body feel stable and balanced. Then the qi "sprouts," that is, moves through the whole body, from the crown of the head to the soles of the feet, creating vitality and long life.

The bible of Chinese medicine, *The Yellow Emperor's Classic of Internal Medicine*, compiled in the first and second centuries B.C., recommends daoyin to cure chills and fevers and states that the goal of dao-yin is to become like the ancient sages who

were tranquilly content in nothingness and the true vital force [*zhen qi*] accompanied them always; their vital (original) spirit was preserved within; thus, how could illness come to them?[5]

The *Classic* is also the source of an oft-quoted tenet of Chinese medicine: the wise physician cures diseases before they develop, rather than after they manifest. It is difficult to follow this principle in allopathic medicine, because Western biotechnology is often incapable of detecting disease in the very early stages. Some cancer cells, for instance, must replicate and grow for years before they show up in an X ray or blood test. By sensitizing oneself to healthy and diseased states of internal energy, qi, one has an ideal way to begin treatment when the disorder is still subclinical, without detectable or measurable symptoms. In ancient China, qigong was a treatment of choice. If prevention or early treatment failed, the physician prescribed an herbal formula and/or acupuncture treatment.

We see further descriptions of qigong in Daoist philosophical works of the third and fourth centuries B.C. In the classic *Dao De Jing* (The Way and Its Power), Lao Zi, the patriarch of Daoism, writes:

Controlling the yang and yin elements by Embracing the One,
 can you not allow them [the yang and yin] to depart?
Concentrating the qi and achieving utmost suppleness,
 can you become like a child? (Chapter 10)

The myriad things are nurtured by the yin and the yang;
Through the blending of qi, they attain harmony. (Chapter 42)

Lao Zi's disciple, Zhuang Zi, mentions dao-yin by name:

Exhaling through the mouth while exercising the breath,
   Spitting out the old breaths, drawing in the new,
   Moving like the bear, stretching like the bird,
   This is simply the art of longevity!—
And the aim of those scholars who practice *dao-yin*. (Chapter 15)

Zhuang Zi also recognized the spiritual dimensions of qigong. He knew that by cultivating the qi, the mind could become open and receptive. Instead of fasting from food, Daoists prefer to fast from words and concepts.

"May I ask the meaning of 'fasting the mind'?"
"Unify your will. Don't listen with the ears; listen with the mind. No, don't listen with the mind, but listen with the qi. . . . This 'qi' is an emptiness which is receptive to all things. The Dao [Way] is understood through emptiness. Emptiness is the fasting of the mind." (Chapter 4)

Daoism, China's original spiritual tradition, is pragmatic and this-worldly, emphasizing simplicity *(su)* and harmony with nature *(zi ran)*. In order to keep the mind and body healthy, Daoists, particularly those living austerely in the mountains, practiced and developed many styles of qigong. Needham believes that Daoism blends the healing and mystical wisdom of philosopher-recluses, who withdrew from society to find a deeper truth in nature, with elements of Chinese shamanism.[6] Daoist qigong may have incorporated shamanic animal dances and postures. The Daoist word for sage, *xian* (often translated "immortal" because of the Daoist preoccupation with longevity), was in ancient times a picture of a dancing shaman covered with feathers, as though imitating a bird.

The *Daoist Canon*, a collection of 1,120 volumes, contains virtually all of the early texts associated with qigong, including one specifically devoted to the subject, the *Dao-yin Classic*. The text was probably compiled around A.D. 1145, when it was first mentioned in a bibliographic reference. The exercises in it, however, date to the late sixth century. The methods described are remarkably consistent with qigong exercises and meditations still being taught in China. The goal of qigong has also remained the same. According

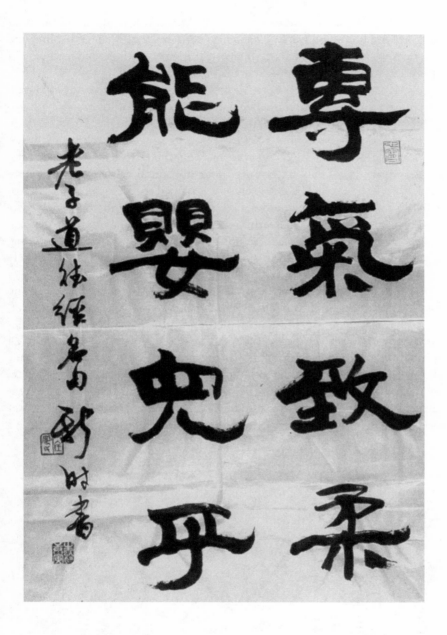

"Concentrating the qi and achieving utmost suppleness,
can you become like a child?" By Tu Xin-shi.
From Chapter 10 of Lao Zi's Dao De Jing.

to the *Dao-yin Classic*, the adept learns to "expel diseases, extend his years and prolong life." The *Daoist Canon* also contains thousands of healing and mystical visualizations. Healing Imagery, the new, cutting-edge medicine of the West, has a long and venerable history in China.

In 1973, archaeologists near the city of Changsha, the capital of Hunan Province, found a relic that has become *the* great locus of information on ancient qigong. When they excavated the tomb of King Ma (ca. 168 B.C.), they found in one of the coffins a folded piece of silk, half soaking in water. Approximately 50 cm. high and 100 cm. long, the restored silk included the earliest drawings of dao-yin postures, four horizontal rows of eleven figures each, forty-four in all. The entire chart was named the *Dao-yin Tu* (The Dao-yin Illustrations). The painted figures represent nearly all the major categories of modern qigong: breathing, stances, movement, and self-massage from standing, seated, and supine postures. Several of the figures are bending, stretching, or twisting. With this discovery, it became possible to not merely read about ancient dao-yin, but to actually see what was practiced.

There are captions near most of the figures on the chart. Some of the captions are names of animals, including hawk, wolf, crane, dragon, cat, bear; perhaps these are the names of the movements. Other captions describe how to move the body: "Bend at the Waist, Wave the Arms," etc. Of great interest are the captions that name specific disorders, such as kidney disease, flatulence, painful knees, lumbago, rheumatism, gastric disturbance, and anxiety, suggesting that by 168 B.C. specific exercises were used to treat specific illnesses. These exercises may have been commonly known "household" remedies or perhaps prescribed by healing specialists.

The Dao-yin Tu, *The Dao-yin Illustrations.*

The figures in the *Dao-yin Tu* are young and old, men and women, peasants and bureaucrats. According to Daoist scholar and Qigong Master Patricia N. H. Leong, the figures' ". . . varied mode of dress seems to indicate that therapeutic exercise and aspirations for longevity were not the province of only one class, but were the interests of a broad spectrum of society."[7]

The *Dao-yin Tu* is the finest example of the consistency and continuity of qigong healing techniques. The majority of exercises look so similar to the postures of modern qigong that it is possible to deduce how they were performed. The rich themes found in the *Dao-yin Tu* run like a fine thread through the fabric of qigong history and evolution.

After the *Dao-yin Tu* qigong literature flourished. In A.D. 142 a Daoist named Wei Bo-yang wrote *Can Tong Qi* (The Kinship of the Three) [Spiritual, Earthly, and Human], the first book on alchemy in the East or West.[8] In it Wei showed how the theory of yin and yang, the Five Elements,[9] and symbols from the *Yi Jing* (Classic of Change) could be applied to alchemy. Alchemy, for these early Daoists, meant creating an elixir of immortality[10] either from the elements of one's own body (*nei dan* "inner alchemy") or by ingesting external herbs and chemicals (*wai dan* "outer alchemy"). It is likely that both methods were practiced together. Alchemists practiced respiratory techniques to refine the qi and also attempted to transform the body with herbs and elixirs. Chinese herbology, dietetics, and cuisine owe much to the alchemists.

Wei described an alchemical theory that became a cornerstone of qigong philosophy: "Things of a similar nature (*tong lei*) will cause changes in each other. This will not happen if there is dissimilarity." Unfortunately, much of Wei's text is written in an obscure style, filled with metaphor and cryptic symbolism, perhaps designed to guard information from the uninitiated and to jar the memory of students who had already learned his methods. Nevertheless, Wei's idea that like affects like—or as I prefer to call it, *the theory of correspondence and affinity*—influenced the development of modern qigong practices. For instance, Wei associated the east and dawn with the wood element. Qigong students rise early and face east to heal the liver, the body's inner wood element. Wei believed that a quiet mind, a peaceful attitude, and persistent practice enables the qi to flow through the entire body, creating a golden elixir of health and longevity.

Wei Bo-yang's work was followed by numerous encyclopedias of qigong and Daoist cultivation, significantly: the *Bao Pu Zi* (Master Who Embraces Simplicity) (A.D. 320) of Ge Hong, a compiler of predominantly southern Chinese alchemy and longevity techniques; Tao Hong-jing's (A.D. 456–536) *Yang Xing Yan Ming Lu* (Record of Nourishing Nature and Lengthening Life), containing chapters on dao-yin, dietetics, and sexual qigong; the *Qian Jin*

Yao Fang (Precious Medical Formulas) by Sun Si-mo (A.D. 581–682), a classic of Chinese medicine; the eleventh-century work *Yun Ji Qi Qian* (Seven Tablets in a Cloudy Satchel), which includes the text of the *Dao-yin Classic* and important commentaries on the great works of Daoist meditation; continuing to the relatively recent classic *Nei Gong Tu Shuo* (Illustrated Explanation of Nei Gong [i.e. Qigong]), written by Wang Zu-yuan in 1881, which includes the first diagrams and details on the practice of today's most popular qigong styles.

OUTSIDE INFLUENCES

Qigong techniques and schools also developed in response to influences from Indian Yoga and Tibetan Buddhism. Tibetan Buddhism, known as *Mi Zong* "Esoteric School" in Chinese, came to China in the eighth century A.D., where it was centered around the capital city of Chang-an. According to Buddhist scholar Kenneth Ch'en, the school rapidly declined after the year 774.[11] Tibetan Buddhist qigong (*Mi Zong qigong*), however, remained. Holmes Welch, a former research associate at Harvard University's East Asian Research Center, writes, "During the Republican period [1911–48], Tibetan lamas had almost as much of a *cachet* in China as they had in Europe. . . . Rich laymen became their disciples to get their instruction in the exercise of paranormal powers."[12] Welch attended a demonstration of Tibetan qigong in Hong Kong during which an eighty-year-old master attempted, unsuccessfully, to use qi to push people without touching them. An acquaintance of Mr. Welch, a former employee of the Shanghai office of *The New York Times*, claimed that his teacher, Yeh Wan-zhi, a disciple of a Tibetan lama, could heal by laying on of hands and had tough, "diamond-like skin" (*jin gang pi*).[13] Both abilities are well-known in traditional Chinese qigong.

One of the celebrated lamas in China during the Republican Period was Lama Kong Kha, teacher of Buddhist scholar Garma C. C. Chang.[14] In Chang's translation of Tibetan texts transmitted by his guru, there are references to qigong-like techniques: exhaling toxins and spiritual obstructions, methods of circulating the breath, "absorbing pranas [qi] of the Five Elements, in five different colors . . .",[15] using animal movements such as the Tiger, Turtle, or Lion to gather or spread the internal energy. These techniques were probably most popular in border regions between Tibet and China. In China's Yunan Province, qigong techniques from the Tibetan Lion's Roar Martial Art (*Senge Ngawa*) blended with Chinese White Crane Boxing to produce unique Sino-Tibetan methods of fighting and qi cultivation.[16] Considering the post-Communist relationship between China and

Tibet, I seriously doubt if such friendly exchanges were common after 1949. Nevertheless, many present-day qigong masters claim a *Mi Zong Qigong*[17] lineage and include Tibetan or Sanskrit chants in their qigong, most commonly *Om Ah Hung* or *Om Mani Padme Hung*, invocations of the Buddhist personification of Compassion.

It is beyond the scope of this book to cover all of the significant events in qigong history, as there are thousands of individual monastic or family styles, transmitted only within particular religious sects and families or to adopted heirs. These "closed-door" styles were not written down, and many have vanished as a result of an irrational fear that martial qigong techniques would be used by one's enemies or that no one was worthy to receive a master's precious techniques.[18] Many qigong practitioners died in China's Boxer Rebellion (1898–1900).[19] The Boxers falsely believed that qigong and shamanistic rituals would make them invulnerable to the invaders' bullets.[20]

RECENT HISTORY

Until quite recently the People's Republic of China had an ambivalent attitude toward its own cultural treasure. Qigong was considered the vestige of early, feudal society and Daoism was branded as individualistic, eccentric, and "counterrevolutionary." Qigong was also linked with parapsychology, a subject widely researched in Western countries and perceived, by the Chinese, as evidence of "the decline of capitalist society." Throughout Chinese history, many qigong practitioners have made claims to supernatural abilities, using magic and trickery to demonstrate such techniques as pushing objects without touching them, stabbing the body without injury, or catching bullets in the mouth. These con artists detract from qigong's credibility and create an impression that qigong is a means to superhuman power rather than a time-honored facet of Chinese medicine.

For about twenty years after the founding of the People's Republic of China, qigong was actively practiced and researched. New methods were explored, and old, traditional methods were systematized and standardized so they could be more readily applied on a wider scale. In 1955, a qigong sanatorium was founded in the city of Tangshan, Hebei Province. A year later, two qigong training centers were established in Hebei. Another qigong sanatorium was founded in Shanghai in 1957. In October 1959, China's Ministry of Public Health officially sponsored a national qigong conference in Beidaihe, Hebei Province, inviting representatives from seventeen provinces to attend.

In 1966 this open door was suddenly closed. During the Cultural

Revolution (1966–1976) qigong was officially prohibited, and interest in it was strongly discouraged. When the revolution was over, qigong was again accepted as a valid field of research, largely through the influence of one of the great figures in Chinese science, Dr. Qian Xue-sen, "the father of Chinese space technology." Qian had studied at the Massachusetts Institute of Technology in the 1930s and earned a Ph.D. from the California Institute of Technology, where he later served as Goddard Professor of Jet Propulsion. At Dr. Qian's request, he was traded back to China after the Korean War, in exchange for American POWs. The U.S. government probably regretted its decision, believing, according to authors Tron McConnell and Zha Leping, "that without Qian, China would not have been able to join the nuclear and space clubs so soon."[21]

In 1980, Qian began to advocate using science and technology to research qigong, Chinese medicine, and human potential. In December of 1985, the government gave approval to the formation of the "China Qigong Science Association." In a February 1986 symposium sponsored by the association, Qian declared, "Many facts show that an intensive scientific study of qigong will lead to a full development of man's mental as well as physical abilities."[22] In his lecture, Qian remarked that he believed qigong could even affect intelligence. He had received a letter from a schoolteacher who claimed that his students had improved their grades by practicing qigong. Given the more open political climate, scientific studies were conducted at major universities and hospitals throughout China. A growing body of evidence showed that qigong could be very effective in treating disease.

In 1987, Dr. Qian was appointed chair of the prestigious Chinese Science and Technology Association, the organization that directs and coordinates China's scientific research. During his first year in that position, he gave a well-known public endorsement of qigong in the Chinese journal *Liao Wong*, (Prospects Weekly): "Chinese qigong is modern science and technology—high technology—absolutely top technology."[23] The same year, China's Department of Education directed universities to establish qigong training courses.

Fortunately, in spite of the vicissitudes of Chinese history, the great, classical styles of qigong have persisted. There have always been simply too many people practicing qigong, with or without the government's approval, for qigong to disappear. By 1987 qigong was being practiced by at least twenty million Chinese.[24] In 1992, Yu Gongbao of the China Wushu [Martial Arts] Academy estimated that there were seventy to eighty million practitioners in China.[25]

Qigong has also gained international recognition. In the late '80s and early '90s, China hosted several international conferences for the exchange of information on qigong science. Two such conferences were held in North America, at the University of California at Berkeley in 1990 and in Vancouver, British Columbia, in 1995. By 1996, there were more than one thousand published abstracts on some aspect of qigong science available in English. Chinese bookstores are now filled with books and periodicals on qigong. In the United States, there have been several popular magazines focusing on qigong and Chinese healing practices.[26] There are probably at least one hundred thousand qigong practitioners outside of China, including several thousand in the United States and Canada and an equal number in Europe. I have received mail from qigong clubs in Russia, Australia, South Africa, Israel, and most countries in Europe. Qigong and Yoga are undoubtedly the most popular healing exercises in the world today.

LIFE ENERGY AROUND THE WORLD

Invisible life energy is a universal concept and is most commonly associated with breath, heat, air, and/or sunlight. Evidence of a shared, perennial philosophy of health can be found among all ancient cultures.

God breathes the "breath of life" (*ruach*) into Earth to create the first human. The Hebrew name "Adam" is derived from the same root as *Adama*, Earth. The Breath of God (*Ruach Ha Kodesh* in Hebrew, *Spiritus Sancti* in Latin) is synonymous with the power of Spirit. A similar idea is expressed in the holy scripture of Islam, the *Qur'an* (Koran). The words *nafas*, meaning Allah's own breath, and *ruh*, meaning Allah's own soul, "are used to mean the human breath and human soul—confirming the fact that we are originally from Allah, of Allah, for Allah, and in the end will return to Allah."[27] Shaykh Hakim Moinuddin Chishti says that "breath" is not the same as air or oxygen. Rather it is a divine energy that regulates human emotions and the equilibrium of the body. "Both the quantity and quality of breath have a definite and direct effect upon human health."[28]

In Greek, the vital breath is called *pneuma*, a word first used by the philosopher Anaximenes (ca. 545 B.C.). Anaximenes said that life begins with the breath. All things come from it and dissolve into it at death. The soul *is* breath and is that which controls and "holds together" (prevents the disintegration or decomposition of) human beings. As air or wind, it encloses and maintains the world. Cambridge University professors G. S. Kirk and J. E. Raven in their work *The Presocratic Philosophers*, label a section of Anaximenes' writings "The Comparison Between Cosmic Air and the Breath-Soul,"[29] ideas that are remarkably parallel to the Chinese words *Yuan Qi*, "Cosmic or Original Qi," and *hun*, "breath soul." Vital breath creates a unity between microcosm and macrocosm. In Kirk and Raven's translation, "The life-principle and motive force of man is, traditionally, *pneuma* or the breath-soul; (pneuma is seen in the outside world, as wind) therefore the life-principle of the outside world is pneuma; (therefore wind, breath, or air is the life and substance of all things)."[30]

Hippocrates (460–377 B.C.) considered the founder of medical science, believed that the forces of life, like qi, must flow. When *chymos*, the body's fluids—principally blood, bile, and phlegm—are in harmony, one is healthy. In *The Nature of Man*, he writes, "A man enjoys the most perfect health when these elements are duly proportioned to one another in power, bulk, and manner of compounding, so that they are mingled as excellently as possible. Pain is felt when one of these elements is either deficient or excessive. . . ."[31] When a component of health is isolated and out of balance with the other elements, in excess in certain places and absent from others, the result is pain and illness. According to Hippocrates, balance is the natural state. The role of a physician is "not to manipulate the patient as one would handle something inanimate, but to remove, both from within and from outside the patient's body, obstructions to healthy recovery."[32]

Among the Kung San,[33] the indigenous people of Africa's Kalahari Desert, life energy is *num*. The num is stored in the lower abdomen and at the base of the spine and can be made to "boil" through ecstatic dance. In *Boiling Energy*, by Harvard lecturer Richard Katz, an elderly healer explains, "The num enters every part of your body, right to the tip of your feet and even your hair."[34] Num makes the spine tingle and the mind empty, without thoughts. The healer or healers "see people properly, just as they are."[35] At this point in the dance, the healers can project healing num or pull sickness from those who are ill. Shamans, *num kausi*, the "masters or owners of the num," might help a student enter the proper state of transcendent consciousness (*kia*) by "shooting" arrows of num into the student's body, often by snapping the fingers. (Some Native American healers project energy in a similar way, by slapping the palms together.) Like modern physicians, the Kung believe that people carry illness within the body. When disease flares up, it can sometimes be cured by accumulating num, increasing the inner reserve of healing power. The Kung are also willing to use modern antibiotics. No treatment is 100 percent effective. As healer Gau says, "Maybe our num and European medicine are similar, because sometimes people who get European medicines die, and sometimes they live. That is the same with ours."[36]

Some fifty or sixty thousand years ago, long before the Chinese spoke of qi, Australian aborigines were cultivating life energy as a key to healing and spiritual power. According to my friend, Yuin Tribe elder and medicine man Gaboo, "People who had this energy could communicate telepathically across vast distances. They formed the aboriginal telephone line." In *Voices of the First Day*, a classic of aboriginal spirituality, author Robert Lawlor notes that, like the Chinese, the aborigines concentrated on an energy center four inches below the navel, "where they said the cord of the great Rainbow Serpent (kundalini) lay coiled. Through the same center the Aborigines drew body heat from the 'rainbow fires' that helped them endure cold."[37] Aborigines, like other indigenous tribes, believe that people today have less of this life energy than in the past. Because life energy is the common source and link between people and nature, the loss of it parallels the loss of connection between human beings and their relations: the plants, animals, stones, water, sky, the earth, and all of creation. Restoring life energy to its original condition of fullness may be the key to recovering lost potentials and realizing that "the Kingdom of Heaven is in our midst."

Native American tribes also recognize the existence of a subtle healing energy. The Navajo say that the Winds *(nilch'i)* gave life to human beings and all of nature. Thus, James Kale McNeley, Ph.D., a teacher at the Navajo Community College, speaks of the "Holy Wind" in his *Holy Wind in Navajo Philosophy*.[38] As the Winds swirled through the human being, they left their mark as lines on fingers and toes. The Winds are also sacred powers, sources of healing guidance. They are considered messengers of God or the Great Spirit. When Native Americans pray to the "Winds of the Four Directions," they become intuitively aware of solutions to life problems. According to one Navajo elder, if the Winds' guidance is not followed, if one refuses to follow God's instructions, ". . . our Holy One takes out the Wind that was within us. He stops our heart."[39] In *SiSiWiss*, "Sacred Breath," an indigenous healing tradition from the Puget Sound region of Washington State, healers project power to their patients through dance, song, and laying on of hands. Some *SiSiWiss* chants include specific breathing methods to either drive away disease or invite helping and healing spirits.

In the Lakota (Sioux) language, the word for soul, *waniya*, is derived from the word for breath, *ni*. In 1896, the Lakota holy man, Long Knife (George Sword), told physician James R. Walker, "A man's *ni* is his life. It is the same as his breath. It gives him his strength. All that is inside a man's body it keeps clean. If it is weak it cannot clean the inside of the body. If it goes away from a man he is dead. . . ."[40] The Lakota sweat lodge healing rite is called *inipi* because it purifies the *ni*. "Inipi causes a man's *ni* to put out of his body all that makes him tired, or all that causes disease, or all that causes him to think wrong. . . ."[41]

In Hawaii, the most powerful healers are known as *Kahuna Ha*, "Masters of the Breath." The sacred healing breath, *ha*, can be absorbed at power places in nature *(heiau)*, through dance (such as the hula), and deep breathing exercises. Some Kahunas learn how to store healing energy in the heart. Then, when the healing energy is projected through laying on of hands, the ha is colored by the healer's love and positive thoughts. In traditional Hawaiian counseling and mediation, all parties in a conflict first calm their minds by breathing deeply. This helps them to be less reactive and to find a better solution. The ha can also be transferred from a healer to a patient by blowing directly on the patient's body. When a Kahuna Ha is near death, he/she may transfer lineage and power by breathing the ha onto a student or family member. The Hawaiian word *Aloha*, often used as a respectful, heart-felt greeting, also means "love." Love is the "meeting face-to-face" (*alo*) of the breath of life (*ha*).

Of course the closest parallels to qi are found in Asian countries, particularly India. In India, the life energy, *prana*, is described as flowing through thousands of subtle-energy veins, the *nadis*. One of the goals of Yoga is to accumulate more prana through breath control exercises (*pranayama*) and physical postures (*asana*). The student is also taught to conserve prana, not to waste either his inborn, genetic store or that acquired through meditation. Some yogis believe that we are given a certain number of breaths at birth. If we learn to breathe more slowly, we use up our endowment at a slower pace and thus live longer.

There are remarkable parallels between Yoga and Chinese yin-yang theory, the philosophy that health is a balance of complementary opposites: fire and water, mind and body, self and nature. Hatha Yoga balances the solar (Ha) and lunar (tha) currents of life energy. By reversing the courses of the two pranic breaths, one fire-like, one water-like, longevity is assured. Fire is made to descend, water to ascend, thus unifying mind (fire) and body (water) and preventing the dispersal of life energy.

The similarity between Indian Yoga and Chinese qigong is not mere coincidence. Yoga is probably even older than qigong and may have influenced its development. Statues of yogis sitting in lotus posture can be seen as early as the Mohenjo–Daro civilization of the twenty-fifth to twentieth centuries B.C. Some techniques were undoubtedly brought to China by early pilgrims and Buddhist monks in the first centuries A.D. By the sixth century the philosophy of *Sankhya*, the Hindu philosophical base of Yoga, was translated into Chinese. Many Chinese recognized India as a cultural center.

Information was traveling in both directions. Joseph Needham explores the history of this exchange in *Science and Civilization in China*, Vol. 5: "In a single year, +692 [A.D.], missions from five Indian countries . . . converged on the Chinese capital carrying tribute."[42] Thirty years later, the king of the Indian state of Kanci "built a temple devoted to China, and asked the emperor for an inscription giving a name to it."[43] In A.D. 644, even as the Chinese were translating Yogic texts into Chinese, the king of Kamarupa ordered that the Daoist philosophical classic the *Dao De Jing* (Classic of the Way and Its Power), be translated into Sanskrit. The ensuing controversy regarding the translation of technical Chinese terms into accurate Sanskrit equivalents reveals India's high level of interest in Chinese culture.[44]

Ancient tales of Daoist recluses and Indian yogis are remarkably similar. Spiritual adepts of both traditions enjoyed meditating in mountain-caves and river-hermitages. In South Indian Tamil literature of the ninth through thirteenth centuries, we read of eighteen magician-alchemists (*sittars*), two of whom came from China. This was also a major period in the development and spread of Hatha Yoga. We can presume that at the same time that Yoga was brought to China, Indian Yogis were carrying Daoist techniques of meditation and qigong to India.

The exchange between Indian Yoga and Chinese qigong continues to the present day. Zhang He, a prominent Chinese writer on qigong, has also written a text on Yoga.[45] Zhang's teacher, Daoist Master and acupuncturist Dr. Henry K. S. Wong, was an early sponsor of the Maharishi Mahesh Yogi and Swami Satchidananda, before their arrival in the West. Dr. Wong taught Yoga in Hong Kong for nearly twenty-five years and developed a unique integration of Indian pranayama and qigong respiratory exercises.

EUROPE'S MEDICAL GYMNASTICS

The European tradition of physical education is partly a derivative of Greek exercises dating from the sixth century B.C.[46] The original pentathlon of foot racing, jumping, discus, javelin, and wrestling were practiced in the nude (thus *gymnastics* from the Greek *gymnos* "naked"). Hippocrates is credited with founding the theory of *medical gymnastics*, which held that such exercises were not merely sport, but, along with diet and massage, essential ingredients in preventive medicine. Europeans continued to show interest in healing exercises through the Middle Ages, Renaissance, and Baroque periods. The general opinion, however, remained close to modern, Western understanding: that gymnastics are the domain of the healthy, whereas specialized medications or procedures are necessary to treat the sick.

In the late eighteenth and early nineteenth centuries in Europe, there was a resurgence of appreciation for the healing benefits of exercise, largely due to interest in Chinese qigong. In 1779, the Jesuit P. M. Cibot became well-known for his illustrated French translation of Daoist qigong texts:

Notice du Cong-fou [Kung-fu] des Bonzes Tao-see [Dao-shi, Daoist priests]. Kung-fu was another name for qigong, though today it more commonly refers to Chinese martial arts practice. Cibot says:

> It follows that the various postures of the Kung-fu, if well directed, should effect a salutary clearance in all those illnesses which arise from an embarrassed, retarded, or even interrupted, circulation.[47]

Europe was ready for Cibot. Only five years earlier, Viennese physician Franz Anton Mesmer (1734–1815) had discovered that by placing magnets on a patient's body or by simply holding his hands over the patient, he could induce a hypnotic state, "mesmerizing," effectively curing many problems. During Mesmer's "magnetic therapy," his patients would sometimes feel a fluid moving through their bodies. This sounds very much like qi and the sensations associated with qi-flow. Mesmer was an influential figure and a household name in European society.[48]

Cibot's descriptions of the Daoist exercises and respiratory techniques were probably the major influence on Per Henrik Ling (1776–1839), the Swede who founded modern gymnastics. For thirty-five years, Ling taught four types of gymnastics: physical education, military training, medical, and aesthetic at his Bernadotte Institute in Stockholm. Designed to both improve health and treat disease, Ling's medical gymnastics were based on a theory of vital energy with many parallels to qigong. In 1857 N. Dally wrote that "Ling's entire doctrine, theoretical and practical, is only a sort of photographic image of Taoist kung-fu."[49] He described Ling's calisthenics as "a splendid Chinese vase overlaid with European paint."

Ling's calisthenics, gymnastics, and his pioneering use of exercise equipment are the foundation of today's system of physical education. His twisting, squatting, and back-bending exercises are practiced in gyms and health clubs all over the world. However, Ling's ideas about vital energy were eventually dropped. As the philosophy of *vitalism* was eclipsed by scientific materialism, Western exercises and physical therapies began to place an almost exclusive emphasis on strength, stamina, flexibility, and coordination. These qualities are certainly important. However, they reflect the Western preoccupation with the *appearance* of health: a beautiful figure and well-defined muscles. Modern Western exercise systems can be considered symptoms of disempowerment. The individual's internal health was believed to be beyond control and, if disturbed, required the external intervention of an expert physician. The body was reduced to a machine, without intelligence of its own, as incapable of self-correcting serious malfunctions as an automobile. This assumption is incorrect.

Western science has circled back to the recognition of vital force, or "bioelectricity," as a source of healing. Scientists have shown that we can control this energy to an extraordinary degree, exerting control over bodily functions that were once considered involuntary. It is time to reincorporate many of the insights of vitalism and of the ancient healing systems that recognized the power of qi.

CHAPTER THREE

The Three Treasures:
A Chinese Model
of Body Energy

*The sages looked up to contemplate the patterns
of heaven, looked down to observe the ways of the
earth. They knew the inner workings of things,
the theories of life and death.*
—THE CLASSIC OF CHANGE *(YI JING)*

In biblical exegesis, we first seek the meaning of classical Hebrew and Greek, looking for the connotations of a term at or close to the time that the text was written. When Jesus used the word *pneuma*, perhaps it meant something different than it does today. Similarly, by doing some linguistic archaeology, exploring the structure and meaning of ancient Chinese words, we learn how the body and mind were understood in ancient times and find universal truths that strike a resonant chord today.

THE ETYMOLOGY OF QI

The Chinese language is pictographic. To understand the original intent of the word "qi," we need only analyze the components of the ideogram. At most, it might be necessary to look up a more ancient form of the character, in which the picture components are more obvious.[1]

One of the earliest characters for qi consists of the word for "sun" and "fire," suggesting that qi, like sunlight, is a source of warmth and is essential for life. A living body is warm; cold slows down the movement of qi and leads to death. This concept of *vital heat* is maintained in a specialized ideogram for qi used exclusively in Daoist literature. The upper part of the character, a picture of a man clearing the land of trees, means "negation." The wood is gone, hence "negation, wanting, lacking, without." The lower part of the character consists of four sparks from a flame. As a whole, the character seems to mean "no fire." Even as extreme cold slows down the qi and is too yin, so excess fire overstimulates and is too yang. Qi requires a moderate, balanced polarity: passive and active, cold and warm. If the qi is healthy, then the energy does not go to extremes.

Some writers interpret the "fire" as a symbol of desire or passion. No fire would mean "no desire." However, ascetic denial of human feelings is inconsistent with the qigong philosophy of naturalness. Balance of emotions is what is important, not being attached to states of anger or joy, and remembering to laugh at oneself. Alan Watts used to say that angels, like Daoist Immortals, can fly because they take themselves lightly! "No fire" is not the absence of emotions, but rather the absence of grasping and attachment. The emotions, like qi, must be fluid and changeable, not stuck in extreme positions.

My favorite interpretation of the "no fire" ideogram is one I learned from a Daoist priest from Hong Kong. He said, "In this character, 'negation' means negation of form, of concepts of anything fixed and rigid. Qi means 'the formless fire of life.' Qi creates life; it is life, but it has no substance, and anything you can measure is not it. It never holds still long enough to be measured." This highlights a difference between Eastern and Western ways of understanding the body. Traditional Chinese Medicine is not as concerned with measurement and quantification. It recognizes that life is a fluid process; qi is more a function than a substance. We can understand it best through what it does in the body and environment.

The qi ideogram described above has strong metaphysical, spiritual, and psychological connotations and is unique to Daoist writings. The most common character for qi, which appears throughout qigong, medical, and popular literature, is 氣. It represents such everyday concepts as "weather" (sky qi), "balloon" (qi sphere), "customs" (habitual qi), "arrogant" (qi high), "oxygen" (nourishing qi), and the "healing exercises" of qigong.

According to the ancient *Shuo Wen Jie Zi* (Dictionary of Chinese Etymology), the three lines at the top of the character mean steam or vapor; the character for rice 米 is on the bottom. Thus, qi means "vapor or steam rising from cooking rice." Some texts substitute the character 火 "fire" for rice. In either case, the implication is that for water to boil and produce steam, there must be fire. Qi then can be defined as *the energy produced when complementary, polar opposites are harmonized.* Vital energy, qi, arises when opposites are unified: fire and water, heavenly (the steam) and earthly (the rice). Other yang/yin polarities include: mind and body, conscious and subconscious, self and environment. In the same way that an electric circuit requires the positive (yang) and negative (yin) pole, so a strong current of qi requires a balance of opposites.

We can also interpret this character symbolically. Rising vapors are a common image for air or breath. In qigong meditation, the breath is sometimes visualized as mist, steaming through various organs or along particular energy routes. Rice, the staple of the Chinese diet, simply represents food. Thus, the character qi indicates the two major sources of qi: air and food, and two ingredients in qigong training: respiratory techniques and diet.

Our understanding of qigong is an expansion and elaboration of themes hidden in the very structure of the word "qi." The various ideograms used to represent qi bring up the following questions: What is the nature of life energy? How can the physical, mental, emotional, and spiritual aspects of life energy be kept in balance? What is the role of breathing and diet in qi development? How can fire and water—all of the disparate portions of myself—be integrated to create harmony and health?

SOURCES OF QI

The Chinese word "qi" is a generic term for life energy. Just as a medical scientist thinks of healing as mutifaceted, including chemical, psychological, electromagnetic, and environmental components, so qigong practitioners analyze the concept "qi" into several different categories.

There are three main sources of qi: breath, food, and constitution. Air or breath (*zong qi*) and food (*gu qi*, literally "grain qi") mix to form the "nutritive qi" (*ying qi*) that travels through the acupuncture meridians to all of the tissues of the body.

Whereas breath and food are acquired qi, the third source of qi is inborn. In Chinese, the technical term for this inherited, we might even say genetic, life energy is *yuan qi*, literally "original qi." Original qi accounts for our constitution and inherited tendencies toward health or disease. A child with weak original qi may have birth defects, be subject to frequent colds and infections, or, in an extreme case, fail to thrive.

Original qi is largely a product of the health of the parents and the care they give the child in utero. If the mother eats healthily, practices good personal hygiene, lives in as nontoxic an environment as possible—or at least spends more time in nature—and keeps her mind peaceful, then the child will have the best chance at a healthy life. Chinese medical theory also states that the parents' sexual compatibility, the "chemistry" between them, creates the child's original qi. If the mother and father have harmonious, joyous, energetic, and pleasurable sexual relations, then it is more likely that the child will be healthy.

Healthy conception and development are also influenced by the age of the parents. It is best for women to conceive when they are in their most fertile years. According to Chinese medicine, children born to parents in their forties or fifties generally have weaker constitutions and are more prone to disease. Men and women share equally in this endowment of original qi. A wealth of anecdotal evidence suggests that qigong tends to delay menopause and can extend the years of fertility. Women qigong masters have been known to conceive during their sixties.

The term "original qi" can mean different things in different contexts. In medical texts, original qi means inherited, genetic qi. I call this *personal original qi*. In metaphysical texts, the same Chinese word, "original qi" (yuan qi) means the primal energy of life, the creative and omnipresent power of the Dao. We are also born with a supply of yuan qi. It is a gift from the universe, inherited from our cosmic parents, the Yin and the Yang. I call this *transpersonal original qi*. Inherited original qi is a given; we cannot go back to the time before conception in order to increase our present supply. We can, however, supplement it by practicing meditation and spiritual development. We can learn to attune to and absorb transpersonal original qi, "the original qi of Heaven and Earth." In Chinese medicine, a child with a delicate or feeble constitution is treated with diet, herbs, massage, External Qi Healing, and possibly acupuncture, depending on the age of the child. Adults have more healing options.

There are several ways to supplement weak original qi. Tranquil meditation helps one tune in to a source of power beyond the personal, which some practitioners identify as God or the Dao. Nature is also a source of original qi. We can learn to harmonize with the great currents of qi in Nature, sensing the healing power of pure mountain air, of trees, and of fertile ground.

The other method is to practice qigong exercises and to take in healthy qi through diet. This is called accumulating "postnatal qi" (*hou tian qi*), a fancy term for qi acquired after birth. However, since postnatal qi is not constitutional, it is more easily dissipated and lost than original qi. Dedication and regular practice are necessary to sustain it. A crash diet or two-week qigong intensive once a year will not result in better long-term health.

Strong original qi and a hardy constitution are no guarantee of perfect health. Resources not acquired through personal effort and training are easily taken for granted and squandered. I have met many people who claim, "I never get sick anyway, so why should I exercise or diet?" We can sometimes get away with this in youth. However, the cumulative effects of self-neglect tend to catch up with us in later years.

But what about the individual who neglects a healthy lifestyle and never gets sick anyway? We have all met people like Jim, a fifty-year-old couch potato who hates exercise, smokes cigarettes, and drinks a bit too much. He has never been hospitalized and has never had any illness more serious than a common cold. Jim is the exception rather than the rule, a combination of a strong constitution and some degree of plain old luck. If you are envious or if you have sour grapes about getting sick in spite of dedicated self-care, then shake your fist at heaven and shout "Injustice!" Let's not forget the lesson of Job, the man who did everything right and yet for whom everything went wrong. Some things may be beyond our personal control.

CATEGORIES OF QI

An entire book could be written about types of qi. The concept is so central to Chinese medicine that virtually all states of health or disease can be qualified by it. Some Chinese martial arts authors write volumes about the qi required for punching, kicking, blocking, parrying, pushing, pulling, etc. Their analytical aptitude does not imply that they know how to fight! More definition does not equal deeper understanding. It is easy for human beings to delude themselves into believing that because they can name something, they understand it or that it enriches their lives. Fulfillment comes through experience. Without the experience of qi, the label means nothing.

To understand qigong, we should be familiar with seven major kinds of qi:

- **Breath Qi**—from respiration
- **Food Qi**—from diet
- **Original Qi**—inherited from parents or universe
- **Internal Qi**—all qi inside the body
- **External Qi**—qi emanating from the body
- **Nutritive Qi**—flows inside the meridians
- **Protective Qi**—energetic barrier against external pathogens

We have already discussed breath qi, food qi, and original qi. The other general categories of qi are internal qi (*nei qi*) and external qi (*wai qi*). Internal qi moves in the body; qigong is practiced to accumulate internal qi and to correct its flow. External qi has two meanings. It is the qi that emanates from and surrounds the body, the energetic field or aura. Disturbances in this field are indications of underlying disease. Heat above the liver, for example, might indicate that the liver is congested, perhaps from too much fatty food. And since the same Chinese word can function as a noun or verb, wai qi can also mean "to externalize the qi," projecting the qi into a patient's body either with or without touch. This ancient Chinese version of Therapeutic Touch is called External Qi Healing.

Nutritive qi (ying qi), sometimes called "true qi" (zhen qi), is a special term for the internal qi carried to the various tissues and cells of the body. Nutritive qi flows through the acupuncture meridians in a manner similar to the way the veins carry blood. (See also Chapter 15.)

Protective qi (wei qi) protects the body against external pernicious influences: extremes of weather, germs, harmful spiritual or emotional forces. It is a component of the qi in the meridians, and it also flows under the skin, forming a kind of porous, energetic armor. When it is functioning properly, it allows healing energy in but keeps harmful energy out. As part of its defensive function, protective qi is responsible for maintaining the warmth of the skin, controlling perspiration, and regulating the opening and closing of the pores of the skin. Protective qi is produced naturally during qigong practice and is most closely associated with healthy respiration. Deep, quiet respiration creates an optimum flow of protective qi around the body.

QI RESERVOIRS: THE *DAN TIAN* AND INTERNAL ORGANS

The *dan tian* is the most important energy center in the body and one of the most frequently used terms in qigong literature. Located in the lower abdomen, midway between the navel and pubic bone, it is the body's center of gravity and center of energy. The dan tian both stores qi, like an energy reservoir, and propels qi through the body, like a pump. Dan tian means, literally, the elixir (dan) field (tian), the field of the elixir of long life and wisdom. The qigong practitioner learns to cultivate, nurture, and harvest qi by concentrating on this energy center.

There are actually three energy centers in the body. The lower dan tian, in the lower abdomen, is associated with sexuality. It stores qi and sexual energy, jing. The middle dan tian, at the level of the heart, stores qi and is related to respiration and the health of the internal organs. The upper dan tian, between the eyebrows (at the level of the "third eye"), holds shen, the energy of consciousness, and is related to the brain. When the term dan tian is unqualified, it always refers to the most important dan tian, the lower dan tian. The three dan tians are like batteries that can be recharged through physical and spiritual healing practices.

The lower dan tian is generally emphasized in qigong. It is like the root of the tree of life. If a tree's roots are in good soil, then it will grow. If we neglect the roots and only prune the branches, the tree will die. Or if we try to build a temple too quickly or too high—working with the upper dan tian before the lower—then the temple will topple over. This is why qigong emphasizes the primacy of rooted standing, breathing, and body awareness. *Body practice is the root of spiritual practice*. By watching the breath, we can find the source of the breath. When we calm the body, the mind can expand without limit.

The internal organs are also important reservoirs of qi. Although all of the internal organs store qi, the relatively solid, yin organs which include the liver, heart, spleen, lungs, and kidneys are better able to maintain their "charge." These organs are known collectively as *zang*, which translates, "to store or hold." The contrasting hollow yang organs, known as *fu*, include the gallbladder, small intestine, stomach, large intestine, and bladder. The fu are involved in digestion and must be hollow in order to transport substances.

Of the five zang, the spleen has a particularly close connection with qi. The spleen extracts qi from food and fluids. This refined qi is brought up to the lungs, where it mixes with breath qi, producing the qi that flows in the meridians. (The turbid, impure parts of food qi descend toward the colon for elimination.) According to the Five Element Theory, the spleen corresponds to the Earth element. It is the fertile ground that supplies nourishment for the body. For this reason, spleen disorders weaken the blood and qi and make us more susceptible to disease. (The connection between the spleen and immunity makes sense from a Western perspective. The spleen stores blood and acts as a pump for both the red blood cells, carrying oxygen, and the white blood cells, fighting disease.)

THE THREE TREASURES

When a Westerner is asked the purpose of qigong, he is likely to say, "To improve health." When a Chinese qigong master is asked the same question, a common response is, *Jing, qi, shen he yi*, "Sexual energy, qi, and spirit unified." These three forms of energy are known as the Three Treasures. Sexual energy and spirit are yin and yang forms of qi, respectively. The former is earthy and is associated with the most intimate form of physical contact. The latter, spirit, is yang and heavenly, linking human beings with the divine. When the term qi is used in contrast to these two, then qi is considered neutral, at the midpoint between the positive and negative pole. It is neither yin nor yang in itself, yet is capable of functioning in either capacity.

Jing

The word "jing" was originally a pictogram of the germ of a grain, probably wheat or rice. The same character was later given an extended meaning: germ of life, life essence, sexual energy, the most refined, quintessential form of anything. An herbal jing is a concentrated extract. Jing gold is refined, pure gold. In qigong, jing is the most yin form of qi. It tends to flow downward, like water, moving toward the genitals and finding expression in fluids related to reproduction: semen, sperm, vaginal lubricants, ova, menstrual blood. All of these are physical manifestations of jing. However, jing, like the other treasures, is essentially a subtle energy. Qi is air, but it is more than air. In a similar way, jing is sperm, but it is more than sperm. Jing is sometimes said to flow or gather even if there is no change in associated physical substances.

Jing is yin relative to other forms of body energy. Yet, jing itself has yin and yang expressions. The yin, earthy aspect of jing, is the reproductive and sexual fluids. The yang aspect is saliva. Although saliva is physically composed of digestive enzymes and protective antibodies, it is energetically linked to sexuality. In sexual qigong partners are advised to swallow each other's saliva as part of foreplay or as a way to exchange sexual qi during intercourse. (See also Chapter 20.)

In Chinese medicine, jing is the energy of growth and development, slowly increasing during childhood, reaching its peak at age twenty-one, and then decreasing, unless checked or supplemented by qigong training. For this reason, diminishing jing is associated with many of the signs of aging, particularly osteoporosis, less responsive immune cells, loss of libido, graying hair, slower reflexes, and poorer memory.

Jing is the energy that creates bone marrow and the gray matter of the brain. (A classical Chinese term for the brain is *sui hai* "the sea of marrow.") One of the most famous qigong practices is *huan jing bu nao* "reverse the jing to repair the brain," a potentially important process for all of us, considering that, in adults, brain cells die off at an average rate of one thousand cells per hour. Jing is said to "reverse" because, instead of flowing down toward the genitals, it is pushed upward through meditative exercises. Although it is unlikely that damaged brain cells can be "repaired," there is a wealth of evidence proving that individuals can slow the rate of destruction and are capable of awakening new areas of the brain.

In Daoist literature, this process is called "the Yellow River reverses its course." A Daoist priest once joked with me, "The easy way to reverse the jing is to stand on your head!" When I shared this bit of wisdom with a

TABLE 2: THE THREE TREASURES

	Jing	Qi	Shen
Energy	sexual	life	spirit
Organ-Source	kidneys and lungs	spleen	liver and heart
Element	Water	Air	Fire
Form	sexual fluids, saliva	breath	light and spirit
Character	yin	yin, yang, neutral	yang
Movement	down	down and up	up
Reservoir	lower dan tian	middle dan tian	upper dan tian
Circulatory System (TCM)*	bones	meridians	extra meridians
Associated System (WM)**	reproductive, endocrine	respiratory	nervous
Gate	genitals	nose and mouth	eyes
Cultivation Practice	sexual	qigong	meditation

*according to Traditional Chinese Medicine (TCM)
**from the perspective of Western Medicine (WM)

friend, he commented, "My grandfather always said, 'If man stands on his head, he will think with his balls.'" This might not be such a bad state of affairs. In Western society, mind, heart, and genitals are far too independent from one another. Qigong emphasizes the importance of thinking and feeling with the whole body, so that one will be able to make better life decisions, informed by the whole being rather than a particular, dissociated part.

Increasing the reserve of jing stimulates hair growth. The hair also has a tendency to return to its original color. Qigong master Yu An-Ren was imprisoned for several years during China's Cultural Revolution. He was in his thirties at the time. During his incarceration, the center of his head developed a spot of gray, which quickly spread, until all of his hair turned silver. At the same time, his spine began to hunch over. His resting heart rate was 90–100 beats per minute, jumping to 120 if he climbed a flight of stairs. On his release, Yu began to practice qigong intensively in order to regain his health. Now at age fifty-seven, he has a full head of black hair, a straight, flexible spine, and a resting heart rate of seventy.

Jing has three external sources. It is inherited from parents, derived from the purified, refined parts of food, and, in Daoist sexual yoga, can be given to and absorbed from one's sexual partner.

EXPLANATION OF THE THREE TREASURES

Table 2 is by no means the final word on the Three Treasures. Each school or system of qigong has its own interpretation. The various categories are not rigid or mutually exclusive. For instance, jing and shen are types of qi (yin and yang respectively). The related practices, sexual healing and meditation, can be considered subsets of qigong. And although shen is connected to the mind and spirit, jing, which nourishes the brain, is also related to spirit, and qi, as respiration, affects our mood state. The Three Treasures Chart may, nevertheless, help us understand qigong as physical and spiritual cultivation and a process of integrating polar energies.

Looking at column 1, Jing, we see that it corresponds to sexual energy, which manifests in the body as sexual fluids, is yin and thus moves downward, like water, filling the lower dan tian and kidneys. Jing-energy tends to drain outward, leaving its energetic "gate," the genitals, whether one is sexually stimulated or not, though jing is lost more quickly if sexual relations are inharmonious. Jing circulates through the bones and, according to Chinese medicine, accounts for the health of the bones, brain, and mind. All forms of qigong cultivate jing. The type of qigong that cultivates jing specifically is sexual qigong, the art of internally strengthening sexual energy and finding greater harmony with one's partner. Cultivating jing probably has a salutary effect on the endocrine system, resulting in better hormonal balance.

Column 3, Shen, is the subtle energy of spirit. It is yang and moves upward, like fire. Shen is stored in the upper dan tian, between the eyebrows, and escapes through the eyes, unless checked by introspection and meditation. Shen flows through the extra meridians and when balanced creates a healthy nervous system.

Qi, the omnipresent energy of life, manifests as breath and easily escapes through the nose and mouth unless conserved by practicing quiet, meditative breathing. Qigong is sometimes described as a method of "inner alchemy" (nei dan) in which fire (yang) flows down and water (yin) flows up, meeting and producing steam, the qi. Shen descends during meditation; the eyes are turned within, illuminating the microcosm. Abdominal respiration stimulates jing-water to flow upward, replenishing the lower dan tian. All three treasures are conserved by cultivating a quiet mind: a state of clarity that Daoists call the Void.

There are also various internal sources of jing. The reservoir of jing is the lower dan tian. Among the internal organs, jing is stored primarily in the *shen*, a word that although usually translated "kidneys" actually includes the kidneys, adrenals, and urogenital system. This word "shen" is not to be confused with another word "shen" meaning "spirit," one of the three treasures. The two are pronounced similarly and thus written the same in English, but are represented by completely different Chinese characters.

According to ancient Daoist alchemical texts (the art of refining the body's energy to create the gold of health and enlightenment), jing is produced internally from the combined energies of kidneys and lungs. Anything that improves the health of these two organs will help increase the store of jing.

Shen

Shen, spirit, is the third of the three treasures. The word "shen" has two meanings in Chinese—spirit and "to stretch." In ancient China, spirit mediums were called shen "stretchers." They would perform yoga-like postures to invite the descent of an ancestral spirit. Later, shen came to mean a more permanent indwelling spirit and the capacity of the mind to be aware and to think. Here "aware" includes both sensual and spiritual awareness, an intuitive understanding of the workings of the universe. A canon of Chinese philosophy, the *Appendix to the Yi Jing* (Classic of Change, approximately second century), defines shen this way: "The unfathomability of yin and yang is called shen" and "One who knows the transformations of nature perceives the workings of shen."

Like jing and qi, shen can be cultivated within the body or harvested from the universe. Shen has been associated with dance and exercise from the very earliest times. According to the *Yi Jing*, Confucius said, "In ancient times, the sages inspired the people with drumming and dancing in order to reach an understanding of shen." All forms of tranquil qigong develop shen. Shen is associated with the heart and liver. When these organs are healthy, their qi combines to produce shen. If they are ill, the spirit is unsettled, and the mind may have a tendency to be restless.

French sinologist Catherine Despeux defines shen in her *Traité d'Alchimie et de Physiologie Taoïste* (Treatise on Taoist Alchemy and Physiology): "Shen is spiritual and psychic energy, the divine part of one's being, and has an essentially luminous nature."[2] Shen is the light of the eyes. It is conserved and increased when we turn the eyes within, practicing introspection and meditation. Shen energy is lost when we spend too much time looking outside, preoccupied by either external events or our ideas about them. Disturbed, muddled, or mad states of mind are diseases of shen. In Western terms, shen can be thought of as the energy of the nervous system, and thus the most highly charged and electrical of the three treasures.

Just as jing flows through the bones and qi through the meridians, shen flows through a special series of channels, known as the Eight Extra Meridians. These are the energy paths commonly focused on during classical qigong meditations such as the Small Heavenly Circulation (also called the

Microcosmic Orbit). Three of the extra meridians are known to most qigong practitioners: the body's yang-qi superhighway, *du mai*, running along the spine; the yin highway, *ren mai*, down the front midline of the body; and the "thrusting channel," *chong mai*, through the center of the body, connecting the perineum with the crown. The energy vortexes of Indian Yoga, known as chakras, are situated along the thrusting channel.

We can think of the three treasures—jing, qi, shen—as body, mind, and spirit. Some religions emphasize denying the body, or "the flesh," to use St. Paul's terminology, and seeking the spirit. Qigong philosophy is just the opposite. It is impossible to find spirit without integrating the experience of the body. This idea is reflected in perhaps the most famous qigong maxim: "Refine the jing to create qi; refine qi to create shen; refine shen and return to the Void." Subtle energies are based on denser ones, in the way that steam rises from boiling water. If you wish to develop your mind, pay attention to the body. If you wish to develop your spirit, pay attention to the mind.

The Void, the state of empty, clear mindedness, remains both the goal and the source of practice. We don't achieve the Void, we "return" to it. The Void is your original mind, an inner purity that has *never* been clouded by concepts and images. Some wise advice from Daoist Master K. S. Wong, "Don't make the process of refining jing to qi to shen too complicated! Since returning to the Void is the goal, why not make this the basis of your practice? If the mind is empty and attentive, then jing, qi, and shen all reach fullness and health."

CHAPTER FOUR

Qigong Science:
Correlates of Healing Energy

God cures and the doctor sends the bill.
—MARK TWAIN

IS IT SCIENCE?

Before we can discuss qigong science, we need to ask, "Is qigong an art or a science?" The Chinese have always said, unequivocally, "both." Qigong is an art because it is a conscious arrangement of posture, movement, and breath that creates beauty in the human mind and body. It is also an art in the sense of being a skill achieved by diligent practice.

Qigong is a science because it includes the testing and investigation of healing techniques through centuries of trial and error and careful observation. The Chinese philosophy of energy storage and flow provides a theoretical explanation of how qigong works. Qigong has also been rigorously tested according to the standards of Western science, producing measurable, statistically significant, and replicable results. Like his or her Chinese counterpart, the Western scientist asks, "How does qigong work?" He analyzes and evaluates experimental results using ideas consistent with the Western paradigm. Instead of theorizing about life energy or acupuncture meridians, he is likely to discuss electromagnetic energy and nerve cells or to look for modern equivalents of ancient concepts. The modern explanation does not invalidate the older Chinese one. Rather, they are complementary explanations of the same observed phenomenon—that practicing qigong causes specific healing effects, with a high degree of reliability.

Of course, each theoretical model has its strengths and weaknesses. A Western scientist sees one billiard ball hit another and theorizes a cause-and-effect relationship. Ball A *caused* ball B to move. This theory can help a scientist predict the outcome of other analogous events. If I eat too much food (the cause), I will probably gain weight (the effect). A Chinese qigong master sees something different. As one ball touches the other, there is one linked *process*. He does not see a separation of events: ball A hitting ball B, *then*, ball B moving. Instead, there was a continuous hit-move action. Discrete causes and effects are illusions of the dissecting intellect. The qigong master realizes that life is change and relationship; there are no simple explanations. In any case, the Chinese man reminds his friend, "Never mind how they move, just get the eight ball in the side pocket!"

The Chinese have traditionally had a pragmatic attitude toward qigong: it is important to use what works and to consider what is obvious to the human senses, rather than getting too caught up in the elegance of the theory. There is an enlightening Buddhist parable about a man who is shot with an arrow. The doctor comes along, but before the doctor removes the arrow, the man wants to know, "Who shot the arrow? What is the arrow made of? Where was it shot from?" Altogether the doctor is asked more than a hundred questions. The Buddha says, "This man will die before the arrow is removed." The expedient and intelligent thing to do is to remove the arrow. Theory can come later. For the qigong student, the practice is what is most important. How can one understand qi without practicing qigong? Perhaps the best book about qigong is a journal of your own experiences.

The classical theory of qigong has withstood the test of time. It will not be supplanted or disproved by medical science. Instead modern science provides a congruous and complementary theory as well as some powerful experimental evidence that confirms qigong's efficacy. We know that the sun is shining, but it is, nevertheless, deeply satisfying to human curiosity to know how and why it shines.

THE CENTIPEDE AND THE SNAIL: DESCRIBING THE INEFFABLE

In a classic Chinese tale, a snail asks a centipede, "How do you move all those legs?" When the centipede tries to reply, he becomes utterly confused and is unable to move at all. We may find ourselves in a similar predicament. At the level of feeling and body-knowing, we understand how to move our legs and wiggle our fingers. Yet the actual process by which movement happens is so complex that there seems to be a cause behind a cause behind a cause, an almost infinite chain of ever more microscopic and interconnected events. If we had to learn through the intellect how to wiggle a finger in order to move it, it would never happen!

Similarly, at the level of body-knowing, we *know* the difference between healthy and diseased qi and can train ourselves, through qigong, to sense this more accurately. The intellect, by contrast, divides and labels experience, comprehending only limited, measurable aspects of qi.

It is interesting that the Sanskrit word for intellect, *vikalpa*, means to divide and break apart. Our English word "matter" is from another Sanskrit word, the root *ma*, meaning the illusions *(maya)* created by intellect as it confuses these bits and pieces and descriptions with that which is described—the experience. The word or concept "tree" is obviously not the same as the actual tree. When we experience a tree, we see the earth it grows in, the play of sunlight and wind in the branches, the ants climbing up the trunk, and all of this is colored by our feelings, memories, and associations. The actual tree is not a static, unchanging concept, but a fluid, always changing experience. By definition, the intellect can never understand the whole.

Moreover, if ancient Chinese cosmology is right, if the self *is* qi, then how can qi ever be fully known? Who would do the knowing? Can the subject be the object of its own knowledge? As my old friend Alan Watts was so fond of saying, "Can a sword cut itself, can an eye see itself?" Thus, as we discuss the knowable science of qi and qigong, it is important to maintain a healthy respect for the unknowable, the mystery.

The only sensible way to analyze qi is in terms of *correlates*.[1] In the same way that thunder is a correlate of lightning, but is not the same as lightning, so electrical, biochemical, bioluminescent, volitional, and probably some as yet unmeasured phenomena are correlates of qi. The concept of "correlates" allows a scientist to discuss healing without offending the mystic.

In the West many studies in the fields of physics and medicine have, while not testing qigong directly, examined energies and biochemical substances that accompany or promote healing. It is reasonable to infer that by measuring correlates of healing energy, scientists are also measuring correlates of qi. This view is supported by the majority of scientists cited below and by many others conducting research in the emerging field of energy medicine, the study of how energies interact with the human psyche and physiology.[2]

THE ELECTRIC CORRELATE

Bioelectricity: The Current of Healing

Most of the evidence of measurable correlates of qi have been amassed around the phenomenon of bioelectricity. Although qigong causes obvious physical changes—relaxed muscles and improved respiration and posture—some of its most powerful healing effects are due to its influence on the body's electromagnetic energy. A healthy body creates healthy energy, and, conversely, healthy bioelectricity—the qi—creates a healthy body. Physical changes are programmed by electrical messages passing through the nervous system.

Just as computers can be made to run more efficiently through a process called "optimization," so qigong optimizes the human "computer," shifting data to make our bodies run more efficiently and erasing old, unneeded information that clutters the system. By changing the way electrical signals are relayed in the body, qigong restores the body's original "program" to health.

Robert Becker, M.D., orthopedic surgeon and researcher, has demonstrated that the *perineural cells*, or nerve sheaths, carry a direct current of electricity, prompting the body to grow, heal, regenerate, and repair itself.[3] For this reason, any change in health is always accompanied by electrical changes, both at the site of injury or repair and as an electromagnetic field around the body.[4] The strength, polarity, and delivery of electricity determines how and if we heal.[5]

Becker is well-known among his medical colleagues for developing a widely used method of electrical osteogenesis, the electrical stimulation of bone growth. If a fracture refuses to heal properly, electrodes are inserted on either side of the break. Running a minute electric current through the bone stimulates the regrowth of cells. The physician artificially creates a "current of healing," mimicking the body's normal repair mechanism. In a dramatic example of this connection between healing and electricity, Becker amputated the leg of a salamander, then exposed the salamander to an electromagnetic field in which the polarity (positive and negative poles) was the reverse of that normally required for healing. The salamander grew an extra arm in place of the leg.

If electricity is essential for healing, it must be an important correlate of healing qi. Experiments in both China and the United States confirm this hypothesis.

There is evidence that during qigong the conductivity of acupuncture points—that is, the ability of these points to conduct an electric charge—changes dramatically. When a qigong practitioner concentrates on a particular acupoint, the skin resistance at that point goes down relative to other acupoints on the body. Researchers tested this hypothesis at Beijing's Institute of Space Medical Engineering and reported their results at the Second World Conference for Academic Exchange of Medical Qigong in 1993.[6] The qigong group consisted of ninety-six subjects who had practiced qigong for two to three years. The control group consisted of fifteen nonpractitioners. Both skin resistance and skin microvibration (a low-frequency muscular vibration) were tested at three acupuncture points associated with the three dan tians: *Yintang* at the third eye, *Shanzhong* on the sternum, and *Qihai* on the lower abdomen. Another point, *lao gong*, in the center of the palm was also tested. Qigong students often experience these various points as warm, tingling, and highly charged during and after practice.

Both groups sat quietly with their eyes closed for ten minutes, then spent several minutes focusing on specific points. During meditation both groups demonstrated an ability to excite the four "main points," mentioned above, relative to other acupuncture points on the body. This was measured as %/minute of skin resistance change. When microvibration at the points was analyzed on a frequency spectral analysis graph, results showed a percentage of microvibration of 49 ± 6.1 percent in the qigong group vs. 16.7 ± 8.3 percent in the control group. The amplitude of microvibration waves increased on the main points and either decreased or changed only slightly on the other points, again demonstrating relative electrical excitement at the points of focus. Both the qigong group and the untrained group were able to cause a change in skin conductivity at the main points; however, the qigong group was able to elicit a much greater change, thus demonstrating the value of qigong training.

One of the famed pioneers in Chinese medical research, Hiroshi Motoyama, Ph.D., director of Tokyo's Institute for Religious Psychology, has found a specific connection between abnormal skin conductivity (too high or too low) at acupoints on the tips of the fingers and toes and disorders in associated internal organs. Motoyama designed a machine that could stimulate an acupoint with a three-volt DC charge, taking measurements of the skin current at the point before, during, and after the charge is administered. "Through measuring over two thousand subjects with this machine and comparing their data with the results of other medical examinations and with their professed subjective symptoms, we have been able to draw up criteria of normality and abnormality for the values obtained before polarization, after polarization, and polarization."[7] For instance, if the point on the big toe, associated with the liver, has values that are too high, one might suspect past or present liver disease. Low values in the heart-related acupoint on the little finger may indicate heart failure.

Kenneth Sancier, Ph.D., of the Qigong Institute in San Francisco has also conducted a preliminary study on the electrical conductance of acupuncture points on the ends of the fingers and toes. Using a meter calibrated from 0 to 100, he found, "A reading of 50 indicates that the organ associated with the acupuncture point is free of pathological problems. Higher readings (higher conductance) are associated with inflammation and lower readings (lower conductance) with degeneration of an organ."[8] Such data may help predict a disease tendency before the disease actually manifests and thus has enormous importance for preventive medicine.

Other experimental data that clearly indicate an electrical component to qi include brain-wave changes among qigong practitioners (outlined in the next chapter) and changes in the electrical activity of the heart (less abnormal EKG). The connection between qigong and EKG measurements may be an especially significant area for future research. It is possible that the heart, being the most powerful electrical organ in the body, has an entraining effect on the energy and functions of other organs, including the brain.[9] As strange as it sounds, science may yet prove that a loving heart produces a healthy mind and that "waves of loving energy" is more than a New Age cliché.

The Copper Wall Project

In the West, the most impressive research to document electrical correlates of healing energy is a project originally called "Physical Fields and States of Consciousness," and later known as the Copper Wall Project, conducted by Elmer Green, Ph.D., and colleagues at the Menninger Clinic in Topeka, Kansas. The Copper Wall Project progressed through various stages from 1983 to 1995 and has been reported in technical papers published in the peer-reviewed journal *Subtle Energies*.[10]

The project was conceived when Dr. Green came across a letter, dated August 13, 1882, from a Tibetan Buddhist meditation teacher to A. P. Sinnett, editor of *The Pioneer*, the best-known English-language newspaper in India.[11] The letter described a method "for developing lucidity in our chelas [student monks]."[12] A monk sat on a wooden stool supported by a glass platform, facing a wall of polished metal, chiefly copper. A bar magnet with the north pole up was suspended over the crown of the head. The monk meditated in solitude while gazing at the wall.

This description suggested intriguing avenues for research. Is it possible that a meditator electrically isolated from the ground because of the glass platform builds up an electrostatic charge? Is this charge or "body potential" linked with clarity of mind, "lucidity," and how does the presence or polarity of a suspended magnet influence a meditator's experience? Additionally, Dr.

Green realized that the copper wall, an excellent electrical conductor, might provide a way for scientists to measure electrical field changes around the bodies of meditators or healers. If healers produce unusual body potential or electric field readings, this suggests that electricity is a correlate of healing energy.

A copper-walled room was constructed, consisting of a copper floor, copper ceiling, and a copper wall to the front and back. Each copper panel was separate from the others and thus electrically independent. Individual electrometers (sensitive instruments that measure the difference in potential between two points) were attached to each copper panel. The research subjects included "sensitives" widely known for their energetic or parapsychological sensitivity, and control groups of "regular" subjects[13] untrained in energy sensitivity. Each subject sat on a chair on a glass base, facing a copper wall, while scientists measured body potential changes and electric fields.

As might be expected, in six hundred experimental trials with regular subjects (twenty subjects, thirty sessions per subject), there were no unusual or large electrical surges. However, when the sensitives were tested, the results were suprising.

In a series of experiments conducted over a two-year period, from 1988 to 1990, seven male and seven female sensitives were individually studied as they meditated for six forty-five-minute sessions in the copper-wall room. Subjects were asked to keep their eyes open and maintain simple awareness, rather than try to direct the mind toward any particular object or goal. Each subject spent his or her own week at Menninger and thus had no contact with the other subjects. At some sessions, to vary the magnetic properties of the room, a bar magnet was suspended over the crown of the meditator with north or south pole up. Neither the subjects nor the scientists knew whether or not the magnet was present during a session.

Sessions were videotaped by two cameras to rule out spurious electrical readings produced by body motion rather than meditation. A single electrode on the ear of each subject measured, with a sensitive voltmeter, any body potential changes (relative to ground) that occurred during the course of meditation. EKG, EEG (brain waves), finger temperature, skin conductivity, and respiration were also measured. Electric field changes around the subjects were measured by electrometers wired to the four copper panels. All of these measurements were taken simultaneously throughout the meditation sessions and recorded on machinery in an adjacent laboratory.

At the end of each session, subjects filled out a questionnaire designed to elicit their physical, mental, emotional, extrapersonal (psychic), or transpersonal (spiritual) experiences during the meditation. This information was then compared with physiologic data gathered by the researchers.

Nine of the fourteen sensitives were nationally known healers,[14] adept at healing modalities such as visualization or prayer that do not require physically touching a patient. During their last two and a half days at the Menninger Clinic, these healers attempted noncontact healing with volunteers from the Menninger staff. In some sessions, the "patients" sat in the copper-wall room with the healer; in others the patients were in another room in the building. Magnets were not used during this phase of the Copper Wall Project.[15]

During the meditation sessions, body potential surges ranged *from 4 volts to 221 volts*, with these spikes lasting anywhere from 0.5 seconds to 12.5 seconds. These electrostatic charges were evident whether or not a magnet was used. During the healing sessions, the surges were equally unusual, ranging from 4 to 190 volts, and the sensitives generated even more electrical surges per session than during the meditation sessions. It seems that the presence of a patient combined with the intention to heal generates or releases healing power more frequently.

The magnitude of these electrical surges is extraordinary: 10,000 times larger than EKG voltages generated by the body's most powerful electrical organ, the heart, and 100,000 times greater than EEG voltages. These results expand our understanding of both body potential and *human potential.*

As a natural follow-up, the next round of copper wall experiments looked more specifically at the energetic interaction between the healer and the patient. No magnets were used. The same healers—six men and three women—were wired up as well as a new group of patient volunteers. Would healer and patient resonate together? If the healer produced an electric surge, would the patient?

Again there were huge electrical surges registered on the bodies of the healers and, to a lesser extent, in the copper walls. Like the copper, the patients seemed to act as antennae, registering body potential fluctuations in synchrony with the healers, though of smaller amplitude than that of the healers. It is important to note that such synchronized electrical activity was seen only when patients were in the same room as the healer and was not evident when healers attempted distant healing. Occasionally, distant patients nevertheless reported feeling "healing energy" or seeing images that corresponded to images visualized by the healers, suggesting that healing is correlated with more than electrical energy. Other unmeasured or perhaps immeasurable factors are probably involved. Healing volition, the intent to heal, may result in healing even in the absence of extraordinary electrical activity. This is an interesting corroboration of a paradox found in ancient qigong philosophy: *Yi ling qi,* "Intent guides the qi to produce healing." However, according to some qigong texts, intent, of itself, can cause healing— intent *is* the healing power and thus is synonymous with qi.

Some of the healers seemed to be able to turn on their power at will, radiating a measurable electromagnetic field in all directions, like a light-bulb. The charge would generally register strongest on one copper wall or the other. This variability may be a reflection of the healer's type of training, his or her state of mind, or a spontaneous phenomenon reflecting either a unique physiology or an inborn ability.[16]

No one is certain what these electrical surges mean. The important point is that they happen! When renowned Stanford University physicist Dr. William Tiller analyzed the copper wall data from one of the healers, he found that the charge seemed to oscillate between the feet and the crown and to have its source in the lower abdomen.[17] Qigong practitioners have long maintained that healing power is generated from the lower abdomen. Yet we should not hastily conclude that what was true of a particular research subject is true of all healers or all traditions of healing. Commenting on Dr. Tiller's analysis, Elmer Green said, "It is possible that a master healer can generate a charge from *any* part of the body."

Before leaving this discussion of electricity as a correlate of qi, it is important to note the *dangers* of electromagnetism. The electrical currents that control healing and repair are extremely sensitive to external electromagnetic fields (EMFs). Electromagnetic pollution permeates our world in the form of household appliances, computers, radio, radar, and an extensive grid of electric wires and cables. Artificial electromagnetic fields generated by such equipment might be interpreted as information by the human nervous system, and so interrupt the body's ability to scavenge cancer cells, heal broken bones, or keep hormonal levels in balance. Normal biologic processes might be inhibited or exaggerated.

On a positive note, the earth's natural EMF has an entraining effect on the body, keeping it in balance and harmony. Perhaps spending more time in nature can help cure many of the diseases of civilization.

THE BIOCHEMICAL CORRELATE

Every change in our state of health is reflected in numerous electrical and biochemical changes that occur throughout the body. Although we cannot say that any particular compound *is* qi, scientists in both China and the West have noted that certain biochemicals behave like qi and may help explain how qigong works.

Endorphins: Qigong Is as Good as Chocolate

Emotions occur in the mind and body. Emotional states accompany the synthesis of neuropeptides, the chemicals of the emotions, sending them flowing to various parts of the body. This explains why we feel profound restfulness when the mind is contented, a queasy stomach when we are anxious, or a racing heart when we are in love. Two factors suggest a close connection between the neuropeptides and qi. Firstly, neuropeptides, like qi, are produced in response to state of mind and influence the health of the internal organs. Secondly, neuropeptide receptor sites are located on the immune cells. This means that, like qi, neuropeptides form a link between consciousness and immunity, mind and body.

The best-known neuropeptides are the *endorphins*, morphinelike substances found naturally within the body. Endorphins account for moods of well-being or euphoria such as we experience after enjoyable aerobic workouts (the "runner's high"), eating chocolate—scientifically shown to produce endorphins—or dynamic qigong training. Internal martial arts training, the most active type of qigong, also engenders feelings of well-being, both during solo exercise practice or sparring. It is not unusual to see Taiji Quan players smiling happily even while being whacked by a boxing glove! Feeling good is good for you. The endorphins are known to stimulate the immune system and reduce pain.

The sensation of being full of qi, whether as a result of one's own practice or of receiving external qi from a healer, corresponds to an increase in the body's endorphins. If this is the *only* reason why qigong feels good or reduces pain, then administering the endorphin blocker *naloxone* should prevent qi from having the usual effects. This has been experimentally tested in China. When rats were subjected to a painful electric stimulus, external qi treatment reduced their pain significantly. *Naloxone could only partially block this effect.* This means that endorphins are a correlate of qi, but that qi is more than endorphins.[18]

DHEA: The Health Hormone

Researcher Norman Shealy, M.D., Ph.D., founder of the American Holistic Medicine Association, has posited a relationship between qi and a hormone called *DHEA* (dehydroepiandrosterone).[19] DHEA is the most abundant steroid in the human body. It is required for sex hormone synthesis and is found in equal concentrations in the brain and the adrenal cortex. DHEA levels vary among individuals and tend to decline with age. High levels of DHEA have been correlated with youthfulness, less disease, and a more competent immune system.[20] DHEA is generally near its peak during one's twenties and then steadily declines, ebbing more quickly in response to stress or disease. Low DHEA levels have been directly linked with cancer, diabetes, obesity, hypertension, allergies, heart disease, and most autoimmune diseases. From his observation and testing of hundreds of individuals, Dr. Shealy theorizes that if DHEA levels are too low,[21] "that individual is in a stage of adrenal exhaustion and will already have or be on the verge of developing a significant illness."[22]

There is an interesting parallel here between modern science and the traditional Chinese understanding of *jing*, sexual qi. Qigong theory maintains that *jing*, like DHEA, is found in the adrenals and brain, and is an indicator of sexual vitality and resistance to disease. Jing is nurtured by quietness and tranquillity and destroyed by hastiness and stress.

How can we increase DHEA levels? Obviously, by reducing stress and by practicing healing techniques such as qigong and meditation.[23] There is also evidence that moderate sunbathing raises DHEA levels.[24] Ukrainian physicists have found that human DNA vibrates at from fifty-two to seventy-eight billion cycles per second. This same frequency is found in solar energy. There may be a resonance between sunlight and DNA, like one tuning fork causing another to vibrate. Sunlight stimulates the production of DHEA and is, according to Dr. Shealy, "a major factor in maintaining life energy or *qi*."[25]

If DHEA is a correlate of qi, does this mean that we should ingest DHEA? Not necessarily. Electricity is also a correlate of qi, yet it would be unwise to grab a live electric wire! The stress-modulating and immune-enhancing effects of DHEA supplementation suggest the need for further research and clinical trials. Under proper medical supervision, DHEA may be helpful in the treatment of cancer, diabetes, hypertension, AIDS, herpes, chronic fatigue syndrome, and as replacement therapy for aging. However, caution is advised because there is also evidence that DHEA may lead to insulin resistance and increased coronary risk in women.[26] The safest way to increase your body's supply of DHEA is through a healthy lifestyle and the practice of qigong.

BIOLUMINESCENCE: LIGHT AND LIFE

Throughout the world, light is synonymous with healing and energy. In many religious traditions, divine power is identified with a primal light. God created light before s/he created the sun, the moon, and the rest of the world. Scientifically, light seems to defy logical explanation. Light travels at a constant velocity of 186,000 miles per second. The unit of light, called a photon, has no resting mass, making it, like qi, more of a function than a substance. Yet it is a function that has dramatic, measurable effects and is essential for life. The energy of photons is transmitted in whole units (*quanta*), not diminishing as it travels any distance. And time itself must be irrelevant for light, since, according to Einstein's Theory of Relativity, time stops at the speed of light. The great physicist Max Planck said that light behaves with intelligence, always reaching its target along the path that takes the least possible time. This is known in science as the *principle of least action*, a concept with interesting parallels to the Chinese notion of *wu wei*, effortless, efficient action.

Light seems so intelligent, and so far beyond the ordinary laws of space, time, and matter, that scientist and philosopher Arthur Young believes that "it is the basis for free will and is the ongoing dynamic which drives the universe."[27] Since matter can be considered a condensation of photons, and changes or transformation of matter a result of light's interaction with atoms and molecules, Young identifies light with the creative power of the divine, what philosophers call "First Cause."

Living systems literally glow. All living cells emit units of light, *biophotons*. Scientists have been studying this phenomenon of bioluminescence (or "dark luminescence," since the light emission is very weak) since it was first reported by Alexander Gurvich in 1959.[28] Mae-Wan Ho of the Bioelectrodynamics Laboratory, The Open University (UK), explains the biophoton emission succinctly:

> Light is generally emitted from an excited atom or molecule, when an electron in the outermost shell, having been promoted to an excited energy level by, say, a collision with another molecule or absorption of energy by other means, falls back into a lower energy level. Light emission does not always occur, however. The excited electron can often start to move, thus becoming an electric current, or it can be involved in a chemical reaction. . . .[29]

It is also possible for the electron to emit sound or heat as it falls back to the ground state. Such microscopic excitations and energy emissions are happening all of the time as a result of normal metabolic processes. It is also likely that biophotons are emitted from an organized, "coherent" in scientific terms, electromagnetic field that pervades living tissue. Biophoton researcher Dr. Fritz-Albert Popp identifies this field with the "morphogenetic field," the field created by the forms of other members of a species.[30]

The behavior of light seems to scientifically corroborate a mystical truth, that light is a characteristic of life. And I cannot help speculating about the connection between biophotons and the widely held belief that human bodies have an aura. Could some individuals have an unusual sensitivity to dark luminescence? Or are they picking up information kinesthetically and *interpreting* this as varying degrees of light?

Biophoton emission can be a source of important information about an organism's status. When muscles or nerves are activated, the intensity of biophoton emission increases. Biophoton emissions have also been measured radiating from the internal organs. The characteristics of photon emission indicate the health of cells and whether they are multiplying or dying. According to researchers from the University of Catania's Institute of Physics, Catania, Italy, "It is possible to discriminate between tumour and normal tissues by measuring their spontaneous low-level luminescence."[31] In the future, biophoton emission may provide a sensitive tool for cancer detection and to assess the effectiveness of medication or the body's own immune system on the course of any disease. B. W. Chwirot, of the Department of Plant Cytology and Embryology, Nicholas Copernicus University, Torun, Poland, writes ". . . the correlation between the light emission and phagocytosis [immune cells engulfing and destroying bacteria or other pathogens] is so profound that it could be used as a direct measure of phagocytosis itself and of the influence of different chemical compounds on this process."[32] Biophoton assessment has a distinct advantage over many current diagnostic methods, as it does not require disturbing subjects by injecting dyes or isotopes. Instead, information is gathered in a noninvasive way by measuring light emission, a natural activity.

Popp summarizes the types of processes that may be amenable to biophoton research: ". . . molecular interactions, immunological and repair processes in aging, growth and differentiation, pattern formation in development, biocommunication and the nature of consciousness."[33] I would add to this list "human potential and qigong." Light has been understood as a correlate of qi since the beginning of qigong history. One of the early ideograms for qi is a picture of light radiating from the sun. Ancient qigong texts speak of absorbing light energy from the sun, moon, and stars and of the body radiating varying degrees and qualities of light depending on the individual's state of health and consciousness.[34]

CONSCIOUSNESS:
PUTTING THE CHIT IN CHEE (QI)

In a penetrating article published in *Subtle Energies*,[35] Dr. Larry Dossey makes us rethink the very concept of "healing energy." Most scientists investigating complementary healing methods such as qigong assume that healing occurs because energy travels from point A to point B within the body, as in qigong self-healing, or between a healer and a patient. According to the laws of physics, it should take a specific amount of time to bridge the distance between two points, diminishing in intensity as it travels. Electricity, biochemical changes, and light are measurable energies correlated with qi. Dossey asks us to consider the possibility of another, immeasurable correlate that does not behave like "energy": consciousness itself, what Indian Yogis call *chit*. The term "consciousness" connotes awareness, mindfulness, and intent or volition.

Qigong masters speak of *Yi Nian Zhi Liao*, "Mind-Intent Healing," the ability of consciousness to directly affect one's own or a patient's health. A qigong healer thinks of healing a patient; the patient's health improves even without any measurable emission of energy. Mind-Intent Healing is instantaneous and does not depend on the proximity of the patient and healer. This suggests that consciousness can bring about changes unmediated by transfer of energy.

Perhaps, as Elmer Green once suggested, the mind is not in the brain, but rather, the brain is in the Mind. The brain, like a radio receiver, merely translates a signal that is generated by an inclusive and unified consciousness. If, ultimately, there is no distance between you and me, if our minds are in the truest sense one, then how can energy flow between us?

Western scientists are corroborating the power of consciousness with hard scientific data. Since 1979, Robert G. Jahn of the Princeton Engineering Anomalies Research program has been investigating the ability of consciousness to influence Random Events Generators—electrical, mechanical, optical, and acoustic machines that produce ones and zeros in random sequences. Research subjects sitting in front of the various machines, without physically contacting them, have, according to their prestated intentions, been able to influence the machines to increase, decrease, or maintain their output. From 1979 to 1995 approximately fifty million experimental trials were performed. The probability of the documented human-machine correlations being due to chance is about one in a billion.

In his article "Consciousness, Information, and Human Health," Jahn asks the incisive question:

Now, if consciousness, via its own expressed desire, can bring some degree of order into a simple random string of ones and zeros emerging from a rudimentary machine, is it so unreasonable to suspect that it can invoke similar, or subtler, processes to influence the far more elaborate, relevant, and precious information processing systems that underlie its own health?[36]

The Chinese have been saying for centuries that consciousness is a correlate of qi.

CORRELATES OF QI
- Electric
- Biochemical
- Bioluminescence
- Consciousness

Is qi electromagnetic, biochemical, luminous, or some as yet unmeasured potential? Probably these are all partial answers. More important than how qigong works is what it does. For more than two thousand years, qigong has been investigated through personal practice. Today, we can also examine the results of thousands of experiments and clinical trials with qigong practitioners.

CHAPTER FIVE

Does It Really Work?
The Experimental Evidence

*Sit down before fact like a little child, be
prepared to give up every preconceived notion,
follow humbly to wherever and to whatever
abysses nature leads or you shall learn nothing.*
— THOMAS HUXLEY

Active qigong includes stretching, deep breathing, low-impact conditioning, and isometrics. It increases range of motion, builds strength,
increases stamina, and improves balance and coordination. Internally,
qigong movements relax the fascia, the connective tissue that holds the internal organs in place, allowing the organs to work more efficiently. Daoists
even practiced a kind of qigong jogging, running through the mountains,
leaping from boulder to boulder in imitation of the deer or rabbit. The benefits of exercise documented by Western medicine[1] are similar to the findings
of Chinese qigong researchers. But qigong is more than exercise or sports.
Qigong's unique combination of movement, breath, and meditation improves the functioning of virtually all of the systems of the body and has
both preventive and curative effects.

What follows is a summary of significant experiments and clinical observations showing the beneficial effects of self-healing qigong practice. For a
more comprehensive survey of qigong research and published scientific papers, see the Qigong Database™ under Qigong Resources at the end of this
book.[2] Some of the research cited below is qualified by a statistical concept
called the *probability value*. This is expressed as p< "probability less than," p=
"probability equals," or p> "probability greater than." A reading of p<.01

means that there is less than one chance in a hundred that such results could be due only to chance, while p>.01 means that there is more than one chance in a hundred that the results are due to chance. Any value of p<.05 (probability less than five out of a hundred) or lower is considered statistically significant.

HEALTHY HEART AND BLOOD PRESSURE

Qigong strengthens the heart muscle and increases the stroke volume, the amount of blood pumped per minute, so that more oxygen can be delivered to the tissues and more waste products carried away. It also causes the resting heart rate to drop. During more dynamic or demanding forms of qigong, heart rate will increase, but drop afterward. During meditative qigong practice, the heart rate will generally drop below normal, then resume a slow, normal pace as you resume activity. Qigong also lowers high blood pressure.[3] It is likely that relaxation and deep abdominal respiration cause the blood vessels to relax and dilate slightly, creating less resistance to blood flow and thus reduced blood pressure. The precise qigong methods of relaxation, as described in Chapter 8, have been found to be more effective in lowering both systolic and diastolic blood pressure than either simply resting or natural sleep.[4]

One of the finest studies documenting the effect of qigong on hypertension (high blood pressure) and related conditions was conducted at the Shanghai Institute of Hypertension, a division of the Shanghai Second Medical University. Subjects were randomly divided into a qigong group of 122 patients and a control group of 120 nonpractitioners. Both groups took standard hypertensive drugs. Subjects were tracked for a thirty-year period of time. At the end of this period, 47.76 percent of the control group had died. Only 25.41 percent of the qigong group had died. These are very significant results, with a probability of less than one in a thousand (p<0.001) of being due to chance. The incidence of stroke in the control group was 40.83 percent, in the qigong group 20.49 percent. The incidence of death due to stroke was 32.50 percent among the controls, in the qigong group, 15.57 percent. These results are also statistically significant, less than one chance in a hundred (p<0.01). When forty of the patients were diagnosed by ultrasound, the qigong group was found to have stronger heart muscles and better left ventricular function. In a published report, "Effects of Qigong on Preventing Stroke and Alleviating the Multiple Cerebro-Cardiovascular Risk Factors— A Follow-Up Report on 242 Hypertensive Cases for 30 Years," the researchers concluded, "According to both our past and present investigations, we believe that qigong plays a major role in improving the self-regulation and alleviating the multiple cerebro-cardiovascular risk factors."[5] The data is impressive due to the large number of participants and the length of the study.

The basic protocol and results of the Shanghai study were replicated in a six-year study with 204 hypertensive patients, conducted at Xiamen University in Fujian Province.[6] At the six-year follow-up, it was found that the combination of qigong and hypertensive drugs was 19 percent more effective than hypertensive drugs alone. The qigong group had also learned to be less reactive to stressful events, with more stable blood pressure. The mortality rate from all causes was 17.31 percent in the qigong group, and nearly double, 32 percent, among the controls. After six months of practice, the blood of the qigong group showed less tendency to form abnormal blood clots and contained higher levels of the "good" HDL (high-density lipoprotein) cholesterol. Several Western studies have found an inverse relationship between the amount of HDL in the blood and the incidence of cardiac problems such as arteriosclerosis. As HDL levels rise, bad cholesterol (LDL) levels drop. Since HDL helps to transport LDL out of the tissues and blood, higher levels generally lower the risk of heart disease.[7]

Equally impressive results have been found by combining qigong with a Western method of self-regulation therapy: biofeedback. In 1988, scientists at the Research Institute of Traditional Chinese Medicine, Tianjin, reported on 639 cases of primary hypertension treated with a combination of qigong and biofeedback devices. The combined therapy was found to be effective in 85.13 percent of the cases. After eight weeks, most patients had significantly lower blood pressure. In some cases, the blood pressure dropped significantly after only one practice session. Concurrent with the drop in blood pressure, the patients experienced improvements in overall health, mental health, appetite, and sleep. During follow-ups over the next three years, most patients did not have continued access to biofeedback devices. However, it was found that among those who kept up the with qigong practice, 97.7 percent had stable, lowered blood pressure.[8]

Similar cardiovascular benefits have been found for Taiji Quan, an immensely popular form of qigong. Qu Mianyu, dean of the Beijing Medical College, reported that Taiji Quan students have lower blood pressure, greater cardiac efficiency as measured by treadmill testing, and less abnormal EKG patterns than controls.[9] As early as 1963, American physicians, such as cardiologist Louis Brinberg, M.D., of Mount Sinai Hospital, were recommending Taiji Quan as a gentle, daily exercise suitable for cardiac patients.[10]

American hospitals have been shamefully slow to follow his and other scientists' advice.

CIRCULATORY SYSTEM

Qigong increases the volume of blood flowing to the brain, hands, and feet, and in the small capillaries throughout the body. The deep relaxation one achieves during qigong practice causes the blood vessels to gently dilate, enabling them to carry more blood.

Good circulation is extremely important for healthy brain functioning. Although the brain makes up only 2 percent of the body's overall weight, it utilizes 20 percent of its available oxygen. A deficiency of oxygenated blood can predispose one to seizure disorders, migraine headaches, and psychological instability. Greater cerebral blood flow may account for higher intelligence scores among students practicing qigong compared with controls.[11] It may also help to explain how qigong improves memory and retards senility among the aged. Brain cells may die off at a slower rate if they are better supplied with oxygen. It is important to note, however, that qigong's salutary effect on memory may be due to a diminution of adrenal stress hormones in the blood. Some of these hormones bond to and cause deterioration in areas of the brain responsible for memory retention.

One of the signs that qi is flowing is increased warmth in the hands and feet, indicating better circulation in the parts of the body farthest from the heart. Qigong students can learn to self-regulate the diameter of the blood vessels in the hands and feet by paying attention to subjective feelings of warmth and learning how to encourage them. There is evidence that this skill can lead to greater control over blood vessels in other areas of the body, curing or alleviating some forms of migraine or angina.[12]

An accurate method for testing the effect of qigong on peripheral blood circulation is to measure blood volume using a device called a photoelectric earlobe sphygmograph that passes a light beam through the earlobe. The intensity of light changes in response to changes in blood volume. Light attenuation (diminishment), a sign of increased blood volume, is displayed as a higher amplitude tracing on the sphygmograph screen.

The earlobe sphygmograph was used in an experiment conducted by researchers from three major scientific laboratories in China: Beijing University of Aeronautics and Astronautics; Nantong Obstetrical and Gynecological Hospital; and the Nantong Environmental Science Research Institute.[13] As forty-eight qigong practitioners sat quietly, the instrument measured peripheral blood flow during the subjects' ordinary waking state and during qigong meditation. The average amplitude of the sphygmograph wave increased by 30 percent during the qigong state compared to the ordinary state ($p<0.01$). In eight of the subjects, the amplitude increased by over 100 percent and seemed correlated with the subjects' ability to enter a deep state of qigong meditation.

Similar experiments have measured blood flow in the fingertips. At Beijing University of Aeronautics and Astronautics twenty-seven subjects, consisting of twenty-two qigong practitioners and five controls, were asked to sit quietly. Using a laser microcirculation blood flow meter, a device similar to the sphygmograph, researchers found a very significant increase in blood flow, with a probability of less than 0.001, as the qigong group meditated. The change in the control group was not significant, $p>0.1$. Ten subjects were given five sessions of further qigong training. When retested, their blood flow rates were much higher. There was a direct relationship between blood flow and the subjects' length and level of qigong training.[14]

DIGESTIVE SYSTEM

There are many humorous stories told in China about "burping beginners" and the alleged digestive power of qigong masters. One of my favorites involves ninety-years-young Taiji Quan Master T. T. Liang. Taiji Quan is a beautiful, flowing qigong exercise that looks like swimming in the air.

One day two women observed a class, watching the students performing the slow, almost eerie-looking exercise. After the class, Master Liang sat on a chair to read the Chinese newspaper. The two young ladies approached Master Liang and asked, hesitantly, "Could you tell us what is the purpose of that dance?" Liang looked up for a moment and said one word: "Fart!" One of the women said, "Excuse me, what was that?" Liang repeated in a strong voice, "Fart. More fart, more burp, impurities come out. Purpose of Taiji Quan." In fact, beginning qigong students commonly experience strange stomach rumblings and digestive noises during the first few months of their training. This is interpreted as an expulsion of noxious qi and the body's adjustment to a stronger, more efficient digestive system. Experienced masters are known to brag about or demonstrate their ability to digest almost anything, in almost any quantity, or to fast, not eating at all for extended periods of time. Not that qigong masters make a habit of eating immoderately, but rather they are *capable* of eating immoderately for brief periods without serious harm. The reason? They have greater self-control over many aspects of their metabolism. Their digestive systems return more easily to a state of balance. My teachers always seemed better able to digest fried chicken dinners or tolerate hot sauce than I could.

There are many reasons qigong benefits digestion. Abdominal breathing massages the digestive organs. As the diaphragm drops and rises, the muscles involved in peristalsis (the pushing of food through the esophagus toward the stomach) are stimulated. Qigong master and scholar Dr. Jiao Guorui believes that weak peristalsis is strengthened and excessively strong contractions are reduced.[15]

It has been well-documented that qigong improves the appetite. This may be due to an effect on salivary and gastric enzymes, though experimental proof of this is still weak. Almost all qigong practitioners note greatly increased production of saliva both during and immediately after practice. It is possible that qigong practice also gently stimulates hydrochloric acid production in the stomach, so that optimal levels are maintained with advancing age. (Reduced hydrochloric acid levels and poorer digestion are usual signs of aging.)

As blood circulation improves and students make necessary adjustments in diet and lifestyle, hemorrhoids often shrink or disappear. General bodily relaxation, so important in qigong, may account for the cure of psychosomatic digestive disorders and some types of ulcers. Many qigong techniques involve contracting the anal sphincter. This may improve the muscle tone of the smooth muscles involved in elimination and so also aid in the cure of hemorrhoids and constipation.

These benefits have been documented in numerous clinical studies. At the Tangshan Qigong Convalescent Hospital, Dr. Wang Shubin treated 126 patients with severe constipation with a combination of *Nei Yang Gong* (Inner Nourishing Qigong, described in Chapter 11), abdominal breathing, and focusing the mind on the lower dan tian. After ten days, Taiji Quan practice was added. In most cases, constipation disappeared after seven days. Eventually all recovered daily regularity.[16]

There is an especially large body of information about the qigong treatment of ulcers, a problem that is quite common in China. The Qigong Department of the Tianjin Workers Convalescent Hospital No.1 reported on 515 cases of gastric and duodenal ulcers, including 230 with a duration of five to ten years. Inpatient qigong therapy lasted an average of 72.7 days. Such extended hospitalization for ulcers is unheard-of in the United States, yet it does afford an opportunity for the patient to reap the full benefits of qigong in an environment shielded from the social, environmental, and job-related stresses that may contribute to the condition. Patients gained an average of 9.7 pounds, and 70.8 percent of the group were cured of their ulcers.[17]

Most of the evidence about qigong's effect on ulcers is in the form of clinical observation rather than controlled research. Zhao Liming, a doctor of Traditional Chinese Medicine from Harbin, reported on the use of qigong in treating 1,278 ulcer patients:

> Of the 190 cases of gastric ulcer, 154 recovered, 34 improved, and 2 were ineffective. Of the 955 cases of duodenal ulcer, 742 cured, 202 improved, and 11 were ineffective. For the whole group, the recovery rate was 77.4%, improved 20.9% and no effect 1.7%. . . . Of the 175 cases under long-term clinical observation, disease recurred in 59 cases including two who persisted in Qigong exercise, 3 practicing it on and off and 54 who gave it up.[18]

This is a clear indication that regular practice of qigong is essential in order to prevent the recurrence of certain diseases. Several Chinese hospitals have reported even more impressive cure rates of patients with gastric ulcers: the Worker's Sanatorium of Zhejiang Province (91.1 percent), People's Liberation Army Hospital No. 31 (96.99 percent), and the First Affiliated Hospital of Beijing Medical College (86 percent).[19]

Qigong improves mechanical aspects of digestion by strengthening the muscles that push food through the alimentary canal. There is also scanty but strongly suggestive evidence that qigong can improve the chemical aspects of digestion, helping the breakdown of food into nutrients and promoting the elimination of pathogenic bacteria. Researchers at the Pharmaceutical Department of Jiamusi Medical College used ultrasound to examine the gallbladders of twelve qigong practitioners before, during, and after qigong meditation. Results showed an increase in the diameter of the gallbladders and an increased secretion of bile. When the same scientists examined the feces of seven qigong practitioners, it was found that the number of pathogenic bacteria was less than in controls, and the number of beneficial, anaerobic bacteria was higher. Thus, the researchers concluded that qigong promotes healthier microflora in the digestive tract.[20]

Many digestive problems have a strong psychological component. An individual can become constipated from defensive, uptight attitudes or from the burden of unassimilated feelings or thoughts. The efficient breakdown of foods is disturbed by confusion, anger, frustration, and fear. These stresses cause the nervous system to produce chemicals that can lock onto cells in the digestive organs and prevent their efficient functioning. Certainly some of the positive effects of qigong on digestion result from simply learning to relax and become more self-aware.

THE BRAIN:
STATE OF BODY AND STATE OF MIND

Some of the clearest evidence that qi effects the brain can be inferred from experiments involving External Qi Healing. It is likely that qi emitted from a healer's hands affects nerve cells in a manner similar to the way they are affected in the practice of self-healing qigong.

Several experiments have shown that when a healer emits qi to cultured rat neurons, electrical impulses travel more quickly down the cell membranes, causing as much as a 40 percent increase in current.[21] External qi has also been found to protect nerve cells from damage caused by *free radicals*, the hyperactive molecules that bond wildly and easily to cells, interfering with their functioning.[22] Researchers at the Beijing College of Traditional Chinese Medicine exposed two groups of cultured rat neurons to damaging hydroxyl free radicals. One group was treated by an external qi healer; the other group was untreated. The treated cells showed less swelling or degeneration. The researchers concluded that emitted qi may act as a free radical scavenger (like vitamin C), protecting nerve cells from damage.[23]

Many studies have shown that qigong practice causes a shift in the brain waves, reducing abnormal patterns in diseased patients and improving functioning in the healthy. When 158 cases of cerebral arteriosclerosis were treated with an approximately three-month course of qigong breathing exercises, 16 percent of those with abnormal brain waves returned to normal.[24] It is known that long-term hypertension can interfere with oxygen delivery to the brain and impair brain functioning. A study at the Shanghai Institute of Hypertension suggested that qigong treatment of hypertension results in fewer abnormal brain waves.[25] If poor oxygen delivery can produce abnormal brain waves and predispose one to psychological problems, then it follows that better breathing can improve brain and psychological health.

The Qigong EEG

In the 1980s, Chinese researchers documented the existence of a Qigong Electroencephalogram (EEG), a unique brain wave pattern that can be seen in the majority of healthy qigong practitioners tested and most prevalent in long-term practitioners. The Qigong EEG is unusual because of the type and amplitude (strength) of brain waves, location, and degree of coherence (synchronization) recorded.

Scientists recognize four types of brain waves, each categorized by a specific frequency range measured as Hz or cycles per second. All frequencies can be seen in the spectrum of electrical activity of a waking or sleeping human brain, though certain ones clearly predominate at different stages of life or during particular physical or mental states. The slowest is *delta* (.5–4 Hz), prevalent during infancy or, in adults, during deep sleep. Healers sometimes produce delta while awake, a graphic example of connecting with the wisdom of childhood and accessing the deepest levels of consciousness. The next is *theta* (4–8 Hz), present during drowsy, barely conscious states and often accompanied by dreamlike images. Trained meditators can produce theta while fully awake by relaxing the mind, emotions, and body. The third is *alpha* (8–13 Hz). Alpha indicates an ability to maintain a state of relaxed concentration, such as focusing on internal images during visualization, paying silent attention to a sight or sound, or observing the working of one's own mind. Most people can increase alpha by simply closing their eyes and relaxing. Alpha is the frequency most commonly produced during meditation.

The quickest brain waves, *beta* (13–26 Hz or higher), characterize adult waking consciousness most of the time. Elmer and Alyce Green, in their classic *Beyond Biofeedback*, describe beta brain waves as "usually associated with active attention, often focused on the outer world but including thinking concretely."[26] Beta predominates when an individual is reading a book or trying to solve a specific problem. The beta predominant state is euphemistically called "awareness," but is most prevalent during states of "free floating anxiety," when the mind is restless, according to energy medicine researcher, the late Ed Wilson, M.D.[27] It is likely that a large percentage of the adult U.S. population is chronically stuck in beta while awake. We tend to "think about" rather than experience silently. Thinking is a useful and essential means of interpreting experience, but it is pathological if it dominates consciousness. Alan Watts frequently reminded his students, "If you are always thinking, there is nothing to think about except thoughts!"

As the mind slows down, the brain waves also slow down. Qigong helps the mind to "downshift" from beta to alpha, theta, or a combination of the two. Qigong generally creates a preponderance of *high-amplitude alpha*, measured in microvolts. Before qigong practice, alpha might appear on the EEG like ripples on a pond. During qigong, alpha changes into high-crested ocean waves. This is not an increase in frequency of brain waves. Rather, more brain tissue is doing the same thing at the same time, producing a greater electrical charge, and hence, a higher amplitude.

If the practitioner is meditating on an object, a particular part of the body for example, or directing qi through a certain meridian—then more powerful alpha waves are produced in the left hemisphere of the brain. If the practitioner has no object—practicing silent awareness—then high-amplitude alpha concentrates in the right hemisphere.[28] This is consistent with our understanding of the different functions of the two sides of the brain. The intent to focus qi stimulates the left side of the brain, concerned with cognitive functions. The right hemisphere is intuitive and fosters awareness of connections and relationships and so is stimulated by meditation without an object, the experience of unqualified Being.[29]

During qigong, theta waves also increase, though generally not to the same degree as alpha. It is likely that delta waves become more pronounced too as the qigong practitioner becomes more and more tranquil, although more research is needed to verify this effect. Alpha and theta brain waves engendered by qigong practice tend to be concentrated in the frontal portions of the brain. Usually after three or four minutes, there is a measurable shift of alpha and theta concentration from the rear occipital regions to the frontal lobes. This corresponds to a quieting of the language and evaluative functions of the brain and an increased focus on wholistic experience in which subject and object feel unified. Instead of labeling, categorizing, and judging experiences (beta), the qigong practitioner is sensing, experiencing, and silently feeling.

The degree of *coherence* between different portions of the brain also increases during qigong, in proportion to the expertise of the practitioner. Coherence means that different portions of the brain are producing particular frequencies—delta, theta, alpha, or beta—which are phased together, the peaks and valleys occurring at the same time. Similar excitation might be found between the right and left hemispheres, the front and back of the brain, or globally across large portions of the brain. We can infer from this that qigong practice may create a harmonious and integrated sense of self.

Brain wave coherence has been found in many qigong experiments. A typical one was performed at the Beijing College of Traditional Chinese Medicine, Institute of Qigong Science. Thirty-two college students practiced Standing Meditation, one of the most important and popular qigong styles (described in Chapter 10), forty minutes every day for one year. A baseline reading of their degree of EEG coherence was taken before they began learning qigong, and additional readings were taken after six months and after one year. At the one-year mark, there were significant increases in coherence between the two hemispheres in the frontal ($p<0.05$), occipital ($p<0.001$), and temporal ($p<0.001$) areas of the brain. Such findings suggest that brain wave coherence might be an objective measure of success in meditation.[30]

As a practitioner experiences subjective states of peace and harmony, the brain waves actually look more harmonious on the EEG. The different sides of the brain and the different aspects of consciousness—especially the cognitive and creative/intuitive—communicate with each other. Wholeness is not merely a metaphor for health. It is a scientific fact. Such coherent effects are not found as frequently in experiments involving healthy, untrained individuals. When qigong students and nonpractitioners close their eyes and sit quietly, the amount of coherence in the qigong students' EEG is statistically significant when compared with the nonpractitioners.[31]

Perhaps an intriguing avenue of research would be to explore the possibility of coherence not between different portions of a single individual's brain, but between two people. Do powerful healers or psychics produce resonant effects in their clients? Do their brain waves and heartbeats synchronize? Could such research reveal a physical or energetic basis for shared thoughts and feelings between lovers?

When I lecture about the Qigong EEG to Western physicians, there is invariably a neurologist who asks, "Aren't slow, synchronized brain waves a symptom of brain injury?" The Qigong EEG is consciously produced and has a harmonious, well-organized appearance. These qualities clearly distinguish it from the slow pattern seen in head injury patients. Car accident victims, for example, frequently display uneven brain waves, with jagged, irregular patterns and low amplitudes compared to the high-amplitude waves seen in meditative states. Head injury patients often have an inability to produce even normal quantities of alpha, which makes it difficult for them to focus or organize their thoughts. Coherent waves occur after brain injuries because different aspects of consciousness are unable to function separately, as if the damaged brain is confused by a homogenized jumble of thoughts, images, and feelings.

The Qigong EEG is powerful evidence of qigong's psycho-spiritual benefits. The predominance of alpha indicates that qigong induces a relaxed and focused state of mind. The simultaneous presence of theta means that the practitioner is becoming aware of deeper levels of consciousness. The increasing degree of coherence suggests that conflicting aspects of the self are being harmonized. The practitioner is becoming a whole, integrated human being. And very importantly, the qigong master has a high level of self-control. He or she can shift in or out of altered consciousness at will.

MENTAL HEALTH

Unfortunately many of the studies on qigong and mental health have been flawed. Many have lacked control subjects or have used sample sizes too small to be meaningful. Though available in China, standard psychological scales have not always been used in testing qigong, and there is also the question of whether or not such scales can be accurately applied or interpreted in a non-Western culture. Chinese researchers sometimes report vague and imprecise diagnostic labels such as "neurosis," "hysteria," or "neurasthenia."

Essential variables such as a subject's degree of family and community support and previous mental health history, which may be concealed from a researcher because of the Chinese cultural stigma against expressing personal problems, have sometimes been ignored.

Nevertheless some meaningful research has been done. One of the best studies was conducted by Wang Jisheng at the Institute of Psychology, Chinese Academy of Science.[32] Dr. Wang evaluated the mental health of 153 individuals who had practiced qigong for less than two years (Group 1) compared with 119 individuals who had practiced qigong for more than two years (Group 2). Group 2 scored positively ($p < 0.05$) in such areas as less obsessive-compulsive traits, anxiety, or phobic anxiety, and better general indications of mental health. Even greater statistical significance ($p < 0.01$) was found when other results were compared. Group 2 showed more interpersonal sensitivity, less depression or psychosis, and better overall scores. Wang concluded that a longer period of practice has positive effects on most aspects of mental health.

Wang also investigated the effect of qigong on Type A behavior—aggressive, stressed, pressured by time and schedules—which is considered a risk factor in heart disease. In a study of 233 subjects, of whom 89 were qigong practitioners and 144 were nonpractitioners, Wang administered a Type A questionnaire to all subjects. The percentage of Type A behavior in the qigong group was 22.43 percent, compared to 51.39 percent in the control group. A drawback of this study is that Wang did not have Type A scales for the qigong group before they had begun learning qigong. I cannot help wondering if these individuals were drawn to qigong because it matched their relaxed temperaments or because they needed qigong to cure preexisting Type A behavior. Additionally, it would be useful to pinpoint how much of qigong's effect on Type A behavior is actually due to the unique healing qualities of qigong and how much is simply the result of the patience required to learn any healing discipline or the friendship and social support one receives by learning in a group.

A study conducted by Shigemi Hayashi of the Sino-Japanese Qigong Institute found that qigong practice results in subjective states of emotional well-being.[33] Based on a 1992 survey of 226 Japanese qigong practitioners, qigong was found to engender emotional stability, increased joy of life, decreased selfishness, more open-minded attitudes, increased enthusiasm and willpower, and greater caring for others. Hayashi mentions that similar benefits have been found among students of the Aosora Qigong School, who practice qigong thirty minutes every weekday before going to work. They report improvements in open-mindedness, willpower, health, and happiness.

Mental health is often the result of improved physical health. It seems reasonable to assume that as physical problems are cured or alleviated, the mind becomes clearer and better able to cope with or find solutions to personal problems.

RESPIRATORY SYSTEM AND ASTHMA

Qigong increases vitality because it conserves energy by lowering the metabolic rate. The body relaxes; the heart beats more slowly and regularly; the mind becomes quiet. The respiratory rate decreases from an average resting rate of sixteen breaths per minute to three to five breaths per minute. Both inhalation and exhalation are smoother, with fewer pauses or breaks compared with untrained subjects.

High levels of stress in our society create a tendency to breathe rapidly and shallowly by opening and closing the chest. Qigong practice emphasizes a more efficient way of breathing using the abdomen. Once the body experiences the pleasure of healthy, relaxed breathing, it becomes natural and habitual.

In qigong breathing, the lower abdomen moves out with inhalation and in with exhalation. During inhalation the diaphragm drops, pushing the abdomen out as the lungs expand and fill with air. During exhalation the diaphragm relaxes and moves back up, the abdomen gently contracts, forcing air out. This method, called either "abdominal" or "diaphragmatic" breathing, conserves energy since less is required to move the abdomen than to move the chest. Most importantly, it creates the most favorable conditions for absorbing oxygen and releasing carbon dioxide. X rays have shown that qigong practitioners move their diaphragms three to four times more than do most individuals,[34] indicating that they are breathing more fully. When skilled qigong practitioners were studied under a fluoroscope screen while practicing meditative qigong, their diaphragm movement significantly increased, but the *number* of movements per minute (respiratory frequency) decreased.[35]

Diaphragmatic breathing continuously strengthens and tones the abdominal muscles. It may be as essential for a beautiful appearance as exercises such as sit-ups. What is the use of a daily morning "ab" workout if, during the rest of the day, the diaphragm is asleep and not exercising properly? Healthy breathing makes all of the muscles involved in respiration both stronger and more elastic.

There is evidence that the lung capacity of qigong practitioners is greater than the average. Certainly anyone who practices qigong can attest to the subjective feeling of easier breathing and increased lung capacity.

Scientists from the Sino-Japan Friendship Hospital in Beijing measured changes in respiratory health among a group of fourteen elderly individuals suffering from cardiac or pulmonary disease.[36] Eleven had smoked for more than twenty years. After eighteen months of practicing various qigong exercises, including Taiji Quan, lung functions were markedly improved. The *vital capacity* (the volume of air that can be expelled from the lungs after a full inhalation) increased by an average of 3.31 percent. The *total lung capacity* (volume of air in the lungs after the deepest inhalation) increased by an average of 7.34 percent, with four subjects showing an increase of more than 15 percent. The most significant improvement was found in the actual strength of respiration, as measured in *forced vital capacity*, the volume of air exhaled when the patient exhales with maximum effort and speed. All patients increased their forced vital capacity by an average of 16.11 percent (p<0.001). It is true that this experiment was performed with few subjects and without the contrast of untrained controls. The positive results highlight the need for further research.

The respiratory benefits of qigong were also noted in clinical observations by Li Ziran and colleagues of the Research Institute of Traditional Chinese Medicine, Tianjin, and the Tianjin Thoracic Surgery Hospital.[37] Researchers measured the effects of a three-month course of qigong combined with standard drug therapy for twenty patients suffering from chronic respiratory diseases such as chronic bronchitis, asthma, emphysema, and cor pulmonale (enlargement of the right ventricle of the heart, caused by lung disease or pulmonary hypertension). When contrasted with ten controls who were only taking drugs, combined therapy was found to be more effective in relieving symptoms and improving general conditions such as appetite, sleep, and energy. Respiratory rates were also significantly different between the two groups. During the treatment period the breathing rate of the control group decreased from 20.1 breaths per minute to 18.2. The combined therapy group went from 19.3 breaths per minute to 6.6.

Of the chronic respiratory diseases, asthma, because of its prevalence in China, has commanded the most attention and drawn the best research. In 1986 Hua Huang, of the Shanghai No. 6 People's Hospital, reported that since 1958 he had been using qigong as a primary treatment for bronchial asthma.[38] He administered Western drugs only to control acute attacks. A group of 111 chronic bronchial asthma patients were taught to practice qigong methods of deep relaxation (*fang song gong* "relaxation qigong"; see Chapter 8) and tranquil breathing for twenty to thirty minutes, two to three times daily and other methods such as concentrating on particular acupoints (*yi shou gong*), quiet meditation, and self-massage. All practices were done from a seated position to maximize relaxation and lessen the likelihood of asthmatic attacks. The course of treatment lasted between one and two months. Four years later, out of ninety-nine cases, thirty patients had been free of attacks for at least one year. Thirty-nine showed marked improvement, as evidenced by significantly less frequency, severity, and duration of attacks, less drug usage, and clearly improved capacity for physical labor. Twenty-four cases improved in more than two of the five items mentioned above. Only six cases showed no change or improvement. Hua Huang and colleagues have documented similar favorable effects of qigong on chronic bronchitis.

THE IMMUNE SYSTEM AND THE BIG "C"

Qigong has always been considered an immune-enhancing system of mind-body healing. Although the concept of "immune system" is modern, the classical Chinese term *bu qi, bu xue* "tonify the qi and blood" has very similar connotations. According to Chinese medicine, when qi and blood are strengthened, we are better able to fight off infection and disease.

The most compelling evidence of qigong's immune-enhancing effect is found in cancer research. In China, qigong is commonly prescribed as an adjunct to chemotherapy and radiation.[39] It is known to lessen the side effects of these therapies. Qigong is frequently recommended as the primary therapy for advanced, inoperable, and medically untreatable cancer. In these cases, qigong can ameliorate pain and other symptoms and slow the progression of the disease. More rarely, qigong practice results in long-term remission.

A famous Beijing actress, Guo Lin, attributed her remission from advanced, inoperable uterine cancer to the practice of qigong, particularly the Five Animal Frolics (see Chapter 12). In the 1970s Madame Guo began teaching her own synthesis of qigong techniques, at first in public parks and later in hospital clinics. By 1979, twenty "terminal" cancer patients attributed their cures to her qigong instruction. Guo Lin's example inspired and encouraged China's wider acceptance of qigong. It is ironic and tragic that in the United States qigong practitioners are prohibited from treating cancer unless closely supervised by medical doctors. Patients often find it difficult or impossible to find such open-minded physicians.[40]

A clinical study conducted by Sun Quizhi and Zhao Li at the Kuangan Men Hospital, Beijing, contrasted the efficacy of two forms of cancer therapy: standard drug treatment compared with drugs combined with qigong practice.[41] One hundred and twenty-seven patients were divided into two groups: ninety-seven in the drug and qigong group, thirty cases in the control group. All had been diagnosed with various advanced malignant cancers.

TABLE 3: QIGONG THERAPY FOR ADVANCED CANCER PATIENTS: DRUGS WITH QIGONG VS. DRUGS ALONE

Measured Effect	Qigong Group	Control Group
Normalized Liver Function	20.62%	6.67%
Normalized Erythrocyte Sedimentation*	23.71%	10%
Phagocytosis Rate**	Increased 12.31%	Decreased 7.87%
Regained Strength	81.7%	10%
Improved Appetite	63%	10%
Free of Irregular Defecation	33.3%	6%

*Erythrocyte Sedimentation: an important measure of immune function, this is the rate at which red blood cells settle in a blood specimen.

**Researchers measured the rate at which macrophages, a type of immune cell, engulf and destroy invading organisms such as bacteria and cancer cells.

Similar drugs were given to both groups. Members of the qigong group practiced two hours a day for an average of three months.

Looking at changes in symptoms, body weight, and standard immunological indices, researchers found significant results.

Studies such as the one above have been replicated several times with similar positive findings. Favorable results have been obtained treating virtually all forms and stages of cancer with a combination of qigong along with allopathic drugs, surgery, chemotherapy, radiation, acupuncture, and herbs. When qigong is omitted from the prescription, the patient requires a longer period of treatment or declines more quickly and is less likely to experience remission.

For the cancer patient, the emotional effect of qigong may be as important as the energetic effect. The cancer patient knows that his body is out of control, with cancer cells replicating wildly and his own immune system unable to distinguish friend from foe. He feels disempowered in the hospital environment, having turned his life over to highly specialized machines and strangers in white coats. By practicing qigong, the patient feels that there is finally something he can do for himself. There are aspects of his body that he *can* control. Numerous studies in the West have shown that feelings of "self-efficacy" can have powerful healing benefits on the course of almost any disease.

Qigong can also help some patients feel closer to God as they become more aware of the spiritual dimensions of themselves and the world. Pain is assuaged by transcending it or, from another point of view, by reaching underneath it to a level of being that is more fundamental. Qigong may or may not cure the disease. But if it inspires acceptance, faith, and hope, it is a good prescription for the soul.

QIGONG: THE 120-YEAR PRESCRIPTION

The first step toward achieving longevity is making every attempt to eliminate the things that are shortening your life! Qigong will be far less effective if you are smoking; taking illegal drugs; drinking excessively; eating too much; living in an ugly environment; staying in a destructive relationship; breathing polluted air; worrying, depressed, lonely, or hostile; not taking time for yourself. Qigong cannot make you healthy if your lifestyle makes you sick.

Qigong cannot miraculously change your *chronological age*, but it can change your *functional age*. A fifty-year-old has the health and vitality of a thirty-year-old. Chinese research has shown that with long-term, regular practice qigong can improve many of the biomarkers of aging, including vital capacity, blood pressure, cholesterol levels, hormone levels, kidney function, mental acuity (especially memory), vision and hearing, skin elasticity, bone density, reaction time, physical strength, and immune function.

Jiao Guorui, renowned qigong master and doctor of Chinese medicine, reports in his English-language work *Qigong Essentials for Health Promotion* on a survey of elderly qigong practitioners compared with seniors who did not practice.[42] The qigong group scored better on hearing, vision, blood pressure, memory, and ability to work.

Important experiments have been conducted to measure the activity of the enzyme superoxide dismutase (SOD) in qigong practitioners. SOD protects the cells against damage from superoxide, a highly toxic free radical. Superoxide is a reactive variety of oxygen that can cause aging of the body's tissues, including wrinkling and changes in skin pigmentation, the appearance of "age spots," in the same way that exposure to air causes food to rot or go stale. Superoxide can cause the breakdown of cartilage[43] and synovial fluid,[44] the cushioning and lubrication between bones, leading to arthritis and joint damage. When it penetrates the cellular DNA, superoxide may induce cancer and other immune system disorders. Chinese scientists hypothesized that qigong should increase SOD levels and thus decrease superoxide.

Xu Hefen and associates at the Jiangsu Provincial Institute of Traditional Chinese Medicine reported on SOD activity in their paper "A

Clinical Study of the Anti-Aging Effect of Qigong."[45] Two hundred retired workers, aged fifty-two to seventy-six, were divided into a qigong group and a control group of nonpractitioners, each consisting of fifty men and fifty women. The qigong group practiced qigong exercises,[46] relaxation, and self-massage for at least a half hour per day for approximately one year. Levels of active SOD increased dramatically for both men and women in the qigong group compared with the controls ($p<0.001$).

In a related experiment, Ye Min, Zhang Rui Hua, and other researchers at the Shanghai Academy of Traditional Chinese Medicine and the Shanghai Qigong Institute found a significant increase in SOD activity in 116 subjects after a two-month course of qigong.[47] These same researchers measured blood levels of estrogen in seventy-seven qigong practitioners compared to twenty-seven controls. During two months of observation, there were no significant changes in hormone levels among the controls. However, in the qigong group, estrogen levels tended to decrease for men and increase for women, including those over age forty-five. These are considered healthful changes, especially in postmenopausal women. Reduced estrogen after menopause causes a loss of calcium from the bones and increased risk of osteoporosis and heart disease.

Since 1958, the Shanghai Institute of Hypertension has focused much of its research on hypertension in the elderly and the treatment and prevention of geriatric diseases.[48] In one twenty-year study, qigong practitioners were found to have stable, lowered blood pressure compared with controls, as well as significant relief from such other age-related disorders as coronary heart disease and diabetes. At the Shandong Institute of Traditional Chinese Medicine, a study conducted with thirty-one middle-aged and elderly diabetics found that qigong had beneficial effects on blood sugar levels, insulin levels, microcirculation (measured in the nail bed), and disease resistance.[49]

More research is also needed to analyze the significance of many common observations: For instance, elderly practitioners frequently note improved sleep and cure of insomnia. Preliminary studies suggest that qigong can improve myopia and hearing. Qigong also seems to make the bones stronger and denser. It is well-known that the bones of elderly qigong practitioners do not break easily, even during a fall. In China, there are elderly qigong martial artists who enjoy demonstrating how they can withstand direct punches to the torso that might break the bones of a younger man.

Qigong can help us *fan lao huan tong* "reverse old age and return to youthfulness." In addition to physical practices, it is important to remember the spiritual side of longevity. We do not age if the mind stays young, renewed, and refreshed by each moment of life. In the words of the ancient

Chinese philosopher Mencius, "The sage is the one who keeps the child's heart and mind."

When an old Daoist was dying, his disciples tried to give him longevity elixirs. He admonished them, "Get away from me. Don't disturb the process of change. Heaven and Earth, yang and yin are my true father and mother. Where could they bring me that would not be in harmony with the Dao! It would be unfilial of me to prolong my life beyond nature's plan." We can achieve this spiritual longevity by shifting our frame of reference, identifying with the universe rather than our limited egos. We live long as the mountain lives long. Human beings are born from the forces of nature; death is a return to what has always been. As Zen philosopher Alan Watts was fond of saying, "You never die because you were never born; you've just forgotten who you are."

SECTION II

Qigong Basics

CHAPTER SIX

The Time and Place
of Practice

To everything there is a season . . .
    —ECCLESIASTES 3:1

Qigong is more than exercise. It is a healing discipline for the body, mind, and spirit. Some of the rules that govern qigong practice differ significantly from those that apply to calisthenics, aerobics, or working out at a gym. Since one of qigong's goals is greater harmony between inside and outside, between yourself and nature, when and where you practice can influence the effectiveness of qigong techniques. Even good qigong exercises are less effective at the wrong time of day or in uncomfortable surroundings.

THE MORNING WORKOUT

Most people practice qigong in a daily "wellness workout," designed to prevent disease and improve or maintain health. The workout, lasting from ten minutes to an hour or longer, consists of dynamic exercises, self-massage, and, sometimes, meditation. Additionally, we all experience times when particular parts of the body are calling for attention, whether due to disease or just feelings of discomfort. To cure a specific problem, we practice therapeutic qigong techniques, either instead of or in addition to the normal daily practice. The daily workout occurs at a fixed time each day. Therapeutic qigong is practiced whenever it is needed.

The period from 12 midnight until 12 noon is called *sheng qi* "the time of the living breath." It is best to practice your qigong wellness workout in the middle of this period, at about 6 A.M. The early morning is the "spring-time" of the day. The winter portion of the day, from noon until midnight, is called *si qi* "the time of the dead breath." Seeds planted in the early spring bear the healthiest fruit; those planted during the winter are less hardy. The living breath peaks at sunrise, the ideal time for qigong training. The effects of morning practice are long-lasting and cumulative. You are likely to still feel pleasantly energized in the afternoon. As each day passes, your supply of qi increases.

While you are learning new qigong techniques, it is a good idea to have at least two practice times, one just for yourself, to build the qi and enjoy, and another "homework" time to review and memorize techniques and details. Do your homework after the morning wellness workout, whenever your schedule allows. Review instructions and practice the exercises slowly and carefully, over and over again until your body can do them automatically. But remember that the time for yourself is the early morning. If you have to get ready for work or prepare the kids for school, try getting up an hour earlier. You can't take care of others effectively if you are not taking care of yourself. Your family will appreciate that the more qi-full you are, the more cheerful you are. (And breakfast seems to taste better if the cook is happy.) If your schedule just doesn't permit early-morning qigong, then find whatever time you can.

On the other hand, if you have time to spare, there is no prohibition against more than one wellness workout per day. This would be in addition to the important morning practice and your "homework" review session. If your normal workout is at sunrise, try another one at sunset. Qigong is a wonderful way to punctuate the daylight hours. The energetic and beautiful exercises feel completely natural at these times of day, probably the human equivalent of birdsongs.

No matter what time of day you practice, always wait at least two hours after eating a meal. There is a saying, "If the belly is filled with food, there is no room for qi." A full belly interferes with breathing and movement. Digestion uses qi, making less available for qigong. It also diverts qi to the digestive system, away from the areas of the body that are the focus of your exercises. If you eat *after* practice, wait at least one half hour after your session to allow time for residual effects of qigong practice. After the half hour "cooling down" time, the qi will be settled and you will be ready for normal activities.

HARMONIZE THE YIN AND THE YANG

There is a simple, commonsense way to harmonize your exercise routine—the wellness workout, "homework" sessions, or Western exercises—with the time of day and the season. In the morning, progress from stillness to movement. Start your workout with relaxation and quiet meditation. Then practice more active forms of qigong. Save jogging or aerobic activity for the last phase of your morning workout. In the evening we naturally want to unwind, slow down, and prepare for sleep. Start with the most vigorous exercise, progress through slower and gentler techniques, and finish with silent meditation. Thus your actions are in harmony with the yin and yang cycles of the day.

Similarly, in the spring emphasize dynamic qigong exercises to open the body to the currents of fresh energy in nature. In the winter, emphasize meditation and gentler, slower exercises to conserve energy and build warmth.

THERAPEUTIC QIGONG

Western science has found that the strength of the immune system fluctuates through each twenty-four-hour period.[1] It is strongest at about 7 A.M. and weakest at about one in the morning—an interesting parallel to the Chinese idea of living and dead breaths. Chinese medicine maintains that the circadian rhythm governs the health of not only the immune system but of each internal organ. Thus, practicing qigong at a certain hour affects one organ more than another.

As the qi circulates through the body, the internal organs experience periods of peak and minimum functioning (see Table 4 below). For instance, at 12 noon, the heart is stimulated by a strong flow of qi. Martial artists are advised never to strike someone in the chest at this time, as it could damage the heart. However, this is a propitious time to do heart qigong. The stomach qi peaks between 7 and 9 A.M. This is when digestion and assimilation are most efficient and is thus the best time for breakfast. One could also use this period to practice qigong for curing ulcers or weak digestion. As a general rule, use the peak periods to work therapeutically on specific organs.

In *Between Heaven and Earth*, Harriet Beinfield and Efrem Korngold point out that disease symptoms also tend to appear at fairly predictable times. "Symptoms of excess appear during peak hours, those of deficiency during the ebb tides of Qi."[2] To find the period of "ebb tide" of an organ just look across the chart to the opposite time period. For instance, lower back pain, which is often a symptom of excess kidney qi, is likely to be more pronounced between

TABLE 4: PEAK PERIODS OF VISCERAL QI

11 P.M.–1 A.M.	Gallbladder	11 A.M.–1 P.M.	Heart
1 A.M.–3 A.M.	Liver	1 P.M.–3 P.M.	Small Intestine
3 A.M.–5 A.M.	Lung	3 P.M.–5 P.M.	Bladder
5 A.M.–7 A.M.	Large Intestine	5 P.M.–7 P.M.	Kidney
7 A.M.–9 A.M.	Stomach	7 P.M.–9 P.M.	Pericardium
9 A.M.–11 A.M.	Spleen	9 P.M.–11 P.M.	Triple Burner[3]

5 and 7 P.M., the time when kidney energy peaks. If the kidneys are deficient and weak, then one will probably experience low vitality between 5 and 7 A.M. Heart attack, a symptom of excess qi, occurs more frequently around noon. On the other hand, heart failure and symptoms of insufficiency such as shortness of breath tend to be more pronounced at midnight. Looking opposite the heart, to the gallbladder, we see that gallstone pain will be more severe late at night. However, if the gallbladder is weak and not producing enough bile, it will be difficult to digest heavy, oily foods between 11 A.M. and 1 P.M., its period of minimum functioning. Even healthy individuals should avoid eating heavy foods at this time.

HOW DAOISTS DEAL WITH CRISIS

In order to overcome a serious, life-threatening condition, the ancient Daoists of China advised practicing qigong frequently and intensively, during "the Four Sacred Periods": Sunrise, Sunset, Midday, and Midnight. In the course of the year, these periods correspond to Spring Equinox, Autumn Equinox, Summer Solstice, and Winter Solstice, respectively. At such times of transition, when yin is changing to yang or yang is changing to yin—whether during the day or the year—we are more susceptible to disease. We can also use these periods to maximize the benefits of qigong in curing disease.

One of the most extraordinary Daoist scholars and practitioners I have met is Mr. Xie, a retired government employee from Hong Kong. When Mr. Xie was diagnosed with incurable and inoperable cancer, he began to practice qigong for eight hours a day, two hours at each of the Sacred periods. He also took Chinese herbs, as prescribed by an acupuncturist. Three months later there was no trace of cancer. Today, fifteen years later, he remains in excellent health. Mr. Xie advises most individuals to practice qigong at sunrise and sunset, with the greatest emphasis placed on morning practice. Only in extreme circumstances, add midday and midnight training.[4]

Mr. Xie would be the first to admit that in general qigong practice, more is not necessarily better. The golden rule is *moderation*. Water your garden a little bit every day. Harrison Moretz, director of the Taoist Studies Institute of Seattle, astutely notes, "Even if you know your garden will require ten thousand gallons of water in the course of the year and x amount of sunlight, this does not mean you should, at the beginning of spring, dump this water all at once or expose your seedlings to a thousand ultraviolet lamps!"[5] Increase the length of qigong practice gradually. At the end of your practice, you should feel more alive and pleasantly satiated, as after a good meal. Start with ten or fifteen minutes a day. Each week add a few more minutes to your routine. After several months, you should be familiar enough with the effects and benefits of qigong that you can find your own optimal length, according to your schedule, needs, and abilities. This is no fixed rule. Most long-term students enjoy about forty minutes in the morning and twenty minutes in the evening. I will present some suggested training schedules in Chapter 16.

A MATTER OF ORIENTATION

It is important to practice in a quiet, well-ventilated area with as much natural lighting as possible. Outdoors is ideal if the weather is comfortable. Extremes of heat, cold, damp, or wind should be avoided, since these "pernicious influences," as they are called in Chinese medicine, can cause disease. Many qigong masters advise practicing in a forest of pine, spruce, or other evergreens. These trees are symbols of longevity, maintaining their color through the four seasons. The forest's balance of light and shadow helps restore balance of internal yin and yang. Water also has a positive influence on qigong. Practicing near a small stream had a resonant effect on the internal energy, helping the qi to flow smoothly in the meridians. Lakes calm the mind and create a serene mood. Does this mean that you must live in the wilderness in order to practice qigong? You can find nature wherever you are. In Beijing, Shanghai, and other Chinese cities, millions of people go to the parks each morning to practice qigong.

Even the direction you face can influence the efficacy of qigong techniques. A popular traditional practice is for men to always face north, women to face south when practicing qigong. North is the direction of cold, yin. When men face north, they absorb yin qi, balancing their yang. South is the direction of warmth, yang. When women face south, they absorb yang qi,

TABLE 5: THE FIVE DIRECTIONS

East	South	Center	West	North
Spring	Summer	Late Summer	Autumn	Winter
Liver	Heart	Spleen	Lung	Kidney
Gallbladder	Small Intest.	Stomach	Large Intest.	Bladder

balancing their yin. However, even these rules must occasionally be varied according to circumstances. Men who are weak, debilitated, or excessively withdrawn and introspective may need the firelike energy of the South. Women who are out of touch with their nurturing side and who have problems controlling anger or aggression may need the yin of the North.

Some qigong practices require facing a specific direction. For instance, Taiji Quan, perhaps the most popular healing exercise in the world, is named after Beiji,[6] the Polestar. The Polestar teaches stillness within motion; it is the unmoving pivot around which the constellations seem to turn. Both male and female Taiji Quan players face north to absorb the influence of this star.

In the philosophy of Wei Bo-yang, discussed in the second chapter of this book, nature is seen as a web of interconnected phenomena. Things of a similar nature, such as the east and springtime or the west and autumn, are linked together and influence each other. This philosophy led to the qigong practice of coordinating direction, season, and organ (Table 5).

For instance, in the spring, face east to bring more qi to the liver and gallbladder. In the summer, face south, the direction of the heart and small intestine. During late summer (what we might call "Indian Summer," a separate season for the Chinese), face any direction, while imagining the qi coming up from the ground. This adds healing qi to the spleen and stomach. During the fall, face west in order to harmonize with the qi of the season and to heal the lungs and large intestine. In the winter, practice qigong facing north, letting the winter qi heal the kidneys and bladder.

Qigong recognizes that nature is an important facet of healing. We are part of the natural environment; we grow out of it in the same way that a wave emerges from the ocean or a tree grows in the forest. While practicing qigong, let nature become part of your experience. Do not "space out" or become preoccupied by internal sensations. In quiet meditative qigong, you can sense the power of the seasons and directions, the feel of the ground, the sun and gentle breeze on the skin. The ears are open and hearing the sounds of nature. In more active qigong, the eyes are generally open and allowing the natural world in, a pure, innocent appreciation, with no need to think about or label.

Isn't nature always practicing qigong? The trees "expel the old breaths, draw in the new." The clouds are moving fluidly, without sign of excess, depletion, or stagnation. The animals, because they are in harmony with nature, demonstrate balance, coordination, and grace, the qualities of a qigong master.

CHAPTER SEVEN

The Posture of Power

In stillness be like the pine.
In movement be like clouds and water.
—QIGONG PROVERB

GOOD POSTURE MAKES HEALTHY QI

Almost all qigong techniques, whether standing, moving, or meditating, share common principles of alignment and posture. Correct posture enhances relaxation, balance, proper breathing, and energetic flow. It is essential that you understand and practice the basic physical mechanics of qigong, what the Chinese call *diao shen* "regulating the body," before concentrating on subtler, internal aspects, such as coordinated breathing or specific ways of focusing the qi. How can you feel or move the qi if the body, the vessel of qi, is crooked? If you maintain correct posture, tense, weak, or energetically stagnant areas of the body come more quickly to the foreground of awareness so that you can more easily discover and correct your areas of imbalance.

The basic principles of qigong posture are simple. The spine should feel long and open, with the shoulders relaxed, neither slouched nor pulled back. The elbows, knees, and fingers are all slightly bent rather than rigidly locked. The feet are generally flat on the ground. The chest feels easy and open, neither puffed out nor depressed. The abdomen and solar plexus are free of tension, allowing the breath to become slow, quiet, and deep. The whole body is alert, relaxed, and more fully alive.

THE QIGONG STANCE

The various elements of posture are combined together in "the qigong stance." Although the qigong stance may be practiced from a standing or seated position, it is most beneficial to practice from a standing posture. Standing creates the greatest ease of breathing because it allows the most space for the lungs, diaphragm, and abdomen to move.

All qigong techniques are based on the qigong stance. Like a musical composition, the stance is the theme, and the other qigong movements are the variations. In later chapters on qigong exercise and meditation, you can assume, unless otherwise noted, that you begin from the qigong stance and try to maintain as many of the postural principles as possible throughout the practice. In qigong exercises, the stance is also held for a moment while making a transition from one technique to another. For instance, to do a qigong bend, first stand in the qigong stance, with the feet shoulder-width apart and flat on the ground. Then slowly bend down until your upper torso is hanging. Hold that posture for a few seconds, with the knees slightly bent and the breath as relaxed as possible. Next gradually straighten the spine, resuming the stance.

Holding the qigong stance is a powerful way to increase the flow and accumulation of qi and is considered qigong in and of itself. It is the subtlest type of qigong because you can practice it in secret anywhere, at any time. Use the stance to review principles of good posture while waiting in line for movie tickets or sitting at the bus stop. One of my students practices qigong while sorting mail at a large computer firm. He concentrates on a straight spine, relaxed joints, and deep breathing as he tosses mail into hundreds of mailboxes.

The Chinese language has a specific, highly specialized vocabulary to describe posture and movement, which makes it a wonderful medium for describing the qigong stance. At first, go through each of the principles described below one by one. With practice you will be able to apply several principles simultaneously, maintaining the previous principle in mind and body as you go on to the next. "My joints are open *and* my shoulders are relaxed, *and* my spine is straight." Eventually you will memorize the principles and will be able to supply them as needed. You may find yourself remembering them when something feels out of balance. "Why does my shoulder feel sore? Ah, I'm raising my shoulder and lifting the sternum." The qigong stance creates a specific, pleasurable feeling of balance, ease, and rootedness. As you become familiar with this feeling, you will be able to return to it as a whole, without going through individual postural points.

FROM THE CHINESE QIGONG CLASSICS

While practicing the qigong stance or other forms of qigong, wear loose, comfortable clothing, with flat-bottomed shoes, or go barefoot if the ground is a comfortable temperature. If you do not need eyeglasses to read instructions, take them off. Also remove any rings or other jewelry, since these may interfere with qi circulation. It is easiest to get the feel of these principles from a standing position. If standing is difficult for you, sit down. Most seated qigong practices, such as breathing exercises and visualization, are practiced from a chair. Exceptions will be made clear in this book. Sit in the middle of a straight-backed chair, without leaning against the backrest. Avoid over-stuffed chairs that you disappear into, as they make it difficult to maintain a healthy posture. Whether standing or sitting, the legs are uncrossed, the feet shoulder-width apart and flat on the ground. The hands rest comfortably at the sides or, if seated, in the lap.

Here are the most important principles of qigong posture and the elements of the qigong stance:

Relaxation

QUAN SHEN FANG SONG

"Whole body relaxed." The word fang means "to release," and it implies that relaxation is not merely the lack of tension. It is an activity. Quan shen fang song is alive, alert relaxation. It means eliminating unnecessary tension, being supple and alert to the environment. Relaxation is the first and most important principle of qigong. It is often considered a system of qigong in itself (see Chapter 8).

GUAN JIE SONG KAI

"Joints relax open." The joints are the points of articulation between the bones—hinges and connections that allow movement to occur. Obviously, if the joints are tense, movement is difficult. Tension means shortened muscles and restricted range of motion, creating the possibility of bone irritation and inflammation (arthritis) and damage to the cartilage. In qigong, the joints are considered gateways that allow the passage of qi. It is important to keep these gateways open by consciously relaxing and releasing all of the joints. Do not lock the elbows or knees. Keep the wrists soft. Release tension in the shoulders, fingers, hips, ankles, toes. Imagine all of the vertebrae supple, like a rope, capable of unrestricted motion. Relax *open* these joints; think of the relaxation as a gentle expansion from the center, toward the periphery. Become aware of places where you contract inward. By lessening friction in the joints, you will preserve the health of bone and cartilage, adding years to your life and life to your years.

Among the most difficult joints to relax from a standing position are the knees. Relaxed knees are slightly bent knees. Slightly bent does not mean walking six inches closer to the ground, as though imitating Groucho Marx. Simply make sure that you do not have the habit of standing or stepping with locked knees. Maintaining a slightly bent position is difficult for us because the preponderance of flat surfaces to walk on in the civilized world causes our joints and leg muscles to weaken. Bent knees allow the springiness necessary to adapt to a changing terrain. As the knees bend the spinal vertebrae compress and release, open and close, and the pelvis remains loose. As Ruthy Alon observes in her beautiful work *Mindful Spontaneity*, springy knees induce springy, supple joints in the rest of the body—". . . your back is agile and alive to the degree that your knees are agile and alive."[1] It is easy to understand why bent knees are emphasized in all sports. Try jogging or jumping with locked knees. Have you ever seen a pitcher throw a fastball while keeping the front knee locked? Even a tennis serve loses power.

Relaxing open the joints helps the qi to flow and helps *you* to flow, to move gracefully and beautifully. You may have noticed this quality in accomplished dancers and athletes. But you don't have to be a dancer to be graceful. The key is in following correct principles of posture and movement. The qigong stance can remind you of these principles.

Head and Neck

XU LING DING JING

"Empty the neck, let energy reach the crown." Release the muscles of the neck both outward, toward the surface, and down along the back. Think of the muscles gently lengthening and opening. The head becomes light and free, delicately balanced on the upper spine.

Our society is becoming more and more top-heavy, emphasizing the head rather than the heart or feet. I believe that this obsession with intellect creates tension in the head and cervical vertebrae and poor upper body alignment. With chin pushed forward, back, or cocked to one side, we seem desperate to get somewhere a-head of the rest of the body.

In Daoism, the head is considered the abode of the inner gods. It is visualized as a sacred mountain, containing caverns for training and initiation. When the neck is tight, the energy cannot reach the head. We lose touch with the "inner gods," that is, the intuitive mind. The spirit becomes dull. On a physical level, qi and blood flow are both restricted, contributing to headaches, eyestrain, and confusion.

DING TOU XUAN

"Suspend the head." The soles of the feet connect us with the earth; the crown of the head connects us with the heavens. The Chinese have devised an ingenious image to help relax the head and neck and to stand with greater poise and balance. Whether standing or sitting, imagine that the head is suspended from above, as though a string were attached to the crown, holding you up. Be careful, however, that the head maintains its alignment with the neck. Do not lift the chin away from the chest or push the chin downward. With the head suspended, the eyes naturally relax and gaze level, looking neither up, down, right, or left.

Holding the image of a suspended head is a way to create "breathing space" in the body and to counter the unappealing effects of gravity and age: the tendency to grow shorter and wider. Ida Rolf, Ph.D., famed creator of the Structural Integration (or "Rolfing") method of body therapy, reminds us in her classic, *Rolfing: "The inevitable action of gravity anywhere at any time on any soft, pliable mass is to bring it nearer to a formless, chaotic, spherical unit.* Thus in human bodies, gravity acts to shorten, thicken, and compress. Only the bones prevent bodies from becoming a thick, amoebalike ball."[2] Interestingly, Dr. Rolf says that if we could only put the human body on a "sky hook" many of these abnormalities would be corrected.

SHE DING SHANG E

"Tongue touches the roof of the mouth." Keep the mouth relaxed, the lips lightly touching. Unless otherwise specified or unless you are exhaling through the mouth, it is best to keep the tongue gently touching a comfortable place on the upper palate. This is useful for two reasons. First, it generates saliva, which should be swallowed when necessary, preventing the mouth or throat from drying out. According to Daoism, saliva is the body's "longevity liquor." The second reason is that the body's major yang meridian ends at the upper palate while the yin meridian begins at the tip of the tongue. By touching these points together, an important energy circuit is closed, allowing the qi to circulate with a stronger current. A stronger current means more energy and vitality.

Shoulders and Elbows

CHEN JIAN ZHUI ZHOU

"Sink the shoulders, drop the elbows." Chronically lifted shoulders are a common symptom of tension and anxiety,[3] often resulting from fear and a need to protect oneself against a perceived threat. When our shoulders are raised, the ribs lift; breathing becomes shallow and thoracic. Other tensions quickly follow in a kind of chain reaction. The midback becomes tight, freezing the shoulder blades and preventing them from expanding with the breath. From the back, tension moves into the neck and head and along the arms. Raised shoulders create a feeling that the arms are disconnected from the rest of the body.[4]

Shoulder tension often results in elbow tension and a habit of locking the elbows. The converse is also true; locked elbows cause the shoulders to tighten. Locked elbows slow down circulation to the hands; the fingers become cold, numb, and insensitive. It is also easier to damage the elbows when lifting heavy objects.

Sinking the shoulders and relaxing the elbows makes it possible to transmit whole-body power through the arm, an essential skill in baseball, tennis, golf, and in many other sports. In the qigong stance, it is imperative that the shoulders sink down. Be careful not to slump the shoulders forward or pull them back. Let them sit straight down. At the same time, loosen the elbows; relax them open. The elbows, like the knee joints, are never locked during qigong. The elbows are "dropped," that is, slightly bent. When shoulders and elbows drop, it is easier for the qi to drop, to fill the dan tian, the vital reservoir in the lower abdomen.

Back and Chest

ZHONG ZHENG

"Central and erect." This refers to the straight spine and centered feeling while practicing the qigong stance and most qigong exercises or meditations. The spine is the highway for electrical messages to and from the brain; it is also the highway for qi. If it is bent, crooked, or leaning, the qi cannot flow evenly. With a centered and stable spine it is easier to feel the bones stacking, one over the other. The skeletal structure is used to maintain the erect posture without unnecessary tensing of the muscles. The weight drops evenly through the feet, maximizing contact between the feet and the yin, earth-qi of the ground.

Think of the spine as a flexible rope rather than a stiff pole. It should be straight, but not stiff. The rope is gently stretched and pulled at both ends: the head lifting and tailbone sinking. Or imagine that the spine is a string and each vertebra a bead on that string. Let there be a comfortable space between each "bead," no cramping or crowding. Give your vertebrae room to breathe.

"Straight" should be interpreted as relatively straight, not swaybacked, hunched, or twisted. Straight does *not* mean absolutely straight, as though the spine were a wooden plank. The healthy spine has four fluid and graceful curves—at the neck, chest, lumbar region, and sacrum. This axis of opposing concave and convex spinal curves allows the body to shift various positions and to carry the weight of the body upright. An infant is able to walk only when these curves and the supporting muscles and ligaments have developed sufficiently. According to *The Columbia University College of Physicians and Surgeons Complete Home Medical Guide*, "If these natural curves are altered too much, stress is placed on the vertebrae, and pain can follow."[5]

Many qigong instructors, both Chinese and American, advise *eliminating* the sacral and lumbar curves and are unclear about whether this posture is to be maintained outside of qigong practice.[6] Although it is true that qigong posture helps eliminate *excess* curvature, it is not advisable to attempt to eliminate *all* curvature. How straight then is "straight"? Maintain the feeling and image of an elongated spine, and allow the hips to roll *slightly* under. If you place one palm on the sacrum with the fingertips touching the tailbone, it is easy to feel a gentle tucking of the pelvis. The spine feels straight, though there is still some natural curvature. This posture facilitates awareness of the lower abdomen and stimulation of the *ming men* acupoint below the second lumbar vertebra, which harmonizes kidney function. After qigong practice, the back resumes its normal curves.

The words "central" and "erect" also imply that the spine is plumb erect, perpendicular to the ground, rather than straight on an incline, like an airplane taking off. Do not lean to the front or back, right or left. You are in a position of maximum potential, capable of moving with equal ease in any direction. This is also called *zhong ding* "centered and stable," a posture of poise, rootedness, and fine balance. Returning to the image of a tree, if the body is centered and stable, it feels like a tree with deep roots and flexible branches.

HAN XIONG BA BEI

"Sink the chest, lift the back." This description has given rise to misunderstanding among Chinese as much as Westerners and illustrates the need for special training in translating qigong literature. *Han* does not mean depress or collapse the chest inward. Such a concave posture would place a great deal of pressure on the heart. Instead, the sternum is sunk down and relaxed. The point is not to raise or puff out the chest. Lifting the sternum creates tension in the diaphragm and makes abdominal respiration more difficult. In martial arts practice, a raised chest exposes the sternum to attack.

Lifting the back does not imply a kind of "coat-hanger posture," as though the seventh cervical vertebra were suspended on a meat hook! The Chinese word *ba* refers to a special kind of lifting. It does not mean grasping an object from above or holding it from underneath. Ba means to draw a sword out of a scabbard. "Lift the back" means to extend and lengthen the spine. The two phrases "Sink the chest" and "Lift the back" go together. If the back is extended naturally, the chest will be neither concave nor convex. In terms of qi circulation, lifting the back helps the yang, heavenly qi, to rise up the back. Sinking the chest helps the yin, earthly qi, which flows along the front of the body, to sink toward the ground. Thus the heavenly and earthly, yang and yin, are able to follow their natural courses and create greater internal harmony.

Hips

SONG KUA[7]

"Relax the kua." The word kua refers to the inguinal area, the creases at the junction of the thighs and trunk. This is a core and pivotal area of the body. Relaxing the kua can facilitate relaxation of the hips and the deep muscles, including the psoas muscles, which attach to the hips. This improves sexual performance and responsiveness and helps strengthen the reproductive system. The hipbones form a protective shell around the lower abdominal energy center, the dan tian. When the muscles and tendons around the hips are relaxed, the dan tian qi can spread more easily through the rest of the body. It is also easier to feel qigong movements as *inner directed*, propelled by the movement of qi in the lower abdomen.

Mind and Qi

YONG YI, BU YONG LI

"Use intent, not force." It is difficult to find a single word that captures the meaning of the Chinese word yi. Yi may be translated "intent, volition, concentration, or mindfulness." Because the qigong stance is relaxed and balanced, minimal force (li) is required. Do not strain. Applying this principle to qigong exercises, if it is difficult to do a movement, then do less or just imagine the movement. It is a scientific fact that imagining a movement can cause the same neurons to fire as doing the actual movement. Thus, a golfer who frequently imagines his stroke, can improve his performance on the golf course. Intent seems to clear the neural pathways, making it easier to do the actual technique at a later time.

There is a qigong saying, "When the intent (yi) arrives, the qi arrives." This means that the more your mind is focused on what you are doing, the more qi you can develop and control. It is impossible to benefit from qigong if you are trying to watch TV or listen to music or prepare the shopping list while practicing.[8] *Qigong does not work without awareness and focus.* All qigong techniques are designed to strengthen and refine intent, so that eventually the techniques can be dispensed with, and you can direct the healing energy just through concentration.

QI CHEN DAN TIAN

"Qi sinks to the dan tian." When I was studying Taiji Quan with Master William C. C. Chen, he would often correct my technique by saying one word, *Chen* "Sink." In Taiji Quan and other qigong practices such as breathing, exercise, meditation, and the qigong stance, every part of the body seeks its lowest level in the field of gravity, moving and flowing downward like water. The shoulders sink, the abdomen sinks and is allowed to hang out and down (no forcibly flat stomachs for qigong and self-healing!). In standing, the knees bend, the weight of the body sinks through the feet into the ground. In sitting, the body rests gracefully in the chair and the feet are rooted into the ground. The breath also sinks, dropping deep within the body. With every inhalation the dan tian expands (expanding the lower abdomen and, to a lesser extent, the lower back); with every exhalation, it contracts. This method of breathing massages and stimulates the dan tian. In time, as the dan tian accumulates a greater supply of qi, the student will experience a feeling of warmth, fullness, and inner strength, at first only during practice, but eventually all day long.

An intent to drop energy downward, to sink the qi, increases balance and stability and facilitates proper breathing. It is important not only in qigong training, but to improve performance in any sport. Famed martial arts instructor and scholar Adam Hsu puts it clearly when he writes, "In the upper levels of traditional kung fu, even when the practitioner sends the qi to other areas of the body, the *dan tian* is never totally emptied. Any of China's traditional body disciplines—health exercises, *neigong* [qigong], Beijing Opera, folk dance, acrobatics, kung fu—always require the qi to sink down."[9] Hsu notes that if the qi is mistakenly centered in the chest, the breath becomes short and shallow, damaging the health. As we will see in "Healthy Breathing" (Chapter 9), this view is supported by medical research.

Practice the qigong stance for a few minutes whenever you feel the need to review principles of the standard qigong posture. As you practice various qigong techniques described in this book, go back to this chapter and work through the principles one at a time. If the stance needs to be varied, my instructions will make this clear. For instance, if a qigong meditation may be practiced cross-legged, then obviously the feet cannot be flat on the floor. Or if an exercise requires bending down followed by bending back or leaning to the front, then the back is zhong zheng, "central and erect," only during the transitions from one posture to another.

In active qigong—compared to tranquil qigong, where one posture is held—apply principles of the stance while moving through space. This creates a feeling of inner calm, of meditation in motion. The qigong stance is a posture of dynamic potential. You feel balanced and capable of initiating movement in any direction at any time. In Japanese samurai movies, such as Kurosawa's *The Seven Samurai*, the samurai paces his enemy while maintaining a straight, balanced spine, slightly bent knees and fluid, gliding motions. As soon as the opponent leans to one side, raises the shoulders, or in any way varies from the stance, he loses the ability to react and move with speed and freedom. The samurai who loses the qigong stance loses the battle. In everyday life, the qigong stance helps one move with grace, ease, poise, and dignity. Like the samurai, one is less likely to be defeated by life's battles, and can react in a healthier way to stress.

There is a Daoist saying, "When a child or a drunk falls from a carriage, their bones don't break." This is because they are embodying the qigong principle of *song relaxation*, and so are able to adapt to the ground as they fall. (The ultimate sign of a stubborn attitude is expecting the ground to adapt to your body, rather than the other way around!) Qigong cultivates a powerful and unique form of relaxation. When filled with qi, the body is like a tree branch filled with sap; it can bend and flow with the breeze, but it does not snap or lose its connection with the root. On the other hand, a stiff, dead branch is easily broken. Thus the adage of Lao Zi, "Concentrate the qi and you will achieve the utmost suppleness. . . . Suppleness is the essence of life."

Qigong posture is the opposite of military posture (figs. 1 and 2). In military posture, the chest is out, stomach in, knees locked. In qigong posture, the chest is down, the stomach out, and knees bent! Military posture is designed to cut off autonomy and independence, to influence the soldier to follow orders.[10] When the abdomen is pulled in, it becomes virtually impossible to feel our weight sinking through the feet into the ground. The soldier loses touch with the unconscious—the "ground" of the mind—and with deep feelings. Theoretically, he will not hesitate when given a command. Being cut off from deep feelings may be a desirable state for a soldier, but it is unhealthy for qi development. Qigong posture is designed for *self-empowerment*, to help the student feel internally strong and capable of unrehearsed action.

There is an easy exercise that will help you appreciate the difference between qigong and military posture. Face a partner, standing in the qigong stance. Have your partner gently push against your chest, until you start to lose balance. Both of you should try to remember how much force was required. Then stand in military posture, and ask your partner to push you again. Now how much force is required before you start to lose balance? Probably about a tenth, compared to qigong posture. In military posture one

Figure 1. Military posture   *Figure 2. Qigong posture*

easily loses balance when exposed to outside pressure, that is, one is more easily controlled by another's will.

In summary, when practicing qigong, keep in mind the following: relax the whole body, especially the joints; keep the neck relaxed and the head suspended delicately over the spine; the jaw is also relaxed, with the tongue generally touching the upper palate; sink the shoulders and elbows; maintain a relaxed but erect spine, centered and stable; maximize contact between the feet and the ground, feeling your body's weight dropping *through* the feet; release the sternum; the spine is long and extended; the hips are relaxed. Do not use force! Be aware of what you are doing! The abdomen is relaxed, and the breath feels as though it is sinking into it.

By practicing these postural principles the whole body can be replenished by the energy of life, qi.

CHAPTER EIGHT

Fang Song Gong:
The Art of Relaxation

Learning to inhibit unwanted contractions of
muscles that function without, or in spite of,
our will, is the main task in coordinated
action.

—MOSHE FELDENKRAIS,
THE POTENT SELF

The Chinese word *song* (pronounced sung) has very different connotations from the equivalent English word, "relaxation." When we say "relax" in English, we often mean eliminating *all* tension, becoming almost limp. Song, however, implies greater aliveness. As my teacher, Charlotte Selver, used to say, "A flower is relaxed." Song is not merely the absence of tension, but rather *the absence of unnecessary tension.* Song is the art of becoming aware of and inhibiting the habitual contraction of muscles due to emotional stresses and poor habits of posture, breathing, and movement.

The complete Chinese term for this qigong is *fang* (doing or releasing) *song* (relaxation) *gong* (work). We can translate the entire phrase as "active relaxation." Active relaxation is a form of qigong in itself; it is also essential preparation for all styles of qigong. It includes the following attributes: *awareness and tranquillity, effortlessness, sensitivity, warmth and rootedness.*

AWARENESS AND TRANQUILLITY

Active relaxation is a state of being aware and alert to both oneself and the external environment. Vitality is not wasted on unnecessary tension. The

model for such relaxation is the crane. In the Chinese language, the word for
tranquil observation or contemplation, *guan*, is a pictogram of a crane. The
crane stands perfectly still at the edge of a lake, as though asleep. Yet it is
fully awake, scooping up fish as they swim by.

It is impossible to achieve this state of aliveness without cultivating
awareness of the body. The golden rule of qigong is "Pay attention." We cannot get rid of tension if we are not aware of *what* is tense and sensitive to *how*
this tension is maintained. In physics the Heisenberg Uncertainty Principle
states that the act of observation changes that which is observed. This principle is especially true of the human body. As we "observe" our areas of
tension, it becomes possible for tension to dissipate. There is a reciprocal
relationship between chronic functional tension (as opposed to tension
caused by injury or disease)[1] and habitual lack of body awareness. A tense
body part lapses into unconsciousness, becoming white noise, like the constant hum of an electric fan, or the drone of passing automobiles. If I am unaware of an area of my body, it is easier for the tension in that area to be
maintained. Yet when I am aware of a tense shoulder, the shoulder begins to
relax. As I become aware of the breath, the breath slows down. Awareness
helps to thaw out frozen diaphragms and locked sternums. It presents the opportunity for change. We can see that awareness might not be comfortable or
pleasantat first; it is, however, the first stage in cultivating tranquillity and
deep relaxation.

EFFORTLESSNESS

Active Relaxation trains the body to use the minimum effort necessary for
any task. If four ounces of strength are necessary, why use five? The extra
ounce is wasted energy and, if exerted routinely in daily life, a continuous
drain on vitality. In Taiji Quan, a gentle martial art that includes much
qigong training, there is a saying, "A feather cannot be added; a fly cannot
alight." This means that the posture is held so precisely, so delicately that
if a feather rests on the shoulder, the knees will need to bend because of
the added weight. If a fly alights on the extended arm, the arm will drop.
Obviously, some effort is required to keep an arm extended. The point is not
no-effort, but rather minimum effort creating a subjective feeling of effortlessness and ease, no matter how much energy is actually expended. This
quality is also apparent to observers. A great ballerina appears to float across
the stage. A master sculptor seems to fluidly and effortlessly free the image
from the stone.

By contrast, when an action is poorly and inefficiently performed, there is always a subjective feeling of strain, friction, or resistance. According to Moshe Feldenkrais, Ph.D. (1904–1984), founder of the Functional Integration system of neuromotor education and reconditioning, ". . . the sensation of effort is the subjective feeling of wasted movement."[2] A good example would be clenching the teeth and facial muscles in order to lift a heavy object, or tightening (thus, shortening) the hamstring muscles at the back of the leg while walking. (The latter inhibits the rotation of the femur in the pelvis.) Or, very commonly, tightening and furrowing the brow while concentrating for a school test. Is the brain a muscle that works better by tensing the skull?

In a culture that emphasizes hard work, it may take some critical thinking and introspection to realize the futility of effort as it is so often understood. In order to perform an action more efficiently, one must generally do less, and actually learn *how to not make an effort*.

In the Daoist classic *Zhuang Zi* (third century B.C.), there are two famous stories illustrating this principle:

A man jumps into a raging, torrential river and goes for a swim. Confucius runs frantically along the shore, certain that the man will be drowned. When the man later pulls himself gracefully up on the riverbank, Confucius asks him how he managed to stay afloat. The man replies, "I just go in with a swirl and out with a whirl. I follow the way of the water and don't think of myself."

Another tale concerns Daoist butcher Ding who moves his knife "with a zing and a zoom, keeping perfect rhythm, as though performing a dance." King Hui asks the butcher how he developed such skill. The butcher replies, "Your servant only cares for the Dao [the Way], which goes beyond skill." He explains that he always cuts precisely through the hollows and spaces, never touching a ligament or bone. Thus he has kept the same blade for nineteen years. When he hacks at the piece of meat, it just falls apart, "like a crumbling piece of earth." "Excellent!" exclaims King Hui. "By listening to the words of Butcher Ding, I have learned the essence of nurturing the forces of life [*yang sheng*, a synonym for *yang qi*, nourishing the qi]."

In the Chinese martial arts, one must similarly balance effort and effortlessness. Relaxation is the key to speed and quicker reaction time. A skilled fighter moves so fluidly, easily, and quickly that he seems to have no bones. Yang Zheng-fu, one of the great figures in Taiji Quan history, would tell his students, "Relax, relax; be calm" at least ten times a day. A modern-day Taiji Quan Master, T. T. Liang, once corrected a tense student by reprimanding him, "Are you practicing hard-style Karate or Taiji Quan? Who are you trying to hit, the opponent or yourself?"

One of my favorite stories about effortlessness was recounted to me by

Taiji Quan master Paul Gallagher, one of Master Liang's senior students. Master Liang was once practicing the Taiji Quan exercise in a park in Taiwan. An old Daoist priest walked by and told Master Liang, "Why don't you try holding the posture you are in?" Liang had just assumed the graceful "Golden Pheasant Stands on One Leg" posture in which the body is balanced on one leg, the other knee raised high in the air. Liang held the posture as a standing meditation, while the old Daoist observed. About five minutes later, while Master Liang was still balanced in the Golden Pheasant posture, the Daoist stepped over to Liang and lightly grasped his calf. He shook his head disapprovingly and said, "Why is your calf tight? Your Taiji Quan is like a stiff piece of wood." To illustrate his point, the Daoist raised one knee in the air, demonstrating the same Golden Pheasant posture. Master Liang relaxed and stood at the side. After five minutes the Daoist asked Liang to feel his calf. It was completely relaxed and as soft as cotton.

Minimum effort creates optimum health. However, there are times when minimum effort implies more tension, rather than less. Obviously the ability to increase tension may be essential therapy for problems such as paralysis, urinary incontinence, or to gain control over atrophied muscles. In some forms of meditative qigong, one must learn to gently tense the muscles of the perineum or coccyx (coccygeal muscles) in order to stimulate the circulation of qi through the spine. It is important to remember that qi cannot flow through a tense, knotted muscle or a locked joint. Nor can it flow through a limp wrist or flaccid belly. True relaxation is often compared to water: soft, supple, alive, and powerful!

Learning to use only as much effort as necessary is a way to improve health and vitality and an important ingredient in curing stress-induced fatigue, including the fatigue of busy-mindedness. As the body relaxes, the mind becomes tranquil, aware, and alert.

SENSITIVITY

Master T. T. Liang, in his text *T'ai Chi Ch'uan for Health and Self-Defense*, has an excellent definition of song. He says that the principle of song "implies loosening one's muscles and releasing one's tensions, giving up one's energy externally but preserving it internally so that one's body will be sensitive and alert enough to adapt itself to any circumstance."[3] He explains that a collapsed body, the opposite of song, is unable to react appropriately in an emergency. Thus, active relaxation is a process of becoming more sensitive to what is happening both inside and outside the skin.

Sensitivity is possible because relaxation helps release fixed attitudes of body and mind. *Physiologically*, the body is in a state of balance, *homeostasis*. This does not mean that there is a complete absence of disease, but rather that the body returns to balance more easily and quickly after it has been disturbed. I am reminded of the weighted Joe Palooka punching doll I played with as a child. When I hit it, it would bounce toward the ground, then quickly spring back to an upright position. Qigong practitioners cultivate the center *(shou dan tian)* in a similar way. The winds of life might knock them off balance, but they quickly spring back.

Psychologically, the relaxed state of mind is *kong*, "empty," free of rigid beliefs about oneself or others. One might react to emotional disturbances, but reactions tend not to be prolonged or out of control. Holding a grudge is poor qigong. We can say that "emptiness" creates a centripetal force, drawing one back to the point of tranquillity and balance. One is sensitive to states of balance and imbalance and thus able to move spontaneously (authentically) and appropriately respond to life events.

A relaxed body-mind can feel. A tense body-mind is insensitive. Simple experiments can verify and illustrate this principle. Stand barefoot on the floor or, ideally, outside in a grassy meadow. Feel the texture and temperature of the ground. Allow yourself to appreciate where and how such feelings are registered. Do you feel the ground with your feet? Do the feelings rise through your legs, into the abdomen? Can your whole body feel the ground? Now, while continuing this self-inquiry, tense the thighs and/or buttocks. How has this affected your feeling and sensitivity?

Next, fill a small basin with hot water and another with cold water. Place your hand in the hot water and then in the cold water. You should experience slight discomfort. Now, tense your hand into a fist and tense the muscles of your upper arm, the biceps and triceps. Again, experience the hot and cold water. Can you feel the temperature as clearly? Do you react as strongly to the discomfort? Even so-called spontaneous, natural reactions to extremes of heat or cold are tempered by tension. Thus, as in Master Liang's explanation above, a tense individual might not respond quickly enough to a dangerous situation.

Tension also decreases sensitivity to other people. Try shaking hands with a tight shoulder. Or stroke a loved one's hair while grimacing. In the martial arts, relaxation is essential in order to react to subtle cues about how an opponent is going to strike. According to the Taiji Quan classic, the *Explanation of the Thirteen Movements*, at a high level of training, "if the opponent doesn't move, I don't move. If he makes the slightest move, *I move first*."

Here's an enjoyable way to test your level of relaxation and sensitivity. Ask a partner to try this "Qigong Dance." Stand facing each other, each of you with one arm (either arm) extended. Lightly touch your hand or wrist to your partner's hand or wrist. The exact point of contact can shift and change as necessary during the "dance." Imagine that your wrists are adhering to each other, like two pieces of paper stuck with glue. Move your arm smoothly (not changing the speed or rhythm) in different directions. Your partner follows your movement, staying attached, never breaking contact (fig. 3). Do this for a few minutes, then change roles, so your partner leads. If you or your partner can follow the other's movement very easily, then move the arm with varying rhythm and speed. The exercise should be challenging but not impossible. You will find that your ability to sensitively "listen" and adhere to your partner's arm is directly proportional to your degree of relaxation. If your arm is tense, it will be virtually impossible to follow your partner. With practice, you will be able to gently follow your partner's movements without changing the pressure of contact. You will feel like two feathers that have met in midair and are moving together in a gentle breeze. The "dance" will feel like a delightful energy play, a way for you and your partner to train each other to a higher degree of awareness, relaxation, and sensitivity.

There is a famous anecdote about a qigong master whose "adhering ability" was challenged by a boxer. The boxer asked the qigong master to place his hand on the boxer's shoulder and dared him to stay attached. The boxer began to run about, swaying and shifting his body, frequently changing direction and speed. After a few minutes he came to a low brick wall. He jumped over it, somersaulting in the air, and landed on his feet. To the boxer's amazement, the qigong master was still attached, the pressure of his hand unchanged on the boxer's shoulder!

Figure 3

During the Second World War, Taiji Quan master Zheng Man-qing was strolling through a grassy field with one of his students. They were engaged in conversation. Suddenly the master drew his foot back, as though touching a hot coal. He took a few steps backward, knocking his student over, causing him to stumble and fall. The master's toe had just touched a buried wire connected to a land mine. His quick action, withdrawing his foot before an ounce of weight had passed through it, had prevented the mine from exploding.

WARMTH AND ROOTEDNESS

Relaxation creates deep and efficient abdominal respiration, resulting in more complete oxygenation of the blood. Relaxation also helps to dilate blood vessels and lower blood pressure. It also affects blood chemistry, including normalization of the acid-base (pH) balance and reduction of blood and tissue levels of calcium, which can help prevent or eliminate tremors, spasms, and tension in the muscles. The overall result is improved circulation and oxygen delivery to all parts of the body. This is especially noticeable in the hands and feet, which often feel pleasantly warm both during and after qigong.

According to Chinese medicine, relaxed abdominal breathing is an *energetic pump*, sending qi through the meridians. In the *Explanation of the Thirteen Movements*, we read, "Qi is rooted in the feet, controlled by the *yao* [waist and abdomen], and manifests in the hands." Like a reservoir filling with water, abdominal breathing causes the dan tian energy center to fill with qi. Once the dan tian is filled, the surplus of accumulated qi begins to overflow into the meridians, bones, and, eventually, all the tissues of the body, creating a general sensation of warmth.

By contrast, chest breathing all too frequently results in tension, constriction of the blood vessels, poor oxygen delivery, cold hands and feet. The dan tian is empty, the body weak and fatigued.

Qigong masters are famous for the warmth of their hands. External Qi Healers lightly touch a client's body in order to transmit warmth and healing qi. Dr. K. S. Wong once commented to me, "Sometimes, if a patient is sick, I begin the treatment by just shaking hands!" Another famous qigong master, the late Wang Shu-jin, used to teach qigong outdoors in Tokyo during the bitter winter season. If a student couldn't stand the cold, he could grasp the master's hand for a quick warm-up.

Hand-warming is also one of the goals in biofeedback training. Deep relaxation results in warmer hands. Conversely, an individual who learns, through self-regulation, how to warm the hands has also learned how to induce relaxation. Clinicians have found that hand-warming often generalizes to a greater degree of control over vasodilation and constriction throughout the body. This can sometimes result in the cure of migraine headaches and other vascular disorders.

Another common side effect of Active Relaxation is the feeling of weight, rootedness, and "sinking," corresponding to a reduction of tension and release of worry and mental baggage. Relaxation and sinking (*chen*) are synonymous and are used interchangeably in qigong literature. The sinking sensation may be especially pronounced in modern societies, in which left-brain, intellectual dominance produces a feeling of top-heaviness. When we say that someone is "stuck-up, hung-up," or "too much in his head," this is an accurate assessment of qi imbalance.

Eighty-years-young Taiji Quan master Gao Fu constantly advises her students, "Relax *through* the feet, into the ground." We should not be "standing on our own two feet," but standing on the ground! This creates a feeling of balance, support, and comfort. An individual who is standing relaxed and sunk feels "stable as Mount Tai" (a majestic Daoist holy mountain in eastern China) and rooted like a tall tree. If the roots are deep, the tree will sway, but not topple.

When I teach qigong classes, I am always amazed at the external signs of sinking. Faces release their lines and worries. The eyes and jaw loosen and relax. The shoulders, which may have been raised, sink and sit on the torso. The breath is now sinking and moving more freely in the lower abdomen.

After a qigong session, I sometimes ask students to saunter about, paying attention to differences in their balance and quality of movement. Even before the usual exclamations of "I feel heavier. I feel grounded," we all notice how the floor now shakes, as though the students have turned into a herd of elephants! Yet no one is stomping. Each student feels more finely balanced and walks with greater coordination and confidence.

The connection between warmth, weight, and deep relaxation has been known in the West since the turn of the century. In 1932, German psychiatrist Johannes H. Schultz developed Autogenic Training (AT), a kind of Western qigong, in which a patient concentrates on various parts of the body while imagining that they are heavy, warm, and relaxed. Schultz described AT as a "method of rational physiologic exercises designed to produce a general psychobiologic reorganization in the subject which enables him to manifest all the phenomena otherwise obtainable through hypnosis."[4] The subject learns how to create favorable psychological and physical changes that en-able him to control and improve his own health. AT is quite popular in Europe and has been used to treat or to speed up recuperation from anxiety, hypertension, ulcers, chronic pain, headache, and numerous other disorders. The psychological shift that occurs during AT—a state of tranquil alertness—has also been found useful in retrieving information from the unconscious or in reprogramming the unconscious toward more health-promoting behavior.

To practice AT, the subject should lie down or sit with the eyes closed, passively concentrating on various parts of the body while silently repeating phrases, called *autogenic formulae*, for periods of anywhere from thirty seconds to two or three minutes. For instance, "My *right arm is heavy*," beginning with the dominant side (the left arm for left-handers). Then he opens his eyes, breathes deeply, and gently flexes the body, noticing how the feeling of heaviness has remained or perhaps spread to the other arm or other parts of the body. This process is repeated several more times. Then he switches to the opposite arm, repeating the phrase "My *left arm is heavy*." Again followed by opening the eyes, flexing and noticing the residual effects. Other phrases, practiced in the same slow and methodical way, include:

Both arms are heavy.
Right leg heavy.
Left leg heavy.
Both legs heavy.
Right arm warm.
Left arm warm.
Both arms warm.
Heartbeat calm and regular.
It breathes me.
My solar plexus is warm.
My forehead is cool.

Schultz's method is remarkably similar to fang song gong. It results in a feeling of warmth and heaviness in the hands, calm emotions, natural and effortless breathing. As in qigong, the abdominal region ("solar plexus") is warm and the upper body ("forehead") relatively cool. The autogenic formulae are an excellent description of qigong relaxation. Like fang song gong, Autogenic Training requires patience and dedication. It may take as long as a year before one can relax and warm the hands at will.

It is interesting to compare AT with a particular method of meditative qigong called Nei Yang Gong, "Inner Nourishing" (Chapter 11), which also uses the repetition of specific phrases to induce a relaxed state.

THE METHODS

Now we come to the essential question. You say, "I understand that relaxation is important. But how do I relax? How can I relax if every effort to relax makes me more tense?" Actually, *relaxation is a matter of effortlessness with intent*. It is true that trying to relax is counterproductive. This would be like trying to float, an action that results in sinking more quickly! It is easier to teach children to swim or ride a bike than adults because children have not yet learned to interfere with their natural abilities so consistently! They know that skills like floating, bike riding, or relaxation require three essential ingredients: awareness, letting go, and practice.

To relax we need to pay attention to what we are doing, setting aside worries and thoughts. The Chinese are fond of repeating, "To relax, you must be tranquil." And we need to regard relaxation as a process of surrendering to a deeper wisdom, rather than acquiring, through effort, a new ability. Developing large muscles requires effort; cultivating relaxation requires letting go. Adopting this attitude will help us to stop *trying* to relax.

Practice is essential. Through regular practice, you will become familiar with the feeling of being relaxed. You will soon find that you can achieve results with shorter and shorter practice sessions. You will become like a pianist who is ready to play a beautiful Mozart sonata as soon as her hands touch the keyboard.

The three principal methods of fang song gong are: 1. *Sequential Relaxation and Sinking*. 2. *Floating on the Ground* (Tensing and Relaxing). 3. *Relaxing the Three Lines*. Experiment with each. Practice any one or combination of relaxation techniques that work best for you, every day, morning and evening. Your practice sessions can last anywhere from five to twenty minutes.

Before beginning any of these exercises, it is helpful to do a *body scan*. Simply spend a few minutes doing an experiential self-inquiry, "How do I feel today? How am I breathing? Where am I comfortable? Where am I tense?" At this point, do not censor, reject, or think about the meaning of tension, discomfort, or other sensations. Simply observe, innocently accepting and appreciating what your body is telling you.

1. Sequential Relaxation and Sinking

Trying to relax the entire body at once is generally fruitless; it may only increase tension or shift it to other areas. You are tense because you have lost or never fully developed the ability to differentiate parts of your body that are tense. It is best to proceed systematically through the body and, in the process, to discover where you are working at odds with yourself, where you are tensing inappropriate muscles or where you make an effort when none is necessary. As Feldenkrais observes in his seminal work *The Potent Self*, "The correct approach is to disentangle at least one thread of the knot of cross motivation, and then at once one discovers more hidden treasures of capacity and vitality in oneself than anybody suspected."[5]

Stand with the feet shoulder-width apart or sit in a comfortable, erect posture. Close your eyes or leave them half-open, with a soft, unfocused gaze. Starting at the crown and working your way down toward the feet, become aware of and ask each part of the body to relax and sink toward the ground.

First bring your mind to the head. Relax the muscles of the crown, forehead, eyebrows, eyes, cheeks, jaw, gums, ears, all the muscles of the face. Feel these muscles letting go, releasing downward.

Become aware of the neck. Relax the muscles on the front, sides, and back of the neck. Relax and mentally open the vertebrae of the neck, so the upper spine can be soft and open. Let your head float easily on the upper spine, like a cork floating on water.

Relax the shoulders, letting them sit on the torso. The shoulders sink straight toward the ground, neither pulling back nor slouching forward. Allow relaxation to spread through your arms and hands, so you become aware of the weight of your own arms. If you are sitting, release the weight of your arms onto your lap or thighs. Relax the elbows, wrists, and fingers. The fingers are neither spread open nor curled into fists. Feel the natural extension and weight of the fingers.

Relax the collarbones, the shoulder blades, the ribs, and breastbone. Let the ribs hang and release down. Relax the chest muscles, including the pectorals and the muscles between the ribs. Release the muscles of the upper back and along the spine. Relax the entire spine—upper, middle, and lower—feeling the spine opening, gently extending to its natural length. Note that when the spine is relaxed, it is open, not compressed. You should feel a comfortable space between each vertebra. Now let your open, relaxed spine be finely balanced and connected with the ground, like a tall tree. Release the muscles of the lower back (the sacrum) and the tailbone, so the spine can balance with minimal tension, without extra, muscular help.

Relax the entire torso, especially the internal organs, letting go of tension on the surface of the body and inside the body. Release the solar plexus, diaphragm, and abdomen. Let the abdomen hang out and sink down. For a change, don't worry about how you look; rather, be concerned about how you feel! Allow the body to breathe without interference. Let the breath relax, so it can sink deep in your body.

Relax the hips. Relax the inguinal area and the groin. Relax the buttocks and the anal sphincter. Become aware of the connection between the top of your leg bones (the femur) and where they attach to the hips. Let there be a comfortable space and freedom at the head of the femur.

Release the thigh muscles, including the backs of the thighs, the hamstrings. Release the knees, again allowing a comfortable openness, so the articulation has the potential for easy and natural movement. Relax the lower legs, the calves, the ankles, the bones of the feet, the toes.

Again, check your body to see if it is relaxed and sunk, yet appropriately open, with the fullest potential for movement. Let gravity work for you, allowing each part of your body to seek its lowest level, like water flowing downhill.

An interesting variation on this technique is to imagine yourself inhaling into each part of the body sequentially. With each exhalation, release all unnecessary tension toward the ground. Qigong therapists have found that inhalation helps the mind focus; exhalation helps one to release tension.

Sequential Relaxation may also be practiced lying on your back. The method is essentially the same. Instead of imagining tension dropping toward the feet, start at the top of the head and allow each body part to sink toward the floor. When you have relaxed all parts, imagine that the ground is soft clay. What kind of impression does your body make? Has your weight been fully released down into the ground? Can you eliminate unnecessary spaces between your body and the ground, trusting the ground to support you?

2. Floating on the Ground

This method is identical to the Corpse Posture of Indian Yoga. One of my qigong instructors called it "The Dead Cockroach." Not a very inspiring title! I prefer to think of it as "Floating on the Ground."

Lie on your back on a comfortable, flat surface: a thick rug, exercise mat, or very firm mattress. As you focus on each part of the body sequentially, tense that part of the body and then release it into the ground. Tense your muscles only within comfortable and safe limits. There is no need to strain or to tense as much as possible. (This method should be practiced only by those without serious medical conditions. For instance, it may not be safe to tense a herniated disk or diseased heart.) Tighten the crown and the muscles of the face, then let go. Tighten the neck, let go, and so on. You may tighten each arm and fist one at a time or simultaneously. The same is true for legs and feet. Gradually work your way down. At the end, tighten and clench the toes, then release them. Many students find that this technique helps them to become more precisely aware of each body part and to more fully relax.

Some physical therapists use a similar technique to help clients become aware of areas of chronic tension. When a tight muscle is tensed even further, the difference between it and surrounding tissue is more pronounced. As unconscious tension becomes consciously uncomfortable, the client improves his/her ability to sense the difference between tension and relaxation.

You may also combine this technique with breathing. Inhale to the body part. While holding the breath for a moment, tense and contract. Then exhale and release tension down to the ground.

At the end, imagine that the ground is a wonderful, buoyant lake that easily supports your body. Enjoy the sensation of floating, relaxed and carefree.

3. Relaxing the Three Lines

From a standing, seated, or supine posture, with the arms naturally extended at the sides, imagine the body has three lines. First relax the line from crown to coccyx, including the entire spine. Next relax the line across the shoulders and arms, down to the fingertips of each hand. Finally, relax the line of the hips and legs, all the way down to the toes. Feel each line relaxing, sinking, opening. Proceed slowly, at your own pace, and repeat each line or the entire exercise as often as you wish, until you feel you have achieved satisfactory progress.

This technique is a powerful way to work on the body as a whole, helping healing qi to circulate more fully along the major meridians. Although the three lines are not themselves acupuncture meridians, the exercise relaxes part of the body through which important meridians pass. It is especially helpful for qigong meditations such as the "Great Heavenly Circulation" (*Da Zhou Tian*), sometimes called the "Macrocosmic Orbit," in which qi is directed up the spine, along the arms, over the front of the body, and along the legs (see "Purifying the Meridians" in Chapter 11).

However, the Three Lines does not work as precisely on particular body parts as the first two methods and so may not result in a satisfactory level of relaxation. Beginning students may prefer practicing this method *after* either "Sequential Relaxation" or "Floating on the Ground."

Closing

Just as you began your relaxation session with an introspective "body-scan," when you finish your session, again observe areas of comfort and discomfort, relaxation and tension. Has anything changed? Do you feel different? How? Don't answer this with words, but rather by focusing your awareness and listening to your body. The body, like the mind, learns through appreciating differences. You could not see the black print on this page without a white background. The more you are aware of the contrast between how you feel before and after practice, the easier it will be to change old habits.

After your second body-scan, place your hands gently on the lower abdomen and take a few minutes to focus on quiet and gentle breathing. This will help you feel centered and ready to move on to other forms of qigong, to the day's activities, or to a sounder sleep.

CHAPTER NINE

Healthy Breathing

*The Lord blew into Adam's nostrils the breath
of life, and Adam became a living being.*
—GENESIS

The word qigong has often been translated as "breathing exercises." This makes good sense, as the word *qi* commonly means air or breath and the subtle energy carried by the breath. It is the air we breathe, the oxygen delivered to the cells, and the energy that sustains life. Awareness of the breath is a constant feature of both moving (active) and tranquil (passive) qigong. One of the ancient names for qigong, *tu gu na xin*, "expelling the old, drawing in the new," sounds like a modern description of the gaseous exchange that occurs during respiration. On inhalation, fresh air is drawn into the lungs and a nutritive component of it, oxygen, is carried by the red blood cells to the tissues. On exhalation, carbon dioxide, a waste product, diffuses from the blood into the lung's air sacs and is expelled. One of the goals of qigong is to maintain the balance and efficiency of this exchange, so that the entire body receives the energy it needs.

It is important to note that efficient, healthy respiration is not the same as deep breathing. A common fallacy is to assume that by expanding the chest cavity, one is thereby sending more oxygen to parts of the body that need it. Rapid expansion and contraction of the chest cavity actually causes oxygen to bind too tightly to the hemoglobin molecules, so that less is released to the cells. It also causes a constriction in the blood vessels, further preventing the oxygen from reaching its target. Oxygen delivery depends more on the *quality* of breathing—ease, grace, and efficiency—than the quantity of air forced into the lungs with each cycle of respiration. In fact, as we will see later, if breathing habits are poor, then the respiratory rate increases in order to keep approximately the same amount of oxygen flowing to the cells each minute. This quickened pace is a drain on body energy. Healthy breathing increases vitality and creates the most favorable conditions for gaseous exchange. Abdominal qigong breathing causes even the tiniest blood vessels, the capillaries, to relax and gently dilate with a greater flow of blood, oxygen, and qi.

In this chapter, we will explore healthy ways of breathing and look at the causes and results of poor respiration. Unless otherwise noted, all of the exercises and meditations can be practiced while seated in a chair, on the floor (cross-legged or lotus posture), or while lying on the back on a comfortable but supportive surface, such as an exercise mat or thick carpet. Make yourself as comfortable as possible. If you are lying on the floor, you may use a pillow and/or prop up the back with a cushion, if this creates easier breathing.

FOUR ASPECTS OF BREATHING: A SELF-INQUIRY

Before attempting qigong breathing, it is important to discover your usual breathing pattern. Check periodically to see if this pattern has changed in order to track if qigong is really improving your habitual way of breathing. It may be easy to breathe correctly when you are trying to do so. However, the goal is to breathe correctly in everyday life.

During a period of rest and quiet, practice the following self-inquiry. This inquiry is, of itself, a qigong exercise. As you learn to focus on all the fine details of your breathing, places of comfort and discomfort become more obvious. The act of observing the breath changes the breath. Body awareness causes a shift of energy and intent away from the daily hassles and worries toward the needs of the body.

1. **How does the breath feel?** Does it feel smooth or choppy, deep or shallow, clear or turbid, light or heavy, quiet or noisy, easy or difficult, healthy or diseased? Pay attention to the subjective feelings and thoughts evoked by the breath. Is your breath a slow-moving stream or is it dammed

by tension and anxiety? Images that rise spontaneously to consciousness are also important indicators of the quality of breath and qi.

2. Where do you breathe? How does the breath enter and leave? Where does it go to, how deep in the body? Can you feel it moving through the nostrils, down the trachea (windpipe), in and out of the bronchi and lungs? Do you breathe with your nose or mouth or a combination? Do you feel the breath moving in your chest, in your abdomen, in your back, anywhere else? Can you feel the breath moving in your hands or feet? There is no right or wrong in this inquiry. Your *experience* of the breath does not have to concur with your knowledge about breath. For now, let yourself forget medical dogma and anatomical charts. Discover what your own senses have to teach you.

3. Which part of the body moves with inhalation and exhalation? Does your chest open or close or move at all with inhalation? Does your abdomen move as you breathe? A good way to answer this question is to place one hand on the chest and one on the abdomen and to notice which hand rises or falls in response to inhalation and exhalation. Another method is to lie on the back and place a lightweight paperback book on the abdomen and notice whether it rises or falls as you inhale and exhale. At the same time, does the lower back seem to press into or release from the ground as you breathe? Now place the book on your rib cage and again note the response to inhalation and exhalation. If you use two books, one on the left side of the chest, one on the right, you can find out if the two sides of the body expand and contract with equal ease. The back might also feel as if it presses into and releases from the ground. We sometimes forget that the ribs are designed to move front, sideways, and back. What about the sternum (breastbone)? How does it move as you inhale and exhale?

4. What is your breathing rate? How many breaths do you take per minute? Look at the second hand on your watch and count how many exhalations you make in a minute. Do this while you are calm and meditative, not during a period of physical or mental activity. Make sure you loosen your belt and are wearing comfortable clothing. A constricted abdomen will automatically speed up the breath.

At least once a week, go through these four steps and write down your response in a Qigong Progress Report. Empty your mind of the shoulds and should-nots. With an innocent and noncritical attitude observe your breathing. Since it is likely that the majority of the U.S. population breathes in an unhealthy and inefficient manner, normal breathing may not be the truly natural way to breathe. With qigong practice, your normal breathing can become natural.

NOSE OR MOUTH?

In all of the following exercises, it is best to breathe only through the nose. The nose contains fine hairs (*cilia*) and mucus that help trap and filter out dust, pollutants, and germs. Some of these harmful particles are swallowed, thus removing them from the respiratory tract. Others are discharged by blowing the nose, coughing, or sneezing. Because the mucous membranes contain a rich supply of capillaries and white blood cells, bacteria trapped there can also be disinfected and destroyed. The nose has often been compared to a humidifier; it conditions the air before it enters the windpipe and lungs. The air is warmed by the blood flowing through the nose and its mucous membranes and by residual warmth left from the previous exhalation (if one exhales through the nose). The air is moisturized by water vapor rising from the lungs and by a combination of mucus and drainage from the sinuses and tear ducts.

The upper end of each nasal passage has spiral-shaped bones called *turbinates* or *nasal conchae* (Latin for "seashell," referring to their appearance). Here the nasal passage narrows, and the air divides into various passages. As air moves past the turbinates, swirling currents are formed, further warming and moistening the air and affording more opportunities for relatively heavy particles to settle on the nasal lining or be trapped by its mucus. After this final filtration, air continues down the windpipe. As air is inhaled and exhaled past the turbinates, approximately two quarts of water are conserved and returned to the lungs.

On a psychological level, nose breathing encourages meditative awareness. This is why one breathes through the nose during Zen meditation. The air feels warm and comfortable and is thus less distracting. The mind does not have to control the opening and closing of the mouth, allowing fuller relaxation and focus on the object of meditation. Naturally, if one is suffering from a sinus infection, a cold, or other disorder that makes it difficult or uncomfortable to breathe through the nose, then by all means use the mouth or a combination of nose-mouth breathing that is most comfortable and effortless.

NATURAL BREATHING

The foundation of qigong breathing is *shun hu xi*, "natural respiration." Shun actually means "free-flowing, going with nature's current." It is the opposite of swimming upstream. Natural breathing is also called abdominal or diaphragmatic respiration. On inhalation, the diaphragm muscle contracts and moves downward, pushing the abdomen out. This increases the volume of the lungs, creating a partial vacuum and sucking air in. During exhalation, the diaphragm relaxes upward, the abdomen releases inward, pushing air out. *Thus, inhalation: abdomen expands; exhalation: abdomen contracts* (figs. 4a-b). This is the most efficient and natural way to breathe. The dropping of the diaphragm opens the lower lobes of the lungs, where most of the oxygen exchange takes place. Contrary to a popular misconception, breathing abdominally creates more internal space, more room for the lungs to expand than expanding the chest. This also means that a greater volume of air will be exchanged. The rising and falling of the abdomen also gently massages the internal organs.

Readers should not, however, confuse abdominal breathing with tensing or restricting the chest. Healthy breathing means that the breath adapts and responds to the body's needs. In any aerobically demanding activity, such as swimming or playing tennis, the chest *and* abdomen will be moving in order to breathe more quickly and deeply. We need to allow the body's natural responses to activity. Even during times of utmost quiet and stillness, the chest is free to expand, though it moves ever so gently and slightly. Most of the movement of quiet respiration is in the abdomen, and it may require concentration and sensitivity to even feel the movement of the chest cavity (ribs and sternum).

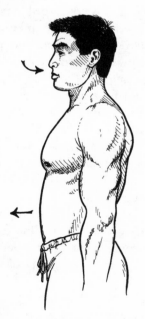

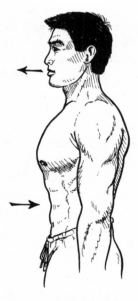

Figure 4a. Inhalation   *Figure 4b. Exhalation*

By breathing abdominally, respiration can become slow and relaxed. The average adult resting respiratory rate is about 16 breaths per minute (bpm). Yet someone mentally and physically relaxed should breathe at about 5 breaths per minute! I am not suggesting that you should breathe this slowly if you are reading an exciting novel or cooling down after a workout. Rather, the breath can slow to 5 bpm when your body is completely still, the mind quiet and untroubled, the environment and temperature comfortable, and the clothing loose (especially around the waist). Unfortunately, many of us feel incapable of breathing slowly even with ideal conditions. The breath, like the mind, seems to be constantly rushing. We may need to gradually reeducate the body, breath, and mind with qigong.

The key to natural respiration is not forcing the breath. Natural breathing is the way children breathe. Watch an infant's abdomen as she inhales and exhales. The abdomen expands on inhalation, retracts on exhalation. The child has not learned the unique adult talent of interfering with nature! Rather than trying to control the breath, acknowledge nature's wisdom by allowing the breath to move of itself. No need to pull the breath in or push it out; just let it go. Trust nature to breathe you!

As you breathe abdominally, look for *six qualities of the breath*: Slow (Man), Long (Chang), Deep (Shen), Fine (Xi), Even (Jun), and Tranquil (Jing). Slow means a slow respiratory rate and an unhurried mood. Long means that the breath is a long, steady stream of air. It is not gasped or puffed or broken by excitement or anxiety. Deep refers to breath and qi sinking low in the body, filling the dan tian energy center. Fine means smooth and quiet, instead of coarse and loud. Even means a feeling of internal balance and equal ease of inhalation and exhalation. It also implies not favoring any particular part or side of the body. Right and left sides, front and back, are all capable of movement. Tranquil refers primarily to a mind focused on present experience, free of thoughts and worries. According to Hu Bing, chief physician of the Qigong Department, Beijing Academy of Chinese Medicine, "The efficacy of qigong is determined by one's depth of quietness (ru jing): the greater the tranquillity, the greater the benefits."[1] This is an excellent principle to keep in mind throughout your qigong training.

Notice also the *four stages of the breath*: a) inhalation, b) the turning of the breath between inhalation and exhalation, c) exhalation, and d) the natural pause that occurs during the second turning of the breath, between exhalation and the next inhalation. Do not try to prolong any of these stages; simply observe them.

It is fascinating to discover that breathing is more than inhalation and exhalation. During the moments of transition between inhalations and exhalations, we have an opportunity to change dysfunctional habits of tension and anxiety. Can you let the breath fall easily, effortlessly out after inhalation, or do you have an unconscious tendency to push the breath out? After exhalation, are you anxious and untrusting of the body's ability to inhale automatically? Are you trying to control a process that is controlled gracefully and beautifully for you? Can you let inhalation occur when and as the body wishes, with no added effort to pull the breath back in?

Indian Yogis believe that the moments of the turning of the breath are times of deep inner stillness. By paying attention to these brief periods we can remember the time before we were born and have a foretaste of the experience after death. In religious literature, exhalation has often been compared to creation: God *says*, "Let there be light," and there is light. He/She uses voice, breath, and intent, exhaling the universe. Inhalation is compared to the dissolution of the universe, the withdrawal of creation back into the cosmic womb. Between inhalation (yin) and exhalation (yang), we are in a state of nondual awareness, more accepting of the unknown dimensions of ourselves and the world.

UNNATURAL BREATHING: THE HYPERVENTILATION SYNDROME

Relaxed abdominal breathing is, unfortunately, not the norm in our society. In various works on breathing and respiratory therapies, Robert Fried, Ph.D., Professor of Psychology at Hunter College, analyzes the effects of chronic rapid breathing, called *the hyperventilation syndrome*.[2] Hyperventilation is characterized by predominantly thoracic (chest) breathing, little use of the diaphragm, irregular or interrupted breathing, a quick respiratory rate, and frequent sighing. These sighs have an effortless quality and often include a rising and falling of the sternum with little lateral expansion of the chest.

Hyperventilation is a common symptom in the seven major psychosomatic diseases: asthma, hypertension, ulcers, rheumatoid arthritis, colitis, hyperthyroidism, and neurodermatitis. It is also seen in migraine, chronic pain of any origin, seizure disorders, heart disease, and among smokers. Psychiatric disorders have profound effects on both the method and rate of breathing. Chronic anxiety creates and is exacerbated by upper chest breathing and an irregular, rapid breathing rate of 18.3 ($\pm$2.8) bpm. Panic disorder can raise the resting breath rate to 30 bpm. (Conversely, researchers have noted that when psychiatric patients show clinical improvement, their breath rate often drops.) Hyperventilation may be the most common disease symptom in America, by some estimates afflicting more than half the U.S. population.[3]

My own observations of many thousands of qigong students over the past twenty-five years corroborates this opinion.

Hyperventilation may be a common *symptom* of disease, but it does not necessarily follow that it *causes* disease. Diseases have complex, multi-factorial origins, including physical trauma, viruses, bacteria, lifestyle, state of mind, diet, genetic predisposition, previous health history, and environment. Evidence does suggest that improper breathing can be a precipitating factor in many disorders. It can also intensify or prolong pain or disease symptoms. In some cases, proper breathing can provide a cure. In order to grasp what Dr. Fried calls "the breath connection," it is important to understand the physical mechanics of hyperventilation.

For inhalation to take place, the lungs must be capable of expanding. We have seen that the most efficient way to expand the lungs is by contracting the diaphragm and relaxing the abdomen, allowing the abdomen to expand. If the diaphragm is frozen with tension, then the chest and rib cage must move instead. The abdomen may seem to hardly move at all, creating a pattern of almost exclusively thoracic respiration. I have noted this in the great majority of chronic pain clients I have seen. I have also found that teaching these individuals to breathe abdominally has a pronounced analgesic effect. There seems to be a direct correspondence between free movement of the diaphragm and alleviation of pain. From the Chinese viewpoint, pain results from stuck or stagnant qi. Freedom of movement, *physically*, creates freedom of movement *energetically*; qi flows and pain diminishes.

In some cases, thoracic respiration causes the abdomen to move in a chronically reversed pattern—contracting on inhalation, expanding on exhalation. The chest expands as the abdomen contracts and contracts as the abdomen expands. This peculiar movement of the abdomen (with or without an accompanying oppositional movement of the chest) is called "reversed breathing," a term first mentioned in qigong literature and coined independently by Western respiratory therapists. Reversed breathing is generally dangerous for physical and mental health, except under certain conditions or as a specialized qigong exercise, which we will examine later in this chapter.

Thoracic respiration does not allow as much air into the lungs as abdominal breathing. To compensate, the respiratory rate must increase in order to maintain the same amount of air going into and out of the lungs each minute. The breath is rapid, shallow, and primarily in the chest: major characteristics of the hyperventilation syndrome. The breath may appear full and deep, because of the more noticeable and dramatic movement of the chest, but this is the opposite of what is happening.

Hyperventilation has a deleterious effect on blood chemistry. It causes the blood to lose carbon dioxide (CO_2) more rapidly. Because CO_2 is necessary for acid formation in the body, the loss of CO_2 means that the blood's acid-base (pH) balance shifts toward alkalinity (base). This shift decreases the ability of the blood's hemoglobin molecules to release oxygen. Normally, oxygen rides "piggyback" on the hemoglobin molecule, becoming *oxyhemoglobin*. During hyperventilation, the bond becomes too tight; the oxygen cannot let go. Thus even though oxygen is in the blood, less of it is delivered to the cells, which means less energy and an impaired ability to carry on ordinary metabolic processes.

The decreased levels of oxygen in the tissues has especially pronounced effects on heart and brain function, as these organs require a great deal of oxygen. There is also a direct connection between hyperventilation and a tendency toward constriction and spasms in the arteries that feed both the heart and the brain. In 1978, the *Journal of the American Medical Association* reported that hyperventilation decreases the amount of oxygen delivered to the myocardium (heart muscle), causes abnormalities in the EKG, and increases the cardiac workload.[4] Hyperventilation is known to be a contributing factor in ischemic (reduced blood flow) heart disease, high blood pressure, coronary insufficiency, cardiac arrhythmia, and angina.

The brain comprises only 2 percent of the body's weight yet consumes more than 20 percent of the body's available oxygen. According to Dr. Fried's *The Psychology and Physiology of Breathing*, "Rapid breathing [i.e., hyperventilation] reduces brain blood flow, while slow, deep breathing enhances it, other factors being equal."[5] Some forms of migraine are caused by chronic constriction and dilation of the arteries feeding the brain. This can be precipitated by emotional stress, diet, and rapid breathing. A loss of oxygen supply to the brain cells can also cause anxiety, strokes, and increased frequency of epileptic attacks. Wilder Penfield, one of the world's leading neurosurgeons and experts on epilepsy, wrote, "The mechanism whereby hyperventilation elicits change in the EEG and seizures in epileptic patients is still unknown. It may act by causing a partial ischemia [reduced blood flow] due to cerebral vasoconstriction, and there may be some increase in excitability accompanying the lowered CO_2 concentration."[6]

Two of the factors mentioned by Penfield in relation to epilepsy—vasoconstriction and "increase in excitability [of the nerve cells]"—are factors in a number of other common disorders. Vasoconstriction results in a feeling of "poor circulation," including cold hands and feet (Raynaud's Syndrome). Again, hyperventilation leads to constricted blood vessels, reduced blood flow, and thus less warmth in the extremities.

The increased excitability of the brain cells is part of a general state of cellular hyperactivity induced by rapid breathing. As the blood becomes more alkaline, more calcium enters the nerve and muscle cells. This causes them to "fire," that is, respond more quickly and strongly. The net result is a state of nervousness and muscular contraction. This could be a desirable state if one needs to flee from an imminent threat; the sympathetic nervous system is excited, and one is ready for action. However such stimulation is damaging if it becomes a habitual state of the body. The hyperventilation syndrome might become "programmed" into the nervous system if stress is prolonged and one feels incapable of changing or fleeing from the situation. (Perhaps the most common neurosis of mind *and* body is hyperventilation induced not by an actual threat, but in response to a *fixed belief* in a threat: a memory of past trauma and expectation that such a trauma may recur.) Here again we see the connection between hyperventilation and psychosomatic disorders. The state of overexcitation, nervousness, and tension could predispose one to headaches, ulcers, muscular pain, increased blood pressure and heart rate, and many other problems commonly associated with stress.

The good news is that natural qigong breathing can cure or alleviate many of these conditions. It causes the muscles to relax, including those that cause constriction of the blood vessels, improves circulation, and increases oxygen delivery. There is clinical evidence that one can learn to abort, control, and possibly cure migraines, lessen the frequency of seizures, and reduce cardiovascular risk factors, such as high blood pressure. When the breath is relaxed, one is more focused on the present and able to find healthier ways of coping with personal problems.

LEAVE WELL ENOUGH ALONE! A WORD OF CAUTION

Blood is ordinarily alkaline ($pH = 7.4$). Researchers have found that hyperventilation increases this alkaline condition of the blood. If hyperventilation is chronic, blood alkalinity can also become chronic (a condition called alkalosis). Although not life-threatening, this chemical imbalance can have unpleasant effects, causing neuronal irritability and tetany, a disorder characterized by muscular twitching and cramps. Most of us should try our best to correct this problem at its root, by breathing abdominally.

However, certain diseases, such as hypoglycemia, diabetes, and kidney failure, create metabolic acidosis, too much acid. In these cases, chest breathing and a quicker respiratory rate may be a necessary biologic adjustment, a way of maintaining the acid-base balance. If hyperventilation is needed to correct a serious underlying disturbance, then to interfere with it is to court disaster.

Some diseases make it physically impossible to practice "natural respiration"—for instance, a lesion in the respiratory center of the brain or an obstruction in the lungs. *Thus, it is extremely important that qigong students realize that there are times when hyperventilation should not be interfered with and when it might be dangerous to practice slow, abdominal breathing. Anyone with a serious medical problem should practice qigong breathing only with the approval of his/her physician.*

Similarly, anyone receiving allopathic interventions would do well to consider the wisdom of qigong. I do not believe that qigong provides a global solution to all human ills. Nor should allopathic physicians assume that Western medicine has all the answers. I advocate consultation with physicians not because Western medicine is "best," but rather because all systems of healing have much to learn from each other. Medical Imperialism is a threat to human health!

THE CORRECT WAY TO PRACTICE "REVERSED BREATHING"

Although natural respiration is generally the safest and healthiest way to breathe, it is also helpful to occasionally practice "reversed breathing," *ni hu xi,* as a way to stimulate the qi and gain more control over the breathing muscles. Reversed breathing is not dangerous if practiced for brief periods of time. It *is* dangerous if it becomes your normal breathing method.[7]

In reversed breathing, the abdomen contracts during inhalation. At the same time, the chest cavity expands slightly—the ribs opening, the sternum lifting. During exhalation, the abdomen is slightly distended, and the chest closes naturally. In both the inhalation and exhalation phases, the breath is deep, soft, and silent. The abdomen is moving, though opposite to the fashion of "natural respiration." In the *practice* of reversed breathing, the respiratory rate should be slow. This is in contrast to habitual reversed breathing, characterized by a quick breathing rate and symptomatic of tension and anxiety.

It is also important to maintain meditative awareness of the dan tian. Regardless of which method of breathing you are practicing, the dan tian remains the physical center of gravity and the energetic reservoir of qi. As you practice reversed breathing, every now and then ask yourself, "Does my lower abdomen feel alive? Is it relaxed and supple? Am I aware of the dan tian?" When reversed breathing is practiced consciously, the lower abdomen feels alive and empowered. When it is engaged in unconsciously, as an unhealthy habit, awareness centers in the upper body; the abdomen feels un-comfortable and tight.[8]

There are three methods of practicing reversed breathing. The first is to simply pay attention to the physical process, as described above. This is very strengthening for the diaphragm and abdominal muscles. The second is to note the *vertical component* of reversed breathing. While inhaling, qi and in-tent seems to shift to the chest, the middle dan tian. While exhaling, it seems to shift back to the lower abdomen. In this way two energy centers are stimulated, as well as the solar plexus (called the *huang ting* "yellow court" in Chinese). The third method is pay close attention to the *horizontal compo-nent*. In this technique, during inhalation, as the abdomen contracts, imag-ine the breath being drawn back, toward the sacrum. The qi adheres to the *ming men* "the gate of life" opposite the navel. During exhalation, as the ab-domen protrudes, the qi is pushed toward the navel. It may be helpful to imagine a pearl in the abdomen that is pushed frontward and backward with each breath. This is one of the most powerful ways of using the breath to stimulate and strengthen the dan tian energy center, increasing the dan tian's ability to pump qi through the body.

Some Taiji Quan styles, such as the ancient Chen Family Style, require that students coordinate their movements with reversed breathing (primarily the third method described above) as a way of developing martial arts power. Basically, every time one strikes (punches or kicks), there is an exhalation, an expansion of the abdomen, and a feeling of qi sinking to the dan tian. The rapid exhalation increases power; the intent to expand the abdomen and sink qi downward increases balance and stability. One of the great Taiji Quan Masters had such control of the abdomen that he used to demonstrate his qi by lying on his back, placing grains of cooked millet on his abdomen and then shooting them up to the ceiling with a quick (reversed breathing) exhalation. There are Japanese and Chinese martial artists who use reversed breathing to emit a frightening "kiai" shout while striking. Lions and other animals that roar also use reversed breathing, making a loud sound with a sudden expansion of the lower abdomen. As Feldenkrais notes, "In fact, we use paradoxical [i.e., reversed] breathing whenever we must make a sudden, violent effort, even if we are not aware of it. It is therefore important to learn something about it."[9]

However, it is a grave mistake to assume that a training method should become a regular habit. During push-ups, the pectoral muscles and triceps tighten and release. This doesn't mean I should do this while typing on my computer. Reversed breathing is a wonderful exercise, but it does not have the extensive health benefits of natural breathing!

Practice reversed breathing for three minutes *before* beginning natural respiration. Most students find that this frees the diaphragm and abdominal muscles and actually makes the natural breathing much smoother and deeper.

DIFFERENTIATED BREATHING

One of the reasons for practicing reversed breathing is that we should explore all possibilities in breathing. If you are in good health, it is advantageous to try many varieties of breathing. This can fine-tune awareness of all of the muscles and body parts involved in breathing. By practicing both normal and unusual breathing patterns, you will become conscious of your habits and be less likely to return to those that are unpleasurable. We cannot control a bodily function unless we are aware of it. Differentiated breathing also awakens various states of consciousness and teaches us about the relationship between breath and mind. It is likely that differentiated breathing is a form of neurological reeducation. New circuits, new connections are formed; rusty, unused pathways are awakened.

Although differentiated breathing is never mentioned by name in qigong literature, it is clear that this principle was thoroughly exploited in practice. I have observed or read about qigong adepts practicing virtually every kind of breathing imaginable: slow and quick, high and low, shallow and deep, fluid and paused. I have observed a Taiji Quan school where students were instructed to practice while continuously hyperventilating, with rapid bellowslike expansions and contractions of the abdomen. This was followed by a round of Taiji Quan with ultra-slow natural respiration. I know a Taiwanese qigong master who imagines the bellows not inside the body, but outside, as though an air pump is pushing air in and pulling air out of the body. I have met qigong practitioners from Yunan Province who practice breathing not from the lower abdomen, but from the throat. They imagine the breath as a fine stream entering and leaving the clavicular notch, between the collarbones. The Daoist sage Zhuang Zi advised breathing through the heels. Many qigong students imagine that they can breathe through the skin or bones.

Here are some suggestions for the practice of differentiated breathing: Can you breathe extra deeply? Begin the inhalation by expanding the abdomen; then allow the breath to roll into the upper chest with an expansion of the rib cage. Afterward, let the breath fall away naturally. Can you breathe with only the left side of the chest, only the right side? Can you concentrate on the lateral expansion of the ribs, on the upward movement of the sternum during inhalation? Can you breathe with the back? Is anything happening under the collarbones as you breathe? Can you hold the breath comfortably for a brief period of time? While holding the breath, can you alternately expand the abdomen and chest, moving the breath between the lower and upper lobes of the lungs? How does it feel to sometimes pause the breath during inhalation or exhalation? I advise qigong students to playfully experiment with the breath. Books on yogic *pranayama* (Indian qigong) are full of suggestions and useful exercises.[10] In later chapters we will explore especially beneficial qigong breathing meditations and visualizations.

DAN TIAN BREATHING

Dan Tian Breathing is an extremely beneficial variation of natural breathing. The dan tian is the energy center in the abdominal region, about three inches below the navel and midway into the center of the body. The precise location of the dan tian can vary slightly from individual to individual. Some students feel it behind the navel, others locate it closer to the pubic bone. Listen to how your body breathes. The dan tian will be the point or region from which the expansion of the abdomen seems to originate.

When practicing dan tian breathing, both the lower abdomen and the lower back expand with inhalation, and both retract with exhalation. Most of the movement is still felt in the front of the body, but there is definitely a response in the back. If you were to hold your hands on the lower abdomen and lower back of a qigong master during inhalation, you would feel as if a small balloon were expanding in the abdomen and pushing both hands away from each other. The lower spine pushes lightly into your palm and the kidneys seem to expand with a gentle outward and lateral movement. During exhalation, air is let out of the balloon and the hands sink toward each other. Taiji Quan master T. T. Liang says that one of the marks of an "old Taiji hand" is the ability to expand and contract the lower back during deep, concentrated breathing or during the practice of Taiji Quan.

Dan Tian Breathing includes all of the benefits of natural respiration. It makes the mind and body relaxed, decreases unhealthy reactions to stress, lessens anxiety, allows more efficient gaseous exchange, and massages internal organs. Additionally, Dan Tian Breathing stimulates the kidneys, the lower spine, and the important acupuncture point, *ming men* "the gate of life." Ming men controls the proper functioning of the kidneys and, when stimulated, increases the body's overall vitality and energy level. Dan Tian Breathing primes the body's major energetic pump so that qi can spread more efficiently throughout the body.

You may have been familiar with the concept of abdominal respiration, but breathing with the lower back might seem strange and difficult at first. It is important not to force the lower back. Never strain the breath or breathing muscles! If your lower back does not move, then just imagine the movement. Eventually, the back will begin to respond.

It is surprising how few physicians know about this kind of breathing or are even aware that the back is capable of moving significantly with the breath. Medical doctors are expert in recognizing and treating disease and attempt to return the body to average, normal functioning. They are poorly trained, however, in recognizing symptoms of limited human potential or the procedures necessary to create better than average health. This is the domain of qigong healing.

EMBRYONIC RESPIRATION: BECOMING AGAIN AS A CHILD

With practice, the breath can become so slight, so fine, that it seems to have stopped. The Chinese alchemist Ge Hong (fourth century A.D.) says that the sage can hold a down feather in front of the nostrils, and the feather does not move! This is a characteristic of the most advanced stage of qigong breathing, a form of Dan Tian Breathing known as embryonic respiration (*tai xi*, also translated "fetal respiration").

Embryonic respiration refers to the time when the embryo (or fetus) is in the womb. Breathing is an internal process, air and nutrients being exchanged through the umbilical cord. In Daoism, the Dao ("Way of Nature and Spirit of the Cosmos") is considered the Great Mother. When an adult practices embryonic respiration, he/she feels a return to the womb of the universe, nurtured by the primordial qi. Echoing the teachings of the great Christian mystic Meister Eckhart, the child ("Christ") is born within when one becomes "poor in spirit," free of greed, egotism, and the tyranny of intellect.

What is the actual practice of embryonic respiration? Embryonic respiration is sometimes called "stopping the breath." The breath is so slow, easy, and slight that it seems to have stopped. We read in various qigong texts, "Hold the breath for twenty minutes. . . . Hold the breath for two hours, from 11 P.M. to 1 A.M." Obviously, no one is expected to hold the breath for unnatural or dangerous periods of time! Hold the breath (*bi qi*) means the breath feels as though it is held within; it has become an internal, effortless movement. For this reason embryonic respiration is often called internal breathing (*nei hu xi*). The abdomen rises and falls. Air enters and leaves

圖 形 現 兒 嬰

夫蟾蜍之虫
孕蝘蛉之子
傳其情交其
精混其氣和
其神隨物大
小俱得其真

潛龍今已化飛龍
愛現神通不可窮
一朝跳出珠光外
湧身直到紫微宮
　　　　　　　　　長壽聖胎
他日雲飛方見真人朝上帝
神水洽流
洮澆根株
內外無空

此時丹熟更須慈母惜嬰兒
氣穴法名無盡藏
藏包於窈窈包空
我問空中誰是子
他云是你主人翁

行住坐臥
抱雄守雌
綿綿若存
念茲在茲

The Inner Child Manifests. *As a result of practicing Embryonic Respiration,
a new self is born. From the Daoist qigong classic* Xing Ming Gui Zhi,
"Pointing to the Meaning of Spirit and Body," 1615.

effortlessly, spontaneously, the way an infant breathes. The mind is free of thoughts and images. It too has "stopped."

One of the most practical texts dealing with natural and embryonic respiration is *Yin Shi Zi Jing Zuo Fa* (Master Yin's Method of Tranquil Meditation),[11] written by Jiang Wei-qiao (aka Master Yin Shi) in 1914. Jiang was a weak and sickly child. Neither Western nor Chinese medicine was able to improve his condition. In the 1890s, when Jiang was in his twenties, he caught tuberculosis. He set up a meditation hut in his yard and spent a year in retreat, practicing qigong and meditation. His miraculous cure and spiritual realizations were detailed in his text. The *Yin Shi Zi Jing Zuo Fa* is unique in its clarity and originality. Yin writes from firsthand experience rather than hearsay or rote repetition of a previous master's words. His writings were extremely influential on the popularity and development of qigong. Jiang was also an important influence on my own training. In 1972 I met a Chinese Buddhist Abbot who, knowing of my interest in qigong, handed me a thin paperback edition of Jiang's Chinese text. He said, "Read this first, it's the best!"

Jiang makes it clear that no matter which style of breathing meditation is practiced, it is important to breathe through the nose and to gradually slow down and lengthen the breaths. He constantly recommends naturalness and effortlessness. Jiang says that during embryonic respiration, the breath should be so natural that the meditator is no longer aware that he is breathing. That is, subject and object seem to disappear in the experience. I am not breathing. There is only the breath. He calls this "a state of non-respiration in which there is neither inhalation nor exhalation . . . the breath seems to enter and leave through the whole body." Some authors describe this experience as "the whole body becomes entirely qi."

An important contemporary of Jiang, Daoist master Zhao Bi-chen (b. 1860), considered embryonic breathing the key to spiritual enlightenment. He devoted an entire chapter to it in his *Xing Ming Fa Jue Ming Zhi* (Secrets of Cultivating Spirit and Life). Zhao says that during embryonic respiration qi from the universe continues to enter the body, but that no internal qi escapes. (The student can imagine that with each inhalation qi enters the dan tian. During exhalation concentrate on the qi remaining fixed in the dan tian, creating warmth and light, like a luminous pearl.) The continuous influx of universal qi helps to create a new self, a seed or embryo of wisdom and long life. "When embryonic respiration is restored, it neither gathers nor scatters, is without self or other [duality] . . . it unites the yin and the yang." Embryonic respiration, Zhao continues, is really not a matter of how one uses the nose, mouth, or dan tian. Rather, it is a state of being, a condition of utmost serenity. According to Charles Luk's translation, "When the breath remains (nearly) stationary, the (immortal) foetus will be as secure as a mountain and by continuing his practice . . . all phenomena will be absorbed into nothingness and with spirit frozen in this state by day and night, the bright pearl will form in this unperturbed nothingness."[12] He likens this process to death and resurrection, again a reference to the birth of a new self.

To put this in simple terms, embryonic respiration means to allow the breath to become completely effortless, so that it leads you into a state of blissful stillness and serenity. In this state, you are likely to feel as if you are unified with the cosmos, at one with all of life. You will feel spacious ("nothingness"), free of any constraints, as though you have *become* the breath. At the same time, there is a feeling of clarity and luminosity ("the bright pearl"). When the meditation is over, your mind and body will feel refreshed, as though you have recaptured some of the vitality of childhood.

Although embryonic respiration is more a way of being, rather than a particular qigong technique, certain procedures can help the student to achieve embryonic respiration more quickly. According to Zhao Bi-chen, these include: Dan Tian Breathing, as described earlier; a balanced diet; not allowing emotional excesses; circulating the qi internally; and cultivation of inner silence.

THE METHOD OF NO-METHOD

I cannot overemphasize the importance of naturalness and spontaneity (*zi ran*) in breathing. The Chinese term zi ran literally means "self-so," that which happens according to the rules of its own nature, a process of growth rather than external manipulation. A tree grows zi ran; waves occur zi ran; a child grows and breathes zi ran. The word "nature" in Chinese is *da zi ran* "the great self-so" or "the great spontaneity." We learn various methods of breathing in order to find freedom of the breath, so that the body can adapt in a healthy way to the needs of the moment. It would not make sense to breathe slowly and meditatively during a marathon race. Nor should one pant while meditating on passing clouds. If an individual sighs frequently through the mouth while resting, this is a symptom of hyperventilation. However, such sighing during intercourse is a sign of sexual health. Methods are learned in order to unlearn dysfunctional habits and to recover new options, greater freedom of choice for the body. After practicing these qigong techniques, forget them, just let yourself breathe. As you continue training, your daily habits will change *naturally*, not through force.

TABLE 6: QIGONG BREATHING METHODS

Method	Inhalation	Exhalation	Purpose
Natural	Abdomen expands	Abdomen contracts	Establish good breathing habits and overall health
Differentiated	All possibilities	All possibilities	Control of breath, release inhibitions
Reversed	Abdomen contracts	Abdomen expands	Energize, strengthen diaphragm
Dan Tian	Abdomen and lower back expand	Abdomen and lower back contract	Strengthen and cultivate dan tian qi, health, and inner peace
Embryonic	See above, minimal movement, effortless	See above, minimal movement, effortless	Spiritual bliss, expanded awareness

Remember also the "method of no-method," *not* controlling the breath, letting nature work without interference. When the shoe fits, you forget the shoe. When the breath "fits," you forget the breath. Trust nature (the Dao) and appreciate her wisdom!

SECTION III

The Way of Healing

CHAPTER TEN

Standing
Like a Tree

The ordinary is the extraordinary!
—QIGONG MASTER WANG XIANG-ZHAI

S tanding Meditation is the single most important and widely practiced form of qigong, integrating all elements of posture, relaxation, and breathing previously described. It is a way of developing better alignment and balance, stronger legs and waist, deeper respiration, accurate body awareness, and a tranquil mind. Standing Meditation is just what the name implies; one meditates while standing, holding the arms in a rounded position, as though embracing a sphere, and observing the natural flow of the breath. The Chinese term for Standing Meditation is *Zhan Zhuang,* "Standing Post." One learns to stand as still and stable as a wooden post in the ground. Standing has several advantages over seated or supine meditation. The mind is more likely to remain alert, as any lapse in awareness might cause one to lose balance. In Standing Meditation, the legs and feet are naturally extended, uncrossed; thus blood circulation is not impeded and may actually improve.

Most importantly, in Standing, the body is always part of one's experience. Meditation does not become an exclusively psychological or spiritual practice. Standing can be considered an advanced form of Dao-ist meditation, in which *xing ming shuang xiu* "spirit and nature are equally cultivated."

In Standing Meditation, externally, there is no movement, yet inter-nally, the qi and breath are moving. It is thus both passive and active, both yin and yang. The student does not try to *do* anything with the qi, he simply becomes aware of the *quality* of the qi: how it is moving, where it is blocked or free, whether it feels clear or turbid, smooth or coarse.

Qigong Master B. P. Chan once asked me, "Why do you think we learn these complicated healing arts? You know, hold your hand this way, keep the feet parallel, breathe like this, visualize the qi moving from this acupuncture point to that. . . ." He answered his own question. "I want to find out, is this hand really my hand? Is this leg really my leg?" In other words, the purpose of qigong is to understand "the four virtues (*si de*) of being human." What are these four virtues? How to lie down, sit, stand, and walk. It seems so simple, until we try it. Normally, when we are standing, the mind is walking, taking a journey to another time and another place, perhaps worrying about the dinner menu. When we are sitting, the body may be restless and ready to stand or move about. Even when we are lying down in bed, part of ourselves is doing something else; perhaps the breath is racing, unable to let go of the excitement of the day. Through the practice of Standing Meditation, we learn how to unify the body and mind so that every activity is savored with the whole being.

A disciple of Rikyu (1620–91), the founder of the Japanese Tea Ceremony, once asked him the same question which Master Chan put to me. "What is the purpose of Tea Ceremony?" Why the complex and intri-cate choreography of step and gesture? Rikyu replied, "First we boil the water, then we prepare the tea, then we drink it, that is all." The disciple frowned. Rikyu continued, "Show me someone who can *really* do these things and I will become his disciple." The discipline of Tea, like qigong, is a discipline of wholeness and integration. Even a child of three knows what is required to drink tea or to stand, but few sages of eighty can put this into practice!

Thus, Standing Meditation is "a million-dollar secret." It is a secret be-cause it is so obvious, so ordinary that we do not give it the attention it de-serves. It is hidden as the air is hidden, or as the water is hidden to a fish. In the everyday qigong of Standing, we discover the deepest mystery and beauty. We turn Standing into a discipline in order to go more deeply into the quality of what is happening and to bring back to wholeness the con-fused, scattered, and lost parts of the body, mind, and soul.

A BRIEF HISTORY OF STANDING
The Ancient Language of Posture

All ancient cultures used standing postures to induce altered states of consciousness and physiology. In Standing, we learn to shed energetic obstructions to the natural human potential.

It is possible that Standing Meditation began with the need of ancient hunters to keep perfectly still for long periods of time, so as not to scare the prey. This also led to a feeling of attunement and oneness with nature and a recognition of the potential self-healing benefits of such postures. Ancient people quickly discovered a science and psychology of posture. Specific postures induce unique psychophysiological changes. These have been carefully documented in the pioneering work of Felicitas Goodman, Ph.D.,[1] retired professor of anthropology and linguistics at Dennison University and Director of the Cuyamungue Institute in New Mexico.

Dr. Goodman explored ancient examples of sacred and ritual posture found in sculpture and art, from the cave paintings at Lascaux to African petroglyphs. She found similar motifs spread across all major continents, a common language of posture. She posited that the consistency of the human nervous system would allow even modern European and American students to reap the benefits of these postures. Since 1977 Dr. Goodman and her associates tested and confirmed this hypothesis with thousands of students, asking them to hold various postures and note their experiences. Even allowing for individual differences in experience and expression, "we found that each posture predictably mediated not just any kind of vision, but a characteristic, distinctly different experience."[2]

For example, the "Bear Posture," similar to Standing Meditation and virtually identical to the "Crane" qigong stance described in Chapter 11, is found at archaeological sites dated from 6000 B.C. to the present in Egypt, Africa, Europe, both North and South America, and China.[3] A description of the Bear Posture sounds like qigong. Stand with the back straight, the feet parallel and about a foot apart, knees slightly bent, the hands on either side of the navel. Students practicing this posture[4] consistently have waking dreams or experiences associated with the healing power of the bear. Altogether, Dr. Goodman discovered about thirty ancient postures representing "a behavior and no doubt an attendant knowledge having a worldwide distribution."[5] Other postures induce feelings of metamorphosis, soul journeys, divinatory visions, etc. Native Americans continue to use similar postures to transmit healing power during their rituals.[6]

Teachers of Awareness Through Movement,® a system of healing exercises developed by Moshe Feldenkrais, also recognize the consciousness-specific aspects of posture. I have participated in classes[7] in which I was led through the various postures and movements associated with prayer in several world religions—the swaying movements of Jewish *davening*, the palms held together and body still in Buddhist sutra recitation, a knee bending before the image of Christ, and so on. We found that, even without the external trappings of religion, we were quickly induced into a prayerful state of consciousness, a sense of awe and divine presence. This is also true of the *asanas*, the sacred postures of Hatha Yoga, which are sometimes held for long periods of time as tranquil meditations. In Islam, the practice of *salat* (prayer, worship, supplication) requires assuming eight separate postures, holding each for specific lengths of time, while reciting holy verses. Each posture is said to have physical and spiritual benefits.[8]

Standing in China:
The Path of Warriors and Healers

China is the only country in which Standing has been made into an exact science, with specific healing and defensive techniques transmitted from generation to generation. There is historical evidence that Standing has been practiced for healing and transformation since very ancient times: martial postures of the Qin Dynasty Warriors,[9] ancient drawings from the *Dao-yin Tu* ("Dao-yin Illustrations," second century B.C.; see Chapter 2), paintings of Shao-lin monks in low Horse–Stance postures. There is also a wide variety of standing postures in ancient Chinese rock art, many of these parallel to the postures recognized by Dr. Goodman. Jiang Zhenming, member of the International Committee for Rock Art and the China Association of Ancient Bronze Drum Research, notes that "the human-face rock pictures found in the [former] Soviet Union, Canada, the United States of America, and Australia are similar to those in Fujian, Jiangsu, Taiwan, Inner Mongolia and other places in China."[10] Although the petroglyphs are often attributed to ethnic minorities, this does not diminish their relevance to the culture of the Han (Chinese ethnicity). We know that minority people, such as the Islamic Hui, were a major influence on the development of Chinese qigong and martial arts. It is also significant that several rock art panels depict military training,[11] choreographed dances, and animal postures[12] (perhaps hunting dances). Rock art is found throughout China, including China's sacred peaks (e.g., the Kunlun and Wuyi Mountains), areas that in later centuries became centers for qigong practice.

Although Standing has always been an integral part of qigong, the best-known and perhaps greatest Standing Meditation teacher of all time is Wang

Xiang-zhai (1885–1963). Wang was expert in all three aspects of qigong: healing, martial arts, and meditation.[13] As a healer, he believed that Standing could "cure anemia, normalize blood pressure, and make the heartbeat calm and regular."[14] Wang was a renowned, undefeated martial artist. He was also a spiritual teacher, strongly influenced by the philosophy of both Daoism and Chinese Zen (*Chan*) Buddhism. He said, "In movement, be like the dragon and tiger. In stillness, have the mind of the Buddha." He emphasized that the secret of Standing is "emptiness" (kong). An empty mind can sense internal blockages to the flow of qi (qigong healing), can meet the opponent creatively without a preconceived strategy (qigong martial arts), and can realize the nature of the cosmos (spiritual qigong). It is obvious that for Wang Xiang-zhai, Standing was a method of both physical and spiritual cultivation. "After forty years of experience, I have learned that all true strength arises from a primordial, selfless void, and that this void can be gradually comprehended by paying attention to the small, subtle movements of the body."

HOW TO PRACTICE STANDING MEDITATION

General Points

Review the information presented on qigong posture and relaxation in Chapters 7 and 8, and apply this to Standing Meditation. The most important points to remember are: The body is relaxed, yet extended and open. Use minimum effort. Stand with the feet parallel and shoulder-width apart, the toes pointing straight ahead, the knees slightly bent, the back straight but not stiff, the abdomen relaxed. The head is held as though suspended from above. Unify the internal energy by imagining that the breath is able to flow everywhere in the body.

Position of the Feet

The weight is evenly distributed on the feet. Make sure you are standing *plumb erect*, not leaning to the front, back, right, or left. This will allow the body's weight to spread through the feet into the ground, favoring neither toe, heel, inside of the foot, nor outside of the foot. Maximizing contact with the ground creates a feeling of deep roots, easy balance, and abundant internal energy, qi. One feels like a tree, drawing nutrients from the soil. The posture should feel relaxed, harmonious, and natural.

Position of the Arms and Hands

The arms are in a rounded position, at the height of either the abdomen (fig. 5), chest (fig. 6), or face (fig. 7), as though lightly embracing a giant beach ball. The palms can be facing either away from or toward the body. Wang advised, "Don't raise the arms higher than the eyebrows or drop them lower than the navel. Don't cross the right arm over to the left side or the left arm over to the right." Generally, during the practice of Standing, one either holds one position for a long period of time or spends a lesser period holding several positions in succession. For instance, the hands might be held at chest height for twenty minutes. Or the hands can be rounded at the level of the abdomen for five minutes, chest level for five minutes, face level for five minutes, then back to chest, five minutes, and abdomen, five minutes. This gives a total workout of twenty-five minutes.

The height of the arms can vary according to your ability. For instance, if you have bursitis or another problem that prevents lifting the arms to shoulder height, practice with the arms in a comfortable position, below chest level. If you are disabled, apply all the principles of standing to your

Figure 5   Figure 6   Figure 7

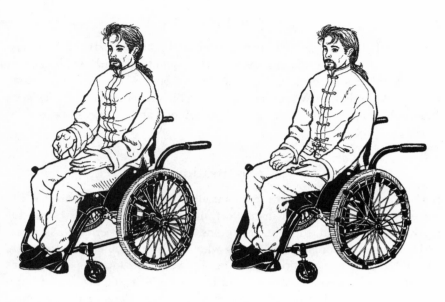

Figure 8   Figure 9

seated position in the wheelchair (fig. 8). If the arms cannot be lifted at all, let them rest on the lap (fig. 9). You can still drop the breath and imagine a deeper, more alive connection with the ground.

Keep the shoulders and elbows relaxed. The fingers are gently spread, the palms feel hollow and receptive. Try to keep the forearm, wrist, and back of the hand in an almost straight line or curving gently. Avoid letting the hands droop down toward the wrists or flex back stiffly toward the forearm. An excessively open or closed wrist joint interferes with the flow of qi and blood to the fingertips.

The Eyes

The eyes should be open and relaxed, looking with a soft focus, straight ahead into the distance. Standing Meditation is best practiced outdoors or near a window with an unobstructed view. Wang advised, "One's inner thoughts do not wander to the outside. Outside events do not encroach on the inside." Another way of putting this is that the eyes are open but not focusing on or grasping at external objects. They see in a disattached way, not distracting one from inner awareness. One is gazing inside *and* outside, allowing the two realms to merge into one seamless experience.[15]

The Breath

The breath is completely natural, relaxed, and diaphragmatic. With every inhalation, feel the lower abdomen gently expanding. With every exhalation, the abdomen retracts. Don't force the breath, just feel its natural rhythm. According to Wang Xiang-zhai, the breath should be *jing, chang, xi* "tranquil, long, and fine." "Fine" means smooth and even, as opposed to coarse and broken.

Concentration

Simply be aware of whatever presents itself to consciousness.[16] This may include feelings of comfort or discomfort, muscular tension or weakness, the rhythm of the breath, thoughts, emotions. Give yourself permission to feel, without either prolonging or rejecting whatever occurs. The goal is to cultivate a state of clear perceptiveness, without exclusively focusing on any particular, passing event. In Zen meditation, there is a practice called "Just Sitting," sitting as a way of hanging out with yourSelf. Here we are practicing "Just Standing." Interestingly, one of Wang Xiang-zhai's Japanese students, Kenichi Sawai, calls Wang's Standing Meditation "Standing Zen."[17]

Use the breath as your focal point. Whenever your mind begins to wander, gently ask yourself, "Am I breathing? How am I breathing?" Physiological awareness brings self-awareness. The mind becomes silently attentive to the subtleties of what is happening in the here and now, rather than thinking about the past, the future, or abstractions disconnected with the present.

Time and Length of Practice

Standing can be practiced at any time of day, but early morning is best. The following recommendations are based on the assumption that you are in relatively good health. Do not stand as long as I advise if you have a joint problem, such as arthritis or any other condition that makes it medically inadvisable to practice Standing for extended periods.

Begin training about five minutes a day. If you are practicing with the arms at the height of the abdomen, chest, and face, divide the time evenly among the postures. During your second week of training, practice for ten minutes a day, fifteen minutes per day during the third week, and so on. Build gradually to a minimum of twenty minutes daily Standing, and a maximum of forty minutes. This is a small investment of time considering that you will probably have more energy during the day and need less sleep at night.

It is possible to judge the length of Standing without looking at the clock. Simply count your exhalations. If you count sixty breaths in a single posture (or twenty breaths for each of three postures), this will probably take four or five minutes, at the normal respiratory rate of approximately 15 bpm (breaths per minute). As time passes and your qigong improves, the breath will slow down, approaching the rate indicative of deep rest, 3–5 bpm. Now you will be standing for close to twenty minutes. You can vary the breath count according to your abilities and needs, increasing the count if you need to stand longer, decreasing the count if you need to stand for a shorter period.

Proceed slowly and systematically. After three to four months of regular training, you will be able to sense the most beneficial length of practice. In qigong, "beneficial" does not necessarily mean comfortable or easy. It *does* mean a length of practice sufficient to deepen self-understanding and to improve health and vitality. The period can vary a great deal from person to person. As Wang Xiang-zhai's student, Tang Ru-kun, explained to me, "I know some old-timers who stand for thirty minutes, others who stand for hours. Standing is like eating. Some people need a lot, some a little to satisfy them." Wang Xiang-zhai compared Standing to a furnace, refining and tempering the students' minds and bodies. The length of "firing" depends on the material.

Concluding Your Session

At the end of your Standing Meditation session, it is important to practice *Xiu Xi Shi*, "the Posture of Rest." Let your hands float down to your sides, and allow them to rest against your thighs for a moment. Then lift the hands so that the back of the hands rest comfortably on the lower back. Now begin to rock the weight slowly from front to back, toe to heel. Do not lift the toes or heels from the ground; simply feel the weight shifting through each part of the foot. Then rock the weight several times from right to left, side to side. After this, rock the weight in a circle, several times in one direction, several times in the other, feeling each part of the feet stimulated: toes, heels, inside of the feet, outside of the feet. Through each of these "shiftings" imagine that you are using the ground to massage the feet. Then, again let the arms settle at the sides of the body. You are ready for the next stage of your qigong or for the day's activities.

Difficulties and Challenges

Standing Meditation is the optimum posture for balanced flow of qi. As a result, all of the places where qi is not flowing come immediately into the foreground of awareness and are experienced as discomfort. One notices places of tension, weakness, constriction, disease. For instance, if your shoulders are chronically raised, after only a few minutes of Standing, the shoulders may ache and feel so elevated that you feel they are touching your ears! If the thigh muscles tense beyond what is necessary, they will soon "burn" with the effort of Standing. If your sacral vertebrae are misaligned, you will really know it when you Stand! If your stomach has a tendency to rumble because of poor digestion or eating habits, it may sound thunderous during Standing.

Long-distance runners and other athletes are often dismayed at their difficulties in Standing. When they first see the exercise, they say, "This looks easy enough. If I can run ten miles, I can certainly Stand ten minutes." Then they try it and experience tension, discomfort, shaking knees. Standing does not test how strong you are, but rather how intelligently you use your strength.

Discomfort reveals places of dysfunction and should be welcomed as an opportunity for improvement. When you experience it, do not immediately change your posture. You may feel like shaking, wriggling, or moving your arms, legs, or torso. If you do so, you will lose the opportunity to discover, through your attentiveness, *how* you are tense.

When you find an area of discomfort, apply any of the following strategies: 1. Do nothing—simply being aware of tension may change it. 2. Inhale into the area, exhale stagnation and diseased qi. 3. Think of the tension or discomfort dropping down, through the feet and into the ground. It is also helpful to practice Standing after you are deeply relaxed, for instance following a massage or a hot bath. This allows you to more accurately sense how tension returns, how it is programmed back into the body-mind system.

If Standing becomes *painful* rather than uncomfortable, then *do not continue*. Pain is a danger signal and should not be ignored. If the pain is a result of poor postural habits, it may have a simple solution, such as checking if the back is straight, the chest relaxed. If, however, it is a result of a medical disorder, it should be treated by your physician and Standing resumed only with his/her permission.

Stages of Standing

Most students pass through three tests in Standing Meditation.[18] First, there is the "test of discomfort," where every joint and muscle seems to be out of place or doing something wrong. This is often accompanied by trembling or shaking in the joints, most frequently in the ankles, knees, or wrists. Trembling results from weakness in the muscles or tendons; perhaps certain muscles have weakened or atrophied because of lack of use. Or trembling may be a sign that "there is water in the pressure cooker." The body is adapting to a greater charge of internal energy. Neither reject nor exaggerate such shaking. Just feel it, and if, after a few minutes, it does not stop of itself, practice the "Posture of Rest" and resume Standing at a later time. Some students may experience cold hands and feet during Standing. Although Standing is a powerful cure for cold extremities, in the beginning such problems may seem to worsen. As the student focuses on subtle, inner feelings, energy seems to move toward the core and away from the periphery.

Test number two is called "the test of fire." Finally, after months of practice, one has learned how to release energetic knots and tensions. The basic body mechanics—how to stand and breathe—are automatic. The places that were formerly depleted are now filled with qi. The hands and feet may feel uncomfortably warm. The forehead is beaded with sweat. The abdomen feels hot. Again, this is a transitory test that may last anywhere from a few days to a few months.

The most difficult test, number three, is called "the test of patient growth." I once asked Master B. P. Chan if the ancient qigong and martial arts masters had superior abilities to those of the present. He said, "In general, yes. But only because they were more patient." It is at this point in one's training, when Standing feels ordinary, comfortable, and *nothing special*, that most students abandon the practice and look for a new form of "entertainment." But it is precisely at this stage that the most lasting benefits of Standing are cultivated. As Wang often admonished his students, "The ordinary is the extraordinary." One can now focus not on unusual sensations, symptoms of imbalance, but rather on the positive, on the miracle of breathing, feeling, and awareness.

WALKING MEDITATION

Walking Meditation is the second stage in Wang Xiang-zhai's qigong system. It is a way of walking so slowly and meditatively that each step is as stable as a mountain. With each step of Walking Meditation, you are practicing Standing Meditation. Stillness and motion are harmonized; the mind and body become tranquil and balanced. Walking Meditation also stimulates the qi gathered during Standing to flow more strongly through the body. The current of qi increases, becoming like a mighty river that can sweep away debris and open clogged passages.

After you finish Standing and the Posture of Rest, raise the arms slightly,

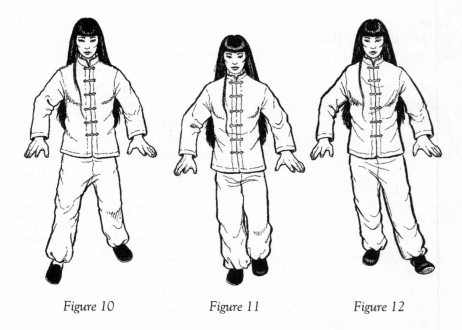

Figure 10   Figure 11   Figure 12

about six inches out from the sides of the body, at the height of the hips, with palms facing the ground and fingers pointing forward. There should be a buoyant feeling under the palms, as though they are resting on the surface of a calm lake.

Step out slowly with your left leg, letting the heel touch first, and then the rest of the foot. Transfer the weight from the rear (right) to the front (left), feeling the way the rear leg becomes "empty" as the front leg becomes "full." The weight passes through the foot into the ground. Now take the rear foot and "post" it, bringing it up to the front foot and just touching it momentarily with the toe on the ground. The weight is still on your left.

Now the posted right foot steps out, again reaching with the heel. Once more the foot comes flat, molding to the ground, and the weight transfers from rear (left) to front (right). Once the weight has completely emptied from the left leg, the foot can post, touching on the toe, near the right. The process is repeated, step after step, for any length of time. Step, shift, post, step, shift, post . . . (figs. 10, 11, 12).

After a while, you can practice the "retreating step." The method is basically the same as forward stepping, except that as you reach back, let the ball of the foot touch first. The weight transfers, this time from front to back. The front foot "empties" and steps lightly on the toe, close to the foot that has the weight. The posted foot reaches back on the ball and sinks flat into the ground. The weight transfers, shifting back, and again the front foot posts.

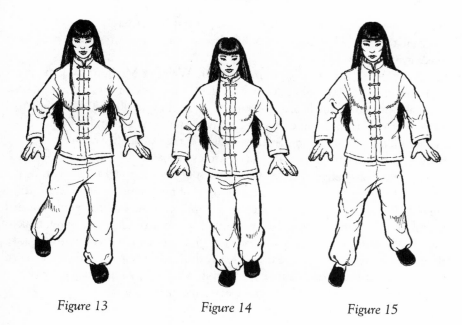

Figure 13   Figure 14   Figure 15

Step, shift, post, step, shift, post . . . (figs. 13, 14, 15). You can practice the Walking Meditation, advancing and retreating, as long as feels comfortable.

You will discover that the feet are actually moving in a crescent pattern, causing the body to zigzag slightly with each step. When Chinese artists make ink, they grind the solid ink stick into a dish of water with the same semicircular motions. For this reason Wang called this exercise *Mo Ca Bu* "the Grinding Step." It takes about ten minutes to make a good supply of ink; it takes an equivalent period to accumulate qi during Walking Meditation. The trick is to move your "ink sticks" (the feet) smoothly. When the feet touch the ground after posting, there is no sound, no "clunk." The movement is delicately balanced. It may help to imagine that the hands are truly resting on a lake's surface. They *slide* along the surface, neither pressing into nor lifting from the water. The body moves on a plane, without making waves. Or you can imagine that the feet are stepping with such fine control that they would not crack dry brush or startle a deer!

After practicing walking with the hands at the sides, you can bring the arms into any of the rounded Standing Meditation postures and continue the exercise. The arms may be held in a circle at chest height, as though embracing a tree. Practice advancing and retreating as above. Here another image might be helpful. Imagine that you are holding a large basin of water, filled to the brim. If you lean from side to side, front to back, or if you break the slow, even pace of the exercise, the water will spill out. Alternately, you can imagine that the "bowl" of the hips is filled with water, and you don't want to make waves.

Now, here's the trick and challenge in Walking Meditation. Can you keep breathing as you move? Can your depth and rate of breathing remain undisturbed? Can your heartbeat remain calm, slow, and even? We want to find a point of stillness amid change, a way to stay centered and tranquil during activity. By familiarizing ourselves with this sensation, we can retrain the body-mind to remain in control during times of stress.

Another challenge: Can you relax each leg as the weight leaves it, as it posts and steps? Obviously, a greater amount of tension is required when the leg is "full" and weighted. But when it is empty, can the muscles empty? Can the thigh and calf relax? Or do you hold on to an attitude of working, making an effort even when none is needed? The ancient qigong masters said that a key to developing more qi is "clearly differentiating yin and yang." It is as if by establishing the positive (yang, full, with weight) and negative (yin, empty, without weight) poles, more electricity (qi) can flow.

EXPERIMENTING WITH ENERGY

Wang Xiang-zhai said that to truly understand Standing and Walking the student should be creative, experientially testing each aspect of the exercise and the various ways of balancing effort and effortlessness. This is known as *Shi Li* "Experimenting with Energy and Strength." A common experiment is to imagine a counterforce while practicing Walking Meditation. While you are advancing, imagine that there are ropes attached to your legs, waist, and arms, pulling you back. When you retreat, the ropes are pulling you forward. Or imagine that your entire body is immersed in water or that the air is thick and viscous. It is important that the student *imagine* resistance but not use increased strength. Imagined resistance helps each part of the body find *the path of least resistance* and least effort. Wang wrote that by imagining counterforce the student recognizes a new, deeper source of coordination and power.

Other experiments can include slowly expanding and contracting the arms while Standing. The arms open and close like a balloon filling and releasing air or as though playing an accordion. This can also be done during Walking Meditation. For example, while advancing with the arms rounded, chest-high, increase the diameter of the circle as you step and shift to the front (fig. 16), and decrease the diameter as you post the rear leg (fig. 17). You can also experiment with various positions of the arms or different ways of coordinating the breath with walking.

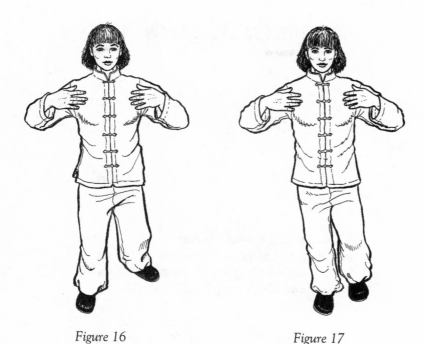

Figure 16   Figure 17

Wang seems to have taught different techniques to different students. He taught Standing postures in which the weight was primarily on one leg or the other, postures held in wide, low, and difficult stances, postures that imitated various animals. It is useless to make a catalogue of "orthodox techniques," as this is against the very spirit of creativity and adaptability that Wang advocated. Wang knew that Standing and Walking could point toward the truth. But this truth had to be realized by each student through his or her own dedicated practice.

CHAPTER ELEVEN

Qigong Meditation

*It [the imagination] is a function or faculty
that gives one access to an intermediary world
between the realm of unfathomable and hidden
mystery and the word of sensible and gross
forms.*

—ISABELLA ROBINET,
TAOIST MEDITATION

Qigong Meditation includes two types of practices. The first and most important is called *ru jing* ("entering tranquillity"). Entering tranquillity means training the mind to be silently aware without any particular point of focus. It is nothingness. The mind is not *thinking about* but rather *experiencing* directly, immediately, without the mediation of thoughts and concepts. Ancient Daoist classics called this "the fasting of the mind." To fast from food is relatively easy. But to fast from words requires perseverance and practice. A Daoist asked his teacher how to understand reality. The master said, "Listen to the stream." It is not easy to just sit and listen, without letting the mind wander about or dance from thought to thought. Yet such listening is extremely satisfying and comforting. It is like tasting the food rather than reading the menu. "Thought is born of failure," said biologist Lancelot Law Whyte. "Only when the human organism fails to achieve an adequate response to its situation is there material for the processes of thought, and the greater the failure the more searching they become."[1] A powerful critique of our intellect-obsessed civilization. The information explosion may be a sign not of progress, but of maladaptation!

Entering tranquillity should remain the goal and root of all qigong practices. Do not let yourself get lost in or entranced by the beauty of qigong

148

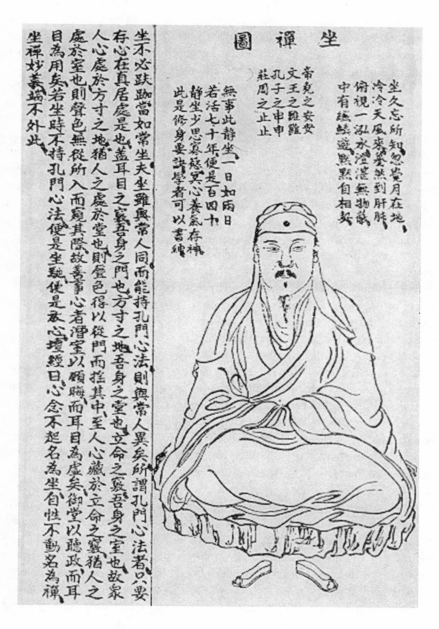

坐禪圖

坐久忘所知忽覺月在地，
冷冷天風來瑟然到肝胜
俯視一泓水澄湛無物礙
中有躍鰍遊默默自相哭

帝堯之安安
文王之雍雍
孔子之申申
莊周之止止

無事此靜坐一日如兩日
若活七十年便是百四十
靜坐少思寡慾冥心養氣存神
此是修身要訣學者可以書紳

坐不必跏趺端當如常生夫坐與常人同而能持孔門心法則與常人異矣所謂孔門心法者只要
存心在真居處是也蓋耳目之竅吾身之門也方寸之地吾身之堂也立命之竅吾身之室也故眾
人心處於方寸之地猶人之處於堂也則燈色得以從門而搖其中至人心藏於立命之竅猶人之
處於室也則聲色無從所入而窺其際故善事心者潛室以頤晦而耳目為虛矣御堂以聽政猶而耳
目為用矣若坐時不持孔門心法便是坐馳便是放心壇經曰心念不起名為坐自性不動名為禪
坐禪妙義端不外此

*Seated Meditation from the Xing Ming Gui Zhi, "Pointing to the Meaning
of Spirit and Body," 1615. The text advises, "Sit tranquilly, lessen thoughts,
reduce desires, expand the mind, nourish the qi, and preserve
the spirit—this is the secret of physical cultivation."*

techniques. Periodically go back to the experience of just Being. Practice silent observation. Observe an internal state, such as breathing, or an external object, such as a tree or passing clouds. A quiet mind can sense imbalance more easily and is better able to direct the flow of qi.

The other kind of qigong meditation consists of *cun si*: healing visualization and concentration techniques. By visualization I mean the conscious production of mental images, rather than images that arise spontaneously during dreamlike or visionary states. Spontaneous images, like dreams, are symbolic of our inner life. They can be helpful in diagnosing or describing an ailment. For instance, an arthritic patient tells his therapist that his fingers seem filled with sandy grit. This is imagery. Healing visualization, on the other hand, is therapeutic. The therapist suggests to his patient that with every inhalation, healing steam flows over and through the joint. With every exhalation, some of the "grit" dissolves and exits with the breath.

Qigong visualization is a training in imagination and volition. In qigong, imagination is not merely a flight of fancy or fantasy, but rather a way of sharpening awareness and correcting health problems by using the creative power of the mind. We learn to substitute positive images for negative ones. Instead of imagining that the body is diseased, rebellious, obstructed, or polluted, we imagine that it is the abode of archetypal forces: colored light, solar qi, and healing breaths. Healing visualizations might eventually result in the state of entering tranquillity, but they are primarily therapeutic and goal-oriented and based on a principle shared by qigong and psychoneuroimmunology: if the mind can cause disease, the mind can also cure it.

Sensual reality is *not* an illusion. The illusion is confusing our ideas, projections, and values with that which is perceived. These ideas create another reality. Instead of seeing the apple, we focus on the idea "apple," the label or word "apple." If these ideas are positive, then eating the apple can have a healing effect. If the ideas are negative, if we believe that the apple is poisonous, then the apple may have toxic effects. Imagination can mean the difference between health and disease. As Mark Twain once said, "You cannot depend on your eyes when your imagination is out of focus." Similarly, a self-image (idea about oneself) that implies hopelessness becomes weakened resistance to disease. Negative images affect health whether they are consciously held or unconscious—drifting to surface awareness in dreams or during times of crisis. Voodoo practitioners are expert at hypnotically suggesting such images to their victims.

But imagination can also cure disease. If burns are treated with an imaginary healing salve made of love and sunlight, they heal more quickly. If a patient imagines his immune cells destroying cancer cells, chemotherapy becomes more effective. Researchers have found that cancer patients' drawings of how they see themselves are good indicators of treatment outcome. "Belief becomes biology," said Norman Cousins. Belief causes physical changes, manifesting in the production of neurotransmitters, hormones, and immune cells and changes in the functioning of virtually all parts of the body.

This does not mean that imagination is the sole determinant of health. Rather, it is a powerful influence on health. Among infants and young children, the genetic program and a strong measure of chance (and perhaps fate or karma) outweigh imagination. An infant's brain tumor is not precipitated by low self-esteem. But in adults, genetics and consciousness may be on equal footing. It is also important to remember a fact virtually ignored in Chinese qigong research: at any stage of life, environment and loving support are essential ingredients in healing. Although a newborn's own imagination might be of relatively minor significance in his recovery, I have no doubt that the images, thoughts, feelings, and prayers of parents and other caregivers can be of vital importance. Parents do not need science to prove this fact.

On a mystical level, images are used to free the mind from the ruts of linear, discursive reasoning so that other dimensions of reality can present themselves. To the Daoists, the Image (*Xiang*) is the inner form of things, the primal idea from which physical reality later manifests. Although the mystic's final goal might be to simply see the apple as an apple, if we can learn to perceive the qi of the apple, we are one step closer to the divine.

Healing visualization is a cutting-edge therapy in the West, increasing the effectiveness of other therapies and offering hope to those for whom conventional medicine offers no cure. In China, this modality is very ancient and widely practiced. The canonical work of Daoism (*Dao Zang*) contains hundreds of texts filled with healing and mystical qigong imagery. Only a few of these works have been translated into English, chiefly within obscure academic books or journals devoted to sinology or East Asian religion. They are still an untapped resource for mind-body medicine.

There is an important difference between qigong visualization and visualization as practiced in Western holistic medicine. Most qigong visualizations can be classified "end state imagery."[2] That is, the body is visualized as fully healed or nourished with healing energy. Western clinicians emphasize "process imagery": tailoring images very specifically to the condition and the patient and adjusting the visualization as the patient's condition changes.[3]

It is possible to integrate the two approaches. While using a highly personalized healing image, the patient can practice the qigong technique of directing healing qi to the diseased area. At the end of the session, the patient imagines the afflicted area as completely healed. For instance, a hepatitis patient might inhale fresh qi into the liver while imagining the virus as tiny dots on a blackboard. He uses a magic eraser to erase the dots, then visualizes

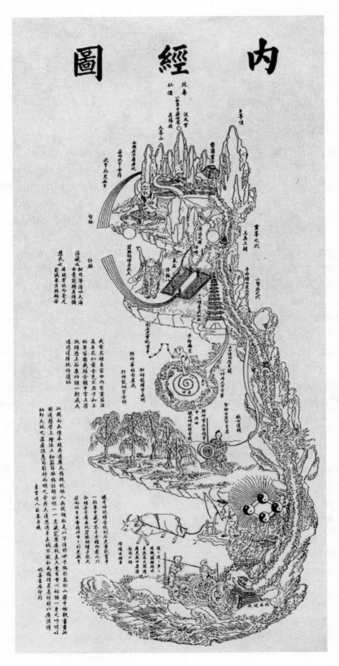

The Chart of Inner Luminosity

THE CHART OF INNER LUMINOSITY

In Daoism qi may be visualized as energy, breath, or luminous spirits. By practicing qigong, the spirits are well-nourished and happy and help to maintain the health of the body. The Chart of Inner Luminosity* is a symbolic representation of the human body and the spiritual forces that dwell within it. The bottom of the chart is the tailbone, the top, the crown. The Chart was carved in stone at the White Cloud Temple of Beijing (seat of the Quan Zhen Sect of Daoism) in 1886 by a Daoist priest named Liu Cheng-yin.

Reading the chart from bottom to top, qigong philosophy interprets it as follows:

- The boy and girl working the water treadmill represent the need to balance yin (feminine) and yang (masculine) energy. They also represent the right and left kidneys, which in Chinese medicine are considered reservoirs of sexual potency. The accompanying inscription says, "Kidney water reverses its course." This means that by practicing meditation, the waterlike sexual energy is conserved and made to flow upward, repairing the spine and brain and recharging the body with vitality.
- Next we see a man plowing with an ox. The inscription says, "The iron bull tills the earth and sows the gold coin." This means that qigong requires the perseverance of a farmer and the stamina of a bull. Regular practice enables one to plant the seed of long life and wisdom ("the gold coin"). The earth element, related to the spleen, is also a symbol of qi acquired through a balanced diet and harmonious lifestyle.
- The four circular yin-yang symbols suspended above a flaming cauldron represent the lower dan tian, the "field of the elixir," below the navel. The dan tian is like an alchemical vessel. By practicing abdominal respiration, the internal energy begins to cook. Eventually it "steams," healing, repairing, and energizing the body. The four yin-yang symbols are radiating energy in all directions.
- The weaving maid and the boy standing above her symbolize the unity of yin and yang. The weaving maid is yin, the ability to store energy, to go inward, to maintain tranquillity. Inner quiet is a prerequisite for energy cultivation. According to Chinese legend, the weaving maid spins a silken garment out of moonlight, which we see as the Milky Way. Here, the silken garment is the internal energy rising up the spine.
- The boy represents yang, the active and outgoing. He stands in a ring of blood; he is the spirit of the heart and the middle dan tian. According to a Chinese legend, the boy, usually called "the cowherd boy," and the weaving maid were once lovers, but because they neglected their duties, the ruler of the heavens, the Jade Emperor, changed them into stars at opposite ends of the sky. One night a year, the seventh day of the seventh month, celebrated as Lover's Day in China, the lovers cross the heavens and meet. In the Chart of Inner Luminosity, a bridge of qi joins the distant lovers. Thus qigong is the means to unify internal energy. The boy also represents

* The name of this chart, *Nei Jing Tu*, is usually translated "The Chart of the Inner Texture of Meditation." Jing (not to be confused with the homonym *jing*, meaning sexual energy) commonly refers to the warp and woof of a fabric. However, I believe that the author is making a deliberate pun on another word with a similar pronunciation that refers to the brilliant spirits (*jing*) sensed in meditation.

spiritual wisdom, innocence, simplicity, and youthful vitality regained through qigong practice.

- We see the stars of the Big Dipper constellation protruding from the cowherd's crown. This means that a qigong student should absorb qi from the stars and seek harmony with the cosmos. Daoists believe that the Dipper handle is like a lightning rod, drawing qi from the stars into the Dipper bowl. During the course of the year, the handle of the Dipper makes a 360-degree rotation. Since it thus points to all of the stars, it is a reservoir of astral power.

- The forest is the wood element and the liver. It represents the largest organ in the body and thus has a prominent place in the Chart. The liver, according to Chinese medicine, controls the even flow of qi. A healthy "forest" is extremely important for success in qigong. However, we cannot improve our health by focusing on only one organ exclusively. Kidney-water helps the liver-wood to grow. Wood provides fuel for heart-fire. Heart-fire creates ashes and nutrients that are necessary for the farmer to reap a good harvest from the earth (spleen). The earth produces gold and metal, the element and energy of the lungs. Metal becomes a molten liquid, feeding the kidneys. The organs thus form a circle of mutual interdependence.

- The twelve-tiered pagoda represents the throat and the back of the neck. During meditation, qi is pumped from the sexual center, up the spine, passing the middle dan tian and internal organs, to the throat, continuing over the crown and then down the front of the body. The throat is an area where the qi is easily stuck, a result of poor posture, tension in the neck, or the concentration required to keep qi flowing upstream. From a Western psychological perspective, qi may be impeded at the "pagoda" because of difficulties in self-expression and communication. The pagoda may also symbolize the importance of having a high vantage point, of not getting bogged down by details.

- To the left of the pagoda we see a rectangular pool of water with the word "drawbridge" written next to it. The pool is the mouth and saliva. The bridge is the tongue. The pool provides water that prevents the mouth from drying out during breathing exercises. Saliva also absorbs qi during meditation; the meditator swallows saliva periodically and imagines it dropping into the lower dan tian, replenishing it. The tongue forms a bridge between two major meridians; the Governing Channel that follows the spine and extends over the crown, ending at the upper palate, and the Conception Channel that begins at the tip of the tongue and descends to the perineum. Touching the tip of the tongue to the upper palate closes the circuit so qi can circulate and flow without leaking.

- Above the pond are two circles, representing the two eyes and the sun and moon. The qigong student closes his eyes and turns their light inward, illuminating the inner world. By practicing self-awareness he becomes a sage such as Lao Zi, the meditating figure above the right eye, or Bodhidharma, the founder of Zen Buddhism, the figure standing under Lao Zi with upstretched arms. The presence of Lao Zi and Bodhidharma, esteemed founders of Daoism and Zen, signify the importance of meditation as the means to awaken intuition and wisdom. They also represent the fundamental unity of different spiritual paths, all leading to the same goal.

- Continuing up the spine, we see the head as a series of sacred peaks. Mountains are funnels that draw down stellar and heavenly energy; this energy is concentrated in caves. Daoists go to mountain caves to meditate and commune with heavenly power.

The human body is a microcosm of the universe, a "small heaven and earth." In the *Nei Jing Tu*, the meditation caves are within the meditator's own head.
- At the top of the head are phrases that read, "Nirvana [Enlightenment]," "Realm of the Sages," and "Longevity." These are the goals of qigong meditation.

the liver glowing with healthy green light. An arthritic patient with bony growths in his hip joint might imagine, as he directs qi into the bones, that he is inside his body polishing the femur, making it smooth. At the end, he practices a qigong "bone breathing" technique, imagining pearl-colored qi flowing through his entire skeleton, unobstructed, like drawing milk through a straw.

The process of healing visualization can also be explored with the help of a therapist. In a typical interaction with a therapist trained in visualization, the patient usually supplies the first image. During a state of deep, quiet relaxation, aspects of the disease normally hidden to consciousness rise to the surface in the form of images. The patient describes what he sees. His therapist attempts to enter an equally deep and intuitive state of mind. The therapist helps the patient create an image that suggests a resolution or at least a clarification of the problem. This creative process is a wonderful addition to qigong self-healing practice. Qigong "end state imagery" may be used before or after the creative "process imagery." Both techniques become more powerful and effective.

Described below are the foundation techniques of Qigong Meditation. I have only explained or translated methods that I, students, clients, and colleagues have personally used with favorable results. The meditations have an advantage over more active forms of qigong in being easy to learn, requiring no special instruction in varying postures or movements. The most effective way to practice is to ask someone to read the instructions to you or record them on an audiocassette and play them back. Make sure to include an appropriate closure to the session, as described below. It is also possible to hear many of these meditations on professionally produced qigong audiotapes. (See Qigong Resources at the end of this book.)

DO NOT ATTEMPT TO PRACTICE MORE THAN TWO OR THREE MEDITATIONS IN ONE SESSION. Think of these meditations as remedies in your medicine chest. You would not take all of them at once. Choose meditations that match your needs and interests. Some meditations can be practiced on an occasional basis as the need arises. For eyestrain, you might practice Brain Cleansing. To prevent a cold, you could practice the Alternate Nostril Breathing daily during flu season. If you are using a meditation as part of a treatment plan for a serious disease, you may, with your physician's approval, follow the Chinese tradition of one hundred days of daily practice.

If your goal is to memorize and become proficient in a particular qigong visualization, then it is best to practice it once or twice daily for at least several days. The length of practice is generally about twenty minutes per session, though this can vary according to the type of meditation and your own experience with it. If the meditation is having pleasurable, healthy effects, then it is probably safe to gradually increase the frequency and/or length of practice sessions. If the meditation feels uncomfortable, try shortening the practice time. If you sense that the meditation is inappropriate for your condition, then cease practicing it. Use your common sense and trust your body's inner voice.

At the end of the meditation, it is common to feel as though you are in an alternate reality (you are!), a dimension of extreme stillness and tranquillity. To bring yourself out of the meditation, let any images evaporate away as your awareness drifts to the surface of your body. Become aware of your skin, your clothes, the temperature of the room, the chair you are seated on or the ground upon which you are lying. When you are ready, slowly open your eyes. After deep rest, you may find that the world looks different. The senses have been washed clean. The mind is like a mirror without dust.

One of the clearest books on qigong in the Chinese language is Dr. Liu Gui-zhen's *Shi Yan Qigong Liao Fa* (Experiments in Qigong Healing).[4] Dr. Liu advises that before practice, students should keep the following points in mind: 1. Let go of troubles and worries. 2. Have a relaxed spirit. 3. Prepare a tranquil, quiet, and simple room for practice. 4. Since the breath is an essential part of many meditations, it may be necessary to take care of any illness that obstructs breathing (such as a cold) *before* practicing certain techniques. 5. Urinate and defecate before practice. 6. Loosen your belt and wear comfortable clothes; don't force the breath; relax the body and lightly close the eyes. 7. Your sitting or lying posture should be natural and relaxed; if you are seated, find a position of comfort and balance. 8. In case of serious disease, it is best to refrain from sexual intercourse for one hundred days, and then resume appropriate and balanced sexual relations.

A. INNER NOURISHING QIGONG
Healing the Body and Mind

Inner Nourishing Qigong (*Nei Yang Gong*) is the most widely practiced method of Qigong Meditation in China today. Because it is extremely gentle,

Inner Nourishing Qigong can complement any other qigong or healing therapy. It is said to strengthen all of the internal organs, reduce stress, and improve sleep and digestion. Inner Nourishing Qigong is indicated for a wide variety of problems, including chronic indigestion, ulcers, chronic constipation, asthma, neurodermatitis, rheumatism, chronic functional heart disease, irregular menstruation, and fatigue. It has the strongest curative effects on diseases of the digestive and respiratory systems. The technique began in Hebei Province toward the end of the Ming Dynasty. At first, it was a secret method handed down from a master to a single disciple, finally passing from Master Liu Du-zhou to a sixth-generation teacher, the eminent Chinese doctor Liu Gui-zhen. Dr. Liu began to teach it openly in 1947, both to the general public and to patients in the hospitals.

Inner Nourishing Qigong can be practiced while seated in a chair, lying on the back with the head or upper body comfortably propped up on a cushion, or while lying on the side. The technique coordinates breathing and the silent repetition of healing phrases. Breathe abdominally and, as you master the technique, keep the mind focused on the dan tian.

Variation A: All of the breathing, both inhalation and exhalation, is through the nose. First spend a few minutes breathing in a relaxed, natural fashion. Next, as you inhale, let the tip of the tongue lightly touch the upper palate. At the same time, think, "I am." Then, for a moment, gently hold the breath, while thinking, "calm and." Now let the tongue again rest in the lower jaw while exhaling and thinking, "relaxed." Continue. Inhale, tongue up, "I am . . ." Hold breath, "calm and . . ." Exhale, tongue down, "relaxed." You are coordinating the phrase "I am calm and relaxed" with the breathing.

After a few weeks of practice, you can gradually increase the number of syllables during the breath-holding phase. For instance, inhale, tongue up, think, "I am." Hold the breath, "sitting calm and . . ." Exhale, tongue down, "relaxed." Or inhale, thinking, "I am." Hold the breath, "sitting calmly, body strong and . . ." Exhale, "healthy."

These are translations of three phrases actually developed by Dr. Liu. "I am calm and relaxed." *Zi ji jing.* "I am sitting calm and relaxed." *Zi ji jing zuo.* "I am sitting calmly, body strong and healthy." *Zi ji jing zuo shen ti neng jian kang.* When reciting in the Chinese language, the first syllable is with the inhalation, the last syllable with the exhalation. Whether you are using English or Chinese, do not exceed nine syllables during retention of the breath.

Variation B: If you are weak, ill, or have respiratory problems, practice a gentler method of Inner Nourishing Qigong. Breathe either only with the nose or with both nose and mouth (only slightly opened) during inhalation and exhalation. Here, the breath is held momentarily after exhalation rather than after inhalation. Inhale while expanding the lower abdomen and holding the tongue against the upper palate, thinking, "I am . . ." Then let the tongue relax and exhale naturally (not holding the breath), thinking, "calm . . ." With the breath out, think "and relaxed." Now touch the tongue again to the upper palate; inhale while returning to the beginning of the phrase, "I am . . ." Continue.

Most of the words in the healing phrase should be recited after exhalation. Thus, the phrase should not be so long as to cause discomfort.

If you have high blood pressure or cardiac problems, it is inadvisable to hold the breath. In this case, you can just let the breath move naturally, coordinating the phrase with inhalation and exhalation, without purposely holding the breath at any point. You may also make up your own healing phrases. For example, after learning Inner Nourishing Qigong, a car accident victim decided to coordinate his breathing with the phrase "My spine is healing."

B. BRAIN CLEANSING
Getting Rid of Mental Cobwebs

Here qi is visualized as a white mist, cleansing and invigorating the spine and brain. It is an excellent technique for headaches, eyestrain, and as an adjunct in healing any neurological condition. It also clears the mind, sweeping away clouds of thoughts and worries. I often use brain cleansing if I have been staring at the computer screen too long. It is an excellent way to take a break from homework or study or to relax and unstress before taking a test. It can give one a fresh start at the beginning of the day or help relax the mind and body before sleep. There are many varieties of this classical qigong meditation. We have qigong master Dr. Stephen Chang to thank for first making this technique available to the West, in both his lectures and his excellent books.[5]

Sit comfortably in a chair. Take a few minutes to just watch the breath, letting the breath deepen and slow down to its usual resting pace. Now, as you take a deep inhalation through the nose, imagine that the healing qi is a white mist. The mist descends to the lower abdomen, or, if you wish, to the base of the spine. As you gently hold the breath, the mist enters the spinal column, through the tailbone. Imagine that the spine is a hollow tube, a hollow conduit for the qi. Still holding the breath, without strain, let the mist rise up the spine. See it passing through the lower back, the midback, the upper back, through the vertebrae in the neck, until it finally reaches the cranium. It exits the spine and swirls about the brain. The qi moves like windblown clouds. Send it through all of the lobes, ventricles, tissue of the brain. Send it to any place it does not reach easily, any place that seems blocked or dark to your inner vision. Again, do not strain. When you need to exhale, even if this is only moments into the meditation, just let the breath fall away through the mouth. Exhale easily. The mist is now tainted, dark colored, blackish or gray. When the exhalation is finished, return to natural breathing. Let the breath come in and out a few times, then repeat.

Inhale white mist to the base of the spine. Hold the breath. The mist rises through the spinal column, entering the skull and swirling through the brain, cleansing and revitalizing. Open the mouth slightly and exhale the poisons—the mist dark and tainted. Again breathe a few natural breaths.

Repeat a final, third time. Inhale white mist to the base of the spine. Hold the breath and see it rising. Still holding, the healing qi moves through the brain. This time, as you exhale toxic qi through the mouth, imagine that you are blowing away the clouds that obscured a clear sky. Return to natural breathing, slow, deep, in and out through the nose. Direct your attention to the crown of your head. You have blown away the clouds, revealing a clear, unblemished turquoise blue sky. Hold this image of the blue color as long as you can. You may feel as though you have become the clear blue sky.

C. PURIFYING THE MERIDIANS
The Qi Superhighways

Qi travels through energy vessels known as *jing luo*, meridians. Jing means literally "to move through." Luo means "a net." The meridians are thus a network of channels. They carry various kinds of qi and fluids throughout the body, providing energetic nourishment and regulating the balance of yin and yang. In these meditations we will clear the main thoroughfares—the superhighways of qi—of any traffic jams and obstructions, so that the qi can reach and heal the parts of the body where it is needed.

Alternate Nostril Breathing

This is the Daoist version of a technique well-known to students of Yoga. The breath is inhaled through one nostril, held for a period of time, and then exhaled through the other nostril. At the same time, the qi is visualized as flowing through various internal channels: two parallel meridians on the left and right sides of the spine and a subtle meridian along the spine itself. The technique was adapted by Dr. Henry K. S. Wong. After more than half a century of clinical observation, Dr. Wong has found that alternate nostril breathing "can help correct any imbalance of hot and cold, yang and yin, in the body." This means that it can aid in the cure of any disease, with the strongest effect on conditions that produce chills and/or fevers. Unlike the Yoga method, the qigong technique includes visualizing and moving the vital energy during the time that the breath is held. As Dr. Wong explains, "If you hold the breath without imagining that it is still moving within, then the qi gets stuck. This can create pockets of congestion and possibly cysts or tumors. Therefore I have improved on the Yoga technique and turned it into a qigong. It has helped many of my patients."

Before starting the alternate nostril breathing, imagine three qi channels. See a hollow tube for qi energy in the midback, extending from the tailbone to the crown. Visualize a yin channel descending from the left nostril, bowing out slightly as it proceeds down the left side of the back, connecting with the central channel at the tailbone. Similarly, a yang channel descends from the right nostril, making a slight bow along the right side of the back and connecting at the tailbone. The three channels can be visualized at any depth, from the back's surface to the center of the body.

Sit on a chair or on a floor cushion. Take a few minutes to observe how you are breathing and feeling before practice, so that after practice you can judge any changes that have occurred.

Close your right hand into a fist. Then open the thumb and little finger; these fingers will be used to alternately pinch and close the nostrils. Begin by holding the right nostril closed with the thumb, inhaling through the left. See the qi as either white light or mist, moving down the left channel, as though drawing milk through a straw. Now gently pinch both nostrils shut. As you hold the breath, see the qi entering the central channel and rising up, until it reaches the crown of the head. Still holding the breath, see the qi descending along the same route, back down the middle channel, until it reaches the tailbone. Now keep the left nostril closed with the little finger, opening the thumb. Exhale through the right nostril, visualizing the qi rising up the right channel and leaving the right nostril. Then, without changing the position of your right hand, inhale through this same right nostril, seeing the qi descending down the right channel. Hold the breath pinching both nostrils as qi rises up the center to the crown and then descends back to the tailbone. Now open the left nostril and exhale through the left channel and out the left nostril. This completes one round.

In left, hold, out right. In right, hold, out left. In left . . . Each time you hold the breath, you are moving the qi up, then down the central meridian. Do a total of nine rounds.

Important points: Regulate the breath so that the inhalation and exhalation are comfortable. There is no need to inhale or exhale completely.

When you hold the breath, stay within your limits. If you are turning blue, you have less qi, not more! Never strain or force the breath. Visualize the qi moving through the respective meridians. Remember that during retention of the breath, the qi washes through the middle channel, moving first up, then down. You can increase control over the breath by counting. Inhale to a very slow count of four: one thousand, two thousand, three thousand, four thousand. Hold the breath, counting four from tailbone to crown and another four from crown back down to tailbone. Then exhale to another slow count of four. This way exhalation and inhalation are the same length. The period of holding is as long as inhalation and exhalation combined. A more advanced method is to count eight for the inhalation, thirty-two for the period of holding (sixteen up and sixteen down the middle channel), and eight for the exhalation.

Qi to the Four Limbs

In the meditations described in this section, do not try to direct the qi along any specific meridians. Rather, as you move the qi through the legs, arms, or torso, notice the path it naturally travels. Qi will find an appropriate route, like water seeking out a furrow in the ground. Inhale and exhale through the nose. The meditations can be practiced standing or seated on a chair.

Route 1: Inhale qi from the feet, up the legs to the perineum (the soft tissue between the genitals and anus). Exhale, sending the qi back down the legs to the feet. Continue nine times.

Route 2: Hold the arms in a rounded posture in front of the chest, with the palms facing toward the ground and fingertips a few inches apart. As you inhale, direct qi from the fingertips of the left hand along the arm to the spine. As you exhale, qi moves from the spine along the right arm to the fingertips of the right hand. Again inhale drawing qi along the left; exhale along the right. The qi is moving through the arms in a counterclockwise circle. Repeat nine times, then reverse direction. Inhale along the right arm to the spine. Exhale from the spine along the left arm. Again nine times.

Route 3: Now we will expand the circulation to include the torso. The route is more complex, but if you follow the directions slowly and carefully, you will see that it is not so difficult to practice. Inhale qi up the legs to the *guan yuan* acupuncture point, approximately three and a half inches below the navel. Continuing to inhale, qi moves straight through the body, reaching the *ming men* acupuncture point, opposite the navel on the lower back (below the second lumbar vertebra). Still inhaling, the qi current splits, moving in two currents around the waist, returning to the point below the navel. Now we are ready to exhale. As you exhale, qi moves from guan yuan, down the midline of the lower abdomen toward the genitals. From there, the current splits and moves down the legs. This completes one cycle. Again, begin by drawing qi up the legs to the lower abdomen, through the body to the lower spine, then around the waist and back to the lower abdomen. Exhale, down the front of the body and back down the legs. Continue nine cycles.

Route 4: Extend the arms in front of the body, at shoulder height, with the palms facing outward, away from the body. Make sure that the shoulders and elbows are relaxed. Inhale through the palms, directing qi along the arms. As you are still inhaling, the qi reaches the spine and then rises up the spine until it reaches the uppermost vertebra in the neck (anatomically, the *atlas*). As you exhale, qi descends down the spine, reaching the ming men. From there, with the continued slow exhalation, the qi splits into two currents, moving around the waist, reaching the guan yuan point below the navel. Now you are ready to inhale again. Inhale from guan yuan, bringing qi back around the waist to the ming men. Continue the inhalation as qi rises from the ming men straight up the spine to the top of the neck. Exhale from this place, moving qi slightly down the spine, then out the arms to the palms. You have completed one cycle. Repeat.

Inhale: qi from palms, along arms, meeting at spine, up spine to atlas (top of cervical vertebrae).

Exhale: down spine to ming men (lower back, opposite navel), around waist to guan yuan (3.5 inches below navel).

Inhale: from guan yuan, around waist to ming men, up spine to atlas.

Exhale: from atlas, down spine, and out along arms to palms. Continue for a total of nine cycles.

These are wonderful meditations. They bring immediate qi sensations of warmth and vibration and can be helpful in improving blood circulation in the limbs and possibly repairing damaged nerves. One of my most moving experiences as a teacher was when I taught a young paraplegic Route 3. After ten minutes the man began to cry, exclaiming that his legs were sweating for the first time since his car accident several years earlier. He could also feel some warmth in his legs. Even if normal functioning cannot be restored, it is important to move the qi through all body parts. Energy circulation is as important as blood circulation.

Small Heavenly Circulation *(Xiao Zhou Tian)*

This is a popular meditation, sometimes called "the Microcosmic Orbit." Qi is directed through the most important yang meridian, the *du mai* "Governing

Channel" in the back and the major yin meridian, the *ren mai* "Conception Channel" along the front. These meridians help to regulate the flow of yang and yin energy in the twelve organ-related meridians. Some texts also describe Governing and Conception Channels as part of a system of meridians that distribute *yuan qi* (original, constitutional qi: see Chapter 3, "The Three Treasures"). One of the goals of qigong is to create a strong flow of qi through these great rivers, so that more energy can reach the lesser tributaries (the organ meridians). Equally important, the two rivers must communicate with each other. The student learns how to *circulate* a continuous current of qi through the Governing and Conception Channels. Qi moves up the Governing Channel, over the crown, and then continues down the Conception Channel. As yin and yang harmonize, health and vitality improve; body, mind, and spirit feel more integrated.

Practice these meditations while seated upright on a chair, the legs uncrossed, with the feet resting flat on the ground. Rest your hands comfortably in your lap. Practice either Method A or Method B, choosing whichever produces the most pleasant and comfortable results.

Method A: Inhale and exhale through the nose. Inhale from the base of the spine to the crown of the head. The crown corresponds to the acupoint *bai hui* ("hundred meetings," because all energy, yang and yin, meets at this point). Exhale from bai hui down the front of the body, to the perineum. Inhale from the perineum to the tailbone and again up the spine to bai hui. Continue nine cycles. Next, let the breath just go, moving naturally. Without any special coordination of inhalation and exhalation, use your intent to direct the qi continuously around the two meridians. It can go at any pace. For some, the qi moves at a low, gradual pace. For others, it goes quickly up the back and down the front. Keep the qi cycling as long as feels comfortable. If you feel as though there is too much energy or if you feel dizzy or uncomfortable in any way, stop the meditation. You may need to practice for a shorter period of time; or it is possible that this meditation is not appropriate for you at this stage in your qigong development.

Method B: Many qigong practitioners imagine a slightly more complex route for yang and yin qi, one that is more consistent with the course of the meridians as outlined in Chinese medicine. Imagine now that the Governing Channel begins at the tailbone (coccyx), follows the spine, proceeds around the head, and ends at the upper palate. The Conception Channel starts at the tip of the tongue and ends at a point in the middle of the perineum (the *hui yin*, meeting of yin). Thus, the circuit is open at two places, between the perineum and tailbone and between the upper palate and tongue tip. You will close the circuit during the meditation practice.

Let the tip of the tongue touch the upper palate during inhalation (through the nose), drop it to rest in the lower jaw during exhalation (through the mouth). Inhale from the tailbone up the spine, around the head, to the upper palate. Now drop the tongue and exhale gently through the mouth, directing the qi from the tongue tip, down the front of the body, to the hui yin point. As you begin the inhalation again, the tongue touches the upper palate. Contract the tailbone muscles slightly (or the anal sphincter if this is difficult) as you suck the qi up into the tailbone, directing the qi to continue up the Governing Channel. Again inhale the qi all the way around the head to the upper palate. The tongue now drops and qi continues down the front of the body to the hui yin. Touch the tongue upward, contract the tailbone, and inhale, continuing. Nine cycles.

Great Heavenly Circulation *(Da Zhou Tian)*

It is best to try this meditation after you have spent a few weeks practicing Alternate Nostril Breathing, Qi to the Four Limbs, and the Small Heavenly Circulation. In the Great Heavenly Circulation, also called the Macrocosmic Orbit, qi circulates through the entire body: the arms, legs, Governing Channel, and Conception Channel. Your posture is the same as in the Small Heavenly Circulation—seated on a chair, legs uncrossed, feet on the ground, hands resting on the lap. The tongue is lightly touching the upper palate throughout the meditation.

Breathe in a quiet, natural fashion, inhaling and exhaling through the nose. There is no need to match your breath with any particular phase of this meditation. You will use your mind-intent to direct qi through the body. First concentrate on your well of qi, the dan tian. Focus your mind there for about five minutes, experiencing how the dan tian moves with respiration. Then direct qi from the dan tian down past the genitals, around the perineum, and up the Governing Channel. It continues down the front of the body, reaching the dan tian. You have completed one round of the Small Heavenly Circulation, the foundation of the Great Heavenly Circulation.

Next, from the dan tian, qi moves again down the front of the lower abdomen, continuing down the outside of the legs (no particular channel—however you experience it is correct). Qi goes all the way to the feet, then winds around to the inside of the feet and is drawn up the inside of the legs. From there, direct qi up the back. As qi reaches the upper back, between the shoulder blades, the current splits and moves down the inside of the arms, winding around the hands and then moving up the outside of the arms, the current returning to the midback. Now qi continues up the back, around the head, down the front of the body, and then, again, down the outside of the legs, up the inside of the legs, up the back. . . . Continue moving the qi as long as feels comfortable.

If it is difficult for you to move the qi with intent only, then you may use an image, such as white light or mist. Send light or mist along the body, as above. You will probably find that after a few weeks, the qi sensation becomes pronounced. There is a distinct feeling of warmth and/or electrical vibration. At this point it is possible to practice qi circulation without images.

D. THE SIX QI METHOD

Healing the Internal Organs

Also known as the "Six Word Secret" (*liu zi jue*), this is a classical system attributed to a Buddhist hermit of the sixth century, in which breath and sound purge the major internal organs of noxious and stagnant qi. The method has become very popular in modern China, thanks to the dedicated teaching of the late, renowned qigong master, Dr. Ma Li-tang.[6] Dr. Ma had excellent results teaching his qigong to students and hospital patients.

You can practice from either a seated or supine posture. Meditate for a few minutes, observing how you breathe, the quality of the breath, and your general sense of bodily ease or discomfort. In each of the exercises below, fresh qi is inhaled through the nose, old qi is exhaled through the mouth while quietly chanting a sound.

1. Lungs: Focus the mind on the lungs. Locate the lungs with your mind. Inhale, imagine healing qi filling the lungs, reaching all of the air sacs, all of the tissues and lobes of the lungs. As you exhale through the mouth, make a barely audible prolonged chant, *See-ahh*. Repeat two more times.

2. Kidneys: Become aware of the kidneys. Feel them with your mind. Inhale fresh qi into the kidneys; exhale unneeded qi with the low chant, *Chrroooeee*. Repeat two more times.

3. Liver: Locate your liver internally. Feel it, be aware of it. Inhale healing qi into the liver. Exhale toxins with the chant, *Shuuu*. Repeat two more times. This sound should be like a "Sh" as though saying, "Hushhh, be quiet." At the end of the sh, form your mouth into the U shape.

4. Heart: Be aware of the heart. Inhale fresh qi into the heart, letting the qi permeate all of the tissues, muscles, chambers, and valves of the heart. Exhale with the sound *Ho*. The sound is identical to hoo in the word "hook". Repeat twice more.

5. Spleen: Locate the spleen with your mind. Feel it, a spongy organ just behind the stomach. Inhale healing qi. Exhale toxins with the sound *Hooo*, just like the word "who." Repeat for a total of three times.

6. Triple Burner: The triple burner refers to a bodily function rather than a specific substance or organ. It is the aspect of qi that helps to control the balance of heat and moisture in three regions of the body: the head and chest, including heart and lungs (upper burner), the solar plexus, including the spleen and stomach (middle burner), and the lower abdomen, including the liver and kidneys (lower burner). Inhale pure qi into the entire torso. Exhale with the sound *Seeee*. While making the sound, form the mouth into a smiling shape and imagine a happy feeling pervading the body, as though your body is smiling. Repeat two more times.

It is best to practice all of the healing sounds in each session. If an internal organ is diseased, then you can emphasize this one by doing extra repetitions. If you have had the spleen removed in an operation, it is nevertheless important to practice the spleen qigong. According to Chinese medicine, the energetic imprint of the organ (like a phantom limb) is still there. The spleen meridian and the psychological and spiritual functions of the organ are disturbed but not removed.

The Six Qi Method is a powerful, ancient qigong that is begging for scientific inquiry and validation. My own enthusiasm for the technique was increased when, in 1982, I received an ecstatic letter from a man in Texas. Although I had never met him, he began, "Thank you for saving my life." He claimed that several months earlier he had been hospitalized for "terminal" cancer of the liver and spleen. He adopted a macrobiotic diet and began to practice the Six Qi Method, following my *East West Journal* article on the subject.[7] Although I would certainly never recommend substituting qigong instruction for doctor's orders, he decided to reject chemotherapy and radiation. He wrote to me that whenever he made the liver and spleen sounds, he also imagined that his immune cells were knights in shining armor, lancing the cancer cells and throwing them out of his body with the exhalations. After three months, there was no sign of cancer left in his body.

Frankly, I did not believe this story until the editor of the *Journal* contacted me a few months later, stating that he had checked with the hospital and confirmed the man's story. Although an anecdote does not constitute proof, I was certainly intrigued by the possibilities of this qigong.

E. COLORED LIGHT MEDITATION
Illuminating the Microcosm

The Daoist sage Lao Zi said, "Use light to develop insight." Color and light are the most common elements in healing visualizations among all ancient cultures. In indigenous Hawaiian counseling, sessions often begin by imagining the body suffused by blue, green, purple, and white light, to bring peace and healing power to the body, mind, and spirit. Native Americans will sometimes imagine specific colors of light carrying their prayers to the patient.[8] In China, the therapeutic use of color is systematized according to the *theory of correspondence*. Just as internal organs are related to various sounds, so they also correspond to particular healing colors. An individual can learn to see these colors internally, as though radiating from the respective organs. If the organs are diseased, they will generally appear a sickly black or gray. The patient trains to project the proper healing color, thus returning the organ's qi to balance and harmony.

The meditation is similar to the one above, only this time we see a color rather than make a sound. Also, we will focus only on the five major organs, not including the triple burner. As above, we follow the sequence of the five elements–five organs. Metal (lungs) becomes molten, creating water (kidneys). Kidney-water grows wood (liver). Wood creates fire (heart). Fire creates ashes, representing the earth (spleen). From the earth, we dig metals (lungs). Thus, we are back to the beginning of the cycle. Inhalations are all through the nose, exhalations through the mouth.

Bring your mind to the lungs. As you inhale, draw a beautiful white light into the lungs. When you exhale, dark light leaves, but the beautiful white color remains in the lungs. Again, inhale into the lungs. White light suffuses the lungs, exhale dark light. As you look within, the lungs have retained even more of the white color. They are beginning to glow on the inside, like luminous pearls. A third time, inhale white light into the lungs, exhale the poisons. The healing white light remains within. You can repeat two more times, for a total of five.

Now focus on the kidneys. Inhale deep, ocean blue light into the kidneys. (In some texts, black is recommended. If you prefer black, imagine a healing gemstone color, like black jade or obsidian.) Exhale the toxins. With each cycle of the breath, the kidneys glow more brightly inside, like blue sapphires. Repeat a total of five times.

Your awareness rests on the liver. Inhale forest green light into the liver, like the green of spring leaves. Exhale the unneeded qi. Five repetitions. As above, with each cycle, the liver retains more of the green light. It glows like an emerald.

Bring your attention to the heart. Breathe healing red light into the heart. Exhale diseased qi. Five times. The heart is beginning to glow with a beautiful rubylike color.

The mind goes to the spleen. Inhale healing yellow light into the spleen, filling it. Exhale the poisons. As you continue, the yellow color becomes clearer and clearer, the spleen appears like a brilliant topaz. Five repetitions.

Now, while breathing in a relaxed, natural fashion, do a quick review of the internal organs, seeing them glowing internally, like five precious gems. With practice, you can hold all of the images in your mind simultaneously. The lungs white pearl, the kidneys blue sapphire, the liver green emerald, the heart red ruby, the spleen yellow topaz. Enjoy this image as long as you wish, then let them dissolve and disappear in simple awareness of the body. Notice if your internal organs feel different. How alive are you now, compared to the beginning of the meditation?

Anti-Cancer Variation

These colors—white, blue, green, red, and yellow—carry the energies of archetypal, primordial forces, five basic kinds of qi. As such, they can also be directed in sequence to other parts of the body that need healing and harmony, rather than to the particular organs to which these colors belong. For instance, one might send the five colors of light to a wound to help it heal more quickly or to inflamed bronchi to aid in recovery from bronchitis. Some external qi healers imagine that they are projecting colored light to the patient as the medium or vehicle for qi.

One of the most interesting variations of this technique is a method of Buddhist qigong found in Sarah Rossbach and Lin Yun's excellent work, *Living Color*. The authors advise that as an adjunct to medical treatment for cancer, look at the following Six Colors—white, red, yellow, green, blue, black—and imagine their qi going in this sequence to the afflicted cancer cells.[9] This color sequence derives from Buddhist philosophy, where it symbolizes the healing power of Guan-yin, the personification of Compassion.

F. THE PLANETS WITHIN

A Mystical Meditation

Not esoteric enough for you? Want to experience something out of this world? If your answer is No, then skip this meditation and proceed to the next.

Instead of journeying to the stars, Daoists preferred to let the stars and planets journey to them, nourishing the body with astral qi. Repeating the above meditation, you can add an additional element, imagining that the colored lights are coming from associated planets.

Inhale white light from *Venus* into the lungs. Exhale poisons.
Inhale blue light from *Mercury* to the kidneys. Exhale poisons.
Inhale green light from *Jupiter* to the liver. Exhale poisons.
Inhale red light from *Mars* to the heart. Exhale poisons.
Inhale yellow light from *Saturn* to the spleen. Exhale poisons.

Whether or not you believe in the correspondence between planet, color, and organ, the meditation, nevertheless, creates a wonderful feeling of connectedness, of belonging to the universe. And since you are not attempting to leave the body, the meditation is safe even for those who suffer from *anima via phobia*[10] (fear of soul travel).

G. HARMONIZE WITH SEASONAL QI
Flowing with Change

Resistance to disease is lowered during times of transition, whether this be a positive or negative emotional change, a change of employment or environment or the change of seasons. An important benefit of qigong is an improved ability to flow with changing situations.

A classic meditation for attuning to the seasonal changes appears in the Daoist classic *Bao Pu Zi* (The Master Who Embraces Simplicity), by the fourth-century alchemist Ge Hong. Based on years of personal experience with this technique, I have adapted and expanded the meditation below. The meditation adds another element to the system of correspondences: the connection between color, direction, and season. Each of the five sections of the meditation is practiced on or shortly after the beginning of the season.

Spring equinox: Stand outdoors facing east. Imagine clouds of healing green qi flowing from the east and entering the body. You can inhale the qi, or imagine it entering through either the crown of the head or the pores of the skin. As green qi fills the body, the body is visualized as beautiful green jade.

Summer solstice: Stand outdoors facing south. See red qi swirling toward your body. Absorb it, as above, visualizing the body becoming red jade.

On a sunny day in late summer (so-called Indian Summer, considered a separate season in ancient China), face any direction you wish. Imagine yellow, earthy qi rising directly from the ground, up into your body. Your body becomes yellow jade.

Autumn equinox: Stand facing west. See clouds of white qi blowing toward you. You absorb it and become beautiful white jade.

Winter solstice: Dress appropriately and stand outdoors, facing north. Imagine healing black qi-clouds approaching you. The black qi fills your body, turning it into radiant black jade.

Practice the technique for five to ten minutes only, once at the beginning of each season. If you have difficulty maintaining balance, it is advisable to keep the eyes slightly open.

Review

Table 7 will help you remember or review the various correspondences used in meditations D–G.

TABLE 7: CORRESPONDENCES CHART

Organ	Sound	Color	Planet	Direction	Season
Liver	Shuuu	Green	Jupiter	East	Spring
Heart	Ho	Red	Mars	South	Summer
Spleen	Hooo	Yellow	Saturn	Center	Late Summer
Lungs	See-ahh	White	Venus	West	Autumn
Kidneys	Chrroooeee	Black/Blue	Mercury	North	Winter
Triple Burner	Seeee				

H. ABSORBING QI FROM NATURE
Healing Resources

The human body is not a self-sufficient system. If you do not believe this, imagine living in a chamber isolated from food, water, air, sunlight, and simple contact with natural environments. Independence? An impossibility! Interdependence is a more realistic concept. We need nature's qi to live. Nature feeds us because it either *is* energy or it is converted into energy by the body. The problem is that although qi is everywhere present, the ability to assimilate it differs from person to person. Qigong visualization can increase awareness of external sources of qi and greatly augment the body's ability to utilize this energy for self-healing and spiritual development.

The principle of absorbing qi is simple. Use intent (and, in some meditation, inhalation) to draw healing qi from any natural source. The most powerful and easily experienced sources are the "three luminaries": sun, moon, and stars.

Sun Meditation

Stand outdoors on a warm, sunny morning. Your arms are resting at your sides, with the palms open and pointing forward. Face the sun, with the eyes shut. Feel the warmth and light on your face, body, and palms. Open your mouth and inhale the sun's light. Exhale through the nose. Imagine your whole body filling with sunlight. Repeat three times.

Variation A: Stand facing the sun, as above. Inhale sunlight through the mouth, imagining that the sun's healing light is mixing with the saliva. Then close the mouth, and as you exhale through the nose, swallow saliva, imagining it dropping into the lower abdomen, like a golden pearl sinking into the sea. After repeating for a total of three times, rest the palms gently over the lower abdomen and concentrate on deep, quiet breathing. The abdomen should feel pleasantly warm and full of healing energy.

Variation B: Sit on a chair, preferably outdoors on a pleasantly warm day, although the technique can also be practiced indoors. Breathe softly through the nose. Imagine the sun directly overhead. The golden light of the sun pours into the body through the crown of the head. The body is a hollow vessel, filling slowly with the light, from the feet all the way to the crown. As the light reaches the crown, it cascades down over the outside, flowing over the skin until it again reaches the feet. Another method would be to imagine the golden light pouring only over the outside of the body, as though taking a solar shower. Either technique is practiced only one time in any session, and not more than once a day. The length of the meditation can vary quite a bit, some students spending three to five minutes filling the body with sunlight, others requiring ten minutes or slightly more.

Variation C: While seated either outdoors on a warm day or indoors facing a window, imagine that your body is made of transparent crystal. Pleasantly warm sunlight moves easily through it.

All of these sun meditations add yang qi to the body and are excellent ways to improve vitality and create a more "sunny" disposition.

Moon Meditation

These meditations are similar to the sun meditations. Stand outdoors on a moonlit evening, ideally under the full moon. If the weather is uncomfortable, then stand indoors, facing a window. As above, the palms face forward and you sense the light and cool energy of the moon. Inhale silver moonlight through the mouth, visualizing the light filling the body. Exhale through the nose. Repeat for a total of three times.

Variation: In the evening, during any phase of the moon, sit on a chair either outdoors or indoors. Imagine the full moon overhead, shining down on your body. As you breathe naturally, inhaling and exhaling through the nose, silver moonlight enters the crown and slowly fills the body, from the bottom to the top, like filling a cup. Silver light continues to pour in. As it reaches the crown, the overflow pours over the surface of the body until it arrives at the feet. Then let the image go and just experience your body, now fully energized with the feminine, yin power of the moon.

The moon meditations energize the body with yin qi and are especially invigorating to the nervous system and the brain. They also improve intuition and expand awareness. Whereas the sun meditations create a sunny disposition, have no fear—the moon meditations will not turn you into a "lunatic." To the contrary, they engender feelings of peace and inner quiet.

The Big Dipper

The stars of the Big Dipper Constellation (Ursa Major) have special significance in Chinese culture. In ancient China, each of the stars in this constellation was related to one of China's provinces. If a court astrologer saw a shooting star moving eastward toward a particular dipper star, he might divine that the province of Chu was about to be attacked from the east. The dipper is also a cosmic timepiece; the handle of the dipper makes a complete 360-degree circuit during the course of a year. In the spring, the handle points east, in the summer south, in the fall west, and in the winter, north, thus exactly corresponding to the season-direction correspondence in Chinese Five Element Theory. In qigong theory, the dipper is a reservoir of cosmic qi, collecting qi from all of the other constellations and stars as it makes its yearly course.

This meditation can be practiced indoors, but it has more powerful effects if practiced outside under a clear, starry sky. First look at the actual constellation in the sky. Then sit down and close your eyes. Imagine the dipper overhead, the bowl of the dipper filled with *zi qi*, purple qi or amethyst-colored light. The dipper overturns, purple light pouring down. As it reaches your body, it flows over the crown, over the face, down over the shoulders, chest, and back, continuing until the whole body has been bathed in purple light.

Another technique follows the method of the sun and moon meditations. Let the dipper qi enter the body, filling it gradually up from feet to crown. When the purple qi reaches the top, it cascades back down over the outside of the body. The body is energized inside and out.

What a marvelous way to experience the universe's healing gifts and graces! The dipper meditation never fails to fill me with a sense of awe, wonder, and vibrant qi. On an esoteric level, the dipper meditations are said to increase the strength of the qi field, the aura, protecting the body against negative spiritual forces.

Tree Meditation

The qi of trees is very compatible with that of human beings. Trees stand upright as we do. They drink water and require air and sunlight. They bloom in summer and retreat to quietness in winter. From the most ancient times trees have been symbols of spiritual growth. Their deep roots and high branches suggest an ability to connect earth and sky, the physical and the spiritual.

In a forest or park find a healthy-looking tree. It can be any type of tree, though the Chinese prefer mountain evergreens, such as the pine. Approach the tree respectfully, as though visiting a wise teacher. Make a mental request or prayer, asking the tree for permission to connect with some of its healing power. Stand several feet in front of the tree and close your eyes. Feel the presence of the tree. Inhale through the nose, intending that healing qi enter your body. Exhale through the mouth, releasing stagnation and disease. Do not send this disease back toward the tree. Rather release it as light or into the ground, as though you are turning your unneeded qi into compost. Practice as long as feels comfortable. Mentally thank the tree again before you leave.

An alternate method is to stand facing the tree, breathing slowly and deeply, in and out through the nose. Again sense the presence of the tree. Imagine that you are able to circulate qi between your own body and the tree. Inhale, drawing the tree-qi up your feet, through the body, following no particular pathway; wherever you experience it moving is correct. As the qi exits the crown, imagine it going to the tree, being absorbed by its branches and moving down through the trunk. As you see it exiting the roots and moving toward your feet again inhale, absorbing it into your feet and inhaling it once again up your body to the crown. Again, exhale as the qi is released from your crown and moves down through the tree. Repeat several times.

Then reverse the circuit. As you inhale, absorb the tree-qi through your crown, moving it down your body toward the feet. As it exits your feet, exhale and imagine the qi being absorbed by the roots of the tree and rising up, like sap, through its trunk. Then inhale again as the qi leaves the tips of the tree branches and moves toward your crown. Continue inhaling as the qi enters your crown and moves down toward your feet. Exhale as you send qi into the tree roots and up through the tree. Repeat several times.

After practicing the tree meditation several times, you may find that you can circulate the qi in this manner without coordinating the breath. Keep the breath moving at its own pace, while imagining a constant stream of energy moving from the tree up your body and back down through the tree. Then reverse direction. The energy can move as slowly or quickly as it needs to. After the tree meditation, stand for a few moments in silence. Perhaps you will feel as though you are more like a tree now, deeply rooted, yet standing tall with dignity and beauty.

I can only suggest here the range of meditations of this type. It is possible to absorb qi from any aspect of nature that you intuitively sense as healing: mountains, a campfire, lightning, sky, earth, clear streams, dewdrops, wildflowers.[11] Qi can be absorbed into the entire body or mentally directed to specific body parts that need healing. It is possible to circulate qi between yourself and nature, as in the tree meditation above. Or you can inhale nature's qi and use it to drive pathogenic qi out the feet.

I have found that these meditations work best with an attitude of respect, kindness, and gratitude. Never *take* from nature; rather, accept her gifts and recognize yourself as part of her world.

I. UNIFYING HEAVEN AND EARTH
Inner Alchemy

This classic and ancient qigong visualization is called *Tian Ren He Yi*, "Heaven and Human in Harmonious Unity." As in the sun and moon meditations, external yang and yin, in this case drawn from sky and earth, increase and stimulate internal yang and yin qi. The meditation also transforms the spirit, leading to a state of oneness with the cosmos.

Stand with the eyes lightly closed. If you feel unstable, you can open your eyes slightly. The arms are relaxed at the sides. Bring your mind to the dan tian, relaxing the breath. Now project your spirit and qi up through your body, until you imagine that your spirit is leaving from the crown and moving up into the heavens, as high as you can go. Then bring your spirit back down, willing it to enter your body and move down through it, until it exits from the bottoms of the feet. Project your spirit deep into the earth, as deep as you can go, perhaps all the way to the center of the earth. Then again draw your spirit upward into and through your body. It leaves from the crown, moving into the highest heavens. Continue for ten to fifteen minutes. When you finish, place your palms lightly over the lower abdomen and focus on the breath.

Some instructors teach that when your spirit-qi moves up, it follows along the back. Then, as you bring your spirit back down, it moves along the front of the body. However, I find it more effective to give the qi permission to follow whatever path it chooses. Don't worry about any particular meridians.

J. CRANE, TURTLE, AND DEER BREATHING
Balancing the Three Treasures

In a state of vibrant health, the three treasures—sexual energy (jing), life energy (qi), and spiritual energy (shen)—are harmonious and abundant. I have already discussed the philosophy of the Three Treasures (Chapter 3). Now we will learn how to cultivate them.

The meditation has three stages, known as Crane, Turtle, and Deer, to cultivate qi, shen, and jing respectively. The same posture is used throughout. Assume the Standing Meditation stance, following all of the guidelines for qigong posture: feet shoulder-width apart, knees slightly bent, back straight and long, abdominal breathing. Whole body relaxed into the ground. Place your palms on the lower abdomen, with the thumbs on either side of the navel, the index fingers lightly touching, just a few inches above the pubic bone. The eyes are closed; open them only if balance is difficult.

First get a sense of how you are breathing and how the breath feels under your palms. Let your palms tell you something about the quality of the breath. Allow the breath to become slow and deep. After a few minutes of self-observation, proceed to Crane Breathing.

THE CRANE
As you inhale, feel the hands filling with the abdominal breath. At the same time, the upper body rocks back ever so slightly. The hips are pushing toward the front and the weight shifts a bit toward the toes. The back sways, like a willow in a breeze. There should be no strain in the lower back. The movement is very slow, and small. As you slowly exhale, press gently in with the palms, as though you are helping the breath out. At the same time, the upper body rocks and bends a little bit toward the ground. The hips are moving back; the weight is shifting toward the heels. Again the movement is very small, slow, and fluid. Continue, coordinating the swaying of the torso with the breaths. Inhale, the abdomen fills the hands, upper body rocks back.

Figure 18   *Figure 19*

Exhale, press the palms in gently, upper body rocks to the front (figs. 18, 19). The upper body is moving as one unit. Be careful that the head stays in line with the spine. As you sway and shift with the breath, the neck does not bend. Practice the exercise for three to five minutes.

The Crane is ultra-relaxed, quiet, and contemplative. The Crane is a Chinese symbol of awareness and balance. She stands at the edge of a lake, perfectly balanced on one toothpick leg for an hour or more. You might assume that she is asleep, until a fish swims by. The Crane is relaxed, yet alert and full of qi.

THE TURTLE

Continue the basic rocking movement of the Crane. This time, as you inhale, rocking back, contract very slightly the muscles at the back of your neck, as though you are a turtle pulling your head into your shell. Imagine the movement, don't use force! The chin does not physically move toward or away from the breastbone. The feeling is that as the breath expands into your palms, the head is being drawn down. Now, as you exhale, rocking toward the front and pressing with the palms, the muscles at the back of your neck release, like a turtle extending its neck. Continue. Inhale, rock back, hands fill, neck contracts down. Exhale, rock forward, hands press, neck re-leases. If you cannot physically contract or isolate the neck muscles, then just imagine the movement. Practice for three to five minutes.

The turtle lives long because he moves slowly and conserves shen during sleep by keeping his head in the shell. He is also constantly exercising his neck and spine.

THE DEER

We are still practicing the basic Crane movement. Now inhale, rock back, and contract the muscles around the tailbone upward, like a deer lift-ing her tail. If you cannot isolate these muscles, imagine the movement. Exhale, rock to the front, press with the palms and release, relax down the tailbone, inhale, lift the tail. Exhale, release. Coordinate with slow breathing and continue for three to five minutes.

The deer is a universal symbol of sexual vitality. Musk oil and musk in-cense, among the world's oldest aphrodisiacs, are taken from the musk glands of the deer. The deer sleeps with one heel pressed into the perineum, thus stimulating the sexual glands.

To close the exercise, return to basic Crane Breathing. Inhale, the ab-domen fills, body rocks back. Exhale, the palms press, body rocks forward. No contractions anywhere. Gradually let the movement become slower and smaller, until you rest in stillness. Keep the palms on the abdomen, feeling the movement of the breath. Very slowly and gently release the pressure of the palms on your body and allow the hands to float to the sides. Notice the feeling that remains in the abdomen. Do you still doubt that the dan tian exists? When you are ready, open the eyes and return to this alternate reality.

K. ALIGNING THE THREE DAN TIANS
Synchronizing Body, Mind, and Spirit

This method can be practiced at any time, though I have found the best re-sults after Crane, Turtle, and Deer Breathing. The body is standing, relaxed, the arms at the sides, eyes closed. Or practice seated in a chair, with the hands on the lap. Imagine three spheres in the center of the body, at the level of the lower abdomen, the chest, and third eye. Notice if the three spheres are lined up, one over the other. Would an axle pass through the center of each? While visualizing the three spheres, will them to find a more balanced and perfect linear alignment. You will probably find that they are still slightly "off" (who isn't?), but with practice and patience, the alignment will improve. The suggested practice time is ten to fifteen minutes.

This qigong was transmitted by Daoist priest Wang Zhenyi to a renowned Taiji Quan and Qigong Master, Wang Peisheng, in the 1930s.[12] Aligning the Three Dan Tians creates a clear mind and opens the major qi channels. It can facilitate a stronger flow of qi in the Small and Great Heavenly Circulation. This qigong is also an excellent method to increase overall vitality and recover quickly from fatigue.

L. EMBRYONIC RESPIRATION
The Breath of No Breath

Embryonic Respiration is primarily a state of being that can occur spontaneously when the body and mind are relaxed, clear, and filled with qi. There are, nevertheless, various techniques that can help the student achieve this state more quickly.

Sit on either a chair or a cushion on the floor with the eyes lightly closed. The hands are resting on the lap, close to the lower abdomen. The left hand is on the right, with the left fist lightly enclosing the right thumb. This "yin-yang hand gesture" (*yin yang shou jue*) aids concentration on the breath and seals newly acquired qi in the body. Begin with a few minutes of quiet, natural breathing. Notice the depth, rate, and quality of your breath.

Stage 1. Deep Breathing: Inhale deeply, visualizing the whole body filling with fresh, healing qi. Exhale through the mouth, releasing all unneeded, stagnant, or noxious qi. Do this nine times. As you continue with the stages below, inhale and exhale only through the nose.

Stage 2. External Breathing: Inhale, imagining the breath and qi reaching the middle dan tian (the heart). As you exhale, the qi drops to the lower dan tian, in the abdomen. Of course, you will still be exhaling through the nose, but in your mind, the breath is staying within the body and dropping down. Thus with each cycle of breathing, the inner supply of qi is increasing. Inhale to the heart, exhale to the abdomen. Continue nine cycles.

Stage 3. Internal Breathing, Mingling Water and Fire: Now imagine that the breath-qi stays entirely within the body. As you inhale, qi rises from the lower dan tian to the middle dan tian. As you exhale, it sinks back down from the middle dan tian to the lower. Practice for nine breaths.

This method is called both Internal Breathing and Mingling Water and Fire (*Shui Huo Xiang Jiao*). As qi rises up and down, the energy of the kidneys (water) rises; the energy of the heart (fire) descends. According to the an-

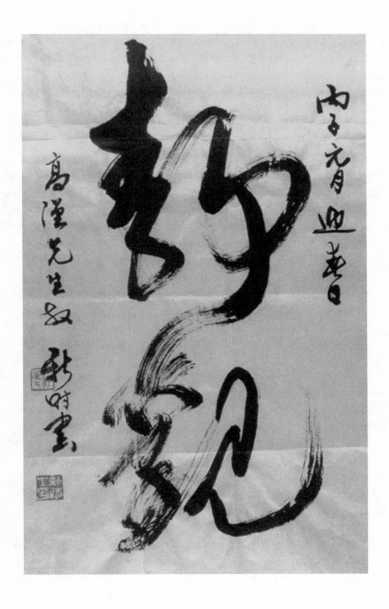

Jing Guan "*Tranquil Contemplation.*" Flowing, "grass style" calligraphy common in Buddhist and Daoist art, by Tu Xin-shi.

cient Daoist theory of body-energy, this has several excellent benefits: Jing (sexual energy, related to water) and shen (spiritual energy, related to fire) increase and are prevented from dissipating. Fire and water meet, producing steam, that is, more qi. The area between the heart and kidneys, including the spleen, pancreas, liver, gallbladder, stomach, and adrenals are washed of impurities. Mind and body are harmonized.

Stage 4. Dan Tian Breathing: Now imagine that the breath stays in the lower abdomen. Inhale, gently expanding the lower dan tian; exhale, let it sink back. Allow the breath to become slow, long, deep, fine, and even. You need not count the breath. After five or ten minutes, you will naturally enter the next stage.

Stage 5. Embryonic Respiration: The breath becomes so slow, effortless, and smooth that you don't even know you are breathing. Imagine that if a down feather were placed in front of your nostrils, the feather wouldn't move. You have become the breath, the qi. Your mind is spacious and free, like the sky, yet deep, like the ocean. Enjoy this state as long as you wish.

M. SPONTANEOUS QIGONG
The Wisdom of Naturalness

Not all qigong consists in following preset, choreographed techniques. Recently the method of *zi fa gong* has become very popular in China. This can be translated "Spontaneous Qigong." It looks like a kind of eerie improvisational dance, with some important differences. Western improvisational dance is expressive of ideas, aesthetics, dance motifs. Spontaneous Qigong is completely effortless. The inner movement of qi is allowed to become external movement. Spontaneous Qigong flows from the inside to the outside. Qi pushes the body into completely unique shapes and movements, opening blockages and tensions and creating a relaxed and alert state of body and mind. Here's how it works:

Begin by standing in the qigong posture, relaxed and sunk, knees slightly bent, back straight, breathing with the abdomen. Practice with the arms at the sides or with the arms at the height of the forehead, chest, or abdomen, whichever position is most comfortable. The elbows should be bent so that the arms have a rounded shape, palms facing each other. The eyes are closed, though they can open slightly if necessary to maintain balance. The posture should feel light and flexible. The position of the arms, feet, or torso may change during practice to accommodate the movement of qi. For instance, the hands might begin at the height of the forehead, then move to the abdomen, the sides, or behind the body. Or you may need to place one foot in front of the other to allow natural shifting and swaying motions. There is no fixed rule. In Spontaneous Qigong, you are not moving the qi, the qi is moving you.

Now we are ready to begin. Imagine that you are projecting your spirit out of your body through the upper dan tian, into the universe. Your spirit fills the cosmos. After a minute or two, imagine that you invite the qi of the whole universe back into your body. It enters the upper dan tian and then pervades your being. You are one with universal qi. Your own ego has disappeared (don't worry, you can reclaim it later). You have become a tranquil emptiness, without objects, without worries.

While maintaining this quiet state, become aware of any subtle movements in the body. Become aware of areas that feel as though they are vibrating or moving. These are places that obstruct or encourage the flow of qi. But for now, don't worry about what your sensations mean. Just experience. After a few minutes, begin to exaggerate the internal movement ever so slightly. This should start the process of Spontaneous Qigong. For instance, you may feel as though the knees are stiff. Your body wants to sway slightly. Let yourself begin swaying; then the swaying will continue of itself. Or you may find that the neck is stiff; the head wants to roll gently and rhythmically, like a cork bobbing on a quiet sea. Perhaps the breath itself causes your hips to sway from side to side or front to back. Or your arms may wish to circle and sway. Movements can be as large or small as needed. Intend that they remain gentle and rhythmic. Do not make quick or violent movements.

In this qigong, you are becoming sensitive to the inner movement of qi. By exaggerating these movements slightly, your body may sway, bob, tremble, rise and fall, shift, rock. The feet are basically fixed, though you may take small steps or readjust the posture if this feels natural and necessary. The qi movements might continue for only a few minutes, switching to a new pattern; or the same movements might continue through the course of the qigong. There may be periods when your body rests in stillness and then begins to move again. The entire exercise should last twenty minutes.

Since you will be in an altered, timeless state during the exercise, it is best to set a timer or ask a helper to gently remind you when the time is up. If you experience pain or other indications that the exercise should end sooner, then finish the qigong at that time. When it is time to close, let the movements come to stillness and rest. Place your palms on the lower abdomen, concentrating on the breath and bringing the qi to rest and stability. Then slowly open the eyes.

If you enjoy this qigong, you can practice it daily, though no more than one session each day. Be patient with yourself. If movements do not occur the first time you try, they may occur during a later session. Master Liang

Shou-yu, who originally taught me this technique, tells a humorous story of three skeptical physicians. Week after week they would stand, neither expecting nor believing that their bodies would sway or move of themselves. Then one day, all three began to bob up and down in synchrony, and then to laugh at themselves. Obviously their bodies were not designed to meet their expectations, nor to remain within the confines of accepted medical dogma.

N. THE MIND DIRECTS THE QI
Ultimate Simplicity

This method embodies the ultimate goal of all qigong: train the mind to send qi where it is needed. It is both the simplest and most profound method of qigong. Simply breathe into the place that feels uncomfortable or ill, imagining that you are sending healing qi to that area. If necessary, you can visualize qi as white mist or light. While exhaling, imagine that the poisons are leaving with the breath. The noxious qi can be visualized as dark light, a shade of black or gray.

For instance, if you have asthma, inhale qi into the lungs, exhale poisons. For eczema, inhale qi into the skin. For a systemic problem, such as lupus, let meditation and introspection guide you to the area or areas of focus. If you are anemic, you may find yourself breathing qi into the spleen, the bone marrow, or the entire circulatory system.

All of the different techniques of qigong are designed to refine the skill at moving qi. The more a student practices qigong, the greater the facility to move qi without following any specific technique. At an advanced level, it becomes unnecessary to use the breath as a medium for qi. Intent alone sends qi to the distressed region. You need more qi in the brain, just send qi there. Mental confusion? Expel confused qi. For those familiar with Chinese medicine, qi can also be directed to specific acupoints. Qigong becomes like self-acupuncture without the needles.

Lao Zi said, "The Dao follows the principle of Naturalness." Remember that there may be times when your intuition advises allowing a disease to run its natural course. For some psychological trauma, denial may be a survival strategy. It could be dangerous to direct qi and awareness to repressed memories without the help of a therapist. In the case of myocardial infarction (heart attack), there is strong evidence that patients who are, at first, in denial of their condition, fare better than those who are either anxious about it or who try to aggressively combat it.[13] Other conditions might require environmental rather than energetic solutions. For instance, if you suffer from hay fever or other allergies, it may be advantageous to move your residence, and *then* practice qigong.

I strongly believe that Nature knows best. Never let your belief in the supposed benefits of a therapy replace this natural wisdom. A good therapy makes Nature's wisdom more accessible. It helps you listen to Nature's voice. The purpose of qigong is not to become proficient in qigong, but to become expert at being more fully who you are.

CHAPTER TWELVE

Active Qigong

"Is Taiji Quan practice the reason for your longevity?"

"Not directly. Taiji Quan helps cultivate a relaxed spirit. Having a relaxed spirit is the secret of longevity."
—INTERVIEW WITH 105-YEAR-OLD TAIJI QUAN MASTER WU TU-NAN

In China, the word "qigong" calls to mind an image of thousands of individuals gathered in a park at dawn, imitating a master's graceful postures. Although meditative qigong is easier to learn and practice on one's own, active or dynamic qigong, *dong gong*, is the more popular form. There are two likely reasons for this. Firstly, active qigong is a social event; learning it requires participating in a class. This means making new friends and being inspired by the example of teacher and classmates to reach for excellence. Secondly, the skills and body awareness acquired through active qigong can be more easily applied to sports or the martial arts. Indeed, many Chinese martial arts are considered styles of qigong. Learning to breathe properly, stand straight, and root into the ground, the student develops a stronger punch and healthier qi.

As we shift toward an ever more sedentary lifestyle, as computers and modems replace human interaction, active qigong becomes increasingly necessary. In any case, most qigong practitioners are frankly unconcerned about *why* they practice. They might begin practicing qigong because they need the exercise or wish to improve their health. Once they try it, they are hooked. They practice because qigong is fun, and it feels good both during and after practice.

It would be pointless to try to catalogue the thousands of styles of active qigong. Instead I will describe the foundation techniques of the great, classical systems of active qigong. These are relatively few in number. What do I mean by "classical systems"? Styles that are referred to again and again in histories of qigong in the Chinese language. I advise learning these techniques first, since they are excellent time-honored self-healing techniques. Learn the theme before learning the variations. Once you learn the classic systems, you will be able to more accurately assess the benefits and evolution of other styles. Learning the classical qigong styles is like learning arithmetic before algebra or becoming a general practitioner before studying a specialized branch of medicine. Without this foundation, the student is easily confused by complex forms or recent innovations.

In this chapter I describe techniques that can be practiced safely and accurately without a teacher's physical demonstration and coaching. However, there are some qigong methods that cannot be learned from a book, and I will not fool the reader into thinking that I can accomplish the impossible. If you do not have access to a qigong instructor, a video can be a helpful way to continue your progress. (See Qigong Resources at the back of this book.)

Any qigong instructor who has done his homework (practice, practice, practice!) can teach valuable qigong techniques. Students should not presume that the styles I present here are the only orthodox or correct procedures. They simply represent the methods that I have found most effective in my own practice and research. I am grateful that other instructors may do things differently. It means we can learn from each other.

Review various styles according to your time, interest, and needs. If a style is improving your health, concentrate on that style. Do not try to practice all systems of qigong in any one session. It is best to spend from twenty to forty minutes in daily morning training. You may wish to alternate styles on different days. Or you can spend a few months on one or two systems, then switch to another. After going through the whole course, you can determine which kinds of qigong are most appropriate. In Chapter 16 I will describe how to combine styles to create a balanced morning workout.

During all active qigong exercises described below, the eyes are always open, with a soft, relaxed gaze. All breathing is through the nose, unless otherwise noted. The joints are never locked, even in stretching postures, because locking a joint blocks the qi.

THE EIGHT BROCADES

Ba Duan Jin means literally "Eight Pieces of Silk Brocade." These eight exercises are elegant, graceful, and essential methods of qi cultivation. They were first described in an eighth-century Daoist text, *Xiu Zhen Shi Shu* (The Ten Treatises on Restoring the Original Vitality), in the *Daoist Canon*. Daoist tradition attributes the exercises to one of the Eight Immortals of Chinese folklore, Chong Li-quan. Chong is frequently represented in Chinese art as a bald-headed, potbellied figure, with a white beard reaching to his navel. Chong had been a general during the Han Dynasty. When his army was defeated in a battle against Tibetans, Chong withdrew into the mountains rather than face the Emperor's wrath. There he met a Daoist who transmitted to him dao-yin (qigong) "recipes" to create an inner elixir of long life. The Eight Brocades was one of these methods. Before he died, Chong inscribed the exercises on the walls of a cave. When another general, Lu Dong-bin, discovered this cave several centuries later, he followed the diagrams and also became a sage-Immortal. According to a statement in the *Ten Treatises*, it was General Lu himself who first inscribed the exercises on stone.

The Eight Brocades are a good way to start a workout. They consist of gentle stretching exercises that lengthen the muscles and tendons and stimulate the meridians and internal organs. There are both seated and standing varieties of the Eight Brocades. The method I teach is similar to the standing set described in *Illustrated Explanation of the Eight Brocades* by Wang Huai-qi.[1] The movements should be done fluidly, but brusquely. Not too fast, not too slow. Find a comfortable pace. I like to repeat each about nine times, though there is no strict rule. Breathe only with the nose.

1. Two Hands Reach Skyward to Balance the Triple Burner

This simple arm stretch gently elongates the body and balances the metabolism of the Three Burners: the upper, middle, and lower body.

Stand in qigong posture. The arms circle overhead. Interlace the fingers and as you inhale stretch them upward, with the palms facing down. At the same time rise up on the toes (fig. 20). As you exhale, the feet rest flat on the ground and the interlaced hands rest for a moment on the crown of the head (fig. 21). Then stretch upward again, inhaling, rising on the toes, this time with the palms facing up (fig. 22). Exhale, again the palms rest on the crown, the feet flat. Repeat several times, each time alternating the direction of the palms.

2. Open the Bow as Though Shooting the Buzzard

Take a wide and deep "horse-riding" stance. If you are strong and

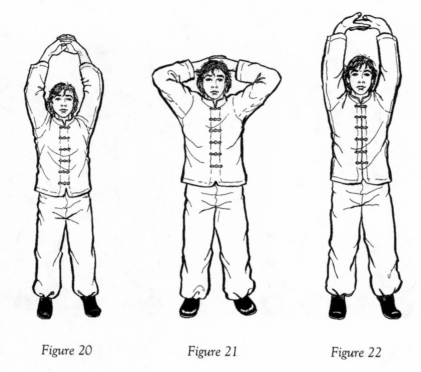

Figure 20   Figure 21   Figure 22

flexible, try standing with the thighs parallel to the ground. Do not stand so low that the knees are strained or collapse inward.

Begin with the hands in fists, rolled inward at chest height, so the back of the hands are facing each other (fig. 23). As you inhale, pull the right fist back toward the right shoulder, with the elbow extended out, forearm parallel to the ground. At the same time, the left hand opens widely as the arm extends straight to the left side, the whole arm parallel to the ground. The left palm is facing outward. To make this exercise more effective, bend the last three fingers of the left hand slightly toward the palm, so that only the index finger and thumb are extended (fig. 24 is a mirror image). Exhale, forming both hands in fists and bringing them back to the starting position in front of the breastbone. Repeat to the other side.

As you open to each side, the head turns and the eyes look toward the extended arm. Whenever the arms return to the center, the head and eyes are facing straight ahead.

Notice how the chest opens as the arms stretch away from each other

Figure 23   *Figure 24*

and how the chest closes when the fists return to the breastbone. This exercise stimulates and strengthens the lungs.

3. Raise Each Arm to Regulate the Spleen

Stand with the feet parallel, shoulder-width apart. Position your left arm overhead, with the back of the hand resting on the crown. The right hand is resting against the side of the right rib cage, with the palm facing down. Push the two hands away from each other, one pushing toward the sky, the other pushing toward the earth (fig. 25 is a mirror image).

Next, with the arms extended, switch them, circling them at the sides of the body, until the back of the right hand is resting on the crown, the left hand facing down and attached to the left side ribs. Again push the hands away, toward earth and sky. Keep repeating from side to side.

It is generally easiest to inhale as the arms stretch away. However, some individuals prefer to coordinate the exhalation with the arm stretch. Both are possible and beneficial. The head and eyes remain facing forward throughout the exercise. There is no need to look up or down toward either hand.

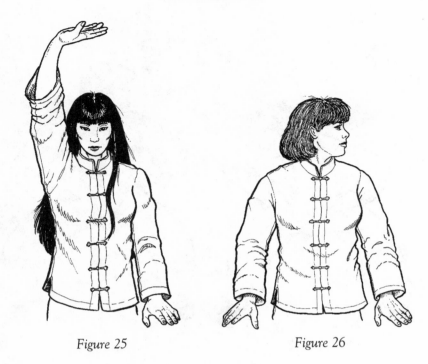

Figure 25   *Figure 26*

As with each of the Eight Brocades, this exercise has an external and an internal aspect. Externally, it stretches the arms and opens and closes the ribs. Internally it compresses and releases the stomach and spleen, gently massaging them and improving their functioning.

4. Looking Behind to Cure Fatigue and Distress

With the arms resting naturally at the sides of the body, palms lifted slightly and facing downward, slowly turn the head from side to side (fig. 26). Don't strain or force the head to turn more than feels comfortable. Do not lift or drop the chin as you turn the head. The eyes can either look in the direction the head is facing, or they can look slightly over the shoulder. That is, if you are turning to the left, you can allow the eyes to look farther to the left and perhaps slightly behind the body. The breath can coordinate however feels natural.

This Brocade is great for getting rid of kinks in the neck muscles. It loosens and strengthens the neck, improves posture and spinal alignment, stimulates cerebral blood circulation, and improves vision.

5. Bending Over, Wagging the Tail to Calm Heart-Fire

We can see from the name of this technique how imaginative the Chinese language can be. The practice is even better than the name.

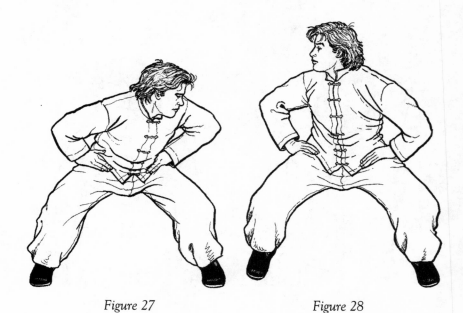

Figure 27   *Figure 28*

There are two ways to practice this Brocade. From a wide, deep horse-riding stance, rest the hands on the thighs, with the thumbs pointing back-ward. Then either:

a) Swing the upper body slowly and smoothly like a pendulum. Keeping the feet planted, turn from the waist toward one thigh. Bend down toward that thigh, exhaling (fig. 27). Swing slowly toward the other thigh, with the body still bent over. Then, as you rise up over that thigh, gradually straight-ening the back, inhale (fig. 28). Continue inhaling as you face the center, re-turning to your starting position. Then repeat, beginning on the other side. Turn toward the other side; exhaling, bend down and swing the body toward the other leg. Inhaling, rise up over that leg and face center.

Or:

b) From the same stance, turn slightly from the waist, exhale as you bend down over one thigh, turn in the bent-over posture only to the center (not to the other thigh, as in option a above). Inhaling, rise up in the center (fig. 29). Then, exhaling, turn to the other side. Still exhaling, bend down on that side, turn the body to the center, and inhale, rising up and straighten-ing. Some practitioners prefer this variation and claim it is more effective.

Figure 29

This exercise banishes excess "fire" caused by worry, stress, emotional disturbances, and overwork. It helps restore balance to the heart and nervous system.

6. Reaching Down to Dissipate Disease

Stand naturally, with the palms resting on your buttocks. As you bend down, exhale and let the hands lightly slide down the backs of the legs, down to the calves, ankles, or as far as you can bend comfortably (fig. 30). The spine is soft and flexible so each vertebra can relax into the bent posture. Then begin to inhale, allowing the palms to move up along the backs of the legs as you resume the straight stance. Continuing to inhale, the hands resting on buttocks, rise up on your toes (fig. 31). For just a moment hold the breath, imagining the body filled with healing qi. Then rest the feet flat on the ground and exhale again toward the toes, palms moving along the backs of the thighs, knees, calves. . . . Repeat several times.

This exercise helps to draw healing qi into the entire upper body. It also stretches the back, stimulates the kidneys, and massages tight hamstrings and calves.

7. Punching with Angry Gaze to Increase Qi and Strength

According to Chinese medicine the eyes and the emotion of anger stimulate the liver, the muscles, and the flow of qi. Staring with an angry

Figure 30   Figure 31

gaze may have been beneficial for ancient Chinese recluses, who probably had low levels of emotional frustration. However, the stress of modern living causes many people to repress or impulsively express anger. Therefore, it may not be healthy for students to cultivate an "angry gaze." Instead of increasing strength, an angry gaze is more likely to make us tense. So let's think of "angry gaze" as "intense" or "focused" gaze. Having an intense gaze while punching stimulates the liver and helps it to purify toxins and spread healing qi more efficiently.

Stand with the feet about three feet apart, knees slightly bent. Your stance is slightly wider and deeper than usual, but it is not the strenuous horse stance of Brocade two or five. The eyes are gazing intensely, as though you are a hunter looking for the deer that will feed your family. Both hands are in fists, palms up, under the shoulders. The elbows are pulled back, behind the body. Punch slowly (no jerky or snapping motion) forward with one fist, the hand rotating as the arm extends. By the time you have finished the punch, the palm has rotated downward. Stop the punch while there is still a little bit of bend in the elbow. Do not lock the joint. Now, as the extended fist draws back, palm up under the shoulder, the other fist rotates and extends out. Keep rotating in this way, one fist out, the other back. Punching fist:

Figure 32

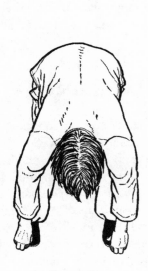

Figure 33

Figure 34

palm down; fist under shoulder: palm up (fig. 32). Let the breath coordinate with the movements however it wishes. Do not force it.

8. Toe Touching to Strengthen the Kidneys and Waist

Stand in a natural shoulder-width stance. As you exhale, slowly bend toward your toes, allowing each vertebra to participate in the bend. Do the movement slowly enough that you can sensitively relax and release areas in your spine that seem to be adhering together or preventing a full, relaxed bend. If you can reach your toes without straining, grasp them and pull your upper body even closer to your legs (fig. 33). DO NOT ATTEMPT THIS IF YOU HAVE A SPINAL INJURY OR CONDITION FOR WHICH BENDING IS INADVISABLE. Once your body has bent as far as is comfortable, spend a few moments breathing naturally. Notice how the front of the body is compressed, the back of the body open. Let yourself breathe with the kidneys. Feel the lower back expanding and releasing as you inhale and exhale.

Now, after your next exhalation, slowly return to a standing position, inhaling on the way up. Let the vertebrae build, one on top of the other. Stand up slowly, sensitively, with awareness. Continuing to inhale, bend gently back into a bowed-back posture (fig. 34). Now, as you briefly hold this posture, return to natural breathing. Feel how now the back is compressed, but the front of the body is open. The lungs easily expand and contract with the breath. Let it happen! Now take an inhalation, and as you exhale, return to a straight posture and continue exhaling down toward your toes. Repeat the technique several times.

This Brocade looks like ordinary toe touching, but it is really quite different, since its intent is to use the external movement to strengthen inner health. In addition to stretching the spine, it works the kidneys, adrenals, and lungs.

BONE MARROW CLEANSING

The Bone Marrow Cleansing (*Xi Sui Jing*) includes healing postures, gentle movements, and concentration techniques to cleanse the marrow of toxins.[2] It is attributed to the fifth-century Buddhist sage Bodhidharma, and is closely associated with the Buddhist monastery he established, the Shao-lin Temple on Mount Song. Bodhidharma is also credited with two other related qigong styles called the Muscle/Tendon Transformation Classic (*Yi Jin Jing*) and Eighteen Lohan qigong (*Shi Ba Lo Han Gong*). Historical research suggests that these systems probably date only to the sixteenth century[3] and may have been attributed to Bodhidharma in order to give them a more authentic-sounding lineage and to confuse several generations of scholars. Many popu-

lar English-language works on qigong maintain the Bodhidharma association. The authors work on the misguided assumption that "if my master said
so, it must be true."

The style of Bone Marrow Cleansing I teach affects more than the
bones. It strengthens the immune system, increases the strength and density
of the bones themselves, stores qi in the dan tian, and stimulates the flow of
qi through the skin and various acupuncture points. Here are the four basic
movements.[4]

1. The Meditating Buddha

Stand in a natural qigong posture with the hands in front of the dan
tian. Line up the palms, so that the center of the hands are about twelve
inches apart, as though holding an energy ball (fig. 35). Slowly raise the ball
up to the level of the chest. Then bend the elbows and move the palms toward each other, until the hands are together in a prayerlike gesture, with
the thumbs resting on the breastbone (fig. 36). While maintaining the posture, focus inward on dan tian breathing. Let the mind become silent and
calm. Keep this stance for a comfortable period of time, generally about two
or three minutes. Then let the hands separate and sink down to the sides.
Relax.

Figure 35

Figure 36

Figure 37

2. The Cosmic Being

Slowly raise the arms up laterally, from the sides of the body, with the elbows slightly bent and the palms facing forward. When the arms reach shoulder height, turn the palms outward, facing away from the body, the fingers pointing toward the sky (fig. 37). Holding this posture, imagine that your body is filling the universe: your head touches the heavens, your feet reach to the center of the earth. Your right arm is extended infinitely to the right, your left arm infinitely to the left. You are the cosmic, primal being. Instead of the universe being inside your body ("Meditating Buddha"), here your body has expanded into the universe. Additionally, imagine that the pores of your skin are open. There is lightness, an openness, a porosity to the entire body. Universal healing qi can flow easily through you. Forget about your breath, just let it go as it wishes.

Maintain this focus for about two or three minutes, then bring your mind to the dan tian. Feel your breath moving within, let your spirit return to body-awareness. Then float the arms down to the sides and relax.

3. Wash the Marrow with One Hand

Your left hand slowly floats up behind the body, until the center of the back of the hand is resting comfortably on the lower back, opposite the

Figure 38a   Figure 38b

navel. You have lined up your rear lao gong acupoint on the hand with the ming men (gate of life) on the back (fig. 38a). This improves the functioning of the adrenals and kidneys. As your left hand moves into place, your right hand is rising up from the right side of the body until the palm is about six inches over the crown of the head, facing downward (fig. 38b). Feel the connection between the center of the right palm (the lao gong point) with the point on the apex of the head (the bai hui point). It is as if you are feeling your own energy field, the qi emanating from the crown. This focus helps to balance all yang and yin energy in the body. The bai hui acupuncture point is the point where the yang energy of the back meets the yin energy of the front of the body. This is why the crown point is known as bai hui, literally "hundred meetings." It is where multiple forms of energy converge.

Hold this stance for only a moment, just long enough to feel a pleasant stimulus at the lower back and crown. Then slowly lower the upper hand down the front of the body. As your right hand floats down, imagine that pure healing qi is flowing through the bone marrow. If an image helps you to focus, you can visualize the qi as a healing steam or white light. Qi moves through the bones of the skull and face, down through the vertebrae in the neck; it flows through the collarbones, shoulder blades, ribs, down the spinal column. Your hand is still floating down, ever so slowly. Qi washes through the marrow of the hips, the thighbones, knees, lower legs, feet. As your hand relaxes at the side, the hand at the lower back releases and also floats down. Now see the impure, noxious qi washing out of the feet, sending it at least three feet under the ground. I like to imagine that this unneeded qi is becoming compost or transforming into light. (I believe that impure qi can create psychic, energetic pollution unless we dispose of it properly.)

Now you are ready to switch to the other side. Your right hand slowly rests on the lower back, center of the hand on the spine, opposite the navel. The left arm rises up until the palm faces the crown: lao gong energetically connected with bai hui. Float the left hand down the front as you wash the marrow. Send the impure qi out the feet. Relax both hands at the sides for a moment before switching sides again.

Keep washing the marrow alternately with one hand, then the other, anywhere from three to five times with each hand. There is no need to coordinate the breath with any particular part of the exercise. Breathe naturally. Relax and center yourself for a moment before moving on to the last stage.

4. Wash the Marrow with Both Hands

Raise both hands up the front midline of the body, palms facing up (fig. 39). As the hands reach the breastbone, turn the palms away and push them overhead. The arms are stretched overhead, palms facing the sky (fig. 40).

Figure 39   Figure 40

Hold this stance for about ten seconds, imagining that you are like a tree, with deep roots and tall branches, connecting sky and earth. Then turn the palms to face the crown and lower them only slightly, until they are about six inches over the crown. The hands are not touching each other. The fingers of the right and left are separated by a few inches. While holding this position for a moment, feel the energy of your crown, your "aura." As in "Wash the Marrow with One Hand," you are connecting the lao gong points, this time of both hands, with the bai hui point. Then float both arms down the front of the body, imagining the pure, healing qi washing through the bone marrow, exactly as in "Wash the Marrow with One Hand." As the hands reach the sides, the impure qi is pushed out of the feet, under the earth. Relax. "Wash the Marrow with Both Hands" is done only once, closing the set.

THE FIVE ANIMAL FROLICS

The Five Animal Frolics (*Wu Qin Xi*) are graceful, dancelike exercises modeled after the Crane, Bear, Monkey, Deer, and Tiger. They are a complete qigong system, developing strength, grace, flexibility, balance, and an abundance of healing qi. The Five Animals are *medical qigong* because they circulate the qi and improve health. They are also *martial qigong* because they encouraged the development of various Animal martial arts: Crane Style, Tiger Style, etc. And the Frolics are *spiritual qigong* because they teach harmony with the animals and all of nature.

The Five Animal Frolics is the most ancient qigong system still practiced today. It is also one of the oldest continuously practiced healing exercise systems in the world. The Frolics were created by Hua Tuo (A.D. 110–207), often called "the Father of Chinese Medicine." The theories of diagnosis, treatment, and prognosis attributed to him are still considered the foundation of traditional Chinese medicine. Hua Tuo's *Classic of the Central Viscera*[5] was selected by the Chinese Ministry of Health and Hygiene as one of the eleven most important premodern works on Chinese medicine, out of a library of more than ten thousand. According to Daoist legend, Hua Tuo received this text as well as instruction in the Five Animals from two recluses living in a cave on Mount Gong Yi.

Hua Tuo's two disciples, Wu Pu and Fan A, following their master's medical advice, lived to age ninety and past one hundred, respectively. Hua Tuo once told Wu Pu, "The body should be exercised, but not to excess. Exercise improves digestion and keeps the meridians clear of obstructions. In this way, the body will remain free of illness. A door hinge does not rust if it is frequently used. Therefore the ancient sages practiced dao-yin. . . .

I have created a dao-yin method called the Five Animal Frolics. It can eliminate sickness and strengthen the root."[6]

The modern resurgence of interest in the practice of the Five Animals is largely due to the influence of a famous Beijing actress, Madame Guo Lin (1906–1984). After an eight-year battle with uterine cancer, doctors pronounced her inoperable and gave her six months to live. Madame Guo began to practice the Five Animal Frolics two hours a day at dawn. Six months later, she was in remission.[7] In the 1970s, almost thirty years after her fatal prognosis, Madame Guo became a national hero in her campaign to introduce qigong into hospitals and clinics throughout China. She wrote the first book specifically devoted to qigong for cancer.

Another very strong influence on the spread of the Five Animal Frolics is qigong master and doctor of Chinese medicine Hu Yao-zhen. Hu taught qigong to many of the best present-day instructors, including the famed Taiji Quan Master, Feng Zhi-qiang. The Five Animal Frolics Hu describes in his book, *Wu Qin Xi*,[8] is almost identical to the style I learned from Dan Farber, a student of retired Hong Kong master Qin Xu. Dr. Hu's book is probably the best work on the subject in the Chinese language. One of his students, Jiao Guorui, learned the Five Animals from Dr. Hu in the 1950s and includes significant portions of *Wu Qin Xi* in his English-language work *Qigong Essentials for Health Promotion*.[9] Excellent translations of the principles of the Five Animal Frolics (again from Hu Yao-zhen) can be found in the writings of a Western qigong master, Paul Gallagher.[10]

I will describe the practice of the two foundation exercises of the Five Animal Frolics: the Crane and Bear. The Crane is the symbol of meditative stillness and longevity. In Chinese mythology, the crane is the companion of Shou-lao, the God of Longevity. Daoists say that enlightened sages ride to heaven on the back of a crane. The Bear is a symbol of strength, power, and healing wisdom. In ancient China, the shaman-healers wore bear masks and may have imitated the stepping of the bear in ritual dance.

The Crane and Bear are the yang and yin of the Five Animals. The Crane is light, relaxed, excellent for the heart and to keep the body cool in summer. The Bear is heavy, strong, stimulates the kidneys, and warms the body in winter. Practice both of them during the same workout. This will keep yang and yin, fire and water, in balance. The Crane and Bear can be practiced safely and with excellent health benefits even if one does not know the other three.

When you practice the animals, do not imitate the animals, become them! Ideally, one could observe the animals (from a safe distance) in their natural environment and practice in that environment. I love to practice the Crane by the edge of a lake and the Bear in the forest. Be careful, however; if there is a bear nearby she might think you are a relative! At the very least, visit the zoo and see how the animals actually move and behave. A monk asked a Zenmaster if a dog has the Buddha-nature. A qigong practitioner asks, "Does a Buddha have the dog-nature, the bear-nature, the crane-nature?" An enlightened being feels connected with all "creature teachers."[11] There is an ancient biblical midrash (commentary) that asks, Why is the plural used in "Let *us* make man in our own image"? The midrash answers its own question, "The 'us' refers to all of the animals, which were created first." The spirits of the animals helped to create the first human.

The Crane

All Crane Frolic techniques begin from the Crane Stance. Maintaining the principles of qigong posture, stand with the heels together, a forty-five-degree angle between the feet. The knees are only slightly bent. The body is tall and open, like a great pine tree. The eyes gaze long, into the distance. Throughout the Crane the body should also have a lightness and porosity like a cloud. You should feel finely and delicately balanced. A Crane can stand for hours, balanced on one toothpick leg, completely still, as though

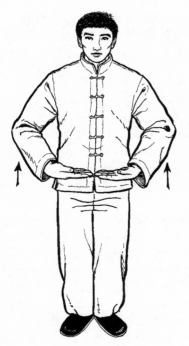

Figure 41a

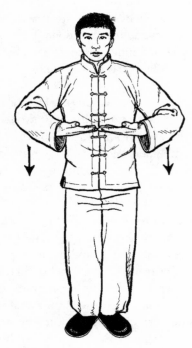

Figure 41b

Figure 42   Figure 43

asleep, yet it is perfectly alert. When a fish swims by, whoosh! it is caught. In the Chinese language the word for contemplation, *guan*, was originally a picture of a crane.

Crane movements are practiced at a relaxed, slow, and even pace, as though swimming in the air. The Crane is like a meditative dance with six distinct techniques. Repeat each technique nine times, then pause for a moment and move on to the next.

1. Standing Crane: Hold your hands palms up just in front of the dan tian with your fingertips almost touching. As you inhale, raise the lower arms and hands up to the lower tip of the breastbone (fig. 41a). Be careful to keep the shoulders relaxed; don't raise the shoulders or chest. As you exhale, keeping the palms facing upward, lower the hands down to the dan tian. Continue, inhaling, hands raised to chest. Exhale, and drop hands to lower abdomen (fig. 41b).

2. Crane's Beak: Hold the arms out at the sides at shoulder height, palms facing down (fig. 42). There is a straight line along the shoulder, upper arm, forearm, wrist, and hand. The elbows are slightly bent. As you inhale, raise the arms about six inches higher. At the same time, let the fingertips of each hand touch together, forming a point, the crane's beak (fig. 43). As you exhale, relax open the crane's beak and float the arms down to the starting position, arms and hands outstretched at shoulder height.

3. Crane Flaps Wings: Begin the same as Crane's Beak: arms to the sides at shoulder height, palms down. As you exhale, lower the arms until the

Figure 44

hands are the height of the waist (fig. 44). As you inhale, raise the arms back to shoulder height. The hands stay open the whole time, swimming gracefully through the air. After the last repetition go straight into Crane Squatting.

4. Crane Squatting: We continue from the end of Crane Flaps Wings.

Figure 45

Figure 46   *Figure 47*

The hands are resting at the level of the waist. As you inhale, slowly squat. Let the heels lift from the ground; the knees bend and bow out to the sides. You are going into as deep a squat as comfortable. At the same time, lift the arms and turn the palms up. The arms rise until they are as high as the shoulders (fig. 45).

Now, as you exhale, slowly stand up. At the same time, the hands turn palms down and float down to waist height. Repeat.

5. One-Legged Crane: Begin with the hands palms down at waist level. While exhaling, squat and reach down with the arms, as though embracing the knees (fig. 46). As you inhale, stand back up, shift the weight to one leg, and cross the arms in front of the chest, palms facing the body. Still inhaling, raise one knee up in the air until the thigh is parallel to the ground. At the same time circle the arms overhead and out to the sides, until they are extended laterally at shoulder height. Hold this balanced position for a few seconds (fig. 47). Then again slowly exhale, go into a squat, and embrace the knees. Inhale, going back to the erect posture, hands crossed. One leg lifting, the arms continuing overhead and out to the sides of the body. Hold for a few seconds and repeat.

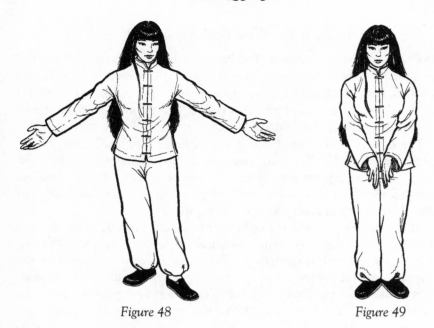

Figure 48   Figure 49

6. Crane Spreads Wings: Begin in the standing posture, heels touching, arms at the sides. As you inhale, draw both arms slightly back behind the body. One foot takes a step out and touches the ground lightly on the toe. All of the weight is on the rear foot (fig. 48). Now, with the exhalation, bring the extended foot back, balance the weight evenly on both feet, and bring the arms to the front of the body, with the back of the hands facing each other (fig. 49). Then, again inhale, reach out with the other leg, touching the toe, arms behind the body (not too far, don't strain the back!). Exhale, heels together, weight even, arms rolling in toward the front of the body, back of the hands facing. Keep repeating side to side.

Make sure that each toe-step is light and delicate, as though you are not bending a blade of grass.

Now that you have finished the basic Crane Frolic, stand in quiet meditation for a moment, then take several steps, walking about for a minute or two. What has changed? Most students feel as if they are as light as a feather and that their arms and legs have grown a few inches longer.

The benefits of the Crane include relaxation, balance, loosening and opening the joints, strengthening the heart and lungs, cooling the body, shrinking inflammation, and relieving congestion.

The Bear

The Crane is light and ethereal. The Bear is heavy and rooted. Will you for-give a playful stereotype? In the United States I like to teach the Crane in New York City, to lift students out of the rat race and paranoia of crowded streets and busy subways. I emphasize the Bear in California: a good antidote to excessive sunshine and alfalfa sprouts.

The essence of the Bear Frolic is to feel sunken, stable, heavy, ponder-ous. According to Hu Yao-zhen, your movements should also be easy and fluid, "as though you have no bones." Lightness, agility, and alertness are concealed within. This is consistent with the nature of the bear, who can amble about slowly or charge with surprising speed.

The Bear Stance, used throughout the exercises below, is a wide, low horse stance, with the feet turned forty-five degrees out. Advanced practi-tioners can stand with the thighs parallel to the ground. Pregnant or men-struating women should not attempt the deep posture. Rather, find a stance that is comfortable and causes no strain. The eyes have a quiet, relaxed gaze. Qi is sunk in the dan tian. As in the Crane, the movements flow one into the other with only a slight pause between techniques. Each technique is re-peated nine times to each side.

1. Bear Turns: While in the Bear Stance, hold the arms at the sides of the body, elbows bent to ninety degrees, hands facing upward at the height of

Figure 50

Figure 51

Figure 52   Figure 53

the ears (fig. 50). Slowly turn from your waist to the left, exhaling (fig. 51). Be careful to turn only from the waist, do not shift the weight or turn the hips or thighs. The stance is fixed and immobile. Turn as far as you can comfortably, without strain. Then, as you inhale, return to center. Now exhale and slowly turn to the other side. Inhale, face center. Keep turning side to side, coordinating with the breath. The hips are fixed, the waist is turning. It is this differentiation of waist from hip that massages the internal organs and benefits the kidneys. After the last repetition, go straight into Bear Pushes Behind.

2. Bear Pushes Behind: This time, as you exhale, turning to the left, push the left hand out behind you, keeping it at shoulder height, palm facing away, fingers toward the sky (fig. 52). As you inhale, face the front and bring the left hand back to the original bear posture, elbow bent to ninety degrees, palm facing up. Then turn to the right, exhaling and pushing the right palm out and away from the shoulder, fingertips pointed up. Inhale back to center. Repeat side to side.

3. Bear Pushes Down: Continue the basic movement of Bear Turns. This time, as you turn to one side, exhaling, push one hand down by the hip (fig. 53). For instance, exhaling, turning to the left, push the left hand down behind you, until the palm is facing down near the left hip. Inhale, facing center and bringing the hand back to the starting posture: both hands palm

Figure 54   Figure 55

up at ear height, as though holding a wooden plank overhead. Then exhale, turning to the other side, the other hand pushing down by the hip. Inhale, back to center.

4. Bear Offering: Bring the hands to rest on the lower chest, just below the breastbone, palms facing up (fig. 54). As you exhale and turn the waist to the left, extend the left hand, palm up, away from and at the height of the shoulder. The right hand extends slightly out to the left and rests palm up on the middle of the left forearm (fig. 55). Inhale, face center, both hands returning to the chest, palms facing the sky. Then turn to the right, the right hand reaching out, palm up, until it is extended laterally, at shoulder height. The left hand is palm up and resting on the middle of the right forearm. Inhale, back to center.

5. Bear Push: Begin as above, both palms facing upward under the chest. This time, as you turn and exhale, push both hands out to the side. The palms are facing away. The hands push on a plane, as though both palms are resting on a wall at your side (fig. 56). Inhale, face center, hands returning to the chest. Exhale, push to the other side.

As you finish this set, resume a comfortable, shoulder-width stance and let the hands rest at the sides. Stand in quiet meditation, then saunter about for a minute. Notice how different you feel now compared with how you felt

Figure 56

after the Crane. What effect has the Bear had on your standing and breathing, on the weight of your body, on different parts of the body? It is common to feel as though the body is so grounded that you have become a moving mountain. You may also notice that the lower back and kidney region are pleasantly warm.

The Bear should be practiced all year. However, its benefits will be most appreciated in winter. The Bear warms the body, improves kidney and adrenal function, deepens the breath, and greatly strengthens the legs and waist.

Readers can find further information about the Animal Frolics by consulting materials listed in the Qigong Resources. The Five Animal Frolics continues with complex Crane and Bear walking exercises and frolics based on the monkey, deer, and tiger. The Monkey has a light, agile quality and helps to loosen the joints. The Deer stretches and twists the spine and hips, creating flexibility and grace. The Tiger is fierce and powerful, strengthening the muscles and tendons.

TAIJI RULER

The Taiji Ruler (no relationship with Taiji Quan) is a sacred and secret qigong first made public in 1954 by Master Zhao Zhong-dao. It is called the Ruler (*Chi*, sometimes spelled *Chih*) because during the basic exercise the hands are held about a foot apart.[12] The Taiji Ruler system consists of gentle rocking and swaying movements that build qi in the feet, the dan tian, and the hands. It can be used for self-healing or as a preparation for any form of massage therapy or therapeutic touch. Your hands will feel warm, vibrating, full of healing power after a few minutes' practice. In the United States, several bizarre variations of the Ruler have become popular, many with little relationship to Zhao's original techniques. The method I present has been synthesized from direct students of Zhao, several second- or third-generation students, and then corroborated by comparison with Zhao's original Chinese text.

The Ruler has a fascinating and venerable history. The Taiji Ruler is one of several forms of qigong attributed to the tenth-century Daoist recluse Chen Xi-yi.[13] Chen lived on Mount Hua, the Daoist sacred mountain in Shenxi Province. The Jade Spring Temple at the foot of the mountain was designed by Chen and contains a statue of him. The monks still recount a legend that after Chen died, his bones glowed with red light. A visitor once stole the shinbone. This so infuriated the monks that they moved his remains to a secret location, never again revealed.

For many years Chen was friends with a young visitor named Zhao Kuang-yin. Zhao loved the beauty of the mountains and frequently journeyed to Mount Hua to join Chen in two of his favorite pastimes: playing Chinese chess (wei qi) and practicing qigong. Years later, when Zhao rose to power as the first emperor of the Song Dynasty, he taught Master Chen's qigong methods to his children. Chen's Taiji Ruler method was maintained within the imperial family, passed down from generation to generation as a precious heirloom and secret to good health. Toward the middle of the nineteenth century, the art was transmitted to a direct descendant, Zhao Zhong-dao (1844–1962). Just before Zhao's grandmother died at age 108, she told her twenty-two-year-old grandson, "Although the Taiji Ruler cannot make you an immortal, it can certainly rid you of disease and increase your life span. Do not overlook it."

Zhao kept up the family practice, and in 1954 he founded in Beijing "The Gentle Art of Taiji Ruler Health Society," the first school to publicly teach the Taiji Ruler. The Society was like a university teaching hospital. Scientists and qigong practitioners from all over China came to learn the art. Patients with debilitating and chronic diseases arrived for treatment. The Society was very successful treating digestive and nervous system disorders, insomnia, high blood pressure, and numerous other problems that had failed to respond to medical treatment.

According to Master Zhao's biography, when Zhao passed on at age 118, "He did not have the appearance of a flickering lamp. On the contrary, he had a child's complexion and silvery hair. His face exuded a healthy reddish glow and he could chat for hours. One glance and you knew this was an exceptional human being. . . . His hearing and vision were sharp. He had strong teeth, unwrinkled skin, and he slept and ate like a young man."[14]

The Ruler is a complex and complete system of qi development that includes numerous solo exercises, exercises with training equipment, and two-person routines. Almost all teachers of the Ruler begin with the same foundation exercises.

The Basic Rock

Stand with your feet about 10.5 inches apart. The left foot is pointing straight ahead. The right foot is at a forty-five-degree angle. The left foot is about five or six inches in front of the right, so that the toes of the right are on a straight line with the left instep (fig. 57). Bend both knees until, as you look down, the front knee is directly over the toes, hiding them from view.

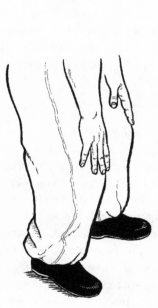

Figure 57

Figure 58

Now lean slightly forward, letting the hands slide down the front of the thighs until your fingertips are almost touching the top of the kneecap. The body is in a stooped-over posture. Do not slouch the shoulders or bow the upper back. Rather, bend from the waist. This allows you to maintain a straight line from tailbone to crown. This is the Taiji Ruler Stance (fig. 58) and is the foundation of The Basic Rock and The Basic Ruler, which follow.

Keeping the left hand on the lower thigh, draw the heel of the right hand into the right *kua*, the crease between the thigh and hip (the inguinal area). The fingers of both hands are facing down.

While keeping this position, begin the Basic Rock. Rock the body ever so slightly to the front. As you do so, raise the rear heel an inch or two in the air. Then rock slightly back, lifting the front toe slightly off the ground. Keep rocking, back and forth, like a rocking chair. Find a way to rock back and forth with almost no shifting of weight, as if your body can move only as a whole, in one piece. One foot is always flat on the ground. Front toe up, rear foot flat. Rear heel up, front foot flat. Do this for a few minutes. Then switch sides.

Right foot in front, pointing straight. Left foot forty-five degrees. Feet separated by about 10.5 inches. Right heel in line with the left instep. Bend the knees until your knees cover the toes. Then bend the back until the fingertips almost reach the kneecaps. (Of course, in the bent-over posture you *can* see your feet.) The back is straight. Keep your right hand above the knee but rest the left hand on the left kua. Now begin rocking. Rear heel up, front foot flat. Front toe up, rear foot flat. Practice for a few minutes. Then go directly to the next exercise. They should be performed in sequence.

The Basic Ruler

Now switch sides again. Go into the Ruler Stance. This time the hands are held a few inches in front of the navel, about ten inches apart, as though holding an energy ball. The palms and fingers are gently spread open. The centers of the palms are lined up. Begin the Basic Rock. As you rock to the front, rear heel lifting, dip the hands slightly down, about three inches below the navel. As you rock back, front toe lifting, the hands lift up and circle inward. You are carrying the energy ball in a circle, down, away, up, and back, coordinated with your rocking (figs. 59, 60). The navel is the center of your circle. As you rock back and forth, the ball is circled about three inches above the navel and three inches below it. Do thirty-six repetitions.

Then try it on the other side. Circle the hands in exactly the same way. Rock to the front, the ball drops. As you rock back, the momentum of the

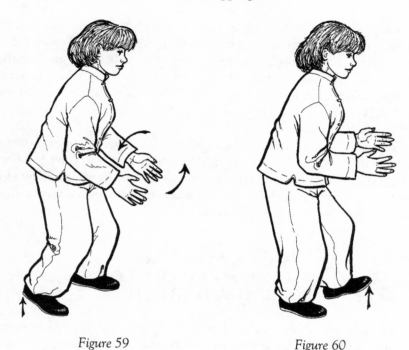

Figure 59   *Figure 60*

backward movement causes the ball to effortlessly lift up and draw back toward the body. Repeat thirty-six times.

Make sure that the breath is relaxed and natural as you practice the Ruler. Don't force or stop the breath. Just let it go. To close the exercise, gently stop rocking. Let your body settle into stillness. Then slowly straighten the legs until the knees are only slightly bent. Then very gently straighten the back. Relax all the way down to your feet.

In just five minutes, the Ruler gives a powerful workout. The Ruler exercise stimulates the Bubbling Well acupuncture points in the feet, the points that feed the kidneys and bones with earth-qi. It also puts a stimulating pressure on the ming men point on the lower back, opposite the navel, increasing overall vitality. The bent-over posture feels almost fetal and compresses breath in the dan tian, increasing its store of qi. Provided you are not bending excessively and the back is straight, long, and open, you should still be able to breathe easily. The legs, waist, and back become stronger.

However, if you have a lower back problem, such as arthritis or a damaged disk, you may need to practice this exercise without inclining the back. If you are overweight, have high blood pressure, are menstruating or pregnant, practice from a plumb erect posture with the knees only slightly bent to avoid putting pressure on the dan tian. If you have a disability that makes it painful or impossible to stand, then sit in a chair and practice the hand-circling movements of the Basic Ruler without the toe-heel rocking. This Seated Ruler has similar, though less dramatic, energetic effects on the body's qi. Naturally, it does not have the same physical effects of strengthening the back and legs.

Remember, if you have any doubts about the advisability of this or any other qigong, check with a health professional. Even if you can't practice, maybe you can inspire your physician to try it. (If your health-care provider already knows everything there is to know about health, please suggest that he affix himself to the altar at Church.)

ARM SWINGING: THREE MINUTES TO BETTER HEALTH

This method is probably a recent innovation, yet it is so simple, gentle, effective, and popular that I include it here among the "classics." Arm Swinging gives a quick charge-up and is an excellent way to improve blood and qi circulation and to begin any kind of exercise routine. If you go early in the morning to a park near any Chinatown in North America, you are likely to see seniors standing in place and swinging their arms back and forth without stopping, sometimes for as long as five minutes. Arm Swinging is the most popular qigong for the elderly.

Stand with the feet parallel, shoulder-width apart, your whole body in a relaxed qigong posture. The arms are relaxed at the sides. Breathe naturally; don't worry about or focus too much on the breath. Throughout this qigong, the toes gently curl inward as though gripping the ground. At the same time, imagine that the heels are pressing into the ground. You will feel as though the arch of the foot, the Bubbling Well point, is lifting up, creating a kind of suction that draws qi into the body.

Now, gently swing the arms front and back, like a pendulum. Not too big a movement, perhaps a foot or two front and back, less if you have bursitis or painful shoulders. Find a comfortable, fluid rhythm. You will find that once you start, the movement seems to continue of itself, effortlessly. Continue for three to five minutes. Then slowly and gradually make the swinging movements smaller and smaller, until they settle into stillness, like a bouncing rubber ball settling into the ground. Release any gripping in the toes or heels. Stand for a minute enjoying the feeling of greater aliveness.

HONORABLE MENTION:
A THOUSAND CHANGES,
TEN THOUSAND TRANSFORMATIONS

All of the styles of active qigong described in this chapter are technically classified as *soft qigong (rou gong)* or *inner qigong (nei gong)*, because they use minimal strength and emphasize the gentle and gradual cultivation of health and awareness. Other excellent styles of soft qigong that are becoming popular in the West include the Swimming Dragon, Soaring Crane, and Coiling Silk.

In contrast to soft qigong, hard qigong (*ying gong*, also called external qigong, *wai gong*) consists of vigorous methods of conditioning and strengthening the body. In China, hard qigong is often practiced by athletes engaged in the martial arts or other contact sports. Qigong does not disparage muscular or aerobic conditioning. It only warns that this not replace the deep internal healing methods.[15]

All Chinese martial arts emphasize qi development at the higher levels of training. But the *inner martial arts (nei jia quan)* teach numerous hard and soft qigong training techniques from the beginning. The three most popular inner martial arts are Xing Yi Quan, Bagua Zhang, and Taiji Quan (also spelled T'ai Chi Ch'uan).[16] All three include both freestyle, full speed sparring training as well as precisely choreographed solo exercises that can be practiced as qigong.

The inner martial arts are becoming increasingly popular in the United States. Teachers of each of these arts can be found in most major cities. Martial arts tournaments generally include competition categories for each style. Magazine articles describing Xing Yi Quan, Bagua Zhang, or Taiji Quan appear frequently in the martial arts magazines. There are also specialized journals devoted to each of the three arts.

The inner martial arts are far too complex to learn accurately from a book. However, for a more complete appreciation of qigong practice, it is important to at least be familiar with their major characteristics.

Xing Yi Quan

The name Xing Yi Quan means Form (Xing) and Intent (Yi) Fighting, suggesting the integration of body and mind. Although legend traces the art to General Yueh Fei (960–1127), the documented founder is a man named Ji Long-feng, who learned it from a Daoist hermit in the middle of the seventeenth century.

Of the three inner martial arts, Xing Yi Quan is the most martial in

appearance. Xing Yi Quan consists of linear strikes, in which the entire body
is driven forward like a battering ram. The five basic strikes are based on the
Five Elements and have healing side effects. For instance, the metal strike
chops like a metal ax and benefits the lungs. The wood strike looks like a
shooting arrow and is generated from the liver area. Water drills and spirals
into the opponent in an uppercut, with power rising from the lower back and
kidneys. Fire shoots explosively from the chest, like a cannonball, and stimulates the heart. Earth, for the spleen, is a side-to-side, lateral strike directed
to an opponent's side ribs. The Xing Yi Quan system also includes twelve
animal-like movements: the Dragon, Tiger, Monkey, Horse, Lizard, Chicken,
Hawk, Sparrow, Phoenix, Snake, Eagle, and Bear.

Xing Yi books in the Chinese language are filled with sound advice on
qigong: the importance of relaxation, sinking qi to the dan tian, natural
breathing, postural alignment, etc. Xing Yi qigong also includes standing,
breathing, and range-of-motion exercises similar to those found in the
qigong classics.[17]

Bagua Zhang

Bagua Zhang is the most mysterious of the inner martial arts. The movements are circular, coiling, spiraling, like a dragon or snake. The name Bagua
Zhang means Eight Direction Palm, and includes elusive, swift changes of
posture and direction. It was probably originally practiced as a series of palm
strikes, blocks, and evasive maneuvers around eight wooden posts. When applied in combat, the Bagua fighter spirals around the opponent, striking,
trapping, locking, or throwing him.

Bagua Zhang is well-known for its unique qigong training technique,
known as "walking the circle." The student walks in a circle while holding
various postures. The gait is extremely narrow, as though walking on a circular tightrope. Every aspect of the posture is choreographed with extreme
precision: the angle of the feet, the position of the elbows, the amount of
twist in the waist. All of these elements help to cultivate strength, flexibility,
and qi.

We know little about the origins of Bagua Zhang. The first references to
the art occur at the end of the eighteenth century. The founder, Dong Hai-
chuan (1798–1897), supposedly studied the art for eleven years from two
Daoists in Mount Omei, Sichuan Province. Dong kept the art to himself until commanded to demonstrate before Prince Su, a relative of the Qing
Dynasty emperor. When Dong defeated the Prince's champion boxer, the
head of his Royal Guard, Dong became quite well-known at court.

The most entertaining story of Dong concerns his death. When his students attempted to raise his coffin, they couldn't budge it. It was so heavy that it seemed bolted to the ground. As they tried to lift it again, they heard a voice from inside the casket saying, "As I always told you, none of you has achieved even a tenth of my skill." With that Dong *really* died; the casket became light and was carried to the funeral.

Taiji Quan

Among the three inner martial arts Taiji Quan is by far the most popular. The best-known styles of Taiji Quan, called the Yang Family and Wu Family Styles, include relaxed and slow-moving exercises, one posture flowing into the next without break, like a stream. The other, more ancient style, Chen Family, consists of dynamic changing rhythms, with more obvious martial applications. The Chen Family Style includes slow storing of energy (yin) followed by dramatic explosions of power (yang). It has been compared to the ocean, with crashing waves and slowly retreating tides.

Taiji Quan is practiced by millions of Chinese every day and by thousands of Americans. The name Taiji means "Undifferentiated Unity." Quan means boxing or martial art. Taiji is a philosophical concept referring to the harmonizing of yin and yang. If yin is the shady slope of the mountain and yang the sunny slope, then Taiji is the peak where they meet. In ancient Daoist texts, Taiji can also mean the Polestar. Again, this connotes the balance of yin and yang. The Polestar is the unmoving pivot around which the constellations seem to rotate: stillness within motion, yin balanced by yang. The Taiji Quan exercise cultivates these qualities of balance and harmony.

Taiji Quan is often attributed to a Daoist monk named Zhang San-feng, who supposedly lived almost a thousand years ago. However, Zhang is probably a fabrication of spirit mediums who channeled his biography hundreds of years after his supposed death. The documented history of Taiji Quan actually begins in the sixteenth century with a general named Qi Ji-guang (1528–1587). General Qi (not to be confused with the similar-sounding word "qi" used in qigong) defended the Chinese against seafaring invaders by feigning weakness, enticing the enemy to enter more deeply into Chinese territory. Then his army would massively and decisively counterattack. In General Qi's *Boxing Classic*, this strategy became the basis for hand-to-hand combat. He called his art *rou shu*, the gentle art (*jujitsu* in Japanese). Yield out of the way of an attack, respect the opponent's opinion. If he wants to go a certain direction, avoid the blow and help him along! With the enemy off balance, your own attack will be much more effective.

The martial postures described in the *Boxing Classic* became the basis for Taiji Quan. A contemporary of General Qi, named Chen Wang-ting, incorporated most of these postures into the first Taiji Quan form. Chen considered Taiji Quan primarily a martial art. However, it is also likely that Chen was influenced by Daoist qigong and meditation techniques. We know that Chen enjoyed reading a difficult and secret text on Daoist meditation, the *Yellow Court Canon*. He may have intended the Taiji Quan exercise to be a kind of meditation in motion: martial art, qigong, and meditation all rolled into one. In recent years the healing aspect of Taiji Quan has become very well-known. Many students are completely unaware of its martial and military origins.

I have often been asked if qigong is form of Taiji Quan. It is just the opposite. Taiji Quan can be considered a form of qigong. The solo exercise follows all of the guidelines for qigong posture and breathing. It shares with *Yi Quan* Standing Meditation a strong emphasis on developing a particular qigong skill, *peng jing*, commonly translated "ward-off power." Peng jing means that any particular part of the body or the body as a whole has a buoyant fullness, capable of rebounding incoming force. The body is filled with qi in the same way that a basketball is filled with air, the force evenly distributed across the rounded surface. When an object hits the ball, it bounces back. Of course, the ball must be firmly rooted, connected into the ground, so that there is a base from which the rebound can occur. In the martial arts, peng jing means that one can discharge an opponent with little expenditure of energy. Peng jing is also healing because it can prevent or lessen injury from any kind of impact.

Taiji Quan is a whole body qigong, encouraging free and unobstructed circulation of qi. According to Taiji Quan instructor Stuart Olson's work, *The Intrinsic Energies of T'ai Chi Ch'uan*, "The idea of 'free circulation' is to permeate all the bones and flesh, every minute cranny and crevice, with not only ch'i [qi], but blood as well. This is what the Chinese call 'nourishing life' (*yang sheng*)."[18]

CHAPTER THIRTEEN

An-Mo Gong:
Self-Healing Massage

All truths wait in all things,
They neither hasten their own delivery nor
*   resist it.*
They do not need the obstetric forceps of the
*   surgeon,*
The insignificant is as big to me as any,
(What is less or more than a touch?)
    —WALT WHITMAN, "SONG OF MYSELF"

Self-massage has been an integral part of qigong from the most ancient times.[1] Lightly chafing and warming the skin over various vital centers, acupoints, or sore muscles stimulates the qi and relieves congestion. Practice self-massage from either a standing or seated position.

ROUTINE 1: YOUTHFUL COMPLEXION
AND SHARP SENSES

Practice each of these techniques ten times.

Rub your hands together to generate warmth. Then lightly circle the palms over the face. Don't forget to run your fingers through your scalp.

Next, chafe one palm back and forth, right and left, across the forehead. Massage away those worry lines and wrinkles!

Place the middle finger of each hand on either side of the mouth. Now run these fingers up along the sides of the nose, all the way to the hairline. Then bring them back down along the sides of the nose to the mouth. Keep going up and down. This is excellent for the sinuses and has a healing effect on the large intestine.

Close your eyes. Use either the middle fingers or the knuckles of the thumbs to lightly circle around the eyes, pressing into the bone that surrounds the eyes. Do not press on the eyes themselves! The hands are each making opposite circles, one clockwise, one counterclockwise. After ten circles, reverse the directions of each hand. Do this movement slowly and with moderate pressure, enough to create a pleasant feeling of stimulation, but certainly not so much that there is pain. When you finish, rub the hands together until they are warm. Then place the palms over your closed eyes. Let yourself enjoy the warmth, quiet, and darkness for a few minutes. Then you can open your eyes again.

Lightly stimulate the gums by tapping around your mouth and cheeks with the fingertips. Imagine healing qi permeating your gums and teeth.

Place the back of one hand under your chin. Gently rub your hand right and left, moving from one side of your jawbone to the other. This can improve circulation, helping to prevent or eliminate a double chin. It also strengthens the immune system by improving qi flow in the lymph glands.

Next, gently knead the earlobes between the thumb and index fingers. According to acupuncture theory, points affecting every part of the body can be found on the ears.

Warm your hands again, rubbing them together. Place the palms lightly over the ears with your fingers pointed toward the back of the head. While holding the ears, tap the fingertips on the back of your head. You will understand why this ear-healing technique is called Tapping the Heavenly Drum.

Close the facial massage by repeating the first technique, circling the hands over the entire face and scalp, until the face feels glowing and warm.

ROUTINE 2: WHOLE-BODY QI MASSAGE

This is an excellent sequence to practice at the very end of your qigong workout. It spreads qi through the whole body. Repeat each technique ten times unless otherwise noted. You may practice it either clothed or unclothed, without any powders or oils, as these can interfere in the transmission of warmth and qi. You may also do this routine immediately after the facial massage, above.

Rub the palms together, generating heat. Begin by circling the palms around the face, repeating the first step in the Youthful Complexion massage. Then place either palm over the crown of the head and gently circle (you are stimulating the bai hui point).

Next place one palm on the breastbone, one just below it on the solar plexus. Circle both hands in opposite directions. Now switch hands so the other one is above. Again circle.

Move your hands to the abdomen, one palm above the navel, one palm below. Circle both hands in opposite directions. Switch hands, circle again.

Now the palms rub across the torso diagonally. Place your left hand just under your right shoulder. The right hand rests on top of the left. Run the hands diagonally across the body to the left hip. Keep going back and forth, right shoulder to left hip to right shoulder. Then switch to the other side. Begin with the right hand under the left shoulder, with the left hand resting on top of it. Rub across to your right hip. Back and forth. Left shoulder—right hip—left shoulder.

Use your right hand to rub up the outside of the left arm, from fingers to shoulder. Then rotate your arm and continue, using your right hand to rub down the inside of the left. Continue, up and down.

Switch to the other arm. The left palm rubs up the outside of the right arm, then down the inside.

Next, massage the legs. Using both hands, rub up the inside of the legs, from the ankles to the upper thighs, then circle to the outside or back of the legs and rub down the outside to the ankles or feet. When you finish this, very lightly and caringly circle the palms over the tops of the knees. Then rub the backs of the knees up and down.

If you have been standing, you will need to sit for the next stage. Place one foot on the opposite thigh. Pull the toes of the foot gently back with one hand, so that the arch of the foot feels pleasantly stretched. Use the other hand to chafe vigorously across the arch, fifty times. This stimulates the Bubbling Well point and increases qi flow throughout the body. Then switch sides. The other foot rests on the other thigh. Pull back the toes and massage the Bubbling Well fifty times.

We close with a dan tian massage called *Yuan qi gui yuan,* "Returning Original Qi to the Origin." First use either the back of your hands or your fists to lightly circle around the kidneys, lower back, and ming men points. Then, men place the left palm on the navel, right hand on the left. Women place the right palm on the navel, left palm on the right. Both men and women begin to make small counterclockwise circles on the abdomen, gradually larger and larger. The navel is the center of the circle. Circle thirty-six times in all. By number thirty-six, you should be circling as large as the lower tip of the breastbone and the upper part of the pubic bone. Then reverse direction. Large circles at first, gradually smaller and smaller. By number thirty-six, your hands are resting quietly over the navel. Close your eyes and relax, feeling the breath moving quietly under your hands.

ROUTINE 3: WAKE-UP!

This method combines stance training with light, percussive massage. It is an excellent way of warming up before an aerobic workout or sports practice. In China, martial artists often practice this qigong at the beginning of a training session. Some consider it a form of hard qigong, because it conditions the body against injury.

First practice either Standing Meditation, as described in Chapter 10, or *ma bu*, the "horse stance," a classical martial arts stance. To practice the horse stance, stand with your feet at least twice shoulder-width apart and parallel to each other, toes pointing straight ahead. The stance is held in as low a position as possible, with the buttocks not lower than the knees. The palms are pressed together in a prayerlike gesture, fingertips pointing upward, about six inches in front of the breastbone. Keep the breath as relaxed as possible. Practice the horse stance for ten minutes every day, gradually increasing the length of time, up to a maximum of forty minutes. Doing the horse stance builds tremendous strength and stability. It is, however, inadvisable if you are in poor health or suffer from arthritis in the lower part of the body.

When you finish, stand up gradually. Then *lightly* but vigorously slap the body with the palms. Make sure that this is a slap of awakening, not punishment! I like to slap the shoulder muscles, upper back, lower back, abdomen, hamstrings, inner thighs, outer thighs, and calves. This unique and ancient form of self-massage improves circulation, disperses toxic qi, and feels wonderful. However, you may not wish to practice it in public, as others may interpret your actions as self-flagellation rather than self-care!

ROUTINE 4: NATURAL SELF-MASSAGE

Whenever you finish a workout, whether qigong or Western calisthenics, it is a good idea to massage and warm the skin over any area that feels congested. Your massage can include rubbing, pressing, gently kneading, pinching, light slapping, or just resting a hand on the skin. This improves circulation, helps to heal strained or sore muscles, and makes the qi penetrate more deeply into the tissues. Let your body tell you where this massage is needed. You can also include this natural method within Routine 2, "Whole-Body Qi Massage." As you massage the various areas of the body, add methods of your own.

CHAPTER FOURTEEN

The Energy of the Emotions

I don't get depressed; I grow a tumor instead.
—WOODY ALLEN

The word "emotion" is derived from the Latin *e-mot*, "outward moving," meaning the outward expression of inner feeling in tone of voice, facial expression, and gesture. Emotions are thus both mental and physical. They imply a movement of energy both within oneself and between oneself and others. Qigong practice can help to clear obstructions to the flow of emotions, so that they are expressed gracefully rather than repressed or released impulsively.

Qigong can help to heal and balance the emotions by making one aware of physical components of emotional distress—tight shoulders, anxious digestion, suspicious eyes, depressed breathing—and by teaching practical methods to resolve these problems on the energetic level. In this respect qigong is similar to Western systems of body-centered psychotherapy such as Bioenergetics or Reichian Therapy. However, unlike these Western systems, qigong does not incorporate counseling. The emotions are only dealt with as they influence the qi or express themselves in poor physical habits of posture, breathing, and tension. Qigong can nevertheless be an important adjunct to counseling or a first step in emotional healing.

Many Western psychiatrists believe that all serious emotional disturbances have an organic basis in brain chemistry and should be treated primarily with physical interventions, such as psychiatric drugs. The assumption is that the mind is nothing more than the body; what we call mental events are actually only manifestations of physical phenomena. This viewpoint is qualitatively different from the wholistic philosophy implicit in qigong, that body and mind exert reciprocal influences on each other. The emotions influence the body. We armor anger into the body by raising the shoulders, tensing the neck, and inhibiting the flow of qi to and from the liver. The body also influences the emotions. Certain habits of breathing and posture or visceral problems can create psychological attitudes. The qi is the unifying principle, the interface between mind and body that allows us to treat both problems at once. The qi is not only in the brain or the heart, but circulates throughout the entire body. When the qi is healthy, the whole system—mind, body, emotions—is healthy.

PSYCHONEUROIMMUNOLOGY: A LONG WORD WITH A SIMPLE MESSAGE

Recently, Western medicine has begun to recognize the ancient wisdom of Chinese medicine. Researchers in psychoneuroimmunology explore the connection between the psyche, the nervous system, and the immune system. They are corroborating that state of mind and state of health go together; mind and body influence each other.

The link is created by neuropeptides,[1] "the chemicals of consciousness," that are synthesized in response to thinking and feeling. Neuropeptides flow through the body like qi, carrying information to/from the brain, nervous system, and other parts of the body. Like a key fitting a lock, they bond to receptor sites on various tissues and then act as information networks helping to coordinate activity throughout the body. For instance, when your body requires fluid, a neuropeptide called angiotensin bonds to a part of the brain associated with emotions and feelings, known as the amygdala. When this happens we feel that we are thirsty. Angiotensin simultaneously locks on to receptor sites on the kidneys, telling the kidneys to conserve water. Thus, the neuropeptide integrates feeling, awareness, and physiology.

Feelings cause specific neuropeptides to be synthesized and to flow to specific sites, influencing how the body works. Physical sensations such as pain, hunger, or the scent of a flower also stimulate the production of neuropeptides and thus change our moods. Candace Pert, Ph.D., research professor in the Department of Physiology and Biophysics at Georgetown University, has shown that there are receptor sites for the neuropeptides virtually everywhere in the body. The internal organs, particularly the intestines, are rich in receptors. This may explain why emotions are said to be felt in the "gut" or why anxiety has an adverse affect on digestion and assimilation. In Chinese poetry, one is said to be "broken boweled" with sadness, rather than "broken hearted."

The activity of neuropeptides also explains why breathing is such a powerful influence on state of mind. In her article "The Wisdom of the Receptors," Dr. Pert explains that the brain stem, which controls breathing, is "thickly encrusted with neuropeptide receptors and neuropeptides."[2] Emotions directly affect breathing (and qi), either disturbing or deepening it. And conversely, breathing and qigong can create a positive mood, a feeling of empowerment and vitality that causes a flood of neuropeptides (qi) to network with other areas of the body, enhancing health.

Perhaps the most exciting discovery in psychoneuroimmunology is that there are receptor sites for the neuropeptides on the various immune cells. It seems that there are receptors for *every* neuropeptide on the monocytes, immune cells that recognize and ingest invading organisms and aid wound healing and tissue repair. This means that a wide variety of emotional states, both positive and negative, directly influence immune cell function and health. When you are angry, the chemicals of anger are synthesized and flow throughout the body, bonding to and influencing millions of cells. Soon the liver is angry; the white blood cells are angry. If this is unhealthy anger—repressed or inappropriately expressed (as opposed to a positive cathartic release of pent-up feeling)—then the white blood cells and liver may become belligerent, refusing to perform their tasks. On the other hand, if you feel happy and secure, all of the cells feel happy. Even the bones (an important source of immune cells) are happy. According to Dr. Pert:

> . . . These emotion-affecting biochemicals [the neuropeptides] actually appear to control the routing and migration of monocytes, which are so pivotal in the immune system. They communicate with B-cells and T-cells, interact in the whole system to fight disease and to distinguish between self and non-self, deciding, say, which part of the body is a tumor cell to be killed by natural killer cells, and which parts need to be restored.[3]

Moreover, these changes seem to occur outside of the ordinary laws of causality. It is not that your brain sends the message and the body responds. Rather, when you feel a certain emotion, many bodily functions respond *at the same time*. This is not a case of cause and effect. Instead, the entire system transforms at once. Such mind-body connections are a matter of common experience. If you grimace, you immediately evoke feelings of anger. Notice how difficult it is to maintain an angry expression if you remember a joyous experience. Practice slow qigong breathing, and your mood changes. Can you maintain the same calm mood if you mimic the uneven heaving of the chest that occurs while crying? Emotional and physical health or distress occur together, bound by one system of communication: neuropeptides in Western science, qi in Chinese science.

According to psychoneuroimmunology, it is no longer appropriate to think of the mind as restricted to either the brain or to an invisible, mystical realm. Rather, the mind flows throughout the body. Daoist scholar Hidemi Ishida sounds like a scientist when he says that the meridians, the energy channels that conduct qi to and from all of the tissues of the body, "are also the routes by which the mind pervades the body."[4]

RELAXED BODY, RELAXED MIND

Emotions that have been repressed for long periods of time are armored into specific muscular tensions and postural defects. For instance, if we tense our throat when we are unhappy, rather than releasing the pressure of sorrow with tears, this might eventually become chronic neck pain. If we depress the chest in reaction to ridicule, this could result in impaired breathing and respiratory problems. A child who stiffens the spine because of fright could develop a poor, inflexible posture.[5]

Unfortunately, these internalized tensions tend to stay with us. As we become used to tension, it becomes part of our reality and identity. The tension and the situation that engendered it lapse into unconsciousness. This is the root of many chronic psychosomatic disorders.

Through qigong practice, we learn how to bring tense areas of the body into the light of awareness. Awareness is so powerful that it is sometimes sufficient to change a fixed pattern of behavior. Emotions that have been locked into the tension come more easily into consciousness. Old memories and feelings thaw out, released from the frozen tissue. If this does not resolve the issue, it at least makes it available to work with, whether in one's own introspective process or with a psychotherapist. I know this from working with many thousands of students over the past twenty-five years and through personal experience.

When I began qigong, at age sixteen, the experience of relaxed abdominal breathing came as a revelation. My first qigong and Taiji Quan teacher, Mr. Tom Downes, is now a close personal friend and professional colleague. Once when we were teaching a class together, a student asked Tom, "But can qigong really heal the emotions?" Tom replied affirmatively while giving me a wink and a twinkle. He remembered the sickly, insomniac, nervous teenager who came to him for Taiji Quan classes thirty years ago. When I learned how to breathe, I felt centered and relaxed. Deep breathing put me in touch with deeper feelings. I was able to understand and *feel* how my childhood problems with low self-esteem and performance anxiety had affected me physically. In learning to breathe abdominally, I restored freedom of choice to my body and mind. I discovered that there was an option, another way to be. The changes I experienced through qigong practice were reinforced with intensive work in Gestalt, Bioenergetics, and other forms of therapy. I firmly believe that qigong and psychotherapy are congruent and compatible healing modalities. Sometimes either technique is enough to solve a problem; often both are required.

The foundation of qigong is *song*, relaxation and tranquillity. Instead of making an effort and doing more, it may be important to do less! Through regular qigong practice, you learn how to achieve a relaxed, quiet center. It becomes easier to return to this sensation when you begin to feel overwhelmed by emotions or preoccupied with particular thoughts. Thus, your emotions are much less likely to become extreme or out of control. Sometimes all that is required is asking yourself, "Am I breathing? Am I standing on the ground?" Daoists call this psychological state *Taiji*, the same term used in the Taiji Quan form of qigong. Taiji means the balance point between yin and yang, the place of stillness amid change. Finding the Taiji state of mind is equivalent to finding what Thoreau called "the witness self," an aspect of the self that is untouched by life's turmoil and that can be accessed during times of difficulty.

Relaxation is not as easy as it sounds. It involves physical and mental transformation. Physical rigidity always produces mental rigidity and vice versa. Obsessive patterns of thinking accompany repetitive internal tensions. Sometimes these tensions are very subtle, as with tension in the jaw, tongue, or deep connective tissue. People who are constantly thinking, who have forgotten the location of the off switch in their internal TV, are usually speaking to themselves as well. The tongue and jaw contract, release, and make extremely small, invisible movements continuously. The fact that tension is often unconscious or chronic does not make it any less damaging. What you don't know *can* hurt you! Continuous tension, whether conscious or not, is a continuous drain on the vitality and qi. Chinese medicine considers these tensions to be the root of most psychological problems.

Sometimes, even when obsessive thoughts or emotional behavior have ceased, the physical rigidity continues and eventually re-creates the pathological condition. This becomes a vicious circle, a negative feedback loop. The situation can become quite complex, considering the way muscular tension also affects the functioning of the internal organs, particularly the liver. For instance, according to Chinese medicine, the liver controls tension in the muscles and ligaments and also helps spread qi through the body. (This explains the central role of the liver among the organs. Even if one gathers qi with qigong, if the liver is unhealthy, the qi cannot spread and reach the areas where it is needed.) When the body is tense, the liver is not able to function optimally. When the liver is unhealthy, the body becomes tense. Again we have a vicious circle.

Mental/Emotional Tension ↔ *Physical Tension* ↔ *Liver Imbalance* ↔ *Qi Stagnation*

The only way out of this loop is by focusing attention. Awareness is the essential ingredient in relaxation. Once the student is aware, it is possible to *feel* what is wrong and to exercise some control. This is called *ting jing*, "listening to the energy." Listening to the energy leads to *dong jing*, "comprehending and controlling the energy." However, since tension and effort *are* the problems, awareness and relaxation, although certainly involving focus and intent, should be effortless, a process of surrendering. Can you *try* to relax? I think not. Relaxation is a matter of paying attention and *not doing*.

I saw a wonderful clinical example of the power of relaxation very early in my teaching career. A male psychiatric nurse, M., requested a series of private Taiji Quan classes. M. was a large, brawny man, approximately forty years old with no physical complaints or noticeable disabilities. M. had enormous difficulties trying to master even the most basic movements. As soon as he tried to perform the exercise, he became tense, dyslexic, and confused. If I asked him to shift to his right leg, he would shift to his left. If I asked him to stand with a straight spine, his left arm raised, he would lean to one side with both arms dangling. Yet he thoroughly believed that he was following instructions, until I very slowly and carefully pointed out to him the difference between what he was doing and what he thought he was doing. It seemed that he had a neurological or cognitive problem that only became visible in the context of slow, choreographed movement. After several months of practice, he had memorized as many techniques as an average student could learn in the first few classes. I nevertheless demonstrated the entire Taiji Quan sequence for him at the end of each class.

One day I had a sudden inspiration. I took out a set of boxing gloves and asked M. to put them on. He pulled them over his large hands and looked at me strangely, perhaps somewhat nervously, as he knew that I had advanced training in the Chinese martial arts. I put my hands behind my back and told M., "Hit me." "I can't do that, Ken. You're my teacher, and I consider you a friend." I explained that this was a coordination exercise. I would dance out of the way, keeping my hands behind me. I wouldn't hit back. He had to keep trying to hit me until he scored three punches on my face or torso.

At first M. was hesitant, punching slowly and haphazardly. After five minutes, he began to pick up speed and to show a glimmer of the coordination he had lacked for all these months. A few minutes later, M.'s face and body were drenched in sweat. He stopped and asked, "Can I stop now, I'm exhausted." "Not yet, you've only scored once. We can't stop until you've hit me three times, even if it takes all night!" We continued another ten minutes, until M. was near the point of complete exhaustion. I then allowed M. to take off the gloves. Before he could collapse on a chair, I asked him, "Would you please do the Taiji Quan exercise?" He said, "But I only learned the first five movements." "Never mind, just do what you can." M. began the Taiji Quan form. To my absolute amazement, *he performed the entire sequence almost perfectly.* At some unconscious level he had been learning Taiji Quan, even when his conscious mind denied it.

Taiji Quan is an extremely complex choreographed exercise. It would be a near-impossible feat for even an experienced dancer to learn it from observation. Yet here was M. performing an exquisite qigong routine. When he finished, he didn't quite realize what had occurred and asked me, "Was that all right?" Then it hit him. He exclaimed, "Well, I'll be! I wasn't even trying! I wasn't even trying!" Perhaps trying had been his problem all along. He needed to be brought to a state where he was so utterly exhausted that trying was impossible. At this point, "Man's extremity is God's opportunity." Qigong just happened!

This experience was a breakthrough for M., a kind of *satori*, "sudden enlightenment," as they say in Zen Buddhism. From that day on, M. was able to learn Taiji Quan techniques as easily as a normal student. The most interesting aspect of the experience was what I learned from M.'s coworkers. After his breakthrough, M., who had been considered antisocial, began making friends with the other nurses. He also revealed that learning how to relax had cured both his insomnia and his drinking problem.

These effects lasted during the several months that M. continued studying with me and were still evident when I checked with him a year later. M. once told me that I taught him "many important lessons about life." I know that he taught me just as many.

Mastery of relaxation is an ongoing challenge at every stage of qigong training. There always seems to be a deeper level of relaxation we can attain, further places where we can let go and do less. The shift from tension to relaxation parallels a shift from distraction and lack of focus to silent awareness. The brain waves slow down, moving from quick beta waves, which characterize the use of language and intellect, to the slow alpha and theta, demonstrating a focused, aware, and intuitive state. The strong presence of slow alpha and theta waves, commonly seen in the EEGs of qigong practitioners, also suggests that repressed images and feelings can rise more easily to the surface of consciousness.

Thus, we can look at how relaxation can encourage the release and resolution of emotional issues from two complementary perspectives. On the one hand, as tension is released, the emotions locked into tense muscles are also released. On the other hand, physical relaxation creates a slower metabolism, slower pulse, slower and more relaxed respiration, and slower brain waves. The slow brain waves correspond to the opening of rigid boundaries between the unconscious and conscious mind, so that, again, we can become aware of repressed and inhibited emotions and, hopefully, express and release them in an appropriate way.

Relaxation, although the foundation of qigong training, is not the only principle with psychological implications.

THE QIGONG STANCE: A POSTURE OF EMOTIONAL BALANCE

One of the most common physical reactions to fear or emotional trauma is a spontaneous shrinking of the back, as a cat does when reacting to danger. Fear causes a contraction inward, a withdrawal of energy from the periphery of the body, away from the perceived threat and toward the center. The sacrum and neck become tight and feel as if they are moving toward each other. The spine may become measurably shorter. Qigong helps us overcome and correct this by emphasizing "relaxing open the joints" and teaching ways of lengthening and extending the spine. In some qigong techniques, the student imagines that the tailbone is being pulled down at the same time that the head is lifted up. The spine is internally stretched. Indian Yoga can be combined very effectively with qigong to create further opening and extension of the back. Only when the spine is long and supple can we live with backbone. A relaxed spine creates a confident attitude.

The sternum is also relaxed, neither pushed out, as if to say, "Don't get too close," nor sunk in, saying, "I am depressed. I'm not worthy of affection." Individuals with psychological problems often feel constriction in the chest during either inhalation or exhalation. Depression, anxiety, and poor self-esteem create a posture in which the chest is chronically caved in, making inhalation difficult. One is *physically* depressed, unable to expand the chest properly in order to take in the new and be refreshed by the environment.

The opposite posture is one of inflation, the chest chronically distended, as though stuck during inhalation and unable to let go. Here, the individual has an inflated and unrealistic self-image, is literally full of himself. Of course, this is a form of compensation, often hiding a deeper feeling of unworthiness and fear of getting close to people. The individual who says, "I am full, I don't need anyone," may really be saying, "I was hurt in the past and don't want to risk it again." The qigong classics advise, "Release the chest; extend the back. Relax open the joints." This creates a posture of fluid breathing in which the pulse of life, the yin and the yang, the inhalation and exhalation are allowed with equal ease. We neither hold on to the old experiences nor avoid the new.

In all qigong techniques, the shoulders are sunk down. This is an area of the body that responds quickly to anger, fear, and frustration. With lifted, tight shoulders, the natural reach of the arms is inhibited. It is difficult to reach out and receive nourishment from the environment. When attempts at receiving love have been repeatedly frustrated, this is often armored into the body as shoulder tension. Tight, raised shoulders also make it difficult to strike out (the reason boxers must relax the shoulders) and may be symptomatic of repressed anger. Whether the aggressive impulse is exploded out or imploded in, in the form of tension, it indicates that the individual is unable to find appropriate avenues to express anger or may have a problem with impulse control.

On the other hand, when the shoulders seem pressed down and slumped forward they are saying, "Life's a burden" or "I can't stand it." The back begins to bend forward, as though carrying a heavy load. If combined with a depressed sternum, this posture can catalyze the harm caused by other conditions. It puts pressure on the heart, making it more difficult to pump blood—a very dangerous situation if there is already a structural heart defect or a tendency toward heart failure. A stooped spine speeds up the debilitating postural changes that are associated with osteoporosis.

The feeling "I can't stand it" also manifests as locked knees, effectively cutting off the feeling of the ground and reinforcing the wall between conscious and subconscious mind. Locked knees may betray an inability to trust, a fear that the ground will not support us, so we try to lift ourselves up away from it. This actually has the opposite effect, making balance difficult and precarious. Can you imagine walking on a balance beam or tightrope with locked knees? When the knees bend, as in all standing or active qigong, we drop down into our center, into a place of balance and fuller awareness of who we are.

In active qigong, the eyes are generally open, taking in the environment, scanning it without fixing on any particular object. The eyes have a

soft focus. They allow the world to come in, without grasping. The eyes neither look back to what has passed (the past) nor jump ahead to what is not
yet in view (the future). This keeps the mind focused on the present and
helps eliminate phobia, unrealistic expectations, and the need to rehearse
our responses to life events before they happen.

The most transforming yet difficult aspect of qigong posture is *chen*,
"sinking." As the body relaxes, its weight sinking through the feet, the qi
sinks to the dan tian. As in mountain climbing, where descent is more difficult and frightening than ascent, sinking the qi can bring up difficult emotional issues. According to Alexander Lowen, the founder of Bioenergetics
Therapy, there is often an unconscious resistance to sinking energy downward, a "fear of melting or letting down into the fires of passion that burn in
the belly and pelvis."[6] To sink and relax is really to let go and surrender to a
wisdom beyond one's conscious control. It is to face and accept the wild and
mysterious.

Qigong is strongly influenced by the Daoist philosophy of naturalness
and spontaneity. Lao Zi says, "Embrace the uncarved block of wood." That is,
don't try to fit yourself into a mold or whittle down the fullness of who you
are with rules and regulations, shoulds and should nots. Instead, as you learn,
through qigong practice, to identify your imbalances, don't be overenthusias-
tic about correcting them. Balance your desire to improve with a strong dose
of self-acceptance. This will help you grow at a slow and steady pace.

THE ORGAN–EMOTION LINK

Chinese medicine categorizes the major emotions as: anxiety, sorrow, fear,
anger, joy, rumination, and empathy. Each of these, when excessive or fixed
(preoccupying the mind), harms an internal organ and disturbs the qi in specific ways.

Anxiety and sorrow both damage the lungs. The English word "anxiety"
comes from a German root *angst*, "narrow," referring to the narrowing of the
bronchial passages. During times of anxiety, breath and qi are constricted,
unable to flow easily in and out of the lungs. It is well-known that anxiety
can contribute to the development or exacerbation of asthma and other
bronchial conditions. The lungs are also affected by grief as demonstrated by
the heaving that occurs with crying. Grief depresses and weakens the lungs
and, like anxiety, disturbs the easy and full movement of breath. According
to Chinese medicine, the lungs extract qi from the air, regulating the supply
of internal healing energy. When the lungs are weakened by grief, one's general health and vitality diminishes. However, this does not mean that we

should suppress sorrow. It is not healthy to withhold one's tears in response to an upsetting event. Both prolonged grief and unexpressed grief weaken lung qi.

In Traditional Chinese Medicine, the word *shen*, "kidneys," includes both the kidneys and adrenals and, in some contexts, the reproductive system. The shen are most affected by fear. Fear causes pain and disease in the kidneys, adrenals, and lower back and creates favorable conditions for urinary tract disorders and incontinence. When one is afraid, the qi drops down toward the sacrum and in toward the center, away from the surface of the body. The body contracts in self-protection. The circulation of blood and breath slows down, resulting in conditions of excess and stagnation in the core and depletion in the periphery. A common sign of this is cold hands and feet. One is literally "frozen with fear."

Chronic fear can lead to a host of debilitating conditions. Fear and stress cause the adrenals to secrete large amounts of the stress hormones adrenaline and hydrocortisone, which signal the cells to break down stored fats and proteins into sugar (glucose). This makes energy available to fight or flee from a threat—a necessity during short-term threats to survival but devastating if prolonged. As the stores of energy are sapped, we become weak and fatigued, leading to "adrenal burnout." The body's reservoir of hormones is not infinitely deep. If we do not have time to rest and regenerate our supply, our ability to cope with stress is impaired.

The release of adrenal hormones puts many bodily processes on hold, in order to defend against the threat. This includes the shutting down of growth, repair, and reproduction by inhibiting or disabling essential chemicals and immune cells. If stress is constant, the body may forget how to return to the healthy state, losing its ability to defend effectively against pathogens or to repair and heal damage.

In qigong theory, the kidneys and adrenals also control brain function, especially memory. Scientific research has confirmed that fear and stress can weaken memory and create learning disabilities. The stress hormone, hydrocortisone, damages the hippocampus, a region of the brain responsible for memory and learning and rich with hydrocortisone receptors. The connection between the adrenal hormones and memory has also been shown in animal experiments. In the 1960s, German physiologists found that these hormones damage the brains of guinea pigs. On the other hand, when the adrenal glands were removed from middle-aged rats, the hippocampal cells were spared the damage that one would normally expect with aging.[7] The implication of all of this for humans is that by avoiding stressful situations or by resolving or changing our reactions to them, we can restore balance to the *shen*, the kidneys-adrenals, and preserve the health of body and mind.

Anger weakens the liver and causes the qi to rise. In fact, the common Chinese word for anger is *sheng qi* "rising qi." Other expressions used to describe an angry person include *huo qi da* "fire qi great" or *yang qi tai gao* "yang qi too high." Rising qi leads to muscular tension and various liver- and fire-related ailments, such as headaches, eyestrain, hemorrhoids, and irregular menstruation. It is interesting that in English, the word "bilious" also implies a connection between the liver and anger. Weakness of liver qi also contributes to mood swings, as the liver cannot perform its function of spreading the qi and harmonizing its flow.

In the West we distinguish between "healthy anger" and "unhealthy anger." Whereas the Chinese simply say that anger is harmful, Western mind-body researchers have found that honest expression of even "negative" feelings is good for one's health. Unhealthy anger is repressed, chronic, cruel, or violent. This kind of anger does not end after it is discharged; inevitably a trail of other feelings follows it, including resentment, frustration, and guilt. In my opinion, it is only this kind of anger that harms the liver. Many scientists have found that the inability to express healthy anger and other emotions conventionally labeled as "negative" may suppress the immune system and create favorable conditions for the development of cancer.[8] Even mice exhibit different immunologic states depending on their behavior. More aggressive mice tend to have smaller virus-induced tumors.[9] It may be that a strong, fighting (and feisty) spirit goes hand in hand with more aggressive white blood cells. It is important to note, however, that a fighting spirit is different from obstinacy and stubbornness. The challenge for anyone facing serious disease is how to balance determination and willpower with acceptance of human frailty and imperfection.

Lao Zi suggests a distinction between healthy and unhealthy emotion in his classic *Dao De Jing*: "The highest virtue is not virtuous, and is thus virtuous"; that is, true virtue is not self-consciously or compulsively virtuous. Compulsive do-gooders are really afraid of or denying their own aggression and hostility. They try always to do what is "best," preferring to be placating, submissive, or self-sacrificing rather than expressing or fighting for what they genuinely feel, lest they "make waves." "The sage is not a do-gooder," says Lao Zi. The sage is true to his or her nature, neither compulsively following nor rebelling against rules of conduct. The sage is capable of expressing emotions, including anger, as necessary and appropriate to the situation. He or she practices self-acceptance and is thus more accepting and understanding of others. The first step in self-acceptance is giving oneself permission to feel what one is feeling; then inner resistance and friction is lessened and much of one's anger is already gone.

That joy is considered a *negative emotion* is troubling to most Western students of qigong until they realize that in Chinese medical literature the term joy (*le*) means excitability, a tendency toward giddiness, talkativeness, lavishness, and general excess. In some texts, another character for joy is used, pronounced *xi*. Etymologically, this character means the joy derived from eating. According to Chinese medicine scholars Kiiko Matsumoto and Stephen Birch, "In a medical context, *xi* accurately refers more to the notion of problems caused by overeating. . . ."[10] Thus, "joy" disperses and scatters the qi. It can create an uneven pulse and make one prone to cardiac problems.

The excitable, joyous person is the opposite of the Chinese ideal of the sage, who is able to maintain inner composure and calm even in the midst of a storm. There is a Chinese saying, "Though Mount Tai collapses at your feet, the qi remains calm, and the face does not change color." Excitement places sudden demands on the heart. The most extreme form of excitement and thus the most damaging emotion for the heart is emotional shock, whether from a negative event such as the death of a loved one or from a positive event, like winning the sweepstakes. The epidemic of heart disease in the West may be symptomatic of our society's preoccupation with *le*, "joy, excitement." The heart is overstimulated by our quick pace of life, by frightening news reports, TV violence, and an infatuation with sex and romance.

In qigong philosophy, it is believed that the heart likes peace and quiet. It needs a feeling of security in order to keep an even pace as it pumps energy through the body. When the heart qi is disturbed by excitement and excess, mind and spirit are both affected, creating the possibility of insomnia, confused and restless thinking, or in extreme cases, hallucinations, hysteria, and psychosis.

The spleen is damaged by pensiveness. The qi becomes knotted and stuck. Pensiveness means excess concentration, an obsessive preoccupation with a concept or subject. It is the kind of intellectual nit-picking usually required for Ph.D. dissertations. Needless to say, college students often suffer from what Chinese medicine considers spleen-related disorders: gastric disturbances, elevated blood pressure, weakened immunity, and a tendency toward phlegm and colds.

Excess empathy, *bei*, also harms the spleen. Empathy is similar to compassion. *The American Heritage Dictionary* defines compassion as "Deep awareness of the suffering of another coupled with the wish to relieve it." Empathy means that we also *identify* with that person's suffering. This feeling is especially strong when we come in contact with individuals who are facing hardships we ourselves have endured. Empathy is a positive attribute and creates a healing trust in any relationship, especially a therapeutic one.

Empathy is considered excessive and damaging to the spleen when we lose a clear recognition of boundaries, when we feel distraught and upset by someone else's problems.[11] Pensiveness and excess empathy, the two qualities that harm the spleen, are related. We are pensive when we are preoccupied with ourselves; we are overly empathic when we are preoccupied with others.

Empathy is an important and difficult issue for many healers. Too much empathy makes it difficult to treat the patient objectively and may result in "picking up" the patient's physical and/or mental disease. A qigong student knows he is overempathizing when it becomes difficult to feel relaxed, centered, and rooted. To overempathize is to feel disempowered and out of touch with the earth, the element that corresponds to the spleen. Such empathy weakens the spleen, and conversely a weak spleen can create boundary issues.

The spleen carries the qi of the earth. Qigong masters say that the spleen *needs* grounding, time spent in nature. There is a wonderful cure for both of the spleen's emotional pathogens—pensiveness and empathy. "Lose your mind and come to your senses." Spend more time in nature, seeing nature as a positive model of health and balance. The earth supports all kinds of life impartially, without attachment. Let the mind become quiet and the senses open to the environment. Such a cure may seem too simple, nontechnical, perhaps even naive. The important point is that it works! I remember my old friend, Zenmaster Alan Watts, once remarking, "We believe that we haven't thought enough about the difficulties of life. Perhaps the problem is that we have thought entirely too much!"

In summary, each of the major internal organs can be damaged by emotional excess. There are also positive emotions that can help heal the organs. These positive emotions are identical to the five virtues that, according to Confucianism, can make one a "Noble Person." The Chinese word for virtue (*de*) was originally written with the same character as the word "to plant," suggesting that virtue is a power that can be cultivated. Similarly, the English "virtue" comes from the same Latin root as "virile," suggesting a power or potential that creates health.

The lungs are healed by *yi*, often translated "righteousness," in the sense of integrity and dignity. When I studied Chinese philosophy, my professor was fond of a particular example of lack of *yi*—the way people push and shove on crowded subways during rush hour. Yi means giving yourself and others a kind of psychological elbow room, room to live and breathe. The kidneys are healed by *zhi*, wisdom. Zhi implies clear perception and self-understanding, a sure antidote for irrational fears. The anger of the liver is mended with kindness (*ren*). The Confucian virtue ren is a pictogram of two people walking together. It is sometimes defined as the natural feelings

TABLE 8: THE ORGAN–EMOTION LINK

Element	Metal	Water	Wood	Fire	Earth
Organ	Lungs	Kidney	Liver	Heart	Spleen
Harmful Emotions	Anxiety, Sorrow	Fear	Anger	Joy, Shock	Pensiveness, Empathy
Qi Effect	Constrict	Drop	Rise	Scatter	Knot
Positive Emotions	Yi (Integrity)	Zhi (Wisdom)	Ren (Kindness)	Li (Order)	Xin (Trust)

that arise with companionship: benevolence and "human-heartedness." In the *Analects*, Confucius says, "Ren consists in loving others" (*Analects* XII, 22). The excitability of the heart is balanced by peace, calm, orderliness, all implied by the Chinese word *li*. Li is usually translated "ritual." However, Confucian texts make it clear that li is not only ritual, but the state of mind required to perform ritual properly and evoked by the performance. Li connotes "orderliness," setting limits on one's behavior as a means of fostering social harmony. Finally, the spleen is healed by the cultivation of *xin*. This is a rich concept that can mean trust, faith, honesty, confidence, belief. Trust is openness and acceptance, a feeling that emerges when one finds a common ground with another. Trust is a cure for the knotted qi that occurs from both pensiveness (an internal knot and stagnation) and empathy (one's qi tied to another).

The correspondences between the five elements, the organs, harmful and positive (healing) emotions are reviewed in Table 8. This network is also the basis for a powerful qigong meditation called, very simply, "Healing the Emotions." You may wish to either memorize or record the instructions, so you can practice with eyes closed.

HEALING THE EMOTIONS

Sit in qigong posture for a few minutes, with the eyes lightly closed. Make sure you are relaxed and breathing naturally. Bring your mind to the lungs. Use your inner senses to feel the lungs in your body. As you inhale, draw integrity and dignity into the lungs. As you exhale, let the breath carry away all worries, anxiety, and grief. Repeat this several times. Inhale integrity, exhale anxiety and grief. . . .

Now focus on the kidneys. Let the inhalation fill the kidneys with wisdom, with the confidence of inner-knowing. Exhale all fears. Repeat several times.

Locate the liver with your awareness. As you inhale, draw in kindness, filling the liver completely. As you exhale, release and let go of anger. Repeat.

Bring your mind to the heart. Inhale, filling it—all the chambers, valves, the heart muscle—with peace and calm. Exhaling, release excitement, zealousness, excesses of any kind. Inhale peace again. Continue. . .

Now find the spleen. Locate and feel it inside. As you inhale, fill it with trust and acceptance. As you exhale, let go of pensiveness and rumination. Let go of excess empathy, so you can be secure and rooted in yourself. Again, inhale trust. Repeat.

Then bring your mind to the center of your being, to the stillness and silence of quiet abdominal breathing. Let all images and thoughts disappear. Stay with the feeling of pure being, "hanging out with yourself" as long as you wish.

You can also use Inner Nourishing Qigong for emotional healing. As you breathe, think of a healing phrase, for instance, "My emotions are balanced and calm." Inhale, gently expanding the lower abdomen, thinking, "My emotions are . . ." Exhale, letting the abdomen relax, thinking, "balanced and calm." Repeat for about five minutes.

I FEEL; THEREFORE I AM

We can see that qigong approaches the emotions from a very different place than traditional psychotherapy. Qigong considers the way emotions affect posture, breathing, and visceral health. Rather than viewing psychological problems in terms of past influences on present behavior, qigong focuses exclusively on *present energy blockages*. Frequently, psychological problems seem to just evaporate as physical tension dissolves. Although memory is stored in unhealthy tissue, one need not always analyze these memories to achieve psychological health. Many qigong students note, in retrospect, that emotional difficulties they had at the beginning of training are simply nonexistent a few years later.

This is not, however, to denigrate the need for insight-oriented talk therapies. Serious psychological problems often do require delving into reasons and causes. Even if the energetic blockage is released, the patient may still need help breaking a loop of repetitive thought or a behavior pattern that reinforces the problem. It is here that both Chinese medicine and qigong are seriously lacking and must look to Western psychotherapy to fill the gap. Dr. Mark Seem's poignant commentary about acupuncture applies equally to qigong:

> Acupuncture therapy, while unblocking an energetic zone, simultaneously frees up the psyche trapped in that zone, and if attention is not paid to the underlying psychological issues in the patient's life experience, a new energetic zone will soon become disturbed. This results in constantly shifting or wandering symptoms, a kind of energetic hysteria due to the practitioner's inability or unwillingness to focus on the soul as well as the body.[12]

Several years ago I was discussing qigong teaching strategies with a well-known Chinese qigong master, visiting from Guangzhou (Canton). I brought up one of my favorite questions. "How do you help a student who has serious emotional difficulties? Let's say a student who cries every time she begins Standing Meditation." The master replied, "I would tell her *Fang Song*, 'Relax.' " "But what if this only made matters worse? What if relaxing the shoulders also relaxes the tension that controls her emotions and holds back the tears?" Again, the master said, "She needs to relax." No matter how I approached this subject, the answer was the same, like a broken record. I have heard the same answer from more than 99 percent of the Chinese qigong instructors I have questioned.

Relaxation is an answer but not the definitive answer in every case. In the West, we tend to view psychological problems as having to do almost exclusively with the mind. In China, the reverse is true. Psychological problems are *somatized*, interpreted and regarded as physical sensations. This belief could be the foundation of a true mind-body science, but it is not. The attitude throughout most of Chinese history has been that anxiety is *only* a problem in the lungs, requiring acupuncture, massage, herbs, or some other physical remedy. If you have a phobic avoidance of certain situations, your personal experiences in childhood are irrelevant. After all, everyone knows that fear is located in the kidneys. And so on. The five element theory became a way to pigeonhole phenomena in terms of one all-embracing system of thought. It is ironic that a system originally designed to show connections and relationships eventually stunted the development of creative approaches to mind-body health.

The five element classification could be applied to almost everything, sometimes in bizarre ways. If an individual was suffering from uncontrollable anger, the Chinese doctor might recommend a healthy dose of anxiety and worry, since metal (associated with lungs-anxiety) chops and destroys wood (associated with liver-anger). Or if a patient was thinking too much and had a tendency toward obsessive behavior, then anger could be the cure. Again, the rationalization is that in the cycle of the five elements, wood (anger) penetrates and destroys earth (rumination). This system of therapy, called "checking one emotion with another," is still practiced in China.[13]

Somatization is reflected in present-day Chinese medical terminology.[14] Grief is *suan*, "sourness in the joints." Insomnia and irritability are *tou yun*, "head dizziness." Depression is *men*, a Chinese character that pictures the heart trapped in a doorway, suggesting a feeling of being closed in or suffocated. The catchall phrase for most psychological problems is neurasthenia, *shen jing shuai ruo*, literally "weakness of the nerves."[15] This can include anxiety, depression, and hysteria. David Eisenberg, M.D., notes that between one-third and one-half of all patients he saw at Beijing's Dong Zhi Men Clinic complained of "suffering from neurasthenia."[16] Thus most problems a Westerner would consider psychological are defined as physical, requiring exclusively physical interventions.

There are historical and philosophical reasons why emotional individuals may not receive adequate attention in Chinese society. They are difficult to predict and control and care little for convention; thus they are perceived as threats to government stability.[17] In Confucianism, the state religion through much of China's history, emotional expression was disdained in favor of decorum, orderliness, and the performance of one's social obligations. Social roles took precedence over personal experience and fulfillment.

In present-day P.R.C., as in the past, emotional difficulties are first addressed within the family. If no resolution is found, the problem is brought to the attention of the local political leader, who oversees both political and social aspects of his community. As a last resort, the truly disturbed individual might be referred to a physician. If the physician practices Western medicine, the course of treatment is generally medication and/or electroconvulsive shock therapy. Practitioners of Traditional Chinese Medicine will use acupuncture, herbs, massage, and qigong. Still, the personal thoughts and feelings of the individual, so valued in the West, have not been discussed or considered.

Arthur Kleinman, M.D., notes that during research conducted in 1980 at the Hunan Medical College Department of Psychiatry, most depressive patients "did not improve their perceived disability, and few experienced substantial improvement in family, school, or work problems."[18] In a follow-up study of chronic pain patients, conducted in 1983, Kleinman found that none of the patients had experienced a cure due to medical treatment and none of the psychiatric diagnoses had predicted a positive treatment outcome.[19]

Fortunately, there are indications of improvement and broader treatment options. Bogged down by an immense population and complex bureaucracy, changes are occurring at a tortoise's pace. Individual and group talk therapy have made some inroads.[20] Standard diagnostic labels of Western psychiatry are being adopted in research and, gradually, in clinical practice.

Perhaps both China and the West can begin to harvest the best of both worlds. We can combine the energy medicine technology of qigong with the insights and methodology of psychotherapy to create a new and truly effective system of mind-body healing.

CHAPTER FIFTEEN

External Qi Healing:
Chinese Therapeutic Touch

Place yourself in the middle of the stream of
power and wisdom which animates all whom it
floats, and you are without effort impelled to
truth, to right and a perfect contentment.
—RALPH WALDO EMERSON,
SPIRITUAL LAWS

THE HEALING PRESENCE

"You know, Ken, I have become too popular! I have so many patients that sometimes I have to schedule them one or two weeks later. But if their problem needs more immediate attention, this seems very unfair. I had to find a solution."

This is how my old teacher and beloved friend, Dr. Wong, began a conversation as we sat down in our favorite restaurant. It had been several years since my last visit, yet it seemed as though we were resuming a conversation we had begun only the day before. When good friends meet, time is irrelevant. They start up from where they left off. As in the past, many of my "lessons" took place over a meal or informally in his living room.

"Did you find a solution, Dr. Wong?"

"Oh, yes," he said with a twinkle. "Provided the patients are not suffering from a contagious disease, I ask a group of them to meet me in a café for a cup of tea."

"Yes . . . ?"

"Then I shake hands with each of them. By the next day, some of them call me back, saying, 'Dr. Wong, cancel my appointment. I don't know what you did when we shook hands, but I am feeling all better!' "

This was a wonderful lesson, as it reconfirmed an opinion I had long

242

held about the naturalness of healing energy. Every contact with another human being (or with an animal, plant, and perhaps any aspect of nature) has the potential for healing or harm. Our very presence can be a healing help and positive influence on those we care about.[1]

When I questioned Dr. Wong about methods of training or increasing the power of this presence, he said, "Practice qigong." If two acupuncturists apply the same technique, the one with qigong training will be more effective. "When I hold the needle," said Dr. Wong, "the needle is not the needle. My whole body is a needle, an antenna for the universal breath of Heaven and Earth."

At a high level of training, it is possible to dispense with the needle and simply point one's fingers at the acupoint to achieve the same effect. Or one can project qi directly into an afflicted area of the body with or without touch. Qi can be projected during any other method of healing body work such as massage, osteopathic adjustments, chiropractic, Rolfing, Therapeutic Touch, or laying on of hands. It can greatly increase the efficacy of any of these techniques. This unique application of qigong for healing others—projecting qi outside of one's own body and into a patient—is called *External Qi Healing* (EQH, *Wai Qi Zhi Liao* in Chinese).

In China, External Qi Healing usually refers to noncontact therapeutic touch, the hand or hands held approximately six inches above the area of treatment. According to Chinese works on the subject, EQH is excellent therapy for the same range of problems treated by acupuncture. It is very effective in "reducing pain, shrinking infections and swellings, killing cancerous cells, combating arthritis, releasing muscular tension, improving skin tone, stopping bleeding, strengthening the immune system, renewing vitality, etc."[2] Compared to acupuncture patients, those treated by External Qi have less frequency of disease recurrence.[3]

EQH is also the most accessible form of Chinese medicine, the easiest for anyone to learn. Although it *may* be applied as an adjunct to acupuncture therapy, it can also be practiced by those unfamiliar with Eastern philosophy. It does not require knowledge of meridians, acupoints, or Chinese medical theory. Unlike many qigong instructors, I do not believe that EQH is only for the advanced. I do not accept that one must wait ten years before attempting it. On the contrary, we are emitting qi all the time, with or against our will. We need to learn how to use this innate capacity effectively and wisely.

I was inspired to learn External Qi Healing by an experience I had in the early 1970s. One day after practicing qigong in a park, one of my students, a woman in her twenties, asked me, "Have you ever thought of using your qi to heal someone else?" She explained that she had an ovarian cyst. One ovary had already been removed, and a large cyst was growing on the remaining one. Although I didn't know if I could help, I was certain that I would do no harm. I asked her to lie down on her back on the grass. I placed both of my palms about six inches above her abdomen and imagined myself practicing Standing Meditation. I was not trying to project healing qi, nor to change or manipulate her energy. I was simply tuning in.

After about fifteen minutes, I finished and asked her how she felt. She said that she felt warmth and tingling throughout her abdomen. This was a positive sign of qi flow and sensitivity but not necessarily an indication of therapeutic effect. A month later, she told me that when she had returned to her physician for a checkup, there was no sign of the cyst! Of course, I have no way of knowing for certain that I caused its remission, but I am very happy that now, more than twenty years later, she is a healthy and proud mother.

HISTORY OF EXTERNAL QI HEALING: THE ROOT OF CHINESE MEDICINE

The method of transmitting qi probably goes back to the very roots of Chinese medicine in ancient shamanism. The word for doctor or medicine in Chinese is *yi*, a word that originally consisted of two pictograms: a quiver of arrows in the top of the character and a dancing shaman (*wu* in Chinese) on the bottom. The arrows represent spiritual power, qi—either healing qi projected from the healer into the patient or arrows of noxious qi energetically removed by the healer.[4]

In ancient China, doctors *were* shamans. *Yi Zhou Shu* (The History of the Zhou Dynasty) quotes the Duke of Zhou (c. 1020 B.C.) as saying that in the past, "every village had a *wu* medical office." These shaman-doctors were probably China's original herbalists. In Chapter 16 of an equally ancient text, *Shan Hai Jing* (The Classic of Mountains and Seas), there is a list of ten shamans who lived on a mountain "where a myriad of healing herbs grow." The names of these shamans suggest that they also practiced acupuncture, using bone, thorn, or stone needles—for example, Wu Geng (Fish-bone Shaman), Wu Di (Thorn Shaman), and Wu Xian (Needle Shaman).[5] We see the same association between shamanism and doctors in the *Analects* of Confucius: "One who lacks perseverance will make neither a shaman nor a doctor."[6] In a stone relief at the Confucian Temple in Qu Fu (Shandong Province), Bian Que, a physician from the fourth or fifth century B.C., is represented as a feathered shaman, a bird-man, one with nature and soaring beyond the fetters of intellect. These shaman-doctors, like shamans the world over, may have occasionally used healing tools such as herbs or acupuncture needles. However, they were also capable of contacting the forces of nature directly and channeling this power to the patient through intent, prayer, and energetic touch.

One of the ministers of the famed Yellow Emperor, Patriarch of Chinese Medicine, was such a shaman. In *The Yellow Emperor's Classic of Internal Medicine*, a text probably dating from the second century B.C., we read that this minister, Zhu You, preferred to treat illness through exorcistic prayer rather than needles or herbs. Some scholars believe that Zhu You practiced External Qi Healing at the same time that he prayed for patients.[7] This is remarkably similar to the synergism of noncontact healing and prayer in Native American and other indigenous healing traditions. The *Yellow Emperor's Classic* states that in ancient times most illnesses were treated according to the methods of Zhu You. China's great etymological dictionary, *Shuo Wen Jieh Zi*, says that professional "prayer healers" (*zhu*) were once widespread in China. They may have formed a specialized branch of shamanism.

As shamanism fell into disfavor in the Chinese court,[8] Chinese medicine shifted ever more toward the technology of needles and herbs. Confucian scholasticism replaced shamanic intuition and energy sensitivity. The spiritual dimensions of Chinese healing were preserved almost entirely by the Daoists.[9] Today most Chinese doctors dismiss shamanism as "superstition" (*mi xin*) and few have even heard of Zhu You or the branch of medicine he founded.[10]

Originally, EQH was called "Spreading Qi" (*Bu Qi*). Most specific references to the technique are in the works by or about Daoists. In the *History of the Jin Dynasty* [A.D. 265–317]: *Record of Formulas and Techniques*,[11] we read, "Those who cultivate the Dao and nourish the qi are able, when their own qi is abundant, to spread qi to others." This philosophy is elaborated in several Ming Dynasty (1368–1644) texts in the *Daoist Canon*, such as *Master Huan Zhen's Secret for Absorbing Original Qi*. "To heal the sick by spreading qi, first locate where among the five organs the disease is located. Then inhale qi and project it into the patient's body. . . . This will drive out demons and poisons." There is the *Bu Qi Jing* (Spreading Qi Classic) of unknown date. This text mentions a technique still used by External Qi Healers: to strengthen the dan tian, hold one hand on the patient's navel and one opposite it on the lower back (ming men). The Daoists also recognized that a healer could affect the qi of even distant subjects. According to the fourth-century alchemist Ge Hong, "If someone far away has been bitten by a poisonous insect, exhale onto your palm and pray: your left palm for a man, right palm for a woman. The individual will be immediately healed even if he is a hundred miles distant."[12] Such distant healing effects of prayer and intent have been documented in Western medical research and lucidly analyzed in the landmark works of Dr. Daniel Benor[13] and Dr. Larry Dossey.[14]

Many styles of EQH were developed or preserved within particular Daoist and Buddhist sects or monasteries. Some of these traditions are still transmitted only orally and have little written documentation. For instance, on Holy Mount Luo Fu in Guangzhou Province, Long-men Sect Daoists practiced standing and seated qi-projection meditations and developed a unique method of diagnosis.[15] Since the Tang Dynasty (618–907), qigong techniques were widely practiced and prescribed at Buddhist monastic hospitals.[16] Buddhist adepts may have also practiced EQH.[17] EQH methods were also discovered by chance when qigong or martial arts masters attempted to heal their own students of illnesses or injuries.

There has been a renaissance of interest in External Qi Healing since 1980 when Qigong Master Lin Hou-sheng demonstrated the ability to induce anesthesia in surgery patients using External Qi. While Lin pointed his fingers at specific acupuncture points, the patient remained conscious and without pain during a thyroidectomy. Since that time, EQH has often been used to reduce pain during or after many kinds of surgery. External Qi anesthesia and EQH in general have become respected branches of Chinese medicine. Like internal qigong, EQH has gained in credibility and respect because it is capable of being measured and tested scientifically. It works on skeptics, laboratory animals, and cell cultures, allaying concerns that it is only placebo effect. When animals with broken bones are treated by External Qi, they heal more quickly than controls.[18] We can assume that if an External Qi Healer inhibits the growth of cancer cells in mice,[19] the therapy does not work because of the mice's belief in the power and authority of the therapist!

PREPARING FOR HEALING
Healer: Heal Thyself!

The best preparation for External Qi Healing is regular practice of qigong, especially Standing Meditation.[20] It is in this systematic self-training that EQH may have some advantage over Western varieties of healing touch. As you persist with Standing, your qi field becomes stronger and your sensitivity to qi imbalances becomes more precise. This means that you can have a stronger therapeutic effect on a client. Essentially, when you practice EQH, you *are* Standing. You are recalling the same physical and spiritual state. The spine is straight, the weight sunk through the feet, and you are breathing with the dan tian. The hands are filled with qi. Daoist texts advise that to master EQH you must also master Embryonic Respiration. This is because when the mind and body are quiet, they are the most receptive and capable of storing and transmitting qi. When the mind is free of turbulence, it becomes like the surface of a calm lake, a mirror reflecting things as they are.

A thirty-year-old American acupressure massage therapist, Scott, consulted me about how he might use qigong to strengthen and improve his treatments. He did not perceive that there was anything wrong with his technique, but realized that there is always room for improvement. Scott looked anorexic. He was very thin and pale. His eyes were dull, his voice so low that I could barely hear him, and his movements slow and listless. When I asked him how his patients felt after treatment, he said, "They always say that they are very relaxed." "And how do you usually feel after a session?" He exclaimed, enthusiastically, "I feel great, full of energy." This was an interesting situation. The patients were unable to distinguish depletion from relaxation. And the therapist was probably unconsciously addicted to the charge he got from treating his patients (no pun intended). The problem was easily corrected by a three-month program of Standing Meditation and a change in diet to include more yang, fortifying foods, such as meat and spices. When I saw Scott again he had gained twenty pounds and looked in better health. I am sure his patients were also benefiting.

Qigong practice keeps the internal qi pure and balanced, without excesses (too yang) or insufficiencies (too yin). These are important matters for energy healers. If the healer's qi is toxic, stagnant, or congested, he might inadvertently transmit some of it to the patient, especially if the patient is weak and depleted. Energy tends to fill a vacuum, flowing from the positive to the negative. Or if the healer is himself depleted, he might either draw out the patient's sickness and become sick himself, or perhaps even more disconcerting, he might absorb some of the patient's own supply of healing qi. (I do not wish the reader to infer that if a healer feels better after a healing session than before, there is something wrong with the interaction. On the contrary, many studies have shown that healing heals the healer. Altruism of any kind is a powerful immune enhancer.) Unlike some forms of shamanic healing, the External Qi Healer never wishes to take on the patient's sickness or to discharge it from his own body.

In summary, if the healer practices qigong, he will safeguard against:

- transmitting toxins to the patient
- absorbing the patient's diseased qi
- absorbing the patient's healing qi

And perhaps the most important reason for External Qi Healers to prepare with qigong and meditation is that the healer, according to acupressure therapist Janet Murphy, "learns to tap into a Universal Well of Healing Energy."[21] According to two of the greatest spiritual healers of the twentieth century, Ambrose and Olga Worrall, "Too few in healing reach out to the pool of health and well-being that is all around us, the infinite sea, as available to us as the air we breathe."[22]

The source of qi is not personal but transpersonal. It includes the healer, like a drop of water in the infinite sea. The healer needs to maintain an awareness of Place, a sense of where he is, not only how he is. He should seek the same state of harmony with nature whether practicing internal qigong or EQH. Simply maintaining connectedness allows qi to flow *through* rather than *from* the body. The healer funnels[23] qi from a Source, sometimes identified as Nature, Dao, Great Spirit, or God. This belief is universal among all of the great healers, East and West. Again, the Worralls: "A spiritual healer is a person who is spiritually, physically, and biologically adaptable as a conductor between the source of supply and the patient. Under the proper conditions, healing energy will flow from the source through the healer into the patient."[24] Most healers agree that one of these "proper conditions" is compassion for the healee and a genuine desire to be of service. According to the Magus of Strovolos, an esteemed spiritual healer from Cyprus, "I assure you the more people you help, the more you fill up with vitality, assuming that you have love in your heart."[25]

THE QI MACHINE: HOW TO STAY CONNECTED WITHOUT IT

Although there are many qigong healers who accept both the omnipresence of qi and an individual's ability to tap into it, there are also many in China who do not. It is easy to become so fascinated by the movement of internal qi—the wiring of the human body—that one forgets to check if the human instrument is "plugged in" to its source of power. Qigong Master Lin Housheng warns that it may be dangerous to emit qi frequently, as this can deplete the healer's own supply.[26] An External Qi Healer and acupuncturist from the Shanghai School of Chinese Medicine expressed a similar viewpoint: "How can you use qi from nature? Where is nature's qi? This is superstition. When you emit qi, you emit your own qi. That's why I only treat patients with qi twice a week. At other times I use the Qi Machine."

Many External Qi Healers now rely on this Qi Machine, a device that emits a qi-like field of infrared and other electromagnetic frequencies. No one claims that the machine produces qi. It only emits certain energetic cor-relates of qi. How these *known* aspects of qi affect the body in isolation from the *unknown* aspects is anybody's guess. Although the machine is apparently effective for pain, headaches, and other conditions, it is immature and weak compared to EQH, for several reasons:

1. Unlike a human being, the machine cannot modulate the strength or range of the field from feedback it receives from the patient during the on-going process of healing. The machine does not know when the patient needs more or when he has had too much.

2. The development of this technology may be founded on wrong as-sumptions: that a human being must use his or her own limited resources in any therapeutic interaction, and that practitioners will always be relatively rare or inaccessible because it takes so long to develop the ability to emit qi.

3. This technology has not been in use for sufficient time to determine if there are any harmful side effects or contraindications.

4. Scientific evidence suggests that healers cause resonant effects in the patient, like one tuning fork causing another to vibrate. Who wants to reso-nate with a machine? In the third century b.c. the Daoist sage Zhuang Zi warned against becoming "machine minded."

5. A mechanical healer, unlike a real one, cannot use intent or visual-ization to project qi to a distant patient. The Qi Machine's healing ray is neither as powerful nor as precisely targeted as a human being's.

6. The human qi-field or projected qi-wave may be encoded with mental and emotional content, carrying information and positive thoughts/feelings from the healer to the patient. If so, then a Qi Machine would be incapable of producing similar therapeutic effects. Additionally, although energy is cer-tainly a measurable correlate of qi, perhaps some healing effects are a product of consciousness itself, without any need to posit an intervening energy.

An External Qi Healer will not be in danger of losing qi provided he is committed to keeping his circuits *unbroken, grounded,* and *properly insulated.* "Unbroken" implies harmony and communication between the inside and outside (self and environment), upper and lower body, conscious and subcon-scious, and right and left (including the intuitive and analytical hemispheres of the brain). "Grounded" means having your feet on the ground, taking long walks in nature, enjoying physicalness: your own body and the world. "Insulated" means setting limits, not allowing yourself to get exhausted or scattered, knowing when you need to turn inward and away from stressful situations. Insulated does not mean insulated from ... insensitive to. . . . Rather, it implies self-caring and inner-nourishing.

Being committed to these principles does not mean that you will always live up to them 100 percent. That would be a human impossibility. Rather, the dedication to these ideals and the regular effort at achieving them will ensure that the External Qi Healer is functioning with optimal potential and safety.

HEALING ENVIRONMENT

In addition to preparing himself energetically, the healer needs to cleanse the space itself of noxious qi. This principle was understood by the ancient Daoist healers who performed healings in beautiful mountain hermitages or in front of an altar, sweetened and cleansed by plumes of incense smoke; to-day, the healing environment is ignored or considered irrelevant. This is as true among modern Chinese acupuncturists as among Western health-care providers, whether physicians or naturopaths. Allopathic medicine focuses on the disease the person has. Holistic medicine prides itself on emphasizing the person who has the disease. Both tend to ignore the fuller context of healing: the environment of the patient.[27]

The relation between qi and space is a matter of common sense. Have you ever walked into the home of someone who is ill or in a bad mood or who recently argued with his wife—and sensed that something isn't right; the room's energy feels imbalanced or toxic. The same thing can happen when a client arrives for EQH or any other form of therapy. He or she may be affected by the toxins that were discharged by a previous client.

Today, it is impractical to make pilgrimages with our patients or to expect them to visit remote locations. The next best thing is to bring nature to them by using her healing power to purify and energize our places of treatment. This can be done a number of different ways. In China, it would be proper to burn Chinese incense. However, only a local herb can affect the qi of an area. I recommend that Americans burn Native American incense—sage, cedar, or sweetgrass. Respectfully gather whichever of these is local to your area.[28] Dry the plant, then burn a little bit in a container or shell. Make sure that a door or window is ajar, so that negative qi can exit. In order to prevent subtle en-ergy pollution, you should imagine that this noxious energy turns into divine light or sinks into the earth as compost. Another way to purify a room is to wave candlelight through it. If you live near the ocean, you can sprinkle ocean water to the four directions, using a tree branch or large leaf. (This method was also practiced in China, using a willow branch.) Finally, you can imagine a natural healing power suffusing the room—for instance sunlight, moonlight, or a spring breeze. This last method is generally not as effective as the others, unless your powers of concentration are very strong.

Cleanse your space before seeing any clients and between clients if you are working professionally. I recommend this to all health-care providers.[29]

BUILDING TRUST

Chinese works on EQH agree that the patient can most easily absorb qi when he is relaxed and free of worries. However, if the patient is tense, it is not enough for the doctor to say, "Relax." That's like telling someone to float when he's sinking in panic. Rather, relaxation is contagious. The patient will catch it if the healer is relaxed, centered, and calm and if the healer interacts with the patient as one human being with another, rather than from an aloof position of power and authority.

Chinese healers can take a lesson from Mexico's folk healing tradition, curanderismo. Firstly, the patient must ask for healing. The curandera (healer) does not missionize her healing ability. She is not permitted to say, "Come, I can heal you." If the patient doesn't ask, he can't receive. And very importantly, if the patient has not given permission for healing, his energy may be hidden, not as available for purposes of assessment or treatment. One time in a curanderismo training class, a student asked the curandera, "Can you read my aura?" She replied, "If you let your aura out, then I will read it." If, however, the patient is a child or someone incapacitated and unable to ask, then the curandera does not need verbal permission. Instead, as in all healings, the healer must ask her own intuition, "Can I help? Is this patient ready for the kind of healing I practice? Should I make a referral?"

When a curandera greets a patient, there is a warm handshake or embrace. Then they talk about everyday concerns. "How are your children? Are you happy at work? Would you like some coffee?" Gradually and subtly they shift into the matter of healing. Healing is treated as everyday rather than esoteric, and it is certainly not a mere business, a cold exchange of commodities. The healer needs to help the patient feel comfortable, relaxed, and cared for.

Remember, before you begin an External Qi Healing session:

- Practice qigong and meditation
- Cleanse the space
- Build a trustful atmosphere
- The patient must ask (unless incapable)

ASSESSING IMBALANCE

General Assessment

In EQH, the client can remain fully clothed, unless EQH is being combined with Swedish or other massage therapy. It is helpful if the client removes jewelry and shoes.

There is a Chinese saying, "The master physician writes the prescription as the patient walks through the door." How is this possible? If the doctor has trained his/her qi sensitivity to a high level, then he receives a very clear energetic first impression. This first level of assessment is called *qi se*, "qi appearance." The healer may even feel as if he is *seeing* the patient's imbalance (*tou shi zhen duan* "diagnosing through penetrating vision"). Chinese tradition claims that the great physician, Hua Tuo, was a master of this technique. He could see the patient's internal organs. (X-ray machines seem primitive by comparison!) However, I believe that the doctor does not so much "see" as feel. He feels the qi se; he feels the emanations from the diseased area. A healer might also notice discomfort in the same part of his own body. The feeling is interpreted and translated by the mind into an appropriate image. This is sight only in the sense of "insight."

There are many factors involved in qi se: the color of the skin; quality of movement, breath, and voice; the sound of the footsteps; and a general feeling of fullness or depletion of qi. Make a mental note of the qi se of the patient; it indicates the patient's general state of health or disease. Your ability to form this impression will grow as you advance in qigong. Later, you can use various assessment tools to corroborate or determine the accuracy of this impression and to gain more detailed information.

Next, I like to practice "laying on of hands" on energy centers or assessment areas to get a more physical and powerful impression of the client's qi. Although not specified in EQH texts, I have found that noncontact treatment is more effective if preceded by some form of physical touch. The warmth of the therapist's hands helps the patient to relax. As strange as it may sound, touch is often perceived by the patient (even those unfamiliar with energy medicine) as *less* invasive than noncontact treatment. Touch communicates caring; noncontact treatment is more obviously an attempt to change or correct the body's underlying energetic program. The only time when the therapist may need to avoid any form of physical contact is with patients who have suffered physical, emotional, and, most significantly, sexual abuse. For these individuals, touch is often perceived as a threat and an invasion of privacy.

What are these assessment areas of the body?

WITH CONTACT

The client is seated in the middle of a stool or kitchen chair, his or her back not touching the backrest. Use any or all of the following:

Method 1: The Spinal Touch. Place one palm (either hand) on the spine, opposite the navel (ming men point). The other palm rests on the spine just below the seventh cervical vertebra (*da chui* point). Keep the hands there for a few minutes, until you have some sense of the temperature, the vibratory quality of the qi, and any other subjective impressions. Does the energy feel superficial or sunken; is it smooth or coarse, choppy or flowing, warm or uncomfortably hot, cool or deathly cold? Note also if the upper or lower body seems more energized. As you practice with more and more clients and compare your findings with the patient's presenting symptoms or medically diagnosed problems, you will gradually develop the ability to interpret your subjective feelings of qi.

Method 2: Dan Tian. Another area that gives a general and overall indication of the qi level of your client is the dan tian. Place one palm just below the navel, the other palm opposite, on the back. Feel how the breath moves or doesn't move between your hands. Is the body tight or relaxed? You may also feel vital heat and qi.

The dan tian is the place of power and loss of power. It is a sensitive, vulnerable area, connected with sexuality. When children are invalidated, they learn to hold and constrict the abdomen. These tensions often persist into adulthood. For this reason, holding the dan tian can give you information about the client's self-worth and degree of empowerment. I have found it best to assess qi here only with clients whom I have already seen a few times and who do not perceive touching this area as threatening and frightening.

Method 3: Lao Gong. To get a sense of peripheral qi and blood circulation, lightly hold the lao gong point in the center of the palm. Touch the point with your thumb, the other fingers touching the back of the client's hand. You may feel both temperature and a gentle pulsing. With practice it is also possible to intuit the emotional state of the client through this point. It is directly connected with the energy of the heart.

WITHOUT CONTACT: THE ENERGY SCAN

The client can be seated or lying down. Position your palms about six inches away from the surface of your client's body. Then experiment to find a distance that allows the greatest sensation of qi. The distance may increase or decrease as you move over the body, following the contours of the energy field. When an area is too yang, the hands will push away. When an area is too yin, the hands will draw closer to the body. It does not matter if you start at the front or back, the head, feet, or center of the body. Follow your intuition. Remember that you are still not trying to change or correct the qi, only to sense it. If your client was lying on his back, he will need to lie on his front when you assess the other side of the body.

Differential Assessment

In Chapter 4, "Qigong Science," I discussed how researchers found that changes in skin conductivity at specific acupoints on the fingers and toes correspond to states of health or pathology in associated organs. These points are actually the first or last points of the organ meridians, places where the energy of the meridian peaks. What these scientists may not have realized is that they were validating an ancient Daoist method of diagnosis.

The ends of the fingers and toes are lightly grasped, one at a time, between your thumb, middle, and index fingers, while the other hand is held a short distance away from the corresponding organ. You do not have to know the exact location of the acupuncture points. Instead, the practitioner touches the general area of the point, around or on the nail. Since the other hand is placed directly above the organ, the method requires only general knowledge of anatomy and can be practiced by those unfamiliar with the location of acupuncture meridians.

Diagnose a man on his left side (using his left hand and foot), a woman on her right. The client can be lying down or seated. It does not matter which hand holds the finger/toe and which is directed over the organ. While assessing the qi, look for *three characteristics*:

1. **Temperature:** Hot, cold, or comfortable (pleasantly warm). Hot means too much qi, congested, or stagnant. This often indicates infection or inflammation. Cool means weak and depleted. Comfortable temperature generally indicates health.

2. **Rate:** Quick or slow pulse or vibration, smooth and even or broken. Of course, the ideal is a smooth, even pulse.

3. **Subjective Quality:** This can take almost any form. The energy might feel pointed, sunk, coarse, cheesy (congested), angry, depressed, tranquil, etc.

REFLEX AREAS ON THE HAND (FIG. 61)

• **Thumb—Lungs.** Hold the man's left thumb tip, the woman's right thumb tip with either hand, the other palm above the lungs. Do an energy scan of both lungs.

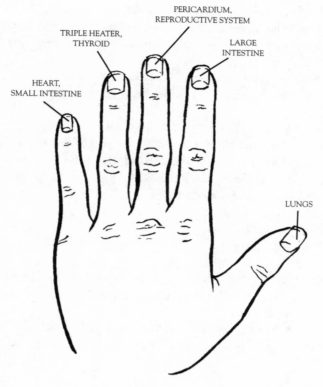

TRIPLE HEATER,
THYROID

PERICARDIUM,
REPRODUCTIVE SYSTEM

LARGE
INTESTINE

HEART,
SMALL INTESTINE

LUNGS

Figure 61

• **Index—Large Intestine.** While holding the tip of the index finger with one hand, the other slowly moves above the large intestine. You can also visualize the organ. This will make your hand position more accurate.

• **Middle Finger—Pericardium and Reproductive System.** The same fingertip is used to tune in, sequentially, to two areas of the body. As you hold the tip of the middle finger, your other hand goes first to the heart. Although this point is related to the pericardium (the membranous, fluid-filled sac that encloses the heart and the roots of major blood vessels), it is practically impossible to distinguish the pericardium from the rest of the heart. So we should consider this as part of heart qi assessment. There will be a second heart reflex area on the little finger. Next bring your palm over the reproductive system: genitals, ovaries, prostate, wherever appropriate.

• **Ring Finger—Triple Heater and Thyroid.** As you hold the triple heater area, the other hand moves gradually over the upper, middle, and lower torso, from the front or back of the body. Note the warmth and qi quality of the three areas to determine which is relatively full or depleted. Then bring your palm above the thyroid. A feeling of uncomfortable warmth or pressure may indicate hyperthyroidism; too little energy may indicate hypothyroidism.

• **Little Finger—Heart and Small Intestine.** As you contact the tip of the little finger, the other hand senses first the heart qi, then the small intestine.

REFLEX AREAS ON THE FOOT (FIG. 62a)

• **Big Toe—Liver and Spleen.** Holding the end of the big toe with the thumb, index, and middle fingers of one hand, the other palm is positioned above the liver, sensing the qi. Then move your palm to the spleen. The procedure is similar for each of the other toes.

• **Second Toe—Stomach.**
• **Fourth Toe—Gallbladder.**
• **Little Toe—Bladder.**

What happened to number three? Am I missing a toe? The third toe does not have a beginning or ending meridian point and is not used to diagnose organ health.

Finally, to tune in to the qi of the kidneys, lightly touch the "Bubbling Well" point (figure 62b) on the sole of the foot, one-third the distance from

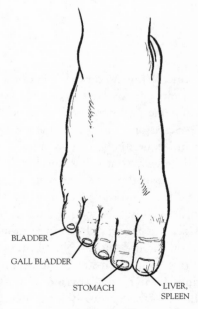

BLADDER

GALL BLADDER

STOMACH

LIVER, SPLEEN

Figure 62a

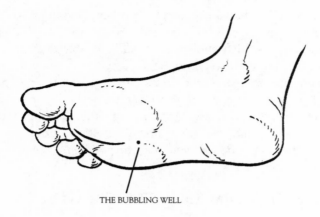

THE BUBBLING WELL

Figure 62b

the base of the second toe to the back of the heel. The other palm reaches behind your client, feeling the kidney qi.

Putting It All Together

You have learned four methods to assess imbalance in qi. 1. Qi se, for a general impression. 2. Light contact on any of three assessment areas (spine, dan tian, palm). 3. Noncontact scanning. 4. Differential assessment using points on the hand and foot. Proceeding in this order, each method adds to your database, giving you more details about what you sensed while applying the previous technique.

For instance, a middle-aged male patient walks into your office. You notice immediately that his movements are determined and aggressive, his face slightly red. The qi se suggests heat, fire, perhaps a "false yang," masking or compensating for inner depletion. When you place your palms on his spine, there is a great deal of surface warmth, with much more warmth on the upper back. You think, Yes, this does seem to be a condition of excess yang, and, in general, too much energy in the upper body, too little in the lower. Then, during a noncontact scan, your hand feels pressure over the heart and liver, and coolness around the kidneys. The finger-toe method confirms your impression: heart and liver hot and yang, kidneys weak.

If you are a health-care professional, you will compare your findings with other systems of diagnosis. For example, a Chinese doctor might feel the pulses and look at the tongue fur to determine the health of the organs. A physician will compare her qi assessment with information received through the stethoscope, EKG, blood work, and any other necessary tests. She might find that the patient above has elevated stress hormones ("adrenal burn-out"), arteriosclerosis, high cholesterol levels (possibly due to a liver malfunction), and a type A personality.

The more you compare your qi assessment with the patient's health history and with standard diagnostic measures—whether from allopathic medicine, chiropractic, Chinese Medicine, or other healing systems—the more you can refine your qi sensitivity and diagnostic abilities.

Now the question is, how do you treat the problem?

TREATMENT STRATEGIES
De Qi: Reaching the Qi

In all aspects of External Qi Healing, whether diagnosing or treating, the most important principle is *de qi* "reach the qi." This means that your hands reach energetically through the clothing, through the skin and tissue, to the underlying life energy, the qi. In China, where patients are more familiar with the electrical sensations associated with qi flow, a beginning acupuncturist will commonly ask her patient, *De qi le, mei you?* "Have I reached the qi?" If the needle is inserted too superficially, it is only in the skin; if too deeply, it can penetrate or damage nerves or other tissues. If it misses the point entirely, there may be pain but no "electricity." The acupuncturist proceeds gradually and may ask the patient for feedback. Essentially, she is asking, "Am I on target?" Later, as the acupuncturist becomes familiar with the electrical, almost vibratory energy that is emitted from the needle, she no longer needs to ask the patient. She can feel the qi.

In External Qi Healing, there is no instrument between the healer and the healee. The healer senses the qi directly with the hands. The healer changes the depth of penetration of her touch not by increasing the pressure of the hands on the skin but by maintaining a calm yet energized qigong-state and simply *intending* to reach in.[30] She knows when she has *de qi* because she senses vibration, warmth, and an indefinable feeling of energy on the patient's body or in his qi field. When the healer feels that she has reached the qi, the patient usually feels it also. It is not uncommon for the patient to exclaim, "What did you do? Your hands suddenly feel like a heat lamp!"

Making Contact: Healing Through Sensing and Yin Yang Polarity

Placing the hands on or above assessment areas is obviously more than assessment. It is the beginning of treatment. *Sensing is healing!* When we interact with another, there is no way to absolutely assess the state of health. As we sense qi, the qi changes and moves toward balance. The observer changes that which is observed. This is why it is important to remember your first impressions and to note how this impression changes as your hands remain on or above assessment areas. The degree of change may be predictive of the patient's responsiveness to therapy.

Sensing, making contact, is the first, safest, and most important method of treatment. After finishing your assessment, return to the places of imbalance—areas where you felt excess, deficient, or diseased qi. Place one or both hands either on that area or in the qi field above it. One of the most effective ways to apply sensing is to position the hands on either side of a diseased area, as though you are doing Standing Meditation with the patient between your palms. I call this method "Yin Yang Polarity."

For example, if the patient has a diseased liver, then one palm can be held in back of the liver, one in front, several inches from the patient's body (fig. 63). Don't worry about projecting qi. Just do your Standing Meditation. You are actually doing qigong together. Your qi field, interacting with that of the patient, communicates a healing message. Unlike Western biotech-

Figure 63

nology, this method requires awareness and intent on the part of the practitioner. The healing message is stronger in proportion to the depth of the healer's centeredness and ability to connect with the patient and with universal qi.

Adapt the Standing Meditation posture to the position of your patient. If your patient is seated or lying on a massage table, it is difficult to reach the patient unless you squat very low or bend your back. This is uncomfortable and awkward and will decrease the amount of qi available. Instead, sit next to your patient. Keep your legs uncrossed, your feet flat on the ground, back straight, breath sunk, and arms rounded. Maintain all of the principles of Standing Meditation from your seated position.

When should you use Healing Through Sensing or the Yin Yang Polarity? These methods may be used for any kind of condition, whether congested (yang) or depleted (yin). It is always the safest method of treatment when you get a confusing impression and are unsure exactly what the problem is. Because the healer is not trying to change or manipulate the patient's energy in any specific way, there is almost no chance of doing harm. For some EQH patients it may be necessary to use only Healing Through Sensing. Generally, I like to begin and end all EQH sessions with Sensing.

Correcting Imbalance: Circling Palms

To understand the principles of transmitting therapeutic qi, try the following experiment. Ask a friend to hold out his left hand, palm up. Place your right palm a few inches above his hand, finding the distance that allows maximum qi sensation. Now as your partner's hand remains still, slowly rotate your right hand in tiny counterclockwise circles, as though the center of your palm is a laser beam, drawing a circle around your friend's palm. Then increase the circumference of your circle, so that your palm is shining light on each of your partner's fingertips and then moving down to the top of the wrist. After several circles, reverse direction, circling clockwise. Ask your friend what he or she felt. Was there a qualitative difference between the two circles, counterclockwise and clockwise? Let your friend try the experiment on you. Is your experiment replicable? Try it with other friends and see if you get the same results. What sensation is produced by counterclockwise circles, what sensation by clockwise circles?

You have already discovered the first principle of therapeutic noncontact treatment. Counterclockwise is cooling (yin) and reduces heat, inflammation, fever, congestion. Clockwise circling creates warmth (yang) and adds energy and stimulation to weak, cold, and depleted areas. If an organ or area feels hot or over-full, use counterclockwise circles, circling above it sev-

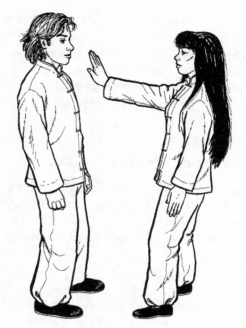

Figure 64

eral times, until you sense that the area is responding maximally and returning to a more normal temperature. If the organ feels cool or deficient, circle
clockwise. If you are unsure, use Healing Through Sensing.

Whereas most EQH treatment methods can be applied with both hands
at once or either hand individually, circling palms is best performed with
only one hand, called the *yang hand*. It does not matter which hand is used to
project qi. Some healers prefer the right, some the left, some are ambidex-
trous, or at least energetically so, and will use one hand or the other according to their mood. The other hand, the *yin hand*, is relatively passive. It is not
used to treat or project qi, but rather rests at the side of the body, fingers
pointing toward the earth. The yin hand connects with the energy of the
earth. Like the healer's feet, the yin hand helps the healer stay grounded. It
will also automatically discharge toxic qi from the healer's body or draw extra healing energy up into the body if there is a need for it. There is no need
for the healer to *think of* emitting or absorbing qi with the yin hand. This will
happen by itself if the healer is relaxed and rooted. *Both hands are simultaneously practicing de qi.* The yang hand reaches the qi of the patient; the yin
hand reaches the qi of the earth (fig. 64).

The circling palms method of treatment is identical to that used by indigenous people. When I explained to my Cherokee mentor, Keetoowah, about EQH methods, he looked at me in disbelief: "How could Chinese people know about Cherokee medicine?" Keetoowah used to hold his hands in front and back of the patient's body, "like two poles of a magnet, the negative and positive." Sometimes he would circle one palm—clockwise to warm the body, counterclockwise to cool it. His other hand was usually pointed toward the ground.

Tapping, Pulsing, Waving

Other effective treatment gestures include Tapping, Pulsing, and Waving. *Tapping* means to lightly and rhythmically tap or pat the qi field with either your palm or fingertips. This is useful to relieve stagnation or congestion and to improve circulation. In *Tui-na*, Chinese Massage Therapy, tapping is applied directly to the body for the same purpose. The therapist taps with either fingers, palm, back of the hand, side of the hand, or fist to produce varying degrees of stimulation.

Pulsing means to ever so slightly open and close the palm. Stretch the fingers and hand open, then let it relax. Do this repeatedly at a steady pace. The qi is emitted from the center of the healer's palm. The indications for pulsing are similar to tapping. It stimulates and improves circulation. Pulsing can be used over any area of the body that requires it, including specific acupuncture points. If you pulse directly over an acupuncture point, it is easy to feel tingling and warmth at the point or radiating along the meridian.

Waving is very useful for congestion or pain. The fingertips sweep down the patient's energy field, as though brushing the pain away. The technique is identical to the "Sweeping" *(barrida)* practiced in Mexican curanderismo healing.

These three methods move qi without adding heat or cold. They can be applied by themselves or combined with clockwise or counterclockwise circling. For instance, if the kidneys are weak and deficient, it may be necessary to use gentle pulsing of qi, followed by clockwise circling. If the shoulders are tight, painful, and hot, you can use counterclockwise circling to reduce tension and waving to relieve pain. For an inflamed, sore throat, you may wish to circle counterclockwise over the throat and then sweep the pain away from the body.

Hand Position

Usually the entire open hand is used to transmit qi. Qi is emitted from the fingers and palm over a broad area. To intensify the "qi beam," emit qi from

Figure 65

the fingertips as a whole or any individual fingertip. This is useful to work on a very specific, small area, such as a cyst or wound. To intensify the beam still further, concentrate on emitting qi only from your palm-center, lao gong point. (Some External Qi Healers emit qi from other acupuncture points, such as the Bubbling Well in the feet or the yin tang point between the eyebrows.)

Acupuncturists or those familiar with Chinese medical theory can use the most specialized hand gesture, known as "sword fingers" (*jian zhi*) to direct qi into specific acupuncture points. The index and middle fingers are gently extended, with the thumb and last two fingers bent into the palm (fig. 65). Here the EQH therapist is actually doing acupuncture without the needles. The sword fingers circle counterclockwise to sedate the energy of the point or clockwise to tonify it. The sword fingers can also tap by moving slightly away from and toward the point. It is also possible to combine EQH with acupuncture. Acupuncturists generally twirl or poke the acupuncture needle to change the quality of stimulation at a specific point. Acupuncturists trained in EQH leave the needle in place and while holding their sword fingers a few inches above the needle, tonify, sedate, or stimulate the point with appropriate EQH gestures.

DURATION AND FREQUENCY

The length of treatment can vary a great deal from patient to patient, depending on what the patient is capable of receiving. For some, five minutes is sufficient. For others, forty minutes is necessary. The therapist can judge the patient's receptivity and degree of satiation (with qi) by noticing changes in the patient's skin color and respiration. If the skin becomes very red or very pale or if the breathing rate becomes consistently quicker, the patient is uncomfortable. If the therapist is capable of de qi, she will also be able to feel when the energy is no longer received. At some point the therapist may feel as though the same poles of a magnet have been brought together. Instead of attracting her qi, the patient repels it. Obviously, the treatment should be closed.

The most important indication of satiation is the patient himself. He needs to know that it is acceptable to inform the therapist if a treatment feels inappropriate, excessive, or insufficient. I have found that when therapists continue EQH against the verbal or nonverbal permission of the patient— with an attitude of "I know what's best for you"—both therapist and patient can become ill. The patient is constipated with unassimilated qi. The therapist is hit by some of her own returning qi, now tainted by the toxic qi field of the patient.

Some patients will experience significant improvement after the first session. Most patients notice definite changes by session four or five. Acute problems are more likely to respond quickly. Long-term, chronic conditions will require a longer course. For instance, I have found that car accident victims with brain injuries usually experience subjective qi sensations after a few sessions, but require anywhere from four to six months before their condition improves according to objective measures. Treatments are generally given once a week. If the condition is very serious, the patient can be treated more frequently.

As with any therapy, not all patients are cured; however, unlike patients treated by allopathic interventions, almost all individuals who receive EQH experience improvements in quality of life, including better sleep, more energy, improved appetite and digestion, and a healthier attitude. In the long run, these qualitative changes may have a stronger effect on the course of serious disease than any specific therapy.

CHAPTER SIXTEEN

The Complete Qigong Workout

*Your stability is as good as your willingness to
risk and lose it, trusting yourself to reach
stability again in a different position.*
—RUTHY ALON, *MINDFUL SPONTANEITY*

In the previous chapters you accumulated a wide repertoire of healing techniques. If you think that the day is not long enough to practice them all,
you are right! One could easily spend all of one's time in self-improvement
and life-enhancing practices and never have time to enjoy life. This is why I
emphasize Moderation as the first of four important principles of qigong training: *Moderation, Gradualness, Patience,* and *Perseverance.*

It is best to begin very gradually, ten minutes of qigong a day. Eventually
you can train for anywhere from twenty minutes to an hour once or twice a
day. Are even longer sessions counterproductive? Not necessarily. It is a very
individual matter. I have some students who reach optimal qi development
with twenty minutes' training per day, others who require two to three hours.

With so many techniques, how do you choose what to practice? How
does one design a "wellness workout" for health maintenance and improvement that can be practiced safely on a regular basis?

Method #1: Choose a maximum of three techniques and concentrate on
these for about three months. Then either continue doing these or switch to
other styles. Through trial and error you will eventually arrive at the most
beneficial training routine.

Method #2: Over the course of a year, systematically try various combinations of qigong methods. In Suggested Routines, below, I have indicated some possible combinations.

Your morning qigong workout should be fun, dynamic, and good exercise. Emphasize active qigong and include the following elements:

- **Relaxation and Centering:** First practice a few minutes of fang song gong relaxation (Chapter 8). Then center yourself with quiet seated meditation, "entering tranquillity" followed by a few minutes of Inner Nourishing Qigong.
- **Stretching:** The Daoists say that longer muscles mean longer life. You can stretch in your own way, working tight muscles and opening locked joints, or practice a formal technique such as Yoga.[1]
- **Detoxification:** You must pour out the old water from a cup before you can fill it with anything new. Get rid of stagnant and toxic energies. The Bone Marrow Cleansing (Chapter 12) fits this category.
- **Gathering and Storing Qi:** Gather fresh qi by practicing Standing Meditation (Chapter 10).
- **Circulating Qi:** Now that your body is charged, circulate and spread the qi by practicing a more dynamic qigong such as Walking Meditation (Chapter 10), the Crane and Bear Animal Frolics (Chapter 12), or both. After these practices, martial arts students can do Taiji Quan or other choreographed forms.
- **Dispersing Stagnation:** At the end of the workout, apply self-massage (An-Mo Gong) to charge up depleted areas and to disperse remaining pockets of congestion and stagnation.

What about meditative qigong? Practice qigong meditations at the beginning of your basic workout or save them for a second evening practice session. Qigong meditations that are ordinarily practiced from a standing posture (e.g., Crane, Turtle, and Deer; Aligning the Three Dan Tians; Spontaneous Movement Qigong) fall somewhere between active and passive qigong and can be added to your morning routines or practiced at other times of day.

SUGGESTED ROUTINES

Begin each morning workout with Relaxation, Meditation (including Inner Nourishing Qigong, if you wish), and Stretching. Then proceed to the techniques listed here. Numbers in parentheses refer to minutes of practice.

The amounts are only rough approximations and will vary according to your individual pace. If your time is limited, you can eliminate any exercise(s) in a sequence, keeping the remaining ones in the same order. I suggest *not* eliminating Standing Meditation from your morning cultivation.

Morning practices are essential for building qi. Evening sessions are helpful, but not absolutely required.

Week 1

A.M.	P.M.
Standing Meditation (10)	Entering Tranquillity (10)

Weeks 2–3

A.M.	P.M.
Eight Brocades (5)	Alternate Nostril Breathing (5)
Standing Meditation (10–15)	Entering Tranquillity (10–15)

Weeks 4–12

A.M.	P.M.
Eight Brocades (5)	Six Qi Method (5)
Bone Marrow Cleansing (7)	Alternate Nostril Breathing (5)
Standing Meditation (10–20)	Entering Tranquillity (20+)
Animal Frolics (7)	
Whole-Body Qi Massage (5)	

TOTAL WORKOUT TIME
A.M. 24 minutes + Standing
P.M. 30 minutes

Weeks 13–25

A.M.	P.M.
Eight Brocades (5)	Six Qi Method (5)
Bone Marrow Cleansing (7)	Colored Light Meditation (10)
Standing Meditation (20–40)	Alternate Nostril Breathing (5)
Walking Meditation (5)	Qi to the Four Limbs (5)
Taiji Ruler (7)	Small Heavenly Circulation (10)
Animal Frolics (optional)	Entering Tranquillity (10)
Whole-Body Qi Massage (5)	

TOTAL WORKOUT TIME
A.M. 29 minutes + Standing and optional practices
P.M. 45 minutes

Weeks 26–38

A.M.	P.M.
Eight Brocades (5)	Six Qi Method (5)
Bone Marrow Cleansing (7)	Colored Light Meditation *or*
Standing Meditation (20–40)	The Planets Within (10)
Walking Meditation (5)	Alternate Nostril Breathing (5)
Taiji Ruler (optional)	Great Heavenly Circulation (10)
Animal Frolics (optional)	Entering Tranquillity (10)
Crane, Turtle, Deer Breathing (9)	
Aligning the Three Dan Tians (3)[2]	
Whole-Body Qi Massage (5)	

TOTAL WORKOUT TIME
A.M. 34 minutes + Standing and optional practices
P.M. 40 minutes

Weeks 39–52

A.M.	P.M.
Eight Brocades (5)	Embryonic Respiration (30+)
Bone Marrow Cleansing (7)	
Standing Meditation (20–40)	
Walking Meditation (5–10)	
Taiji Ruler (optional)	
Animal Frolics (optional)	
Crane, Turtle, Deer (optional)	
Aligning the Three Dan Tians (optional)	
Unifying Heaven and Earth (10)	
Whole-Body Qi Massage (5)	

TOTAL WORKOUT TIME
A.M. 32 minutes + Standing and optional practices
P.M. 30 minutes

After this first year, you are on your own (or better still, working with an instructor while keeping up with practices in this book). Find out what works. Combine techniques creatively. Continue Standing and Entering Tranquillity.

You may wish to practice a *split routine*, where you do a basic workout every day but alternate between various other techniques. These other methods can be added on to your core workout on either a daily or occasional basis. Or you can do a completely different qigong workout twice a week. For instance, some students like to practice only Spontaneous Movement Qigong twice a week. Split routine training prevents you from falling into a rut of habitual practice. Variety keeps the mind fresh and attentive. It also prevents over- or underworking any particular aspect of health or human potential.

You can also add therapeutic or specialized qigong techniques as needed, either as part of your regular practice sessions or at other times of day. For particular health problems practice appropriate techniques such as Inner Nourishing for ulcers and stress reduction, Brain Cleansing for headaches, Arm Swinging to improve circulation, Healing the Emotions for emotional difficulties, or the Mind Directs Qi for any condition. The disabled can do seated variations of almost all qigong techniques and should spend extra time on the qigong meditations.

When a great Japanese Buddhist returned from visiting China, he was asked, "What is the most important thing you learned?" He replied, "Supple mindedness." This is a meaningful concept for qigong students. Keep your mind flexible and relaxed. Try not to approach qigong rigidly or militaristically. Remember that the purpose of qigong is to enhance life. The purpose of life is *not* to practice qigong. I mention this because some people are so bent on self-improvement that they do qigong out of a sense of duty and an almost morose determination rather than enjoyment. Allow me to suggest that if you are trying so desperately to improve yourself, you probably feel very bad about who you are. Clear this self-esteem problem up directly. Seek professional help from a therapist. Then you can practice qigong with freedom and enjoyment rather than compulsion.

If you are open to possibilities, qigong can greatly add to your appreciation of other activities. Before receiving a facial, try the Youthful Complexion self-massage. Your face will be relaxed and sensitive before the session begins. If you are going swimming, do the Wake-Up! self-massage earlier in the day. You may be surprised at how many more laps you can swim. I love to practice Absorbing Qi from Nature when I am in the forest or the Big Dipper meditation on a clear evening. And my favorite place for Standing Meditation is in a particular mountain meadow, facing a clear stream. You will find that many qigong techniques can be practiced "spur of the moment," as the need and inspiration arises.

CHAPTER SEVENTEEN
Benefits and Dangers of Qigong

Life begins at seventy. Everything is beautiful!
—MASTER T. T. LIANG

SIGNS OF SUCCESS

How can you tell if you are doing qigong correctly? What are the signs that you are on track? The four signs of qi flow, the *qi gan* (qi sensations), are *warmth, weight, vibration,* and *expansiveness.* These are generally felt during and immediately after qigong practice.

You feel a pleasant warmth, which is usually most noticeable in the extremities and in the lower abdomen or lower back. This is a sign of improved circulation of qi and blood. Beginners may also sweat even while practicing very relaxed, effortless qigong, though this usually stops after a few months.

You will also experience a sensation of weight, balance, and centeredness, like a tree with deep roots. You feel cool-headed but warm-hearted, the center of gravity has shifted down. The body becomes like a mountain, the mind like the clear sky above it.

Vibration refers to the tingling sensation that so often accompanies qigong. It is very common to feel as though the fingers, palms, or other parts of the body are filled with either pulsing or flowing electricity. Yet this is not a jumpy feeling, like a live wire. Rather, such vibrations seem to accompany a quiet, meditative mind. As the *Taiji Quan Classic* says, "The qi is vibrating like a drum; the spirit is conserved within."

270

Expansiveness means that your body feels open and expansive, without constriction or hindrance anywhere. The very dimensions of your physical being seem to have changed. Some of these changes may actually be occurring. The back lengthens, the joints open. You may be standing taller. But normally, when we speak of expansiveness, we mean the subjective feeling of blending into the environment. Your feet reach through the ground into the earth. Your head joins with the sky. Your skin breathes nature's qi.

There are also many general qigong effects on health and well-being. You should experience some of them during the first few weeks of training.

1. Better Health: Obviously the first sign is that you are feeling better and your health is improving. Even long-term problems such as high blood pressure or poor digestion may start to clear up. Pain is reduced, and you have fewer complaints. You have more vitality and a greater sense of aliveness and joy of life.

2. Sounder Sleep: This is another very common effect, especially appreciated by seniors. I like to tell my students, "If you have trouble going to sleep, don't count sheep, count your breaths." As the breath deepens and slows down, the mind relaxes and drifts easily into sleep. Most people notice this benefit right away.

Notice I say sounder sleep, not necessarily less sleep. We need to dispel a Chinese myth that qigong adepts need only one or two hours of sleep per night. I do believe that if one is getting enough exercise, is living in a beautiful environment, and is emotionally content, then one will probably need less sleep. One or two hours? Not impossible, but I doubt it. Qigong masters who recommend such austerity may be missionizing and rationalizing a sleeping disorder.

As qigong becomes a part of living, we cease overworking and pushing the body. We shift out of overdrive and relax into the body's natural rhythm. Sleep becomes more restful and refreshing.

3. Increased Strength: It is an odd but indisputable fact that after a few months of gentle qigong, you are physically stronger. If your preferred method of building strength has been lifting weights, go back to the gym and notice how much more you are now able to press. Or visit the driving range and see how much farther you are hitting the golf ball.

According to Chinese medicine, internal strength creates external strength. The paradox is that the more relaxed you are, the stronger you can become. Qigong pumps qi into the muscles, which improves circulation, increases the assimilation of nutrients, and prevents excessive muscle breakdown caused by chronic tension and stress. Qigong trains volition so that whatever strength is available can be used and directed efficiently. The practitioner learns how to focus integrated power; posture, muscles, and breath all work together.

4. Clearer Skin: One of the first things one notices about qigong instructors is their clear complexions and soft, almost babylike skin. Qigong causes qi to flow both deep within the body and under the skin, keeping the skin moist, resilient, yet resistant to abrasion and injury.

Clear, healthy skin is a benefit of abdominal breathing. The lungs and skin are the organs of contact between our bodies and the external world. Respiration and perspiration are linked processes, the lungs absorbing fresh qi from the air and emitting old qi, the skin absorbing radiant qi from "the three luminaries" (sun, moon, and stars) and environmental qi from nature and emitting toxins in the form of sweat and invisible toxic qi. The lungs and skin have an internal-external relationship, where the internal organ is of primary importance. Healthy lungs and breathing *creates* healthy skin. Conversely, unnatural breathing (such as hyperventilation) creates more favorable conditions for developing skin disease.

5. More Efficient and Active Metabolism: After practicing qigong, the metabolic rate is generally slower. The body has shifted toward an energy storage mode as evidenced in slower respiratory rate, heart rate, and brain waves. Yet certain aspects of the metabolism are speeded up. The body repairs its injuries more quickly. Digestion is quicker and more efficient. Saliva secretion increases during and sometimes after practice. (If your throat is dry and scratchy after practice, you may be forcing the breath or opening the mouth too often—perhaps breathing with nose and mouth during exercises that require only nose breathing.)

One of the most frequently observed signs of physiological change due to qigong is the accelerated growth of hair and nails. Qigong students remark that they have to cut their hair and nails twice as often as before they began practice. This is believed to be the result of the body shedding its dead cells more quickly. Some Daoists believe that when a sage dies, his body just disappears, blending with the qi of the universe. All that is left behind is clothing, hair, and nails.

6. Increased Libido: Qigong increases the body's supply of qi and jing, sexual essence, and removes blockages to the flow of these vital energies. After a few months of qigong practice, it is common to feel more easily aroused and more sensitive sexually. Daoist and Buddhist monks dealt with heightened sexuality by sublimating sexual energies and impulses with exercises that internalize the jing, drawing it away from the genitals. Individuals living a normal, modern lifestyle need to be careful that they not allow the increased libido to create impulsive or inappropriate behavior.

7. Psychophysiological Self-Control: Qigong students learn how to relax the mind and muscles at will. Imagine being able to practice this skill during rush-hour traffic! A Chinese qigong teacher once remarked to me that he knew his qigong was improving when he remained calm during his United States immigration interview. Greater muscular control leads to improved posture, coordination, and balance. This benefit is of special importance for the elderly, since in the United States about 30 percent of people over age sixty-five suffer at least one fall each year, and 10 to 15 percent of these falls result in serious injury. In 1995, the *Journal of the American Medical Association* reported that a group of individuals aged seventy and over who practiced Taiji Quan showed "significant decreases in the risk of falling . . . (P=.01)" when compared to a control group.[1]

8. Bright Eyes: The eyes seem to sparkle after a few weeks of qigong. This might be due to a happier attitude and a more luminous spirit. As we learn to sense the qi, the eyes also emit qi. Daoists say that a master's eyes glow in the dark, like a cat's.

9. Mystical Signs: Qigong strengthens the intuition. Synchronicity becomes almost commonplace as you find yourself more often in the right place at the right time. You may find that your dreams are more meaningful and can be more easily remembered, perhaps because there is less distance or tension between the conscious and unconscious. Both Daoism and Yoga compare spiritual wisdom to a sweet and fragrant flower rising out of muddy water. When this flower blossoms, that is, when the mind is clear and serene, you will sense a flowerlike fragrance around your body and a sweet taste in your mouth, like honey.

During the first few months of qigong, some students may also experience uncomfortable sensations such as unusual itching, trembling, swaying, or twitching, clicking in the joints, sweating, and sore muscles. Students experiencing these symptoms should rule out the possibility of an underlying skin or neurological disorder. There might also be brief periods of drowsiness or restlessness. It is common to feel the stomach rumbling or to find oneself passing gas more often. These temporary side effects are generally symptoms of neither success nor failure. They are signs that the body is expelling toxins and adjusting to a new level of energy.

DANGER SIGNALS

Because most qigong techniques are so gentle and meditative, it is one of the safest self-healing systems in the world, but if not done correctly even qigong can have some unpleasant side effects. You can avoid negative reactions by following the instructions carefully and by practicing with moderation, patience, and intuition. Abnormal effects can accompany any style of qigong if you maintain a disease-promoting lifestyle or are too eager for results. Always go step by step. A quantum leap in qigong means you land on your back!

Dizziness, Headache, Nausea

If you practice qigong while the kids are clamoring for breakfast, while watching the morning news, or without turning off your phone and answering machine, you may end up with a headache, dizziness, or nausea instead of serenity. The only way to succeed in qigong is to resolve that every day you will spend at least twenty minutes in self-caring. You deserve it! This may mean getting up earlier, practicing a bit later in the morning, going to a park, or renting time in a dance studio a few times a week.

Too much concentration can cause the same symptoms as too much distraction. Excessive visualization or forcing the mind to hold images or thoughts beyond comfortable limits pushes too much qi into the head and drains the dan tian. This can also happen with excess worry or anxiety. As a result, you experience headaches and nausea or a feeling of weakness and queasiness in the stomach. On the other hand, if you force the breath into the dan tian with too much pressure and effort, you will become "constipated" with qi. You may feel dizzy and have uncomfortable sensations in the abdomen such as distension or nausea. The solution is to Do Less and remember the importance of effortlessness and relaxation.

Headaches can also result from practicing qigong outdoors in a strong wind. Wind disperses qi and prevents it from gathering or settling properly. It causes the qi, especially the qi of the liver, to move erratically. In Chinese Medicine, liver imbalance can lead to painful, throbbing headaches.

Hair Loss

Whereas relaxed and meditative qigong makes hair grow more quickly, obsessive and excessive practice of qigong has the opposite effect. Hair is lost in irregular patches when no skin or scalp disease is present.[2] (I am not speaking of genetically determined male-pattern baldness or receding hairlines.) Its poetic Chinese name is *Huo Shao Shao-lin Si*, "Fire burns the Shao-lin Temple." This expression is a pun on the words Shao-lin, which can mean both the name of a famous monastery or, literally, "the little forest." Huo

Shao Shao-lin Si means that the qi is raging like a forest fire and burns the hair follicles (the "little forest"). Why is this "fire" (the qi) out of control? Because it is not held in check by the kidney-water cultivated through quiet, meditative breathing. Huo Shao Shao-lin Si is reversible. I have personally seen cases of hair loss induced through incorrect qigong and regrowth occurring within six months of moderate, correct practice.

Difficult Breathing

Difficult breathing, including breathing that is shallow, halting, constricted, or simply uncomfortable, may occur during or after practice. It can be caused by distraction or excessive concentration or by eating too close to practice time. Physical tension and emotional problems also interfere with breathing. Whenever a problem occurs, look first for the obvious cause and solution. Breathing difficulties may simply be the result of holding an imbalanced or tense posture. If the back is bent, twisted, or compressed, or if the chest is distended or depressed, breathing will feel labored.

Miscellaneous Problems

Qigong exercises are contraindicated for certain conditions. I have noted precautions in previous chapters; let common sense be your guide. If you have any doubts about whether to practice a certain technique, you can also consult your physician. Here are some rules:

- **Do not** practice strenuous qigong or assume low postures if you are pregnant or menstruating.
- **Do not** practice postures that might strain arthritic or damaged joints.
- **Do not** practice qigong that creates subjective feelings of heat if you have an inflammation or infection (hot, yang conditions).
- **Do not** tax your reserves, especially if you have chronic fatigue syndrome, are recovering from surgery, or have any medical condition that requires more rest than exercise.
- **Do not** spend too much time meditating if you need more exercise. Gentle movement is better than static postures for qi or blood stagnation: painful, swollen conditions such as varicose veins, hemorrhoids, swollen breasts, a feeling of abdominal or organ distension.
- **Do not** force yourself to practice slow abdominal breathing if you have a condition that creates metabolic acidosis (for a definition, see Chapter 9), such as diabetes or kidney failure.

And remember these general principles:

- **If the belly is filled with food, there is no room for qi.** Do not practice qigong immediately after eating.
- **Calm weather encourages calm qi.** Do not practice outdoors when the weather is extreme or uncomfortable.
- **If there is pain, there is no gain.** Do not use your willpower to override pain, especially if the pain seems provoked by practice.[3]
- **Never instead of, but in addition to.**[4] Do not substitute qigong for other required forms of therapy, whether allopathic or alternative. Qigong should cultivate flexibility, not stubbornness.

Qigong Psychosis

In the late 1970s I coined the diagnostic terms *qigong psychosis* and *qigong psychotic reaction* as translations for the Chinese expression *zou huo ru mo*, "fire [the qi] wild, devils enter." This describes delusional thinking that results from incorrect and excessive training. It was only in 1994 that the term "qigong psychotic reaction" was included in the "Glossary of Culture-Bound Syndromes" in the *DSM IV*, the diagnostic manual of the American Psychiatric Association.

> **qi-gong psychotic reaction** A term describing an acute, time-limited episode characterized by dissociative, paranoid, or other psychotic or nonpsychotic symptoms that may occur after participation in the Chinese folk health-enhancing practice of qi-gong ("exercise of vital energy"). Especially vulnerable are individuals who become overly involved in the practice.[5]

More is not always better. Powerful medicines can be harmful if the dosage is excessive. Here are two examples:

A thirty-year-old Taiji Quan teacher, whom I will call Bill, came to me for some private classes. Bill had been practicing Taiji Quan for ten years, three to five hours every day. Yet his movements were tense, abrupt, and disconnected. During practice, his eyes wandered about haphazardly. He seemed to have no center, either physically or psychologically. I could recognize his Taiji Quan postures, but someone else watching him practice would probably have thought Bill was on drugs. When he finished, I asked him if he had any particular focus of concentration as he practiced. He said, "Yes, when I do Taiji Quan I am in my third aura!" Qigong does not have a concept of a "third aura." When I asked Bill to explain what he meant, he said that the third aura was his aura's aura. This seemed to hold some deep, mystical significance for him, but, to me, the "third aura" was an indication of delusion induced by excessive and incorrect qigong. It was not so much what he said that disturbed me, but how he said it. Bill was as disconnected and out of touch mentally as he was physically. He expressed his desire to use Taiji Quan as a vehicle for living in his third aura all of the time. Instead of learning more about his body, he seemed determined to get away from it!

Bill had been practicing Taiji Quan in his bizarre way for many years. He was not a drug user and was functional in everyday life. In Bill's case I did not think that delusional thinking was causing him to practice Taiji Quan the way he did. Rather, his excessive practice of grossly incorrect Taiji Quan was causing the problem. I told Bill that he needed to stop teaching and practicing Taiji Quan for at least a year. He agreed, instead, to do *twenty minutes* (not more) of Standing Meditation every morning, followed by self-massage of the abdomen, back, and feet.

A year later, I visited Bill and asked him to try doing some Taiji Quan. Bill performed the exercise beautifully, with none of the previous disturbances. His form was relaxed, fluid, and grounded. Bill continued doing Standing Meditation as a warm-up every day, followed by moderate practice of Taiji Quan. He resumed his teaching career and continued to improve.

Rev. Feng, a Buddhist qigong master, spent twenty-five years practicing alone in a cave. He was revered by Buddhists for his knowledge of meditations, breathing exercises, and mantras. When I met him, I was frankly unimpressed. Engaging him in any sort of conversation required a great deal of effort. His mind was constantly invoking deities. He knew how to talk to God but not to God's manifestation, a mundane friend or colleague. In Buddhist terms, he stunk of Buddhism. In qigong terms, his excess effort at finding the truth had put him out of touch with reality!

The Taiji Quan teacher and Buddhist master are not isolated cases. In more than twenty-five years of teaching, I have met five or six qigong teachers and at least fifty qigong students who developed similar problems resulting from excessive practice, going too fast, or ignoring both instructions and common sense. The dangers of excess are also well-known in China.[6] Dr. Zhang Tongling, professor of psychiatry at Beijing Medical University, runs a clinic for obsessive qigong practitioners. In a study of 145 patients, she found that fanatical practice of qigong could cause latent psychiatric problems to surface and lead to hallucinations.[7]

Qigong has helped millions of people achieve better physical and mental health. The small percentage who harm themselves provides a warning for students of qigong, Yoga, and other healing disciplines that is worth repeating: *Proceed gradually, step by step. Don't short-circuit or overload your qi circuits by trying to do too much too soon. Maintain a balance; don't neglect the joys of everyday life.*

In *The Explanation of the Thirteen Movements*, a Taiji Quan classic, we read, "Let the entire body focus on spirit rather than qi. If you fix on the qi, the qi is blocked." This means that qigong students should prioritize clarity of mind and relaxation. During visualization practice, it is proper to direct the qi with intent, but don't obsessively think about qi when it is not necessary. This could interfere with its natural flow, creating both health and psychological problems.

Does this mean that qigong is risky business? Not at all. I have included in this book qigong techniques that are safe, enjoyable, and that have been used successfully by large numbers of students for many years, both in the United States and China. Any discipline can be harmful if it preoccupies the mind or is practiced incorrectly.[8] Hold your neck and head rigid whenever you swing a baseball bat and I guarantee that after a few years you will have a neck and spine problem. Just use a little common sense; it can go a long way.

SECTION IV

Qigong Lifestyle

CHAPTER EIGHTEEN

The Dao of Diet

He who does not mind his belly will hardly mind anything else.

—SAMUEL JOHNSON

DIGESTION: DISTILLING FOOD QI

Air and food are sources and raw materials for the body's qi, refined and processed into qi through respiration and digestion. *How* you breathe and *what* you breathe both affect the quality of available breath-qi (*zong qi*). Shallow breathing means less oxygen intake and less energy in the cells. Polluted air also delivers less qi because it is filled with toxins and toxic energy. Polluted air contains lead, carbon monoxide, and other chemicals that clog the body and compete with essential nutrients.

Similarly, healthy food-qi (*gu qi*) is derived from the interaction between a healthy digestive system and a diet that is nutritious, uncontaminated, and balanced. Qigong meditations and exercises can do much to improve digestion, assimilation, and elimination. Simply relaxing and breathing abdominally is often enough to cure stress-related digestive problems. But a healthy digestive system means nothing if you don't know what to put in it. The best automobile engine in the world won't run without gas. (Gasoline, in Chinese, is *qi you*, "qi oil." Interesting!) Borrowing a phrase from renowned biotechnician Barry Sears, Ph.D., to "enter the Zone" of optimum health, you need high octane food in appropriate quantities.

Yet food is more than fuel and the body is more than a machine. Once

an automobile is manufactured, the various parts are fixed. They can be replaced, but they do not change their own structure. Although the life of the
engine can be preserved by proper maintenance and regular oil changes, the
automobile cannot fix itself or improve its own functioning. The human
body, by contrast, is not only fueled by food; it is created and repaired by
food. A good diet strengthens the digestive system. Food is a source of qi,
and qi feeds every cell in the body, including the cells of the stomach and
intestines.

Chinese Medicine provides an ingenious model to explain how digestion extracts and creates qi. The stomach and spleen are paired organs, yang
and yin respectively; both are ruled by the Earth phase (or element). Earth
stands in the center of the Five Phases. You can visualize the other four
phases: Metal (Lungs), Water (Kidneys), Wood (Liver), and Fire (Heart), as
surrounding Earth, with Metal to the west, Water to the north, Wood to the
east, and Fire to the south.

Water

Metal   Earth   Wood

Fire

Earth is the mother element; the organs associated with it, the stomach and
spleen, provide energy for the whole body.[1]

Food and liquids enter the hollow organ, the stomach, first. The stomach is like a cooking pot, mixing the ingredients with digestive enzymes and
turning them into a warm soupy mash. According to renowned scholar of
Chinese medicine Dr. Bob Flaws, "the spleen is both the fire under this pot
and the distillation mechanism to which this pot is attached."[2] After the
soup has "ripened and rottened" in the stomach, it is the spleen's job to drive
the pure food qi up to the lungs, where it can mix with the qi from breathing
and create the "true qi" that feeds the entire body. The spleen also takes the
pure part of fluids and drives it up to the heart, to help create blood.
According to Dr. Flaws's excellent guide to Chinese dietary theory, *Arisal of
the Clear*, "The sending up of the pure part of the foods and liquids by the
spleen is called ascension of the clear."[3] Meanwhile, the stomach causes "de-
scension of the turbid," sending the impure food and liquid down to the intestines. In the intestines, the remaining pure energy ("the pure of the
impure") is extracted and converted into kidney energy and various thick
fluids such as cerebrospinal fluid. Whatever remains is excreted as feces and
urine.

We can see why in the Chinese language digestion is called *xiao hua*.

Xiao means "to disperse." Hua means "transformation." Thus xiao hua is "dispersal and transformation," more specifically the transformation of the raw materials, food and liquids, into qi and blood and the dispersal of impure residue. When digestion is not functioning properly, the pure and impure are muddled. The body does not receive the pure energy it needs and is bogged down by putrid energy and substance.

The basic principles that describe how food can strengthen the digestive system and the rest of the body are very simple:

- Food that adds energy is good for you; food that takes away qi, clogs and congests the body, or that requires a great deal of energy to digest is bad for you. (A corollary is to never tax your body by eating late, just before retiring. You will be digesting instead of sleeping restfully.[4])
- The qi of food is influenced by both the quality and quantity of food.
- Different foods and food combinations have different effects on health.
- The method of cooking also influences the energy of food.
- Human beings have general nutritional and energetic needs. However, we are also each biochemically unique, with inherited and acquired strengths and weaknesses and thus unique nutritional requirements.

YOUR DAILY QI TONIC

Both West and East agree that food is medicine. Food is the only medicine that we take in large doses at least a few times a day, every day of the year, for our whole life. The cumulative effects of food on the body's biochemistry and qi makes it more powerful than any drug.

A 1990 report of the United States Public Health Service estimates that one in three Americans will develop cancer.[5] According to *The Journal of the National Cancer Institute*, diet may be an important factor in 35 percent of all cancer deaths.[6] The modern American diet of animal fats and refined carbohydrates has been implicated in the rise of chronic noninfectious diseases, such as coronary heart disease, diabetes, stroke, cancer, arthritis, gallstones, dental cavities, and gastrointestinal disorders.[7] Infectious disease is also on the rise, due to new strains of antibiotic-resistant bacteria festering in our meats and soils.

If unhealthy food can cause disease, then healthy food may cure it. I once offered to buy my qigong teacher a bottle of Chinese tonic wine—a brew of ginseng and other herbs soaked in vodka, purported to increase the body's qi and promote longevity. He reprimanded me, "No need for that. I have my own 'Long Life Wine'—the food I eat every day."

AN EAST–WEST APPROACH

Western medicine has been dominated by a mechanistic view of the body, treating the body as a machine, requiring no more than efficient parts, a source of energy, and a good mechanic. Foods are considered the raw material of component chemicals that nourish the body and have specific biological effects. Vitamins, minerals, and precise nutrient ratios fit well into this analytical model. Chinese medicine emphasizes balance, how the flavor, temperature, and qi of foods affect an individual's state of health. Dietary decisions are guided by the character of food rather than its scientific content, by intuition as much as intellect.

The diet I recommend is a synthesis of East and West, of ancient qigong theory and cutting-edge Western nutritional science. I believe that it is no longer enough to rely on Chinese theories of balance and on one's own intuition—"The body knows what it needs." The body might know, but we don't. We have ignored or interfered with its natural processes for too long. Put a human being in a primitive environment, give him a bow, a fishing pole, and a digging stick and he will eat healthily. Today, our grocery stores present us with too many choices. Foods are not fresh and are filled with invisible toxic ingredients. The diseases of civilization and the diseased, depleted, polluted nature of the soil require scientific as well as intuitive solutions. Christopher Bird and Peter Tompkins direct our attention not only to health, but to survival in their important work *Secrets of the Soil*:

> No creature, not even swine, befouls its nest with such abandon as does *homo sapiens*. . . . Today soils are tired, overworked, depleted, sick, poisoned by synthetic chemicals. Hence the quality of food has suffered, and so has health. Malnutrition begins with the soil. Buoyant human health depends on wholesome food, and this can only come from fertile and productive soils.[8]

Ultimately, we are ailing because the planet is ailing, and I have to admit that looking at the problem from this global perspective, qigong is only a Band-Aid at best. The solution must be ecological and agricultural as well as personal.

What I have said about healing also applies to diet: no single tradition or culture has the complete solution. I have followed the Chinese maxim "Use what is good, discard what is useless" to create a theory that is relevant to today's needs and lifestyle.

RULE 1
EAT FRESH, SEASONAL, LOCAL, NATURAL FOOD

Qigong shares with macrobiotics and virtually all schools of natural medicine the principle that food should be as fresh and wholesome (not refined or processed) as possible. Anyone who has had a garden knows the difference between fresh-picked tomatoes and those picked last week or bought at the grocery. Just the thought of fresh vegetables or ripe apples picked from a tree makes our mouths water. Meat and seafood also taste best and are healthiest when fresh. The traditional qigong diet is not vegetarian. I recommend that about 70–80 percent of your dietary calories be derived from vegetarian sources—legumes, whole grains, fruits, vegetables (including sea vegetables: one or two tablespoons of seaweed daily[9])—and 20–30 percent from lean meat and/or seafood. Limit your consumption of dairy products; the nutrients in them are poorly assimilated.[10]

To harmonize your qi with the place and time of year, try to eat as many local and seasonal products as possible. In Colorado I love to eat buffalo and trout, in Seattle, salmon and halibut. Asparagus and corn taste best and are best for you in the spring and fall, respectively. If you don't have a garden, the next best thing is to shop as though you are foraging in one. Ask yourself, "What grows this time of year? Which animals or fish are local?" Many cities now have farmer's markets that feature regional, seasonal produce. I am not saying that if you live in Alaska, you must live on seal and never again enjoy a chocolate cake made from rich Mexican chocolate. Rather than switching to an exclusively local diet, try to include *some* local foods with most of your meals.

There is a great deal of wisdom in the Native American belief that diseases that arise in an area can be cured by a local plant. The problem today is that many of our diseases are no longer local. The ease of global transportation allows microbes to cross oceans as easily as your luggage. Customs officials cannot prevent microscopic terrorists from entering our territory. Nor can the body's defenses adapt to the strategies of these foreign "invaders." This is why we must rely on multicultural and multifaceted approaches to healing and diet.

Plants should be cultivated and animals raised in a beautiful, nonpolluted environment. High-energy foods come from high-energy landscapes, near clear streams, high mountains, or tranquil plains. As you progress in qigong, you will be able to sense the qi in the land and food as much as in people. When the earth-qi is strong, the food grown on it is more likely to be filled with healing energy.

We don't know the long-term effects of most of the chemicals we add to our food. It is best to avoid processed foods or those that contain additives. Find a health food market that supplies "organic" vegetables, free of pesticides, dyes, preservatives, or other chemicals and grown without synthetic fertilizers or manure from antibiotic-fed animals. *It is also essential to avoid seafood caught in contaminated waters because they may contain high concentrations of hormone-disrupting chemicals that resist breakdown and elimination.*[11] *You should also lessen or avoid all meats that cannot be certified "antibiotic and hormone free."* Farm animals are routinely fed antibiotics, not so much to fight infection as to cause the animals to grow and gain weight more quickly. The problem is that this practice results in the selection and production of deadly bacteria that can grow as easily in a human host as in an animal.

Healthy meats are also called "organic" or "free-range." Free-range animals are allowed to roam about rather than being confined to cages or pens. Animals, like humans, are healthier if they get more exercise. Their meat is leaner and has a higher percentage of protein to fat. According to Chinese medicine, all farm animals, especially chicken and ducks, absorb energy through their feet. If they are cooped up, their meat is low in qi and filled with the confused emotional qi (stress hormones) caused by crowded and unsanitary conditions.

When Drugs Create Disease

What is the problem with antibiotics? For more than forty years tetracycline and other antibiotics have been added to animal feed because they cause extremely rapid growth and lead to quicker profits. Six billion farm animals in the United States—thirty times the U.S. population—are each given daily doses of antibiotics, twenty million pounds in the course of a year. In the presence of regular, small (sub-therapeutic) amounts of antibiotics, an animal's immune system is weakened. Although some bacteria may be held in check, many others, particularly the strong and aggressive bacteria, begin to proliferate. Worse still, any or all of the bacteria may become *antibiotic-resistant.*

Animal bacteria like human bacteria are highly adaptable and creative. They learn how to survive by neutralizing the antibiotic, by attacking the body in a different way, or by mutating and changing their own structure, so that the antibiotic can no longer recognize them. The antibiotic-resistant genes are passed on to their family members. Soon, the rapidly dividing and multiplying bacteria are all antibiotic resistant. The host cannot be cured even by the best weapons in the medical arsenal. According to clinical pathologist and adviser to the World Health Organization Jeffrey A.

Fisher, M.D., "If a microbiologist were designing a laboratory experiment under the most carefully controlled conditions, the purpose of which was to select for the greatest number of antibiotic-resistant bacteria, he couldn't come up with a better scheme than the one carried out on animals every day."[12]

In 1965 six individuals died from an outbreak of food poisoning in England. They were affected by a strain of antibiotic-resistant *Salmonella* bacteria that had also been causing an epidemic among calves. In 1993, three children died and five hundred people became ill when they ate hamburgers infected by *E. coli* bacteria, served at a fast-food restaurant in Washington State. Dr. Fisher continues:

> There are no "cow bacteria" or "pig bacteria" or "chicken bacteria." In terms of the microbiological world, we humans along with the rest of the animal kingdom are all part of one giant ecosystem. The same resistant bacteria that grow in the intestinal tract of a cow or pig can, and do, eventually end up in our bodies.

On July 11, 1995, *USA Today* reported that "the Department of Agriculture estimates 5 million illnesses and 4,000 deaths annually are attributable to consumption of meat and poultry contaminated with microbial pathogens." (This is why it is essential to always cook meat thoroughly—no more medium-rare hamburgers!) Equally frightening, the resistant genes from these bacteria can latch on to other types of bacteria and eventually cause strep, staph, pneumonia, and innumerable other diseases that resist most if not all forms of medical treatment.

Even more shocking is the fact that the food inspection system has hardly changed since it was established in 1907. Federal inspectors look at, touch, and smell the meat, but do no testing for bacterial contamination. In 1995, Michael Taylor, Undersecretary of Food Safety with the Department of Agriculture, admitted that "the current system does not address invisible contamination, the bacteria, which is what makes people sick. The current system lacks . . . any means for holding slaughterhouses accountable for controlling bacteria."[13] Taylor also says that if the inspection process was improved, we could eliminate up to 90 percent of the sicknesses and deaths caused by tainted meats.[14] At this writing (1996), however, politicians and meat industry officials are uncertain how to make the necessary changes. One of the fears is that new and expensive testing procedures would "drive 85 percent of the small meat packers out of business."[15] It's the same old story: economics replacing ethics and "health" of the budget taking precedence over health of the body.

RULE 2
EAT WARM AND BE COOL!
BALANCE THE HOT–COLD
ENERGY OF FOOD

One of the most important principles of qigong is *balance*. In the qigong diet, balance includes a recognition of the warming (yang) or cooling (yin) effects of food on the body's qi. Foods exist on a continuum from cold to hot. For instance, clams are cold and reduce fever; lamb is warming and excellent for weakness and anemia. Healthy individuals should emphasize a diet in which the cumulative energetic effect of the foods eaten in a day is between neutral and slightly warm. This helps maintain the natural internal environment of the body, a warm 98.6 degrees.

The Five Natures of Food are *cool, cold, neutral, warm, and hot* (see Table 9). Vegetables and fruits are generally cooling. Apples, pears, lettuce, raw celery, cucumber, and tofu are examples of cool foods. The coldest foods are those raised in cool, dark places, like mushrooms and bean sprouts and some shellfish, particularly clams, that live on the ocean floor. Other cold foods include seaweed, sugarcane, and watermelon. Anyone with an aversion to cold temperature, a strong need for heat, or cold limbs should completely avoid foods classified as "cold."

Most grains are neutral, close to the middle of the scale. They help to maintain balance and homeostasis by harmonizing yin and yang energies. If you eat an excess of energetically hot food, the heat is diluted and less likely to cause imbalance if you also eat grains. This is why grains are considered dietary staples and should be eaten with most meals. Among the macronutrients—carbohydrates, protein, and fat—grains or other complex carbohydrates should constitute the highest percentage of a balanced diet.

White rice is almost completely neutral, neither warming nor cooling. Most pastas are close to rice energetically, though they become more warming by adding spices. Brown rice, millet, and buckwheat are between neutral and warm, making them better grains to eat in a cold environment. Other foods classified as neutral include grapes, milk, chicken eggs, corn, and Chinese cabbage.

Examples of slightly warm foods include scallions, caraway, brown sugar, red dates, and some root vegetables such as yams and beets. Warmer foods include shrimp, poultry,[16] and pork. The red meats like beef and lamb are somewhere between warm and hot.[17] Deer meat and other wild meats are also in this category. However, because of their high level of activity and vitality, the meat of wild animals is classified as nearly 100 percent yang, in the sense of building and creating energy. This makes sense, since we know that wild meat has far less fat and far more protein, vitamin C, and other nutrients compared to domesticated animals. Hot foods include cinnamon and the hot spices, such as cayenne and black or white pepper. Individuals with hot, inflamed conditions, such as a sore throat with fever or any tendency toward bleeding (including nosebleeds), should avoid cinnamon and other energetically hot foods. Adding hot spices to any food shifts it toward hot.

Three factors—Constitution, Season, and Condition—determine whether you should eat warmer or cooler foods. *Constitution:* People who are very uncomfortable in cold weather or who generally feel cold have a "cold constitution" and should eat warmer foods. If you have an aversion to heat and a tendency to sleep with few blankets, then you have a warm constitution and should eat cooler foods. *Season:* Eat warmer foods in winter, cooler foods in summer. *Condition:* If you have symptoms of heat—inflammation, infection, fever, agitation, a red complexion, extreme thirst—eat cool. If you have symptoms of internal cold—such as diarrhea, anemia, an extreme desire for quiet, emotional withdrawal, an unusually white or pale complexion—then eat warm. Hot and cold symptoms are not always obvious, however, and thus may require the interpretation and guidance of a practitioner of Chinese medicine. The principle is always the same: *if it's cool, balance with warm; if it's warm, balance with cool.*

RULE 3
STEAM, SAUTÉ, ROAST, STEW: NO GREASY SPOONS, PLEASE!

The qigong diet emphasizes cooked foods rather than raw, and both food and drink served at a warm or hot temperature. Remember the image of the stomach as a cooking vessel? If you begin cooking the foods outside of the stomach, then the stomach will have less work to do later. Cooking breaks down the food, making it easier to digest and assimilate. It also destroys pathogenic microbes that might contaminate food. For similar reasons, food should be well chewed. Chewing food thoroughly warms it, breaks it into smaller pieces, and mixes it with digestive enzymes in the mouth. You also eat more slowly and are more conscious of eating. It's a good way to break compulsive eating habits.

Foods or liquids that are served cold differ so much from the internal body temperature that they actually shock the qi and weaken the spleen's digestive fire. This is why anyone who is weak or depleted or who has lost blood—

TABLE 9: THE FIVE NATURES OF FOOD

Cold	Cool	Neutral	Warm	Hot
bean sprouts	apples	almond	beef	black pepper
clams	barley	bass	beets	cayenne
crab	celery (raw)	black tea	brown sugar	cinnamon
grapefruit	cucumber	blueberries	caraway	dried ginger
mushrooms	green tea	cabbage	cherries	soy oil
salt	lemons	carp	chestnut	white pepper
seaweed	lettuce	carrots	chicken	
sugarcane	pears	cheese	coffee	
watermelon	radish	corn	fresh ginger	
banana	spinach	eggs	garlic	
	tofu	grapes	green pepper	
	tomato	green beans	lamb	
	watercress	herring	mussel	
	whole wheat	honey	pork	
		kidney beans	red dates	
		milk	salmon	
		millet	scallion	
		olives	shrimp	
		peanut	squash	
		peas	trout	
		plums	turkey	
		potato	venison	
		rice	vinegar	
		sardine	wine	
		white sugar	yams	

such as after giving birth or after surgery—should avoid raw foods and cold foods and liquids. Warm foods, by contrast, strengthen the stomach and spleen. (Most people can safely eat some raw foods every day, more so in the summer. However, do not eat primarily raw foods, and no raw food fasts for qigong students!)

There are four recommended methods of cooking: steaming, sautéing (especially stir-frying), roasting, and stewing (soups and casserole cooking). It is best to avoid frying, especially deep frying. Fried foods are high in fat and cholesterol and easily produce pathological heat, dampness, and phlegm. According to Chinese Medicine, damp heat is a major contributing factor in such disorders as pelvic inflammatory disease, hemorrhoids, and outbreaks of genital herpes. The *Yellow Emperor's Classic of Internal Medicine* states that fatty, greasy, and oily foods cause a wasting away of the body's energy and may lead to diabetes.

Compared to other methods of cooking, frying drastically increases the fat content of any food. For instance, whereas 100 grams of baked potato has 1/10 gram of fat, 100 grams of french fried potatoes has 39.6 grams fat. A hundred grams of roasted corn has 1 gram of fat; the same weight of corn chips has 33.4 grams. According to S. Boyd Eaton, M.D., "Humans have cooked their food for at least several hundred thousand years, and possibly for over a million, but while roasting, steaming and baking were all commonly employed techniques, frying was not."[18] Our bodies are not genetically adapted to digest fried foods. Heart disease and obesity are the prices we pay.

Light steaming is the best way to cook vegetables. It breaks down and partially softens the food while conserving texture, taste, nutrients, and qi. Seafood and various kinds of dumplings (such as Russian *pirogen*) are also delicious when steamed.

I cannot resist sharing one recipe for steamed food: DR. WONG'S SECRET OF IMMORTALITY. (He's not really immortal, but it's still a catchy title.) This is a recipe that I received from my beloved teacher and friend, Dr. K. S. Wong, Daoist abbot, acupuncturist, and qigong master. The recipe makes a simple, delicious, and qi-filled dinner.

Cook some basmati rice, a fragrant, natural white rice. At the same time steam a mixture of your favorite vegetables. I like to use broccoli, a bitter green like swiss chard or kale, a few mushrooms, and some carrot slices. You may also add tofu. In a separate steamer, cook a whole fish, or if you prefer bake a fish or chicken in the oven in a clay pot. Now the secret: Prepare a mix of two to three tablespoons of miso with enough water to give it a smooth, even consistency. Squeeze in one or two lemons. Grate in a bit of fresh ginger, and add two teaspoons of cold-pressed extra virgin olive oil. Mix it all together. Use this sauce over your vegetables and rice. It is also delicious on fish. And kids love it. I'm convinced that one reason for my daughter's good eating habits today is that when she was very young I used delicious and healthy sauces. A good cook uses sauces to enhance the flavor of good foods rather than to hide or create flavor for bland or unhealthy foods. As Master Chef Mary Taylor writes in her appetizing work *New Vegetarian Classics: Entrées*, "Sauces unify the elements of a dish, and enrichments such as oil, nut butters, milk or cream, smooth out rough edges. Together they transform ordinary dishes into memorable, balanced works of art."[19]

If you are going to sauté, use a very small amount of canola or olive oil. Limit your use of other oils, as many of these increase inflammation and cholesterol levels. The Chinese method of sautéing, *wok stir-frying*, includes steaming. In a curved-bottom wok only a few teaspoons of oil are needed. Bite-sized ingredients are thrown in and tossed for less than a minute in the very hot oil, sealing in the flavor and texture. A small amount of water is carefully added. The wok is covered, and the food steams. More water is added as needed. In fact, much of the art of wok cooking is getting the feel of how much water to add and when to open the lid to toss the ingredients. If too little water is used, the water only splatters in the hot oil; if too much water is used, the mixture turns into a soup and delicious textures are lost. It is important not to overcook. Wok stir-frying is very quick. Most dishes are done in about five minutes.

Roasting and baking are used to a lesser extent, generally to cook large pieces of meat or seafood. Probably the most often recommended method of qigong cooking is clay casserole cooking, whether on the stove or in the oven. Ceramic casserole pots conserve and build the qi in food. In Chinese herbal medicine, clay pots are used to cook meats such as chicken or lamb with medicinal herbs such as ginseng or angelica. Herbs are also frequently added to soups, stews, and rice porridge (congee). The latter has such a long and venerable history in qigong dietetics that it deserves some special explanation.

Rice porridge (*Xi Fan* or *Zhou* in Mandarin, *Jook* in Cantonese) is extremely nourishing, soothing, easy to digest, and inexpensive. It is the single most important food to eat when facing or recovering from illness. And it is an excellent food for strengthening the spleen and stomach, thereby improving digestion and qi. Xi Fan can be eaten any time of day. It makes an excellent, hearty breakfast cereal. Dr. Bob Flaws has written an entire book on the healing benefits of porridge.[20]

Rice porridge is made by adding one part rice to anywhere from five to eight parts water and simmering it for three or four hours until it has the consistency of slightly watery oatmeal. It is also possible to make porridge from other grains or combinations of grains, such as millet or barley. Other common ingredients cooked with porridge include aduki beans, mung beans, yam, ginger, lamb, chicken, chestnuts, and Japanese preserved plum. If necessary, porridge can be flavored with a little salt, sugar, soy sauce, or miso. Chinese doctors frequently recommend that, at the first sign of a cold, you should make a glutinous rice porridge with scallions and ginger. I have found that it works much better than mom's chicken soup.

RULE 4
FLAVORFUL FOOD IS HEALTHY

To many Americans "health food" conjures up images of thin, weaselly look-ing people listlessly consuming tasteless platters of tofu, sprouts, tempeh burgers, lots of brown rice, and little else. This is a far cry from the qigong concept of healthy eating. Qigong theories were an important influence on the development of delicious Chinese cuisine. Taste and aroma are good for you and can entice you to eat the healthiest food. According to the Shanghai College of Traditional Chinese Medicine's textbook, *Health Preservation and Rehabilitation*, "Good food should taste good. Tasteful food is easy for patients to accept and allows them to enjoy their therapy, though they are unaware that it is being administered."[21] Western hospitals should learn this principle!

Just as the warming (yang) and cooling (yin) properties of foods influ-ence health, the flavors of foods stimulate the internal organs. Meals should be varied and full of interesting, diverse flavors so that no internal organ is over- or undernourished. Chinese Medicine usually speaks of five flavors: sweet, salty, sour, pungent, and bitter. Each of these relates to an associated organ and has other general effects on health. Many foods have more than one flavor and so affect more than one internal organ. For instance, barley is both sweet and salty, apples and apricots are sweet and sour, cinnamon is pungent and sweet. Chinese cuisine frequently combines flavors to produce more interesting and healthful dishes: hot and sour soup, sweet and sour chicken, sweet pork dumplings in soy (salty) vinegar (sour) sauce, bitter greens with salted black bean sauce.

The key to using the Five Flavor theory for health-maintenance is to make sure that in most meals you do not eat either too much or too little of any flavor. For therapeutic purposes, Chinese doctors advise their patients to eat more of a certain flavor in order to treat the related internal organ.

Sweet benefits the spleen and stomach. Too little or too much sweet damages these organs. Because the sweet flavor stimulates the spleen-digestive fire, it is also gently tonifying (building qi) and good for some defi-cient conditions. Many people also find that the sweet flavor is relaxing and expansive. However, even as earth opposes water (because earth absorbs it), so the sweet flavor, if excessive, can damage the organs related to water: the bladder and kidneys. Kidney-related symptoms that may be induced by eat-ing too much sweet food include hair loss and pain in the bones. Naturally, if you have a bladder or kidney problem, it is also advisable to eat less sweet foods. Examples of sweet foods include apple, banana, barley, beef, chestnut, chicken, corn, dates, honey, maple syrup, milk, molasses, sugar, yam, and tofu. Sweet, in the form of sugar, is also a major ingredient in snacks and desserts: candy, cake, cookies, pie, and ice cream. I personally do not keep or use any sugar at home, but I am willing to shamelessly ingest moderate quantities of "Vitamin S" when it is disguised in pastries. I limit myself to, at the most, one or two sweet pastry desserts a week. Luckily I do not live near a French patisserie, or I might suffer from temporary bouts of culinary insanity.

The salty flavor benefits the water-related organs: the kidneys and bladder. Salty foods also soften hard nodules such as cysts, inflamed lymph glands, or knotted muscles. Of course, too much salty food can harm the kidneys and bladder and may be completely forbidden for certain kinds of kidney disorders. Most Americans would be well-advised to cut down on the use of table salt, since salt is already added to almost every supermarket item, whether canned, frozen, or dry. Water puts out fire; thus too much salty food can damage the fire organs: the heart and small intestine. Excess salt or salty food also causes the blood to coagulate and clot more easily, again putting some individuals at risk for heart disease. Salty foods include barley, clam, duck, oyster, pork, and seaweed.

Sour foods, like lemons, are associated with wood and help the liver and gallbladder. Sour foods are also astringent and absorbent. They can slow down the movement of fluids, treating diarrhea or excessive perspiration. Wood penetrates and breaks up earth, so excess sour food can weaken the earth organs, the stomach and spleen. Or if you already have a stomach problem, such as an ulcer, it is best not to eat much sour food. Some examples of sour foods are apple, grape, lemon, pear, plum, strawberry, tomato, and vinegar.

Pungent means hot and spicy. Pungent foods are cutting like metal and benefit the metal organs: the lungs and large intestine. Pungent foods also induce perspiration, improve circulation of qi and blood, and stimulate digestion. As with any flavor, an excess of pungent foods will harm these same organs and functions. Metal chops wood; the pungent metal flavor can weaken the wood organs: liver and gallbladder. Thus it is best to avoid or lessen the amount of spicy foods in your diet if you suffer from a liver or gallbladder problem. Eating much spicy food could produce such liver-related symptoms as brittle nails and tight muscles and tendons. In addition to the obvious—cayenne, garlic, black and white pepper, and ginger—the pungent flavor is found in cinnamon, clove, leek, peppermint, radish, and scallion.

Bitter is probably the flavor that most Americans get the least of. It heals the fire organs: heart and small intestine. Bitter also keeps fire under control, reducing fever and feelings of excess body heat. Many Chinese doctors attribute the high incidence of heart disease in America to the lack of bitter foods in American cuisine. Almost the only bitter flavor that

Americans consume regularly is in coffee. However, any heart-healing benefits of coffee's flavor are negated by the harmful effects of caffeine. Studies
suggest that coffee raises blood cholesterol levels and overstimulates the nervous system. Chinese people who are not afflicted with the Imitate Americans Syndrome still prefer tea, a bitter drink that has only half the caffeine of
coffee.

Bitter foods are excellent for the heart and can stimulate digestion,
without, however, adding heat like some pungent foods. Fire melts metal; so
too much bitter could harm the lungs and large intestine. However, there is
probably not much danger of this since we tend to eat too little bitter. Bitter
foods include asparagus, bitter melon (*ku gua*, common in China), celery, cit-
rus fruit peel, coffee, dandelion greens, hops, tea, and vinegar.

Remember the rule of *balance*. Enjoy all of the flavors without overdoing
any particular one. And although it is wonderful to occasionally make
strong-tasting dishes, rich in flavor—such as linguine with fresh pesto—for
regular, daily consumption emphasize simple, wholesome foods that have a
lot of qi but not too much flavor. The Chinese call this the *qing dan* diet.
Qing means pure, clear, unmixed, refreshing. Dan means light, plain, somewhat bland. "Dan water" *(dan shui)* means fresh water. "Dan purple" *(dan ci)*
means light or pale purple. A qing dan diet is one that is nourishing, sustain-
ing, and delicate.[22] It is nongreasy and free of strong flavors created by too
much salt, sugar, spice, or fermented products (e.g., soy, vinegar). It is flavor-
ful but delicately so.

If you are going to emphasize a particular flavor or use strong flavors to
cure a health problem, do so with moderation. You may emphasize a flavor,
but do not limit yourself to it unless so advised by a qualified practitioner of
Chinese medicine.

I learned personally about the dangers of self-prescribing when I was in
my twenties. I had just moved to Montreal, in time for flu season. I got quite
ill and was left with a lingering hacking cough. My physician advised some
over-the-counter cough syrup. I reasoned that eating spicy food and adding
garlic and cayenne to most dishes would tonify the lung qi and help my condition. I became quite good at making Indian curries. After a month I developed a low-grade fever and my cough got worse. My physician diagnosed
"chronic bronchitis" and gave me a course of antibiotics. The cough got still
worse, and I was switched to a stronger cough medicine of codeine and
guafenisen. When I visited the chest clinic, a specialist told me, "My prescription is move to Arizona." I didn't.

Two months later, still coughing, I went to a Chinese acupuncturist.
When he asked me about my diet, he began to shake his head. The doctor
chastised me, "Pungent food *in moderation* can help the lungs. However,

since you have symptoms of internal heat, you need moderate amounts of *cooling pungent foods* such as radish and peppermint, not *heating pungent foods* like cayenne and garlic." My lungs were also weakened and "hot" because of the stress and anxiety of moving to a new location and finding work. (Remember, anxiety is the emotion that weakens the lungs.) The hot pungent food would probably not have harmed me if I had consumed it only in small quantities and continued to eat balanced amounts of the other flavors. Additionally, the buttery curries were not helping. Butter tends to create heat and phlegm. Steaming is much better.

I was treated once with acupuncture, given a week's supply of Chinese herbal teas that seemed to taste bitter, astringent, and sweet all at once. I also switched to a basically bland diet of steamed foods. At the end of the week my cough was gone and did not return.

RULE 5
REDUCE CALORIES, INCREASE NUTRITION

According to ancient writings, the *xian ren*, the Daoist sages of antiquity, preferred a pure diet of breath and morning dew. How do we reconcile this apparent asceticism with the wonderful cuisine developed by Daoists[23] and the Chinese passion for food? Lin Yutang says that the reason the Chinese were late in developing a science of zoology is that they couldn't look at an animal without thinking one thing: "How does it taste?" In fact, "Living on breath . . ." is a plea to, in Lao Zi's words, "embrace simplicity, lessen selfishness, reduce desires." Another way of putting this is that happiness is found by learning how to be satisfied with less, rather than always grasping at more.

In *Bo Wu Ji* (Records of Investigating Phenomena) Zhang Hua of the Jin Dynasty (265–420) states, "The less one eats, the broader the mind and the longer the life span." There is a good scientific rationale for eating less, for paying attention to quantity as well as quality: *The only experimentally proven method of increasing maximum life span is through a combination of maximum nutrition with minimum calories.* Roy Walford, M.D., professor of pathology at the UCLA School of Medicine, calls this the "high/low diet" or "undernutrition without malnutrition." Although some Daoists may have attempted breatharianism, they were probably no more successful than those who added mercury and lead to their elixirs. The majority of ancient qigong practitioners probably followed dietary principles congruent with Walford's gerontology research, a fact that is recognized by some modern qigong authors. For example, Dr. Liu Zhengcai, a qigong scholar and clinician in

Chengdu, notes the importance of small food quantities and proper nutrition in his work on qigong and longevity.[24]

The high/low diet can help one avoid or dramatically postpone age-related health problems, including cancer and other immune system disorders, heart disease, arthritis, osteoporosis, loss of memory and other brain functions, kidney damage, and decreased sexual potency.

Super-Health Under the Microscope

The benefits of low-calorie diets are carefully and convincingly documented in Walford's *The 120 Year Diet*[25] and in Dr. Richard Weindruch's article "Caloric Restriction and Aging," published in the January 1996 edition of *Scientific American*. I will summarize some of their data.

In 1935, Dr. Clive McCay of Cornell University put a group of rats on a low-calorie but highly nutritive diet. After one thousand days, all of these rats were still alive and active, while most of the controls that were fed a normal diet had died. The restricted rats continued living to a maximum life span of eighteen hundred days, equivalent to a human being living to age 150 to 180 years. These rats were "superhealthy." Their hearts were stronger. The females were able to reproduce at an advanced age, and the male rats had high testosterone levels. In 1982, scientists at the National Institute on Aging were able to increase the average life span of calorie-restricted rats by more than 83 percent.[26] Naturally, long-lived strains of laboratory animals—those with good genes—reached the most dramatic extensions in life span.

In one mouse strain, lung cancers developed in 58 percent of those fed normally, compared with 32 percent of those on caloric restriction. Among the restricted mice, breast cancers were nonexistent, and all cancers were less frequent or delayed by an average of two to five months, the equivalent of five- to thirteen-year delays in humans. Other animal experiments have shown that the high/low diet prevents age-related degeneration of connective tissue and skeletal muscles and helps maintain healthier blood levels of insulin and cholesterol. When Rajindar S. Sohal and colleagues at Southern Methodist University in Dallas examined mitochondria, the cells' energy factories, from the brain, heart, and kidneys of mice, they found that those on calorie-restricted diets had lower levels of free radicals and less cellular damage than the normally-fed controls. The high/low diet may also affect intelligence. Calorie-restricted animals are better at solving problems and are more adept at navigating complicated mazes.

Evidence suggests that the high/low diet has similar effects on humans. Other factors—especially nutrition, environment, and heredity—being equal, individuals who consume fewer calories tend to be healthier.

Conversely, obesity is a risk factor in all major diseases, especially diabetes, heart disease, and arthritis. In 1992, the *Proceedings of the National Academy of Science* reported that Dr. Walford tested his theories on a group of human subjects—eight volunteers, including himself. For two years they lived in a hermetically sealed "biosphere," a 3.15-acre experimental enclosure, where they grew and recycled their own food. Despite regular strenuous exercise, the participants ate a calorie-restricted diet of 1,700 to 2,400 kcal/day. At the end of the two years, there were dramatic physiologic changes, including drops in blood glucose, cholesterol, and blood pressure.[27]

Don't Sacrifice Quality

While reducing calories, it is important to maintain a high level of nutrition. Additionally, although nutrition is important for people of all ages, caloric restriction is meant only for adults. Children have different nutritional needs and must be allowed to grow and develop naturally. Similarly, pregnant women should be extremely cautious about reducing calories.

Reducing calories does not mean reducing necessary vitamins, minerals, fats, proteins, or carbohydrates. At least half of the U. S. population suffers from a deficiency in at least one essential nutrient.[28] For instance, 50 percent of the women in the United States consume half the optimal level of calcium and magnesium each day; 25 percent consume less than one third the necessary calcium. The median intake of vitamin E in the United States is less than half the Required Daily Allowance (RDA), the average requirement to prevent nutritional deficiency disease. The American diet is generally imbalanced, with too little of some nutrients and too much of others—such as carbohydrates and fats. Our over-consumption of nutritionally empty calories in the form of pasta, pretzels, pastries, and french fries creates a state of affluent malnutrition. We are the most fat-obsessed country in the world, and ironically, the country with the most fat people.

Therefore, it is probably dangerous to reduce calories or food quantities while maintaining your present diet. This could worsen nutritional deficiencies, excesses, and imbalances. When you are confident of the quality of what you are eating, begin to count calories and, if necessary, reduce the quantity. Optimum qi development requires eating little but eating well.

Calories should be reduced *gradually* to an average of 2,000 calories/day for men, 1,800/day for women, depending on body frame and level of activity. It is not difficult to figure out calories and nutrients. Many supermarkets list calories and nutrients in the fresh produce sections of the store. Packaged goods carry this information on the label. Computer databases are available that catalogue the calories and nutrients in common foods. If you have been consuming excess calories, caloric reduction will cause you to lose weight. However, it is unhealthy to lose more than 1 percent of your weight each week. Most experts agree that forcing the body to suddenly adapt to dramatic changes in diet is counterproductive. Crash diets are more likely to shorten life span rather than lengthen it. The goal of the qigong diet is improved health, increased qi, and long-term maintenance of the best weight for your age and body type. Individuals seem to have a genetically programmed "set point," defined by Walford as "the weight toward which one naturally drifts if he neither under- nor overeats."[29] Thus what is lean for one individual might not be lean for another. "So what counts," says Walford, "is not the absolute weight or the absolute degree of leanness, but the weight relative to the set point of the strain or individual."[30] You do not have to be thin to be a qigong master, just balanced—the right weight for you. Thus, although I do recommend caloric restriction, this must be pursued slowly and sensibly.

RULE 6
LESS CARBOHYDRATE:
SORRY, MACROBIOTICS!

The enigmatic principle "Avoid the Five Cereals or Grains *(Bi Gu)*"[31] occurs in virtually all ancient works on qigong diet. According to Daoist mythology, the three dan tians at the third eye, heart, and abdomen are infested by three worms. These worms live on the impure breaths (qi) created by immoral behavior, putrid food, and the "Five Cereals" which are the basis of Chinese cuisine: rice, millet, wheat, oats, and beans. According to a Daoist text, "The Five Cereals are scissors that cut off life, they rot the five internal organs, they shorten life. If a grain enters your mouth, do not hope for Life Eternal! If you desire not to die, may your intestine be free of it!"[32] A fourth-century Daoist meditation classic, *The Inner Classic of the Yellow Court*, warns that the stench of these grains vexes the soul and stops the embryonic breath.

At first glance this philosophy seems as bizarre to us as it does to most Chinese. We can sympathize with ancient Daoists in their love of mysticism and magic, their rejection of patriarchy, greed, and despotism. But to reject carbohydrates, to avoid croissants, spaghetti, and rice—isn't this a slight against the people of France, Italy, and China herself! Can such a pastaphobic attitude ever be justified?

There is a paradox here, conveniently ignored in most discussions of Chinese dietetics. Some of the very same Daoists who advocated grain avoidance also required five pecks of rice as an admission fee into their sect.[33]

Other Daoists, such as those living on Holy Mount Hua, were far from the rice fields on the plains, yet they supplemented their diet of wild foraged plants with *shan mai*, mountain wheat. If the Daoists, the most ancient masters of qigong, ate grains, how are we to understand the healing benefits of grain avoidance?

Let's remember the historical context. Most Chinese were poor farmers who ate large quantities of grains such as rice and millet and little else. Meat was a luxury. The truth hidden in the concept of "grain avoidance" is that it is impossible to cultivate a full supply of qi or to reach optimal mind-body health if one eats *too much* grain or other carbohydrate. There may also be an implication that agricultural products, in general, weaken the qi.[34] They are certainly responsible for many food allergies.[35] I do not agree that we need to eliminate *all* grains.

The ancient Chinese did not have to contend with refined carbohydrate such as processed white rice, flour, or sugar. We should limit our consumption of these products. However, even an excess of complex carbohydrate, such as whole grains, is unhealthy. In the short term, carbohydrate will increase energy and is certainly better for us than excessive meat or fat. But in the long run, too much carbohydrate—above 45 percent of one's diet[36]— makes one tired, fat, malnourished, and miserable. To understand why we, like the ancient Chinese, need to lessen carbohydrate consumption, we need to review some basic biochemistry.

When you eat a carbohydrate meal or snack, it is broken down into a simple sugar, glucose, that can be readily utilized by the cells. Glucose is the fuel that is required for any bodily process that requires energy. When glucose combines with oxygen from respiration it produces carbon dioxide, water, heat, and ATP (adenosine triphosphate). Carbon dioxide is then carried by the blood to the lungs, where it is exhaled. Water becomes part of intracellular fluid and the metabolic water that is required for life. The heat helps to maintain normal body temperature. ATP provides the energy for muscle contractions and other essential life processes such as cell division and protein synthesis.

To help the body use glucose and in the process to lower blood glucose levels, the pancreas secretes the hormone insulin. Insulin binds to receptor sites on the cell membranes, helping the cells to absorb glucose. Insulin is also necessary in order to convert glucose into glycogen and triglycerides, substances that are stored in the liver, skeletal muscles, and as fat. When energy is needed, stored glycogen is converted back into blood sugar by another pancreatic hormone, glucagon. In an ideal situation, insulin, glucagon, and blood glucose levels stay within healthy limits, each chemical produced in just the right amount.

This delicate chemical machine was programmed into our genes long before the beginnings of agriculture. Our bodies are designed to handle only the amount of macronutrients—carbohydrate, protein, and fat—gathered in the natural environment by our hunter-gatherer ancestors. The ratio of protein to carbohydrate was fairly consistent: approximately 3:4, that is, about 30–35 percent protein to 40–45 percent carbohydrate, with the remainder of dietary energy provided by fat (20–30 percent).[37] This ratio helped to keep the body lean and strong and provided our ancestors with the energy and stamina to hunt with spears and to escape from predators.

With the advent of agriculture, ten thousand years ago, the amount of carbohydrate in the diet increased dramatically. Our bodies are not genetically adapted to respond to this dietary and biochemical stress. In their enlightening article in the *New England Journal of Medicine*, S. Boyd Eaton, M.D., and Melvin Konner, Ph.D., say, "The human genetic constitution has changed relatively little since the appearance of truly modern human beings, *Homo sapiens sapiens*, about 40,000 years ago. . . . Accordingly, the range of diets available to preagricultural human beings determines the range that still exists for men and women living in the 20th century—the nutrition for which human beings are in essence genetically programmed."[38]

When we eat too much carbohydrate in relation to protein and fat, blood insulin levels increase dramatically. (This is especially problematic for the many individuals who are genetically predisposed to secrete too much insulin for the amount of carbohydrate consumed.) When we chiefly consume carbohydrate at every meal and at snack time, blood insulin levels never have a chance to drop.

Now three nasty things can happen: First, overproduction of insulin can cause an abnormal drop in blood glucose levels (hypoglycemia), causing the mind to wander and drift, and producing both mental and physical fatigue (the Two-Hours-After-Pasta-Syndrome; sound familiar?). Secondly, high carbohydrate consumption results in the body storing more fat. Third, the presence of a constant high level of insulin, especially when the body is carrying excessive fatty tissue, may cause the cells to become *insulin resistant*. They no longer produce sufficient receptor sites for the insulin or the receptors do not function normally. Glucose finds no way in; the cells, unable to "burn" sufficient glucose-fuel, become energy starved. One finds oneself craving more and more bread, pasta, and sweets. This can contribute to the most common form of diabetes, *Type 2 diabetes mellitus*, also called noninsulin-dependent diabetes or "adult-onset diabetes."

In a nutshell: at best too much carbohydrate means fat, fatigue, and unhealthy food cravings, the state that Drs. Rachael and Richard Heller call "carbohydrate addiction"[39]; at worst, excess carbohydrate can predispose one to serious disease. The Daoists were right: high grain consumption does not nourish us. On the contrary, it "stops the embryonic breath," and weakens and diminishes qi.[40]

I support Dr. Barry Sears's modern adaptation of the "paleolithic diet" and recommend it to qigong students: 40 percent of your calories should be derived from carbohydrate, 30 percent from protein, and 30 percent from fat.[41] This ratio is consistent with the ancient qigong philosophy of lessening grains and Chinese Medicine's appreciation of the healing properties of meat. According to Liu Jilin's *Chinese Dietary Therapy*, meat is "nutritious and can enrich Qi and Blood, or reinforce the Liver and Kidney."[42] Liu also acknowledges the importance of protein, noting that meat is rich in "quality proteins, fat, inorganic salts (calcium, phosphorus, and iron) and vitamins (chiefly vitamin B)." Correct nutrient ratios will help you build qi more quickly, improve health and vitality, and enter the zone of peak performance, the realm of paleolithic hunters, Olympic athletes, and qigong masters.

"But isn't it unnatural to be counting calories and calculating nutrient ratios? How can I reach a state of integral health with such a left-brained approach?" I suggest experimenting with ratios and recipes for several weeks. You are updating your biocomputer, erasing an old "corrupt" program and installing a new, healthy one. In the beginning this takes some effort. But once you have the feel of healthy eating, trust your intuition and forget the experts! Your spontaneous decisions will now be more intelligent ones, influenced by better habits and more accurate knowledge. You can still use the reference books—but only for reference, not as a religion. If diet is based on a database, it is unnatural and joyless. In the long run, this is worse for your health than a modicum of "bad" foods. The Chinese poet Bo Ju-yi (A.D. 772–846) wrote a poem about ancient Daoist masters who took every kind of medicinal herb yet died young: "Only I, who never followed a diet, have succeeded in reaching a ripe old age. . . . I drink the wine in my cup and trust all else to Heaven's care."

RULE 7
THUMBS UP TO VITAMINS AND MINERALS

I recommend that vitamins and minerals be incorporated into the contemporary qigong diet. Ancient Chinese doctors did not hesitate to use herbs, spices, animal parts, and minerals from other countries. These substances were often refined and concentrated in complex chemical and alchemical operations. In a similar way, qigong has borrowed healing techniques and theories freely from Tibetan Buddhism, Indian Yoga, and, more recently,

Western medicine. Doctor of Oriental Medicine Bob Flaws corroborates my conclusions. He writes, "Therefore, there is no Chinese precedent for thinking that a practitioner of so-called Chinese medicine must only prescribe medicinals which originate in China . . . or naturally occurring substances in their raw or unprocessed form."[43] Many Chinese doctors will prescribe pharmaceuticals *and* herbs and recommend diets based on Western and Eastern nutritional theories.

China has shown a great deal of interest in Western nutritional science. In 1993, the National Cancer Institute and the Cancer Institute of the Chinese Academy of Medical Sciences completed a collaborative study of the effects of vitamin and mineral supplements on 29,584 adults living in Linxian county, Henan Province.[44] This region has one of the highest rates of esophageal cancer in the world, ten times greater than in the rest of China, one hundred times greater than among white Americans. A combination of beta-carotene, vitamin E, and selenium, in doses two to three times the RDA, reduced the occurrence of esophageal, stomach, and lung cancer and significantly reduced the overall death rate. Generally, risk reduction became apparent one to two years after beginning supplementation.

There are several reasons why ordinary dietary sources cannot provide all of the vitamins and minerals necessary for health:

1. We have suffered from nutritional deficiencies ever since the Agricultural Revolution, at least ten thousand years ago.[45] This is because of increased reliance on grains and the fact that the meat of domesticated animals and cultivated crops have less vitamins and minerals than wild equivalents. Prior to agriculture, humans were taller[46] and stronger, had more competent immune systems and less of the "diseases of civilization"—hypertension, heart disease, diabetes, and cancer—in either their youth or old age. Contrary to a popular misconception, this is scientific fact, not romantic idealism.[47]

2. Today many of our foods are gown in nutrient-depleted soils and are heavily processed and refined, with few vitamins other than those artificially added. Vitamins are generally added in small amounts, enough to prevent nutritional disease, but not enough to promote optimum nutritional health. Food storage also destroys essential vitamins and minerals.

3. We consume or are exposed to substances that deplete essential nutrients, interfere with nutrient absorption, and at the same time increase our nutritional needs. These include alcohol, tobacco, refined sugar, some medications, and toxic environmental pollutants.

4. Food allergies also interfere with nutrient absorption and may be the root of many forms of mental illness.

5. The very process of human evolution resulted in nutritional requirements that can never be supplied by diet alone. We may have sacrificed our
ability to absorb or internally manufacture certain nutrients in exchange for
a more complex nervous system. For instance, almost all mammals, birds,
amphibians, and reptiles have an enzyme that allows them to synthesize vitamin C in their livers or kidneys. Human beings and other primates cannot
do this. An ape is smart enough to eat huge quantities of leafy green plants to
make up for this deficit. There is evidence to suggest that our Paleolithic ancestors were probably also this intelligent. Unfortunately, modern *homo sapiens* are not so smart.

The use of vitamins and minerals to prevent and treat disease is called
orthomolecular medicine. Ortho means correct or proper. Thus orthomolecular
medicine means giving the body the correct nutrient molecules in correct
amounts in order to prevent or treat disease. I agree with Dr. Linus Pauling,
that ". . . in general the treatment of disease by the use of substances, such as
ascorbic acid [vitamin C], that are normally present in the human body and
are required for life is to be preferred to treatment by the use of powerful synthetic substances or plant products, which may, and usually do, have undesir-
able side effects."[48]

Take a good multivitamin-mineral supplement daily, with adequate zinc
and trace elements. It is a good idea to also take extra vitamin C (two to
three grams, buffered, in divided doses), and E (generally, 400 units). If you
wish to tailor vitamins and minerals to your individual constitution and
health problems, seek the supervision of a physician or other health-care
professional trained in orthomolecular medicine. Never take vitamins or
minerals in excess of recommended safe dosages.

RULE 8
LEARN THE ACTIONS OF
INDIVIDUAL FOODS

Another principle of qigong diet is *direction*, that is, does the food make qi
rise or sink in the body, go deeper into the body or move out toward the skin.
Knowing this can help combat conditions that create stuck qi in a particular
region of the body. For instance, foods that cause qi to sink can relieve nausea and hiccuping. Foods that cause qi to move from the inside to the outside
can release trapped heat and reduce fever. The direction of food is somewhat
determined by the part of the food eaten. Roots can make the qi sink down.

Leaves and flowers cause the qi to rise. Organ meats, such as chicken liver or pork kidneys, send qi to the same organs in humans.[49]

It is also useful to know the specific actions and contraindications of individual foods, apart from the qualities of hot-cold, flavor, and direction. Which foods are best for headaches; which foods will aggravate them? Here both Chinese medicine and Western nutritional science have much to offer. Western science has unrivaled knowledge of the effects of the chemical components of foods. Chinese medicine focuses on the energetic effects of foods, assessed through thousands of years of trial and error and simply listening to the body.

For instance, pears and pear juice clear the lungs and are used to treat feverish coughs. However, they should be avoided if the patient feels chilled. Lemon is cooling and makes an excellent beverage for summer heat. Chinese sometimes drink it with sugarcane juice. Lemonade, candied lemon, or lemon pickled in salt are considered therapeutic for vomiting and loss of appetite. Soy beans are also helpful for an upset stomach. They strengthen the stomach and spleen and help rid the body of toxins. Soy milk is sometimes taken for mild food poisoning. Chinese white radish (*daikon* in Japanese) is also detoxifying and can reduce phlegm and purge the body of pollution or drugs. Because of this property, they should not be eaten while taking medication. Pine nuts help to relieve dry coughs, and, when cooked in rice porridge, can moisten the large intestine, alleviating constipation. Dried Chinese chrysanthemum flowers are added to tea to relieve headaches and eyestrain. Chicken has an affinity for the spleen and kidneys. It can increase qi and strengthen sexual energy. However, because it warms the body and adds hot qi to the liver, it should be avoided during fevers, headaches, or liver problems. Celery, used as both a food and a spice, helps to cool, cure, and relieve the pain of hot, inflamed conditions such as canker sores and hemorrhoids. The individual properties of foods have been expertly catalogued in the works of Henry Lu and Liu Jilin (see Qigong Resources).

RULE 9
DRINK THE WATER OF LIFE

The two most important beverages in the qigong diet are water and tea. Hot tea, emphasized in Chinese Medicine, harmonizes the qi and is excellent to drink after qigong practice. It is the subject of the entire next chapter. In the West, water is generally considered the healthiest drink. When we are ill, the doctor advices, "Get plenty of rest, and drink lots of liquids." Water reduces fever, dilutes poisons, and nourishes the spirit. I recommend that qigong students drink at least eight glasses of water daily.

Water is the medicine most compatible with our bodies, since our bodies consist of 60–75 percent water. Water in the body makes up *intracellular fluid* (the water within cells, comprising 65 percent of total body water), *extracellular fluid* such as plasma, lymph, interstitial fluid (between cells), and many specialized fluids (e.g., cerebrospinal fluid and synovial fluid—preventing friction between bones). We need to keep drinking plenty of water to replenish these vital fluids.

Water is essential to life for three important reasons:

1. It is a solvent. Water dissolves nutrients, allowing them to be transported to the cells. It dissolves waste in urine. And it dilutes toxic substances, including the chemicals that can form kidney stones.

2. Water is a lubricant, allowing digestion, sex, the movement of the joints, and the trapping of respiratory irritants (through mucus).

3. Water regulates body temperature. This is largely because it changes temperature slowly, a fact appreciated by anyone who lives near the ocean.

Water is also spiritual. Water is the oldest medicine on the planet and our link to ancient healing energies. As Tom Heidlebaugh, Algonquin educator and storyteller, so eloquently puts it, "The cycle of evaporation and precipitation means that the same water that fed the Dinosaurs moves through our own bodies today."[50]

SUMMARY: EATING HEALTHFULLY

Although I can outline general principles of the qigong diet, there is a great deal of variation in how these principles are applied to your unique biochemistry and the satisfaction of your individual nutritional needs. I once met the president of a large Oriental herb company that purported to sell original Buddhist monastery herbal health teas, though at considerably higher cost than the "original" teas foraged from the woods. I became extremely unpopular with this gentleman when I suggested, "I'm certain you are telling your American customers that the formulas are only suitable for celibate monks!"

Qigong teaches adaptability. There is no single medicine suitable for everyone. The diet should be tailored to the individual, guided by knowledge, intuition, and self-awareness. The rules to remember are:

- Eat fresh, seasonal, local, natural.
- 70–80 percent vegetarian, 20–30 percent meat or seafood.

- Avoid meats or seafood that contain hormones or antibiotics.
- Balance hot, cold, and the Five Flavors.
- Steam, sauté, roast, stew. Do not fry.
- Eat Jook (Congee).
- Reduce calories (gradually!) and increase nutrients.
- Maintain the caloric ratio: 30 percent protein; 40 percent carbohydrate; 30 percent fat.
- Take vitamin and mineral supplements.
- Learn the properties of individual foods.
- Drink water and tea.
- *Enjoy* cooking and eating. Boring food makes boring people.

The qigong meal is tastefully seasoned, esthetically presented, and full of variety. Alan Watts, who combined Daoist scholarship with culinary expertise, was fond of saying, "A chicken improperly cooked and not enjoyed as it becomes you, has died in vain."

Healthy cooking and eating are not only ways to improve your qigong; they are qigong! They are physical and spiritual disciplines. A monk asked Zenmaster Yun-men, "What does it mean to attain enlightenment with every atom of your being?" The Zenmaster replied, "Food in the bowl and water in the bucket."[51]

CHAPTER NINETEEN

Have a Cup of Tea!

The first bowl moistens my lips and throat;
The second bowl banishes all loneliness;
The third bowl clears my mind of words and
  books.
At the fourth cup, I begin to perspire—
  life's troubles evaporate through my pores.
The fifth cup cleanses my entire being.
Six cups and I am in the realm of the Divine.
Seven cups—ah, but I can drink no more:
I can only feel the gentle breeze blowing
  through my sleeves,
wafting me away to the Isle of Immortality!
—LU TONG, EIGHTH-CENTURY CHINESE
   POET, FROM *IN GRATITUDE FOR*
   A GIFT OF FRESH TEA

Tea is the most important and popular medicine in China. The classics of Chinese herbal medicine generally have only a few paragraphs on ginseng; but the portions on tea fill several chapters. In China, virtually all experts in qi control—acupuncturists, martial artists, calligraphers, qigong players—drink tea regularly. There are some good reasons why.

WHAT IS TEA?

I am speaking about tea, not herbal tea, but Tea. Black tea or green, it's all the same plant, *camellia sinensis*. The French correctly use the word tea (*thé* in French) to refer only to infusions of this plant. Other herbal "teas"—such as chamomile, peppermint, rose hips—are called *tisanes¹* in French. The color, taste, and quality of true teas differ according to where and how the tea is cultivated, the quality of the soil, the age of the leaf, and the degree of fermentation. The broadest and most generally used categories of tea are green, semifermented, and black, referring to the amount of fermentation of the leaf and, thus, its color. Green tea, the preferred beverage in Asia, is tea in its natural unfermented state. Full fermentation turns green tea black, producing the teas most commonly used in American and European blends, including English Breakfast and Earl Grey. The famous Chinese Oolong Teas are only slightly fermented and so are between green and black tea in flavor and color. The leaves usually have a reddish tint on the edges, but remain green in the center. Semifermented teas have the greatest variety of aroma and flavor, ranging from a light flowery bouquet to a rich "bordeaux." The taste of tea may also be varied by steaming, roasting, smoking, pressing, folding, or rolling the leaf.

HISTORY AND LEGEND

Tea is as ancient as Chinese Medicine. More than two thousand years ago the legendary Divine Farmer (*Shen Neng*) catalogued all of China's medicinal plants. He tasted each plant himself, followed by a cup of tea to neutralize any possible toxicity. (Don't try this. It only works for divine farmers.) He sensed the effect that each plant had on his qi and wrote it in the first edition of the *Shen Neng Ben Cao Jing* (Shen Neng's Classic of Herbal Medicine). The edition of the text we have today, dating to the Daoist alchemist Tao Hong-jing (452–536), remains an important source of information on tea.

Tea has long been associated with the practice of meditation. There is a Buddhist tale that the great monk Bodhidharma (fifth century A.D.) once fell asleep during his nine-year meditation vigil. When he awoke, he was so angry with himself that he cut off his own eyelids. These fell to the ground and arose as the first tea plant in China. Ever since that time tea has been used to keep meditating monks awake and wakeful. (Actually tea is much more ancient than Bodhidharma. Tea is mentioned at least eight hundred years earlier in *Shi Jing* (The Classic of Poetry). The Daoist sage, Lao Zi, is also a patriarch of tea. When Lao Zi left China in search of the Dao, the customs officer offered him the first cup of ceremonial tea.

THE DIVINE MEDICINE

Tea is classified as sweet and bitter flavor and so benefits the spleen, stomach, heart, and small intestine. The green color of the natural leaf is associated with the liver. Tea promotes the function of the liver to spread and harmonize the qi. This is an important benefit for qigong students. The green teas are slightly cooling, black teas slightly warming. Thus, green teas are preferred in the summer, black teas in the winter. According to Dr. Ma Shouchun, of the Northwest Institute of Acupuncture and Oriental Medicine (Seattle), "Tea generates fluids, stops thirst, clears heat, eliminates toxins, dispels dampness, promotes urination, aids digestion, stops diarrhea, clears heart-fire, and raises the spirit."[2] Some of the finest teas are the *Before the Rains Teas*, picked early in the spring before the rainy season. The *Ben Cao* says that these teas "absorb the fresh qi of springtime, strengthen the body's original qi and make the eyes bright and healthy." I would add that all fine teas induce a serene, calm state of mind, sensitive to the beauty of nature. These effects linger, like the taste of the tea. The better the tea, the more the *hui wei* (literally "return flavor"), a delicious, lingering aftertaste. (Go ahead, mark this place and get yourself a cup of tea before continuing.)

Pu Erh, a semifermented Oolong tea from Yunan Province, is probably China's most famous medicinal tea. It has been drunk in Yunan and neighboring Tibet for at least a thousand years. The Pu Erh tea leaves are unusually broad and may be close to the most ancient species of tea plant. Pu Erh is characterized by a mellow, earthy taste, almost smoky or peatlike. In 1986, in Barcelona, Spain, the Ninth International Food Award was given to Yunan Tuo Cha, a type of Pu Erh. My qigong teacher, Dr. Wong, used to carry Pu Erh tea bags with him wherever he went. In Chinese restaurants he would ask for a pot of hot water and make the tea himself.

Pu Erh is excellent for weight loss and digestion and promotes the breakdown of fatty or greasy food. It has also been scientifically demonstrated to lower cholesterol. In 1967, the British scientific journal *Nature* reported an experiment in which rabbits were fed a high-fat, high-cholesterol diet and divided into two groups, one group given water, the other group black tea to drink. The aortas of the tea group suffered far less damage and scarring.[3] This was followed up by a California survey in which it was found that Chinese-American tea drinkers had less coronary and cerebral artery damage than Caucasian coffee drinkers.[4] Similarly, China's Kunming Medical College First Hospital found that Pu Erh tea lowered patients' cholesterol levels by 17 percent and triglycerides by 22 percent.[5] In Paris, when twenty patients with abnormally high blood fat levels were given three cups of Pu Erh a day for a month, their fat levels dropped 25 percent.[6]

It is likely that all teas have healthy effects on the arteries. Jean Carper, a leading authority on health and nutrition, writes, "Tea chemicals can reduce blood coagulability, prevent platelet activation and clumping, increase clot-dissolving activity and decrease deposits of cholesterol in artery walls— all of which help fend off artery damage."[7] Scientists in Japan have found that *catechin*, the polyphenol (sometimes misnamed tannin) found in green tea, is as effective as aspirin in preventing blood clots from forming (and probably with far fewer harmful side effects).[8] In 1993, *The Lancet* published an important study connecting tea drinking with coronary health. When 805 elderly men were tracked over a five-year period, it was found that those who consumed black tea regularly had half the rate of fatal heart disease compared to those who drank less tea.[9]

Tea also has significant anticancer effects. In 1994 the *Journal of the National Cancer Institute* published a study conducted by the National Cancer Institute, Bethesda, Maryland, and the Shanghai Cancer Institute on the effects of green tea consumption on human esophageal cancer.[10] Seven hundred thirty-four esophageal cancer patients were contrasted with 1,552 age and sex-matched controls. After accounting for variables such as diet, alcohol consumption, and cigarette smoking, researchers found that men and women who drank at least one cup of green tea per week for six months had twenty and fifty percent less risk of developing esophageal cancer, respectively. Dr. Allan Conney, Director of the Laboratory of Cancer Research at Rutgers University, has found that polyphenols, as found in tea, "contain significant implications for the future of chemo-prevention of cancer."[11] Dr. Conney found that when he gave mice the same concentrations of green tea that would normally be drunk by humans, up to 87 percent of all skin cancers were blocked, 58 percent of stomach cancers, and 56 percent of lung cancers.[12] In 1991, at a meeting of the American Chemical Society, researchers shared that Japanese smokers who drank green tea had 45 percent less risk of lung cancer than other smokers. Stomach cancer, the leading cause of death in Japan, has its lowest incidence in Shizuoka, a tea-growing district, where green tea is regularly drunk. Similarly, surveys in China have shown that the incidence of stomach cancer and liver cancer are lower in regions where more tea is drunk, compared with other areas of the country. One of the most potent anticancer chemicals in tea is the catechin epigallo-catechin gallate (EGCG). Since roasting and fermentation destroys most EGCG, it is found in high concentrations in green tea. Researchers at Japan's National Institute of Genetics found that EGCG prevents cells from becoming cancerous by inhibiting the mutation of cellular DNA.[13] This also means that carcinogenic substances may be less likely to cause cancer if one is drinking tea regularly.

There's still more. Tea strengthens the immune system. Researchers at the Fujian Institute of Traditional Medicine found that tea increased the activity of white blood cells in mice. Tea does the same in the human body. The Tea Research Institute in Hangzhou has even developed a tea extract to counter the immune-depressing effects of cancer radiation therapy.

Tea is also antibacterial. In ancient China powdered green tea or chewed leaves were sometimes applied as external poultices to stop infection from wounds or insect bites. In vitro studies have suggested that powdered tea can inhibit the growth of staph, salmonella, cholera, dysentery, and other bacteria. According to Dr. Laurence E. Wolinsky, associate professor of oral biology at the UCLA School of Dentistry, tea drinkers have fewer dental problems. Tea destroys bacteria in the mouth, preventing tooth decay. The fluoride in tea strengthens tooth enamel.

The antioxidant properties of tea provide a key to understanding many of its benefits as well as the traditional connection between tea and longevity. *Antioxidants* destroy or deactivate free-roaming and highly reactive oxygen molecules. These "free radicals" essentially do to our bodies what oxygen does to household oils and fats; they turn us rancid and stale. Antioxidants, such as tea, keep us fresh and young. In a 1994 issue of *The Lancet*,[14] Mauro Serafini of the National Institute of Nutrition in Rome reported measuring a 41–48 percent increase in blood antioxidant activity less than an hour after subjects drank a strong cup of either green or black tea.

Tea is also rich in nutrients, though the amount consumed in a cup of tea is naturally quite small. The tea leaf consists of 36 percent insoluble protein. Westerners rarely drink the leaf, unless sipping powdered tea in the Japanese Tea Ceremony. There are more efficient ways to get dietary protein. Similarly, tea has insoluble vitamin A (80 milligrams/100 grams) and chlorophyll (3 percent) not available to us in steeped tea and small amounts of vitamins B_1, B_2, niacin, and folic acid. There is enough manganese and iodine to account for some alleged antacid effects of tea. Green tea is fairly rich in vitamin C (250 micrograms of vitamin C/100 grams), black tea losing some of this vitamin during fermentation. An average cup of green tea (approximately one teaspoon of tea leaves) will release about six milligrams of vitamin C after steeping in water three times. Steeped tea also has significant amounts of potassium, about 58 milligrams in a cup of black tea.[15]

And caffeine? Caffeine in coffee puts the nerves on edge. Some people call this a "boost." I call it "anxiety." Coffee makes one ready for war. The National Academy of Sciences' Institute of Medicine has recommended adding caffeine to the food rations of soldiers. Perhaps they should substitute tea! Soldiers on tea are more likely to be meditative and aware, capable of action but not driven to it. These are qualities that are prized in the Chinese and Japanese martial arts. One reason for the different effects of coffee and tea is that even though both have caffeine, tea contains other substances that may change or mitigate the effects of the caffeine. Also, coffee contains significantly more caffeine than tea. An average cup of drip coffee has 100 milligrams caffeine; an average cup of American brands of (black) tea 50 milligrams—a little less than a can of Mountain Dew (54 milligrams).[16] Green tea has even less caffeine, 22 milligrams in the average cup.

Nevertheless, some precaution must be observed when using this wonder drug. Never drink day-old tea that has been left standing in the cup or teapot. Tea must be fresh in order to have healing benefits. You may need to cut back on the amount of tea if you have insomnia, an irregular heartbeat, or are pregnant. Any drink with caffeine can also interact negatively with some drugs such as birth control pills, ulcer drugs, tranquilizers such as Valium, and antidepressants that are monoamine oxidase (MAO) inhibitors, such as Marplan. Basically, if you have any condition for which caffeine is contraindicated or if you are taking any medications, consult your physician about how much tea you can drink safely.

HOW TO MAKE TEA

There are three ingredients of a delicious and healthy cup of tea: Good Tea, Good Water, and Proper Technique.

I prefer whole leaf tea that comes from one region, "single estate tea," rather than the crushed and blended teas that are used in tea bags. Fine whole leaf teas are picked by hand, two leaves plucked at a time—more than two thousand are required to make a pound of tea. I do not recommend Japanese "bancha tea," a tea that is very popular with American students of natural healing. There is a mistaken belief that bancha is a "tisane," an herbal tea rather than Tea. Bancha consists largely of old, dry, and brittle leaves—the waste left over after good tea is picked. According to Kida Taiichi, an authority on tea, bancha is composed of "discarded leaves and small twigs which were separated out during the process of refinement. Bancha is a general name for these lesser quality teas."[17]

Many supermarkets carry tins of decent black tea: Ceylon, Darjeeling, Russian Caravan, and other teas, in both tea bag and leaf form. Several American companies, such as Celestial Seasonings®, are distributing organic black teas,[18] generally in tea bags. These are available in some supermarkets and most natural food stores. You can usually find some fairly good whole leaf teas in Asian grocery stores. Look for Japanese or Chinese green tea, Indian Darjeeling, Chinese Oolong (two famous, fine Oolongs are Ti Kuan Yin and Shui Xian), and Pu Erh. For truly excellent tea, you will need to find a specialty importer such as the Blue Willow Tea Company or Silk Road Teas. The owners of these companies are true Tea Devotees and travel regularly throughout Asia to sample and bring back the finest estate teas. Grace Tea Company, in business since 1959, uses hand-plucked leaves from choice estates to create consistently delicious blended teas. To contact these tea suppliers, see Qigong Resources.

If you are ordering tea by mail or fortunate enough to live near a fine tea shop, look for the following excellent teas: among the green teas, I like Japanese Sencha and the finer Jade Dew and Gyokuro. However, my favorites are some of the Chinese greens: Long Jing (Dragon Well Tea) from Hangzhou, China; the delicate scented Bi Lo Chun (Jade Spiral Spring); and Shou Mei (Longevity Eyebrow) or Bai Hao (White Down), both made with sun-dried tea buds. Among the Oolong teas look for the rich bouquet of Tung Ting from Taiwan, Pu Erh, Ti Kuan Yin, and Shui Xian from the Wuyi Mountains. There are excellent black teas imported from India, Southeast Asia, and China. These include Assam (often used in "Irish Breakfast" tea), Cameronian—a wonderful, fruity tea from the highlands of Malaysia—fine Darjeelings, and the slightly smoky liquor of Chinese Keemun Tea.

According to the eighth-century *Tea Classic (Cha Jing)*, the best water for tea is from mountain springs and flowing mountain streams. The next best is river water far from human dwellings, followed by well water. In today's world, we need to modify this picture. The best water is from high mountain springs that have been thoroughly tested for chemical and organic contaminants, followed by pure well water, followed by filtered tap water that is allowed to run cold for at least thirty seconds.

Always heat water for tea in a stainless steel or pyrex kettle, never aluminum. Do not use fully boiled water for brewing green or semifermented teas. According to tea expert David Lee Hoffman, "Boiling water 'cooks' the leaves of these teas, destroying their flavor."[19] The best water temperature for green tea is 160–170°F (70–75°C); for semifermented tea, 180–195°F (80–90°C). For black teas, the water should be "bubbling": nearly boiled. Use water at a full, rolling boil to brew Pu Erh tea.

Pour water as soon as it is properly heated. According to ancient Chinese texts, water that is overboiled tastes dull and flat and loses its qi. Keep the water hot for subsequent infusions over very low heat or on a fondue burner.

TEA TECHNIQUE

1. First, the simplest and most convenient way to make tea. I call it the Everyday Chinese Style. Use a tall ceramic cup, ideally the Chinese *gaiwan* that has a cover to keep the tea warm. If none is available, you can use a small dish to cover your cup while steeping. Place a teaspoon of tea leaves on the bottom. Fill the cup with hot water. The leaves will float to the top. When the leaves have sunk back to the bottom, leaving behind their mellow color and aroma, the tea is ready. When you have finished the tea, add more hot water. Good tea leaves can be steeped three times before losing their flavor or fragrance. Often, the second steeping is the most delicious. If you have a tea in which the leaves have been ground into fine pieces or a coarse powder, then you will need a tea ball or strainer. If you are using these or tea bags, the rule is still one teaspoon or tea bag per cup of tea. Infuse for about three minutes, never more than five, as the tea will turn bitter.

2. If you are using a Western-style teapot, first warm the entire pot, including the lid, with hot water. Then add one teaspoon of tea leaves (or one tea bag) for each cup of water you will add. Pour in the hot water and let it steep for about three minutes.

3. Tea can also be an art and a meditation, whether enjoyed by oneself or with guests. Chinese connoisseurs practice a method of preparing fine tea called *Cha Shu* "the Art of Tea," *Cha Dao* "the Way of Tea," or more formally "*Gong-Fu* Tea." Gong-fu can mean not only Chinese martial arts but any discipline that requires patience, perseverance, and practice. In Gong-Fu Tea you use a small pot half filled with tea leaves. The tea is drunk from very tiny teacups. The idea is not to drink a large amount of tea, but rather to truly savor the tea experience.

Utensils: The most important utensil is a small ceramic teapot, somewhere between the size of an orange and a grapefruit—enough to hold one or two cups of water. The very best is Chinese Yi Xing Ware, from the town of Yi Xing in Jiangsu Province. The Yi Xing red clay has been used to make teapots since at least 1500. The pots are generally unglazed to display the subtle earth tones of the clay and to allow seasoning of the pot. They hold the warmth, flavor, and qi of tea like no other utensil. Yi Xing ware is frequently available in the United States at Asian tea and art shops. If you can't find an Yi Xing pot, ask a potter to make a small earthenware teapot for you.

Other utensils needed for Gong-Fu Tea include: some small shot-glass-size teacups (Japanese porcelain sake cups are perfect), a narrow-necked unlidded ceramic cup to use as a decanter, a bowl (the "tea boat") large enough for the teapot to sit in, and a cloth to wipe up any spilled liquids.

THE ESSENTIAL STEPS

- Thoroughly scald the cups and the outside of the teapot with hot water.
- Fill the pot about halfway with tea leaves. Always use a spoon, preferably wooden, to put in the tea, never your hands! (The oil from your hands can affect the taste and freshness of tea.) With practice, you will learn the right amount of leaves to use, so that when they expand they will not block the spout.
- Pour in the hot water, and *within ten seconds* pour this out as waste water. That's right. The first time you add water is only to release some flavor from the leaves. Now you are ready to make tea.
- Again add the hot water. Put the lid on, place the teapot in the tea boat (the bowl), and pour more hot water over the lid, to seal in the heat and flavor. The bowl catches the hot water and keeps the pot hot. There should be one to one and a half inches of water in the bowl, depending on the size of your teapot.
- Steep the tea for a total of about one minute. Never stir the tea. Instead, when the tea is ready, pick up the teapot and make some small, leisurely circles with it around the rim of the tea boat. This will mix the liquid and ensure that there is a harmonious infusion of tea flavor and color.
- Pour the tea into your guests' cups. The remaining tea is poured into the decanter.

As you and your guests drink tea, pour more hot water into the pot. Steep for one to one-and-a-half minutes. When you are ready for more tea, first pour off any tea remaining in the decanter, or pour directly from the teapot if the decanter is empty. Each time you add more hot water to the pot, it can steep a bit longer, though never more than three or four minutes.

When you make tea this way—a very tiny teapot with a large amount of high-quality leaves, steeped for a very brief period—you can keep infusing the tea seven or more times before flavor is lost. This is a simple, elegant way to drink tea. Chinese Gong-Fu Tea is not nearly as complicated as the Japanese Tea Ceremony, yet like the Tea Ceremony it engenders feelings of beauty, refreshment, harmony, and tranquillity. According to Tea Master Soshitsu Sen XV, drinking tea brings peace, a peace that can be shared with others, becoming the foundation for both a way of life and a more peaceful world.[20]

CHAPTER TWENTY

The Art of Clouds and Rain (Your Favorite Three-Letter Word)

A yin with a yang—that is what is called "the Dao."

—*THE YI JING*

DAOIST BACKGROUND

Imagine a country of sheer granite peaks floating above the clouds, vast plains of rice paddies and millet, lovely rivers winding like dragons past thatched huts and tranquil towns. In such an environment, what could be more natural than pure religious adepts, men and women pursuing ultimate truth, forsaking sexual relations in favor of the unity of yin and yang within. *Wrong!* You can take the landscape seriously, but take the rest with a grain of salt. With a population of more than a billion, I doubt if most Chinese have been celibates.

When the mythical Yellow Emperor asked his sexual mentor, Su Nü (the Pure Maiden), whether it was advisable for him to refrain from sex, she said, "If you do not copulate, the *shen* [spirit] and *qi* will be blocked and obstructed; how then will you be able to reach a state of perfect health?"[1] When another legendary patriarch of quigong, Peng Zu, was asked about sex, he said, "Man does not want to be without woman; if he has to do without her his mind will become restive, if his mind becomes restive his spirit will become fatigued, and if his spirit becomes fatigued his life span will be shortened."[2]

In fact, China's original religion, Daoism, is one of the world's only major religions in which food and sex are considered important paths to

317

enlightenment.[3] According to a passage from the Daoist classic *Yang Xing Yen Ming Lu* (Record of Nourishing Nature and Lengthening Life), translated by Professor Douglas Wile in his *Art of the Bedchamber*:

> Those who take the "great elixir," engage in breathing exercises and internal circulation . . . but do not know the root of life, are like trees who have ample branches and luxuriant leaves but are without roots. The root of life is in the business of the bedroom.[4]

The first great Daoist philosopher, Lao Zi, saw mystical union (*bao yi*, "embracing the One") as the path to longevity and health. In the microcosm, this is realized through the harmonious joining of the sexes. As many scholars have pointed out, Lao Zi's writings are free of patriarchal attitudes and the Confucian-puritan ethics that characterized later centuries. Lao Zi makes frequent references to the power of the feminine. The Dao is identified as the Mother. "It is the mother of the universe. I do not know its name, but call it Dao." (See Chapter 25 of the *Dao De Jing*.) Daoists are advised to learn from the feminine principle, to value the yin above the yang and to cultivate the receptivity and humility of the valley.

Sexual yogas and rites were part of both Daoism and qigong from the very beginning. In the second century A.D. Daoists celebrated the *he qi*, "harmonizing of the qi" ritual, in which couples attempted to circulate the vital breaths not merely within their bodies, but between each other, complete with foreplay, changing positions, and a dessert of mutual massage.[5] Men and women had equally important roles and equal political power in the early Daoist church. The gods on the altar were both masculine and feminine.[6]

THE BEST OF BOTH WORLDS

Unfortunately, this happy state was not allowed to continue. The Daoist vision of a classless, egalitarian society was replaced by the Confucian ideal of social and political hierarchy, clear division of labor, and male dominance. Women were tied to their homes with bound feet, a consequence of Confucius' belief in the inferiority of women. By the fourth century, in response to the increasing popularity of Chinese Buddhism among the masses and monarchy, a celibate Daoist priesthood developed.[7] Since that time Daoists have generally considered sexual practices inferior to meditation and abstinence. Although Daoist philosophy states that men and women are equally capable of becoming *xian*, "enlightened sages," historically Chinese society afforded women few opportunities for either education or spiritual practice.

Communism sought to correct some of these evils. Yet, in spite of an ostensible rejection of Confucianism, the Confucian influence remained. Women were still largely confined to their role as "good wives." In *Chinese Women Through Chinese Eyes*, Li Yu-ning writes, "The highest goal of the major women's movements in modern China is national rejuvenation and increase of social well-being, rather than the particular interests of women as women."[8] Confucians and Communists also share a mistrust of sexuality, a belief that individuals seek sexual fulfillment at the expense of social stability, becoming a threat to authority.

In many ways East and West have opposite attitudes toward sexuality and need each other's wisdom to achieve balance. In modern China, in spite of the ancient tradition of sexual healing, sexual expression is frowned upon and the subject is not discussed in polite company.[9] Male tourists are advised to never ride alone in a cab with a Chinese woman, as this could be interpreted as an "insult," that is, a sexual overture, resulting in their prompt dismissal from the country. In the West, both science and psychotherapy have an extensive database on sexual health and pathology and recognize the importance of sexual expression tempered by love. The downside is that Westerners take sexual freedom for granted. Sex is commercially exploited and cheapened in the media. Additionally, an unfortunate consequence of our policy of scientific sex education is that sex is sterilized of mystery, excitement, and emotion. As a result, sexuality is too often impulsive rather than spontaneous, an obsession rather than an expression of love. It probably harms as often as it heals.

East and West have much to learn from each other and from a deep search of their own culture and history.

Some Words of Caution: *The sexual qigong techniques described below are meant to be practiced only between healthy consenting adults who care deeply for each other and who have taken the necessary precautions to prevent sexually transmitted diseases or unwanted pregnancy.* Although information is presented from a heterosexual point of view, much of it is relevant to those with other sexual preferences.

SEXUAL QIGONG

The most important preparation for Clouds and Rain (*Yun Yu*; Clouds: vaginal secretions, Rain: semen) is good health. Sexual interest, libido, menstrual regularity, fertility, and both orgasmic and erectile capability decline dramatically with illness or stress.[10]

All qigong exercises and meditations can improve sexual health. Gentle styles of qigong that emphasize dan tian breathing have a tonifying (energy-building) effect on the kidneys-adrenals (remember these are energetically connected in Chinese medicine). In Chinese medicine, the kidneys-adrenals store *jing*, sexual energy. According to western medical science, healthy adrenal glands can increase sexual desire and responsiveness. Robert M. Sapolsky, professor of Neuroscience at Stanford University, writes, ". . . sex drive goes down following the removal of the adrenals and can be reinstated by administration of synthetic androgens [sex hormones normally produced by the adrenals]."[11]

Qigong relaxation skills also increase sensitivity to sexual needs and our capacity to surrender to the sexual experience. Learning to regulate levels of excitement and relaxation creates the necessary balance that is essential for maintaining an erection and controlling ejaculation. (Technically, one regulates the activity of the sympathetic and parasympathetic nervous systems.) Increased blood flow to peripheral parts of the body also strengthens the erection and improves sexual health of both men and women.

Of the qigong techniques for sexual and reproductive health, the most famous is the Deer. The Deer stimulates, gathers, and moves the jing, preventing stagnation and disease. It is practiced as a solo exercise, without a partner, and is as important for celibate monks as for sexually active individuals. Sexual energy, even if not expressed, must still be exercised. If it is ignored, health will suffer.

The deer is a recurring archetype in qigong. It is the name given to one of the Three Treasure Meditations (Chapter 11), one of the Five Animal Frolics (Chapter 12), and to the exercise described below. According to ancient qigong philosophy, the grace, beauty, and agility of the deer are due to an abundance of sexual energy. The deer conserves and builds up her supply of jing by sleeping in a curled position, with a hoof pressing near the genitals. This prevents the waterlike jing from flowing down or leaking away. Instead, jing is stimulated to flow upstream, strengthening the kidneys, bones, blood, nerves, and brain itself. As the Daoists say, "If it flows away: Death; if you reverse it: Immortality!"[12]

The Deer Exercise causes a similar reversal of jing with healing effects on the reproductive and endocrine systems. Since the kidneys store jing, conserving jing can strengthen the kidneys and all the functions that, according to Chinese tradition, it controls, including bone structure (preventing osteoporosis), blood (preventing anemia),[13] general vitality, and the brain. The brain is said to lose jing as one ages, resulting in memory loss and senility—an interesting parallel to scientific fact: brain cells die rapidly after age thirty-five. According to qigong, such deterioration is not inevitable. By practicing the Deer, the student is able to *huan jing bu nao* "return the jing to repair the brain."

The relation between kidneys, brain, and sexual function has also been documented in Western science. The hormone DHEA, required for sex hormone synthesis, is found in both the adrenal glands, where it is produced, and in the brain. Blood levels indicate adrenal function and general vitality. High levels are associated with enhanced memory, low levels with Alzheimer's. According to doctor of Chinese Medicine Jake Fratkin, "DHEA levels correspond to what Chinese medicine calls kidney yin,"[14] the energetic reserves of the kidneys-adrenals and one's resistance to stress. DHEA is a biochemical correlate of both qi and jing.

Spermine, a nitrogen-rich compound (a polyamine) originally discovered in human semen, but that also exists in the blood and brain of men and women, may be another measurable correlate of jing. Spermine activates RNA polymerase, the enzyme responsible for the synthesis of RNA. Many scientists believe that memory depends on the body's ability to make RNA. Thus, if spermine levels are low, one can predict that RNA levels will also be low and the patient may experience forgetfulness or senility. Dr. Carl Pfeiffer, of Princeton University, writes, "Almost all of the presenile and senile dementia patients seen at the Brain Bio Center show exceedingly low blood spermine levels when compared with controls."[15] Dr. Pfeiffer has also shown that spermine levels decrease with normal aging.

It is likely that the Deer Exercise increases both DHEA and spermine levels and slows down the loss that occurs with aging.[16]

There are different versions of the Deer for men and women. Both are practiced without clothing.

Male Deer

The Male Deer is practiced once a day, preferably in the morning. It is beneficial to practice with an erection. You may masturbate to an erection if necessary. The ideal time to practice is when you have a morning erection and do not have to relieve your bladder. As one old Daoist told me, "Every country raises its flagpole in the morning. At this time, the yang qi is available. Don't always think of spending your 'money.' Rather, put more in the bank. Then you don't have to worry about losing it all or going into debt later on."

Sit comfortably either cross-legged or on a chair. Rub your palms together to generate warmth. Then cup the right hand around the testicles, holding them gently. The right thumb is resting on the top of the "jade stalk's" (penis) shaft, near the base. With the left palm, massage the dan tian area, between the navel and pubic bone, in eighty-one circular motions. Then again warm the hands, hold the testicles with the left hand, the thumb resting on the base of the penis. Circle eighty-one times under the navel with the right hand. (You will circle in one direction with one hand, the other direction with the other. It does not matter if you begin clockwise or counterclockwise.)

Next, rest your hands on your lap, forming them into fists by enclosing the thumbs in the other fingers. This meditative gesture, called *zhang wo* "holding firm," holds or seals the qi in the body. Infants practice zhang wo naturally. Now contract the perineum, the soft muscles between the anus and scrotum. Hold the contraction as long as you can comfortably, generally about one minute. Do not contract or hold the breath; let yourself breathe naturally. (If you cannot isolate the perineum muscles, you may also contract the muscles around the tailbone and the anal sphincter. By placing the index and middle finger on the perineum you can gradually learn to isolate just the perineum muscles.) Then release the contraction and relax for a minute or two before continuing with other qigong or activities.

In addition to its general benefits, Chinese doctors say that the Male Deer helps to cure impotence and premature ejaculation. It strengthens the erection and gives greater sexual control, stamina, and sensitivity. It is also said to prevent prostate disease and sometimes cure sterility, perhaps by stimulating the proliferation and mobility of sperm.

RAISING THE CAULDRON

Raising the Cauldron is another male qigong technique with benefits similar to the Deer. It is part of the Eighteen Monks (*Shi Ba Loghan*) qigong system. Practice while clothed or unclothed and at any time of day.

Stand with the knees bent, toes pointing straight ahead, and feet slightly wider than the shoulders. Breathe only through the nose. Allow the arms to hang down the front of the body, so that the hands rest on the inner thighs. The fingers are gently extended. As you inhale, clench the fingers into fists and raise them to the height of the navel, as though you are lifting a bucket of water by the handle. At the same time, try to draw your testicles upward. You may feel them actually pull closer in to the body; if not, just imagine it. Next, as you exhale, open the fists, and release and extend the hands down to their original resting position against the thighs. At the same time, release the testicles, letting them drop down. Continue. Inhaling, pull the energy up, fists raised. Exhale, let the testicles release, and open the hands. Repeat nine times.

Female Deer

The Female Deer may be practiced once or twice daily (morning or morning and evening), *except during menstruation or pregnancy*. If practiced regularly during those times, the Deer could interfere with the natural hormonal changes. Don't worry if you discover that you are pregnant after having practiced the Deer for several weeks. Just cease practicing at that point.

Sit on the ground or on a cushion, with one heel against the opening of the vagina and exerting a gentle pressure on the clitoris ("the bright pearl on the jade steps"). The other foot rests near the shin. This modified cross-legged posture is common in Indian Yoga, where it is known as *siddhasana*, "the posture of perfection." If your legs or hips are tight, preventing your heel from reaching the clitoris, place a small rubber ball between the heel and clitoris to create the same gentle stimulation.

Warm the palms by rubbing them vigorously together. Then place them over the breasts. Lightly rub the breasts in thirty-six outward circular motions. Don't hold the breasts and move them. Rather, lightly chafe the skin in circular motions, the nipples forming the center of your circle. The hands circle up the inside of the breasts toward your face, out to the sides, down the outside of the breasts, up the inside again. Afterward, rest the hands on the thighs in the holding firm gesture, as in the Male Deer, and tighten the muscles of the vagina as though closing it. One contraction is held as long as you can comfortably, about one or two minutes (rather than repeatedly contracting and releasing, as in the common Kegel exercise). While contracting, it is common to feel a pleasant warmth moving up the inside of the body. The breath is *not* held. Keep the chest and abdomen as relaxed as possible. Then release the contraction, relax, and take a moment to enjoy how you are feeling before moving on to the day's activities.

The Female Deer spreads sexual feeling throughout the body, increasing the potential for clitoral, vaginal, and *whole-body orgasm*. It also increases the strength and tone of the vaginal muscles and sensitivity of the breasts and helps to prevent or cure irregular menstruation, PMS, vaginal discharge, urinary tract infections, ovarian cysts, fibroids, anemia, and sterility. The Deer is famous for its positive effect on fertility.[17] If pregnancy is not your goal, please take appropriate precautions.

MENSTRUATION IS NATURAL AND HEALTHY!

Many qigong texts advise women to "cut the red dragon," to practice a variation of the Deer that completely stops menstruation. The breasts are rubbed as much as 360 times, twice a day.[18] Menstruation usually stops completely within a few months of practice, though for some women it might take six months to a year. If the woman wishes to ovulate again, she simply ceases practicing. From a scientific viewpoint, the Deer activates a reflex loop that connects the hypothalamus and the nipples. According to biologist Robert M. Sapolsky, "If there is nipple stimulation for any reason (in males as well as females), the hypothalamus signals the pituitary to secrete prolactin. And as we now know, prolactin in sufficient quantities causes reproduction to cease."[19] This is also the reason why frequent nursing can prevent conception.

To understand why I differ from many of my colleagues and *do not* recommend cutting the red dragon, either for qi cultivation or birth control, we need to know something about Chinese medicine's understanding of the menstrual cycle. In Chinese medicine, menstrual blood is considered a combination of blood, descending from the heart, mixed with jing, sexual energy, provided by the kidneys. Cutting the red dragon allegedly prevents life energy from leaking once a month and thereby increases qi. It causes a reversed flow of energy, similar to that which occurs during menopause. According to Dr. Bob Flaws, "During menopause, jing moves from the kidneys to the heart. Instead of losing monthly blood, the woman now grows spirit instead. She becomes the wise woman, the sage."[20]

But is it safe to induce menopause early, even if it is reversible? Cutting the red dragon doesn't allow blood to descend. This is probably safe if the woman is capable of the alchemical transformation of blood into spirit, a process that occurs naturally when menstruation ceases because of aging. However, if this transformation fails to occur, perhaps because the woman's spirit is weakened by emotional turmoil or stress, then blood stasis develops. If blood cannot move properly, the body becomes depleted of blood and nourishment, leading possibly to anemia and accelerated aging, sometimes manifesting as age spots and/or wrinkled, dry skin. By contrast, a sign of positive transformation, the successful practice of cutting the red dragon, would be youthfulness, vitality, soft and luxuriant skin, and a general sense of well-being. As Dr. Flaws pragmatically observes, "Stopping the period is probably safe *if* the student is under the supervision of a qualified master, who has remedial treatments should something go wrong."[21]

Deliberately stopping menstruation strikes me as being *yu wei* "forced, artificial" rather than the Daoist ideal of *wu wei* "natural and with the flow." It is one thing for menstruation to stop as a result of hormonal changes that occur during menopause or while nursing, and it is quite another for a qigong practitioner to force this process.[22] "Nature should not be interfered with," says the Daoist Zhuang Zi. Menstruation is a process of yin and yang changing one into the other: yin increases until ovulation, then yang increases until the period. How safe is it to interfere with this cycle? Many Native Americans concur with a basic philosophy in Chinese medicine: if the old—such as static blood in the uterus—is not expelled, the new cannot be created. What effect would stopping and then reinstating the period have on the health of children conceived?

A final note: I cannot help wondering to what extent this variation on the Deer was created by a patriarchy that didn't want to be "inconvenienced" by the woman's period or who believed in the superiority of their own (relative lack of) biological cycles.

THE KEGEL

In the West, the Kegel is a widely accepted exercise for women's sexual health. In China, the same exercise is considered a simple and safe variation of the Deer. From a standing or seated position, exercise your "jade gate" (vagina) by repeatedly contracting and releasing, closing and opening. The contraction should include a feeling of squeezing and pulling up, as though stopping a stream of urine. The exercise strengthens the vaginal muscles and cultivates voluntary control of the pubococcygeus muscle (PCG), the muscle that "contains the nerve endings that provide pleasurable sensations in the outer third of the vagina" (*Merck Manual* 15th Edition, Vol. II, p. 70). The Kegel is recommended by medical doctors for treating "inhibited orgasm." Since the PCG is frequently weakened by childbirth, the Kegel is also an excellent qigong for new mothers. The training schedule given by the *Merck Manual* is sound qigong advice: contract ten to fifteen times, three times per day. There will be noticeable improvements in two to three months.[23]

PREPARATION AND TIMING

In addition to maintaining good health, personal hygiene is an absolutely essential preparation for Clouds and Rain. Wash the body thoroughly with a natural, *unscented* soap. The body's natural scents are extremely important for sexual arousal. As Ornstein and Sobel note in their book *Healthy Pleasures*,[24] good scents make good sex. "Somerset Maugham once inquired of one of H. G. Wells' mistresses why such a paunchy, homely writer had such success with women. 'He smells of honey,' she replied."[25]

An American professor of sociology once commented to me, "I believe that one reason for the high divorce rate in the West is deodorants. If we can't smell each other, we are likely to choose partners with whom we are incompatible." It is significant how often poets compare their lovers to fragrant flowers, musk, sandalwood, or the salty taste and smell of ocean spray.

The room for lovemaking should be aesthetic, clean, and well-ventilated. It is important to have windows and natural light from the sun, moon, or stars, even if filtered through curtains.

Choose a time when you and your partner are in good spirits and when the weather is calm. If atmospheric yin and yang are out of balance, the microcosmic yin and yang do not harmonize as easily. Imbalances include extremes of climate such as heat or cold, a windstorm, thunderstorm, and solar or lunar eclipses.

Other times to avoid Clouds and Rain include:

- within two hours of a heavy meal
- after drinking too much alcohol
- after strenuous activity (when too exhausted to appreciate your partner or provide sexual satisfaction)
- less than twenty-four hours after receiving acupuncture
- while acutely ill
- during emotional upsets
- during menstruation

The last two conditions need some special explanation. Never use sex as an escape from emotional problems or a release from frustration. The *Qian Jin Yao Fang* (Precious Prescriptions), a classic of Chinese Medicine, warns that anger is especially damaging to sexual energy and its appropriate expression.[26] Communicate with your partner and seek to resolve conflicts *before* having sex.

During menstruation, a woman's body cleans out the old cells and tunes in to the cycles of nature. Most ancient cultures recognize this time of the month as a natural period for reflection and meditation. Couples take a short monthly vacation from sexuality and then return to it with fresh energy and a fresh perspective on each other. Respecting nature's wisdom in this way improves sexual health. Menstruation becomes more regular, and, according to traditional beliefs, healthier children are conceived.[27]

FOREPLAY

According to the Daoist sage Lu Dong-bin, "Desiring to have intercourse, one must first embrace the crucible, fondle her two breasts, and suck her lips and tongue. After arousing her passion, one may then insert the yang in the yin and slowly unite."[28]

Couples explore each other's bodies with all of the senses, gently stroking and touching, tasting, smelling, listening to the breath. They should each drink the essences of their partner's "three peaks": mouth, breasts, and genitals.

As your partner becomes sexually aroused, the mouth (the upper "red lotus peak") fills with saliva, "the sweet wine spring." As saliva issues from under the tongue, suck and swallow it down to the dan tian to strengthen the internal organs, the qi, blood, and the dan tian. Deep kissing also strengthens the erection and lubricates the jade gate. Saliva is a physical representation of *jing*, sexual vitality. Drinking it stimulates sexual feelings but also controls the level of sexual fire. The qi in saliva acts like wind, fanning the fire. The water in saliva calms the fire. Kissing can stimulate sexual feelings if excitement is waning, but it can also regulate, and if necessary, lower the level of excitement in order to prolong intercourse. In Chinese Medicine, the tongue is related to the heart and the spirit. In deep kissing, the heart and spirit are aroused. For all of these reasons, kissing is an essential part of clouds and rain.

The middle peak, the breasts, is called "the twin water chestnuts" and its medicinal liquor, "white snow." White snow refers to a subtle energy, rather than a physical substance, found only on the woman's breasts. Although a man may enjoy having his breasts stimulated, his breasts cannot receive or confer the same healing benefits. During arousal and intercourse, the white snow is a sweet honeylike nectar. Like the saliva, the white snow should be sucked and directed down to the dan tian. According to *Exposition of Cultivating the True Essence*, a sexual qigong classic translated by Douglas Wile, white snow "has the ability to nourish the spleen and stomach and strengthen the spirit. Sucking it also opens all of the woman's meridians and relaxes her body and mind."[29]

The lower peak is called the "jade stalk" in a man, and in a woman, the "peak of the purple mushroom" or the "jade gate." When a woman is pleased, it opens like a lotus flower, revealing its sweet dew, the "moon flower." The tongue is like a small penis. The man uses his tongue to stimulate the jade gate and "bright pearl" (clitoris). He also sucks and swallows the moon flower, directing it to the dan tian. When the man is pleased, his jade stalk hardens and pulses with yang qi; it is filled with muscle, bone, blood, breath, and nerve energy. According to Daoist tradition, the mouth is like a vagina. The woman puts it over the man's jade stalk and absorbs his energy, directing it to her dan tian. Remember that it is the energy which is absorbed. The man need not ejaculate for the woman to receive the healing benefits of his *jing*. Man and woman may also use the "69" posture to mutually exchange the energy of the lower peak. The medicine of the lower peak confers longevity and vitality.

THE DANCE OF DRAGONS

After foreplay, when the woman indicates verbally or nonverbally that she is ready, the man should slowly and sensitively insert his jade stalk, at first playing near the entrance. It is important to vary the angle, depth, and speed of penetration. According to the *Dong Xuan Zi*, a seventh-century Chinese sex manual, "a man should not stubbornly cling to one style of union." The text poetically describes numerous ways of moving the jade stalk: "pushing and pulling like seagulls playing in the tide; swiftly alternating strokes, like a sparrow pecking at rice; a steady rhythm of deep and shallow, like large stones sinking in the sea." Playfully explore various positions. Each one creates a different kind of stimulation and causes the sexual energy to flow to different parts of the body.

CONTROLLING THE FIRE, BOILING THE WATER

The man's sexual behavior is naturally compared to fire. The woman is compared to water. Fire is quickly ignited and easily put out. Water is slow to boil and slow to cool down. This means that a greater discipline is required for the man, since he needs to maintain the fire so that the water can boil. There are two secrets to maintaining sexual passion and the erection. A man should build a full supply of qi by practicing qigong and not waste his energy through excessive ejaculation.

Frequency of ejaculation has nothing to do with frequency of sex. Even if a man has sex every day, he should not emit every day. This improves health and sexual stamina, yet is still pleasurable; he enjoys foreplay and, during intercourse, a buildup of intense, erotic sensation over the entire body. Ejaculation frequency is determined by health, season, and age. If a man is in poor health, he should ejaculate only rarely. During the spring and summer, ejaculate more often; in the fall and winter, conserve energy and semen. According to the seventh-century physician Sun Si-mo, one should ejaculate less with increasing age.[30] I recommend that for optimal qi development and health, at age twenty, one may ejaculate once every three or four days, at age thirty, once every five or six, at age forty, once every seven or eight, and so on. There will be some individual variability. If you have a regular sexual partner, you can determine your natural rhythm by simply noting when sexual desires peak during a one- to two-week period of abstention from sex. Explain to your partner in a loving and caring way that this will only be a brief experiment.

Qigong recommends practice of clouds and rain as often as the couple desires. Discipline is required because the man does not emit each time, yet he should always try to promote complete satisfaction of his partner. Whereas a man's health is improved by approaching "rainfall" but withholding, a woman's qi is nurtured by full orgasm, or multiple orgasms. Remember this does not mean that the longer a man withholds semen, the better. Too much abstinence leads to congestion, just as too much indulgence leads to depletion. When it is time to ejaculate, the man should give in to the experience completely.

Ejaculation control: During intercourse, before reaching "the point of no return," stop thrusting and concentrate on drawing the sexual energy upward toward the crown. While inhaling, contract the entire perineum, the coccyx, sacrum, and the penis itself. Some men find it helpful to also squeeze the buttocks. This "Big Draw" method is clearly explained in Mantak Chia's *Taoist Secrets of Love: Cultivating Male Sexual Energy.*[31]

The "fire" can also be controlled by squeezing only the perineum. During intercourse, repeatedly contract and release the perineum muscles while concentrating on inhaling qi into the dan tian. You may do this either while thrusting or during a period of stillness. An even subtler method is to contract and release a specific point on the perineum, called the *hui yin*, the meeting of yin. The point is a small, sensitive hollow midway between the genitals and anus. The more you progress in qigong and energy control, the easier it is to cause sexual energy to rise by contracting or concentrating on this one point.

Drawing sexual qi upward blocks activation of the sympathetic nervous system, thus preventing ejaculation. Energetically, sexual energy is pumped up the spine, away from the genitals. This lowers the level of genital excitement, but raises the level of ecstatic feeling throughout the body.

Many schools of qigong advise forcibly pressing the hui yin point with a finger just before ejaculation to block the flow of semen, preventing it from moving through the urethra. The belief is that the *jing* flows back to its internal reservoirs or is sublimated into higher forms of energy. In ancient China courtesans would sometimes press the point for the man, at his signal. Pressing the hui yin allegedly permits a man to have orgasm without ejaculation and to maintain his erection, prolonging intercourse.

I do *not* recommend this method. Acupuncturists treating practitioners of the "injaculation" method claim that the technique causes jing stagnation and may contribute to prostate inflammation and cysts. If ejaculation is imminent, instead of trying to inhibit the natural process, it is better to seek a harmonious exchange of energies with one's partner. This way no energy is lost. Rather, each individual becomes more whole: the man accumulates yin and the woman gathers yang. It is also important to remember what Wile calls the "exemption clause"[32] in the Chinese sexual classics. The more the harmony and chemistry between the man and woman, the less need to be concerned about losing semen.

EXCHANGING SEXUAL ENERGY

In the 1930s one of my Daoist teachers was traveling with his friend, a Buddhist priest, to the monastery of a Daoist sage who was known as *Jian Xian*, "the Sword Immortal." The monastery was located two days' journey into Holy Mount E Mei, in Sichuan Province. The first evening after their arrival, the master agreed to demonstrate "Daoist sex," to the delight of my teacher and the embarrassment of the celibate Buddhist.

The monastery was dark except for the light of two candles on the altar. The master sat on a chair as a female Daoist entered the room and sat across from him. They were both dressed in long, flowing robes that reached down to their ankles. They each closed their eyes and appeared to enter a state of deep quiet. Then, according to my teacher, there was a whooshing sound, like the wind, as light visibly flashed out of the master's genital area, toward the woman's jade gate, a moment later emerging from the woman's eyes and shooting across to the master's eyes. The light kept circulating in this way several times, and then it reversed direction. Out the master's eyes to the woman, emerging from her genital region across to the master, each time accompanied by the whooshing sound.

With a twinkle in his eye, my teacher, a youthful ninety-year-old, exclaimed, "This is our Daoist sex. Energy circulate. They both smile. They both happy. And not have to lose virginity!"

Are we to believe this story and take it literally? I'm not sure that *I* do. Yet the message in it is profound and can easily be applied to the unclothed varieties of clouds and rain.

The essence of Daoist sex or qigong sex is energy exchange and circulation. The Three Treasures are exchanged through the three points of contact: genitals, lips, and eyes. Jing flows from one to the other through genital contact. By kissing and drinking each other's breath and saliva, the qi is exchanged. Looking deeply into your partner's eyes causes the shen, the spiritual energy, to flow from one to the other.

It is also possible to practice sexual variations of the *Small Heavenly Circulation* meditation (see Chapter 11). Here are some examples.

a) The woman contracts her jade gate, drawing in yang qi from the man. She circulates this qi through her Governing and Conception acupuncture meridians: up the back, along the spine, and over the crown, then down the front midline of the body, passing through the middle of the sternum, past the navel and genitals, and returning to the spine. The man can do the same, imagining that he is drawing in yin qi and cycling it. This can happen simultaneously or the energy can flow from one to the other: The woman draws qi from the man's "jade stalk," drives it up her back, down the front, and *then* asks the man to absorb the energy. He draws it from her jade gate into his organ, sends it around his circuit, and returns it to the woman. One continuous river of qi circulates between them.

b) The man drinks his partner's saliva, directing it down his Conception meridian and up his back. He then gives saliva to his partner. She similarly sends it down her front, up her back. She returns the saliva to the man. The cycle continues.

c) The man draws qi from the woman's jade gate into his jade stalk. He sends it up his back, over the crown, and then asks his partner to drink the energy. She drinks his saliva and sends it down her Conception meridian until it exits the jade gate again. The man again draws the sexual energy up his spine and sends it out his mouth. She drinks. The cycle continues for a while, then reverses. This time the woman uses her jade gate to draw the man's yang qi. She sends it up her spine, over her crown, and out her mouth. The man drinks the energy, directs it down the front of his body, and sends it out his jade stalk. It continues circulating.

With some imagination, you can discover your own variations.

The Mind Directs Sexual Qi

The skills acquired from solo meditation practice can easily be applied to dual cultivation. For instance, with your partner's permission, you can draw the sexual energy to any place in your body that needs healing. Getting permission is important, because you want your partner to know that your priority is loving and giving energy, not taking.[33]

To heal the entire body, you and your partner can simultaneously imagine the sexual energy as a healing light. Draw it up from the genitals, letting it exit the crown and cascade over the surface of the skin. The best time to practice this is during mutual orgasm. As the man emits, the woman pulls the jing and qi upward. Immediately after ejaculation, the head of the jade stalk naturally retracts slightly. The man sensitizes himself to this moment and draws the woman's orgasmic energy upward in his own body.

As with other forms of qigong, close your "meditation" with massage. Instead of self-massage, massage your partner. Take turns to gently stroke the entire body. Make sure you include the head, lower abdomen, lower back, and feet (especially the Bubbling Well points). Apply the principles of External Qi Healing. As you place your palms on any areas that are calling for attention, reach the qi *(de qi)*, making sensitive, loving contact with the healing energy.

DON'T GET TECHNICAL!

The techniques of sexual qigong are tools to help increase sexual harmony and happiness. They are not ends in themselves. In the beginning of a relationship, forget all about these methods. That's right. Do not practice! Your first goal is to allow an uninhibited expression of your love and to develop an appreciation for and understanding of your partner's needs. Later you can bring in various techniques as appropriate. If a method feels unnatural and seems to have any harmful physical or psychological effects, discontinue it. Do not think, "Well, this is *supposed* to be good for me." It either is good for you or it isn't. "Supposed to" has nothing to do with it!

It may seem strange that love is mentioned rarely in the sexual qigong classics—only four times in all of the texts translated by Wile. There are references to passion and ecstasy, to the need for harmony and compatibility, but hardly a word about love. Not that the Chinese didn't love. Although the myths and lore of romantic love may not have played as large a role in the East as the West, one has only to open a book of Chinese poetry to realize the similarity of all human hearts. Perhaps there have been too few poets among China's sexual Yogis or those who wrote about them.

From our modern perspective, the most important benefit of sexual qigong is learning how to better please your partner, as an expression of love. Love, unlike jing, does not have to be conserved. It is the most mysterious form of qi since the more you give it, the stronger it becomes.

CHAPTER TWENTY-ONE

Closing the Circle: Signs of Mastery, Signs of Stupidity

I went there and came back; it was nothing special:
The mountain veiled by misty rain, the river at high tide.
—*THE ZENRINKUSHU* (COLLECTED SAYINGS FROM THE ZEN FOREST), A BUDDHIST CLASSIC FROM THE SEVENTEENTH CENTURY

Are there ranks or belts in qigong, as in the martial arts? What does it take to be considered a qigong master? The answers to these questions are useful in appraising your own progress or determining the expertise of an instructor.

DEFINING THE TERM "MASTER"

I use the term "master" as a respectful way of designating someone who has mastered a craft, without any connotation of ultimate authority or "mastery" over others. In fact, the word I translate as "master" is *Lao Shi*, a term meaning teacher or professor. Thus, Zhang Lao Shi: Professor Zhang, Teacher Zhang, or Master Zhang. Some older-generation Chinese still use the term *Sifu* (Cantonese, pronounced See Foo; in Mandarin, it's *Shi Fu*). This means literally "Teacher Father." In the context of qigong or the martial arts, "Sifu" often relates to the old discipleship system, in which the student pledged his lifelong obedience to a particular master and lineage. I am not a proponent of the guru-disciple system, and so prefer the less ambiguous term Lao Shi.

When new students mistakenly call me Sifu, I usually respond, "Don't call me Sea Food." or "Yes, I like to See Food and eat it. But don't call me that."

DEPTH OF LEARNING

Levels or ranks in qigong are more a matter of depth of learning and practice rather than the accumulation of a set number of new techniques. This point is often poorly communicated by popular writers on qigong—catering to American acquisitiveness, our hierarchical model of education, and our tendency to value quantity over quality. Qigong is like a work of art. One graceful stroke of the brush is far more impressive than an awkward or ugly painting. As the Chinese say, "If you try to draw a tiger, but hold the brush incorrectly, it will look like a dog."

In the wonderful movie *City Slickers*, Curly, the wise old cowboy, tells his young apprentice that the secret of life is in mastering One Thing. I am not denying the importance of broad learning. Knowing many recipes prevents boredom and gives the cook a better understanding of how to create and combine flavors. By exploring diverse qigong techniques, we can evolve a more detailed understanding of the form and function of qi. Diversity is especially important for the professional qigong therapist (or teacher), who must be capable of matching appropriate techniques to the individual client.

However, such diversity is no assurance of quality or mastery. To achieve mastery, we must keep returning to the One Thing, the fundamental theme or themes that underlie all qigong training. How can I relax? How do I breathe? How can I love as a whole human being—mind, body, and spirit integrated—rather than as broken, disconnected parts? Am I aware of myself and my place in the universe? What does it take to master Lying, Sitting, Standing, Walking? The "city slickers" learn this One Thing not in the techniques of horse riding and cattle driving but rather in learning to live and appreciate life more fully and deeply.

YOU DON'T HAVE TO BE CHINESE!

A true master is a humble guide and adviser. When he points to the moon, he wishes the student to look at the moon, not at him! A master never asks for or expects blind devotion. He or she might be demanding, but he is also demanding of himself, always ready to learn more, to improve. For this reason, the master welcomes a student's healthy skepticism and questions.

In this attitude I differ from many of my Chinese colleagues. In China, questions have often been perceived as challenges to the teacher's authority or his supposed ability to know exactly what each student needs. I was once discussing this problem with Madame Gao Fu, a visiting Chinese qigong master. In the middle of our conversation, she suddenly exclaimed, "Oh, now I understand. Americans ask questions because they really want to know the answers!" After this revelation, the teacher began to yield more frequently to her Western students' inquisitiveness. Both she and her students were enriched. At the end of five months in the United States, the master acknowledged that several of her Western students were more advanced than students who had trained with her in China for a much longer period. And if you haven't already guessed—you don't have to be Chinese to master qigong! If an instructor is prejudiced, if he or she is saving the "secrets" for those of a particular ethnicity, nationality, religion, or gender, walk out the door and don't turn back. Such secrets can never reveal the way to mind, body, and spirit harmony.

A BLACK BELT IN QIGONG? NOT QUITE

What then are the levels and stages of qigong mastery? Here I would like to gratefully acknowledge my friend, Qigong master Paul Gallagher, and his teacher, Master T. T. Liang, for this ingenious ranking system.

Level 1: Great Expert

After a few months of qigong, students typically experience so many pleasant changes and improvements in health and state of mind that they are apt to get a bit ego-inflated. Knowing a little, they think they know a lot. This is understandable and forgivable. Our society provides few role models of exceptional human potential. Thus, the students still do not realize that they have taken only the first steps, that there is so much more to learn.[1]

Level 2: Big Potato

Now the student has learned a basic qigong set. He can finally practice on his own and show off to his friends and family. If they are as ignorant about qigong as he is, they will praise him for mastering something so difficult and esoteric. Maybe instead of using 10 percent of his brain, the student is now using 15 percent. Not so much to brag about, Big Potato!

Level 3: Banana Head

The Banana Head realizes, "I don't know so much after all." Like Socrates, he knows that he doesn't know and feels rather silly about his previous self-importance. There is a famous Chinese saying, "Though I live to a ripe old age and study ceaselessly, there is always more to learn." It is both sobering and exciting to discover the depth of qigong philosophy and practice. As you approach the goal of perfect health or wisdom, it recedes into the distance. If you think you have it, you don't. But in realizing that you have not reached an end point, you have understood!

Level 4: Nothing Special

On a physical level, the goal of qigong is mastery of principle and technique. On the spiritual side, the goal is cultivating a profound sense of belonging in the universe, of oneness with the Life-Breath ("the Original Qi of Heaven and Earth"). Qigong is nothing special, yet very special. I stand, I breathe. What could be more natural or more profound? Qigong is a Way, a Dao, to realize mystery and beauty in the ordinary and everyday.

Unfortunately, in China qigong is still often considered a way to acquire special powers. Qigong masters and magicians demonstrate bending steel rods against the throat, breaking stones with their skulls, and pushing objects without touching them.[2] I knew one qigong "master" who claimed that he could make the clouds part, but only under the "right conditions," which occurred about once in every hundred attempts. Focusing on these spectacles is a distraction from the real, life-enhancing goal of qigong. And what could be more magical than healing an injury or disease? The body is still the greatest mystery of all. Noted author and expert on Chinese religion, the late John Blofeld, said, "Yes, qigong can cultivate *powers*: Invisibility—that means going unnoticed in a crowd; Astral Travel—knowing that the real Self is everywhere; Levitation—taking yourself lightly."[3]

So we proceed from Great Expert to Big Potato to Banana Head to Nothing Special. In the end, the complexity of qigong becomes a way to recapture simplicity and innocence. We become more aware of the questions that life presents, but no longer assume that the busy intellect has all the answers.

My friend Paul Gallagher was fascinated by some stories I shared with him about qigong masters who had developed "internal power," the ability to withstand punches or kicks to the body without suffering injury. When he asked his teacher, Master Liang, about these abilities, Liang looked at Paul with a serious, penetrating gaze and said, "Yes, Paul, when you have one, you have many." He repeated, "When you have one, you have many. What is it?" Paul wondered about this profound statement, undoubtedly the essence of qi-power. Could Master Liang be referring to the one and the many, unity in diversity, the complexity of the meridians, and the unity of the dan tian? Or was there some other answer to this conundrum? Paul said, "I don't know, Master Liang, what is it?" Master Liang replied, "Cockroaches, Paul, cockroaches! Don't ask too many questions. Just practice."

Appendices

APPENDIX A

Dates of Chinese Dynasties

Xia (legendary): c. 2000–1600 B.C.
Shang: c. 1600–1028 B.C.
Zhou: 1028–221 B.C.
Qin: 221–206 B.C.
Han: 206 B.C.–A.D. 220
Three Kingdoms: 220–280
Western Jin: 265–317
Eastern Jin: 317–420
Six Dynasties: 420–581
Sui: 581–618
Tang: 618–907
Five Dynasties: 907–960
Song: 960–1279
Jin: 1115–1234
Yuan (Mongol): 1260–1368
Ming: 1368–1644
Qing (Manchu): 1644–1911
The Republic: 1912–1948

A Technical Note on the Concept "Dan Tian"

The dan tian is the elixir or cinnabar (dan) field (tian). It is the energetically fertile part of the body, the place where one can plant the elixir of health, wisdom, and long life. Dan can also mean "alchemy." In outer alchemy (wai dan), the elixir is created by heating and refining herbs, minerals and other elements. In qigong, which is a process of inner alchemy (nei dan), the body provides all of the elements necessary to compound the elixir. The alchemical crucible is the lower abdomen.

The word dan tian first appears in a great third-century classic of Daoist alchemy and meditation, the Huang Ting Wai Jing Jing (Canon of the Outer Radiance of the Yellow Court). "Through respiration, original qi enters the dan tian. The dan tian, three inches below the navel, is the gateway of yin and yang." According to a text in the Daoist Canon, Tai Xi Jing (The Embryonic Respiration Classic), there is a secret reference to the dan tian in a much earlier work, the Dao De Jing of Lao Zi (fourth century B.C.). Chapter six has a line, "The gate of the Mysterious Female (Xuan Pin) is called the root of Heaven and Earth." The Embryonic Respiration Classic says, "The dan tian is the Mysterious Female." It is female because it is a womb, a place where the inner yin and yang coagulate, creating a new self, an "immortal fetus," in Daoist terms.

There are three dan tians: at the level of the lower abdomen, the chest, and the third eye. The lower dan tian is the most important. It is the center of gravity, breath, and energy in the body. Normally when authors refer to "dan tian," they mean this abdominal center: three inches below the navel, in the center of the body. The exact location of the three dan tians can vary slightly from person to person.

In Daoist lore, the three dan tians are infested by three worms. The lower worm destroys the reproductive system. The middle worm eats the internal organs, and the upper worm consumes the brain. The worms are starved through ethical behavior, good deeds, a balanced diet, and healing qi. Daoists do not believe it necessary to wait for a future life to suffer the "karma" of one's actions or to reap the rewards of spiritual practice.

Qigong Master Jiao Guorui correctly notes that certain acupoints are also considered dan tians and may be focused on during Qigong Meditation. The *Front Dan Tian* is located on the front of the body, at the navel. Concentrating here strengthens digestion and abdominal respiration. Many Daoists focus on this point, reasoning that since the umbilicus is the source of fetal nourishment, it is an adult's source of original qi. The *Middle Dan Tian* (the one I generally refer to as either dan tian or lower dan tian) is three inches below the navel, in the center of the body, along the acupuncture meridian known as the Thrusting Channel *(Chong Mai)*. Some authors locate this center at the level of the navel, rather than below it. Focusing on the Middle Dan Tian cultivates qi, improves qi flow in the meridians, strengthens respiration, digestion, and blood circulation. The *Rear Dan Tian* is the *ming men* "gate of life" acupoint, on the spine between the second and third lumbar vertebrae, across from the navel. Concentrating on the ming men is an extremely powerful and popular qigong. It improves kidney function, tonifies both the jing (developmental, sexual energies) and qi, and stimulates the body's ability to absorb original qi from the universe.

In some qigong texts, the lower dan tian is variously identified with any of three acupoints: *guan yuan* "gate source" 3.5 inches below the navel, near the front surface of the body; *qi hai* "sea of qi," two inches below the navel near the front surface; or *hui yin* "meeting of yin," a sensitive point on the perineum, midway between the genitals and anus. I do not recommend concentrating on this latter point for long periods of time, as it is often too stimulating, causing energy "rushes." The guan yuan and qi hai points are extremely potent areas of focus. Jiao says that these points can strengthen the original qi and the constitution.

A confusing point in some Chinese meditation texts is that *qi hai* "sea of qi" is often used as an esoteric name for the lower dan tian, whether located two or three inches below the navel (at the level of either the qi hai or guan yuan points) or in the center of the body—what Jiao Guorui calls "the Middle Dan Tian." We again see how the same word means different things according to different authors or contexts. In acupuncture literature, the term qi hai always refers to a specific acupoint. In qigong literature, qi hai *might* mean that same point or it might refer to the lower dan tian region (which, again, according to some authors is at the acupoint).

In Chapter 3, I described the association between the three dan tians, lower, middle, and upper with jing, qi, and shen, respectively. These correspondences are a theoretical model consistent with the styles of qigong I have presented. Many qigong authorities agree with this map of the body. However, the ancient *Tian Shi Pai*, "Heavenly Master Sect," of Daoism (second century A.D.) draws the map somewhat differently. They agree that jing is stored in the lower dan tian. However, they place shen in the middle dan tian—recognizing Chinese medicine's classical association between the heart and spirit. And they set the upper dan tian as the storage place for qi and the abode of the original qi of the universe. In this system, the upper dan tian corresponds to heaven, the mind, and qi. The middle dan tian corresponds to earth, the heart, and shen. The lower dan tian corresponds to intuition, "gut knowing," and the element water.

Although these various models are not always consistent with each other, they are internally consistent. That is, a work derived from a particular qigong lineage will not tell you, in one chapter, that shen is only in the upper dan tian, and then, a moment later, switch it to the middle dan tian. The fact that there are so many ways of mapping the body or explaining how qi works demonstrates that conceptual models are not absolute truth. This might be frustrating for some, liberating for others.

Double-Blind or
Double Standard?

"If penicillin cannot improve my child's SAT grades, then it is obviously an ineffective medication." What is wrong with this statement? It is, in the words of Shellenberger and Green, a *category mistake*. "A category mistake occurs when conceptualizations appropriate to one category are inaccurately applied to another."[1] The same thing happens when scientists who are familiar with one area of research assume that their methods are equally applicable to qigong.

For instance, the standards of animal and drug research are inappropriate for qigong research. In animal research, a simple stimulus can produce, with proper conditioning and reinforcement, a predictable response. But human beings are not rats (at least not most of them). They attach meaning and value to their experiences. Their responses to stimuli are shaped by a complex web of interconnected and uncontrollable variables, including beliefs, goals, memories, expectations, aversions, conscious and subconscious motivations, spirituality, environment, and degree of social support. These factors make it very difficult to predict an exact response to qigong treatment or to precisely replicate an experiment.

In drug research the "triple-blind" method is an appropriate way to rule out the placebo effect. Neither the subject, the operator (person administering treatment), nor the outcome evaluator knows who is actually taking the drug and who is taking an inactive substance. This is again, quite obviously, an impossible design for qigong research. Qigong practitioners are aware that they are exercising a specific healing technique, and one that, in China, is culturally sanctioned. Qigong instructors, even in the laboratory setting, usually have expectations that they hope their students will fulfill. There is no way to absolutely distinguish specific effects of the therapy from non-specific effects.

Category mistakes also occur with regard to dosage. Qigong, unlike drugs, cannot be administered in standard doses and thus does not lend itself easily to repetitive protocols. Chinese diagnostic labels do not refer to static conditions, but rather to fluid and evolving expressions of the patient's body, mind, and spirit. The condition will differ slightly from patient to patient and from day to day. This means that for qigong to be accurately evaluated, the instructor must be free to change and tailor the methods to the individual patient.

Additionally, qigong cannot be targeted to combat *only* one specific disease. It always has global effects on human health and consciousness. Thus qigong research is in certain respects *more* complex than usual medical research, demanding flexible, creative, and intuitive designs. If we fail to incorporate the qigong perspective into research design, we may end up with, in the words of Dr. Cristina S. de la Torre, president of the American Academy of Medical Acupuncture, "quasi treatment to a quasi diagnosis."[2]

There are also inherent problems with the double-blind protocol, whether applied to allopathic or alternative medical research. It is assumed that if the subjects and the operator are unaware of who is receiving a scientific or sham treatment, it will be easy to demonstrate a cause-and-effect relationship between a particular therapy and a specific outcome. This is not completely true. There is ample evidence that the outcome of an experiment can be influenced by the attitude of the principal investigator: his or her degree of skepticism, optimism, hostility, or hopefulness. Thus, one investigator will consistently get positive results, and another gets negative results even when both are testing identical interventions!

The demand that qigong prove a high degree of efficacy (nearly 100 percent for some critics) in double-blind experiments masks a double standard. Many allopathic interventions have failed to meet these same rigorous standards. In 1978, the Congressional Office of Technology Assessment found that *80–90 percent of medical interventions practiced by physicians are not scientifically proven!*[3] In 1991, the editor of the *British Medical Journal* reached a similar conclusion, observing that "only about 15% of medical interventions are supported by solid scientific evidence. . . . That is partly because only 1%

of the articles in medical journals are scientifically sound and partly because many treatments have never been assessed at all."[4]

Now, I am not proposing that we give up the lifesaving drugs and procedures that are the wonders of modern medicine. I am only suggesting that blind faith in allopathic medicine is as misguided as blind faith in alternative modalities. It is commonly believed that placebo effects account for at least 33 percent of all cures attributed to allopathic medicine. However, when patient and healer believe in the efficacy of treatment, that figure is probably closer to 70 percent. When 6,931 patients were treated with medically ineffective forms of therapy, 40 percent had excellent outcomes, 30 percent good outcomes, and 30 percent poor outcomes.[5]

One of the most shocking examples of the power of placebo was demonstrated in the 1950s, when chest surgery was tested against sham surgeries in randomly selected human subjects. (Thank God that such experiments could never pass an ethics review board today!) At that time the surgical procedure for angina pain involved tying off certain arteries in the chest (internal mammary ligation). In the sham surgeries, an incision was made in the chest, and then the patient was sewed up. *These patients, believing that they had undergone surgery, recovered as well from angina pain as those who had the actual surgery.* Both the "nonligated" (placebo treated) patients and the ligated patients needed less medication and had increased exercise tolerance. Patients remained improved for at least six weeks. In one study, some of the nonligated patients maintained their improved health during the six to eight months they were followed.[6]

Placebo effects are widespread in allopathic medicine. This is to be expected since, according to Herbert Benson, M.D., "between 60 percent and 90 percent of visits to physicians are prompted by conditions that are related to stress and are poorly treated by drugs and surgery."[7] Often it is not the medical intervention that is curing disease, but rather other factors such as caring, hope, greater sense of control, or belief in the power of the physician or the magic of medical technology. So, when a physician points his finger at qigong or other alternative treatments and says, "It's only placebo," look where the other three fingers are pointing.

Carol Schneider, Ph.D., and Wayne Jonas, M.D., remind us that when evaluating the effectiveness of any treatment, it is important to be clear about how one defines success.[8] They list four categories of treatment outcome: *Cure, Care, Empowerment,* and *Enlightenment.* I consider these four aspects of healing, where healing is defined as making whole, a process that might or might not involve curing. Sometimes healing means improving quality of life or preparing for a more conscious and dignified death.

Cure: Both allopathic medicine and qigong are capable of curing or

alleviating symptoms, and each modality has its strong points and weaknesses. The cures accomplished by allopathic medicine are often more immediate and dramatic.

Care: Among the various branches of medicine, East or West, nursing
has turned patient care into a fine art and science, and there is little equivalent in the domain of qigong. I recommend readers to become familiar with
nursing research, as reported in such journals as the *Journal of Holistic
Nursing* (see Qigong Resources). However, qigong has unsurpassed techniques of self-caring and self-management. If a qigong student is taught to
exert even a small degree of control over the course of an illness, this can
boost self-confidence and lead to a more successful treatment outcome. By
contrast, after a typical session with a Western physician, most patients
haven't a clue about how they can improve their own health or prevent a serious problem from recurring.

Empowerment: Empowerment includes the ability to cope with suffering, disease, and the psychological or social consequences of disease. An
individual who feels empowered has a sense of belonging (as opposed to
alienation), value, direction, purpose, and/or meaning. Psychotherapy and
qigong can both help patients feel empowered.

Enlightenment: Enlightenment is often implied in empowerment or is a
spiritual consequence of empowerment. It is self-understanding and the realization of one's relationship to the Divine or one's place in the cosmos.
Qigong excels in this area.

It seems obvious that qigong research with human subjects needs to look
at qualitative and quantitative factors. Psychological scales that measure patient satisfaction, mood, and well-being could be important assessment
tools.[9]

Although it may be difficult to apply the double-blind protocol to
qigong research, there are nevertheless many aspects of scientific methodology that can and should be applied. It would be wise to consider the advice
of Ed Gracely, Ph.D., of the Medical College of Pennsylvania and Hahne-
mann University School of Medicine, "What 'replicability' does entail, in
my view, is that once the type and magnitude of effect for a treatment have
been identified, and the major sources of variation determined, it should be
possible to design studies with an appropriate sample size and methodology
such as to produce relatively consistent results."[10]

In China the scientific method is rarely followed with sufficient rigor.
Whereas some Western scientists reject qigong out of hand because it of-
fends preconceived notions about human functioning (and potential) or because of inappropriate methods of assessment, China accepts qigong research

too readily. Having reviewed several volumes of qigong science conference proceedings from China, I find the following problems with some, though certainly not all, of the abstracts:

a) Too few subjects, no controls, not enough control subjects or not controlling those variables that can be controlled, such as matching subjects by gender, age, education, degree of social support, past and present mental health, and qigong proficiency. For instance, I read a published study on magnetic signals created by qigong practice: three people in the control group, seventeen people in the qigong group, who had practiced anywhere from one to twenty years. It is hard to draw any conclusion with this kind of sample. In another experiment, patients with respiratory diseases who practiced qigong were able to lower their respiratory rate from approximately nineteen to seven breaths per minute. This says little about qigong per se, since we would expect similar results if the patients were simply asked to pay attention to their breath. (If qigong can catalyze this effect, then it is significant.)

b) Not enough testing of qigong against other modalities. China has conducted some excellent research to show that qigong *with* medication works better than medication by itself. I would also like to see research contrasting qigong with standard allopathic medical treatment and other forms of alternative medicine, compared to controls.

Qigong has rarely been tested against placebos such as sugar pills. An interesting placebo would be to treat the patient with a device that the therapist identifies as a "qigong machine" but that actually has only a humming motor inside. *Active placebos* might also be used: for instance prescribing harmless qigong techniques that are meant to treat other conditions and contrasting their efficacy with the correct qigong method.

c) How to measure competence? There is still no clear way to determine the proficiency of an internal qigong teacher or External Qi Healer. In China, popularity, media exposure, and a distinguished lineage lead to assumptions of competence. I suspect that objective measures might sometimes reveal a different picture. In the United States, there is still so little familiarity with qigong that novices may, out of ignorance, assume that they have mastered the subject when they are still at the beginning stages. The fact that they are often successful in clinical practice is a testament to the power of placebo.

Standards of competency need to be established and broadly applied. At the very least, instructors should have trained for a specified minimum length of time (I suggest four years), be proficient in basic qigong skills or methods (perhaps as assessed by a review board), demonstrate an ability to apply their knowledge in clinical practice or as an educator, and be familiar with the literature. Physiological indices of qigong competence could include the Qigong EEG, relaxation levels, peripheral skin temperature, acupoint conductance, and respiratory rate.

d) **Vested interests.** Experiments are often performed by groups that have an emotional and financial interest in finding a positive outcome. For instance, members of a particular qigong school test their style's effectiveness in combating cancer. Such groups are notorious for trying to portray anecdotal case histories as scientific fact, always mentioning their successes and ignoring their failures. This is as much a problem in the United States as in China.

e) **Unconfirmed diagnosis and cure.** In many studies it is unclear if the problem was medically diagnosed or evaluated. When a disorder is "cured," what are the criteria? Is it cured according to X rays and blood work? Or is it considered cured if the patient says he feels better? Was the disease self-limiting, that is, would time have cured it anyway? I have read some claims that I *wish* were true but that I believe are impossible. For instance, Li Hongqi and Huang Jianzhong reported on the therapeutic effects of Yuanji Qigong: "Glaucoma: 120 cases, 62 percent recovered; Cancers: 52 percent arrested, 36 percent recovered; Paralysis: 80 percent recovered; Diseases of aging: 80 percent recovered."[11] An unrelated study found that after eighty-nine days of External Qi treatment, a group of paraplegic pigs could all walk, compared to a control group in which none could stand.[12] As one of my professors used to say, "Don't you believe it!"—Note that's an exclamation point, not a question mark. Grandiose claims are far too common. "I can cure cancer. If I can't cure you, nothing can." That was an alleged qigong master speaking, not God. Such pronouncements create false hope, disappointment, and despair.

f) **Vague or outdated diagnostic labels.** If the problem is cancer, what kind of cancer? If qigong is recommended for "arthritis," is it osteoarthritis or rheumatoid? One is a wear-and-tear condition; the other is an immune disorder. If the same qigong method is prescribed for both, then the diagnosis, the therapy, and the alleged cure are all suspect. When twenty cases of paralysis are "cured," what kind of paralysis was it? What was the cause? Was the spine damaged? Where? In reports of qigong therapy for psychological disorders, it is even more difficult to determine the actual condition of the patient. Most research is directed toward the treatment of *shen jing shuai ro*, usually translated "nerve weakness" or neurasthenia, a vague catch-all phrase for various types of mental illness, including psychosis and schizophrenia. If Western diagnostic labels are used, they should be used accurately.

g) **Sloppy reporting of procedure.** For instance, what kind of qigong did the subjects practice and with what frequency?

Unfortunately even a small percentage of "bad science" weakens the credibility of the whole field. Professional critics and skeptics are likely to dismiss qigong, focusing on anything that can justify their position. And although I disagree with the notion that there is a conspiracy by the medical or pharmaceutical industries to hide or discredit complementary medical research, some people are certainly more concerned with profit than health care. Self-healing is not very profitable for anyone besides the patient. The herding instinct is also alive and well in academia: university professors may fear to differ from the crowd, lest they lose chances at tenure.

For all of these reasons, it is important to promote and seek excellence in qigong research.

Benefits of Internal Qigong: Experimental Evidence

Cardiovascular: Lower resting heart rate, less abnormal EKG, greater cardiac efficiency, stabilized blood pressure, less LDL ("bad cholesterol"), more HDL ("good cholesterol").

Circulation: Improves microcirculation, peripheral circulation, prevents vascular spasms: very helpful for Raynaud's syndrome, angina, migraine.

Digestive: Massages internal organs, improves peristalsis and appetite, less pathogenic bacteria in feces (healthier microflora). Positive effects on ulcers and constipation.

Brain: Slow, high-amplitude brain waves, improved cerebral blood flow, less incidence of stroke, helpful for paralysis and seizure disorders.

Mental Health: Decreased: stress response, Type A, anxiety, obsessive-compulsive, depression. Improved: memory, concentration, interpersonal sensitivity.

Respiratory: Slower respiratory rate, improved gaseous exchange, significant positive effects on asthma and bronchitis.

Immune System: More active immune cells, better targeting of antigens, significant anticancer effect.

Musculoskeletal: Increases strength, flexibility, bone density, improved coordination, beneficial for arthritis and osteoporosis.

Longevity: Improves: BP, vital capacity, cholesterol and hormone levels, kidney function, mental acuity, vision and hearing, skin elasticity, bone density, immune function. Increases physical strength, libido. Deactivates harmful free radicals.

Glossary of
Common Qigong Terms

Active Qigong 動功 (dong gong) Also called dynamic qigong. Qigong techniques that include movement, contrasted with meditative or passive qigong.

Acupuncture 針刺 (zhen ci) The most famous practice in Chinese medicine. The art and science of inserting fine needles into specific "acupuncture points" on the body for the prevention and treatment of disease. Often written 針灸 (zhen jiu) "acupuncture and moxibustion," because acupuncturists may apply the heat of burning moxa (mugwort) to an acupoint to increase the therapeutic effect. Moxa is used in a variety of ways, such as attaching moxa to an acupuncture needle or applying heat directly to a point with a cigarlike moxa stick.

Alchemy 煉丹 (lian dan) Literally, "refining the elixir [of long life and health]." Chinese alchemy consists of *inner alchemy* 內 丹 (nei dan, also translated inner elixir), in which an elixir is created inside the body by practicing qigong exercise and meditation, and *outer alchemy* 外丹 (wai dan, also translated outer elixir), the ingestion of plant- and/or mineral-based pills or substances. In ancient China, it was common for people to practice both forms of alchemy.

Bai Hui 百會 "The hundred meetings." Acupuncture point number twenty on the Governor Channel, at the crown of the head, in line with the apexes of the ears. Qi is directed to this point during some internal meditations and while absorbing qi from nature.

Bubbling Well 涌泉 (Yong Quan) Also translated "Gushing Spring." The first point on the kidney meridian, an essential point in self-massage and meditation. The point is located on the sole of the foot, one third the way from the base of the second toe toward the heel. Stimulating this point calms the spirit and promotes qi flow through the entire body.

Buddhism 佛教 (fo jiao) The doctrine and spiritual disciplines attributed to or evolved from the teachings of the "Enlightened One," the Buddha, an Indian teacher from the sixth century B.C. Emphasizes meditation practice and the realization that suffering is caused by greed. Buddhism has a large following in China, Japan, Southeast Asia, Tibet, and the United States. The Chan 禪 sect of Buddhism, pronounced Zen in Japanese, was established in China by the Indian monk Bodhidharma in A.D. 520 and later brought to Japan. It was strongly influenced by Daoism and combines Daoist philosophy and wit with Buddhist meditation.

Chinese Medicine 中醫 (zhong yi) Includes acupuncture, moxibustion, herbalism, dietetics, massage, and qigong. I use the term to include both pre- and post-Communist traditions. Traditional Chinese Medicine (TCM) refers to the standardized form of Chinese medicine developed in the People's Republic of China. Many American practitioners and scholars of Chinese medicine feel that TCM lacks much of the richness of the earlier, pre-Communist, system due to its frequent use of Western diagnostic labels; greater emphasis on symptomatic, rather than systemic, treatment; and less diversity of treatment methods.

Conception Channel 任脈 (ren mai) The primary yin meridian, extending along the front of the body, from the hui yin point on the perineum to the tip of the tongue. The ren mai regulates menstruation and nourishes the fetus.

Cultivation 修養 (xiu yang) Spiritual development and cultivation of character.

Dan Tian 丹田 "Elixir Field" or "Cinnabar Field," called tanden or hara in Japanese. The center of gravity, breathing, and energy approximately three inches below the navel, where the qigong practitioner plants the seed of health, longevity, and wisdom. Or one of three dan tians in the lower abdomen, chest, and between the eyebrows.

Dao 道 The Way of harmony within oneself, with others, and with nature. The Spiritual Path, similar to the ancient Greek term *logos*.

Dao De Jing 道德經 The Classic (Jing) of the Way (Dao) and Its Power (or

Virtue, De). The philosophical classic of Daoism, attributed to Lao Zi, third or fourth century B.C.

Daoism   A somewhat ambiguous term in English, as it can refer to either Daoist philosophy 道家 (dao jia), the Daoist religion 道教 (dao jiao), or a blending of the two. The philosophy, dating from at least the fourth century B.C., is based on simplicity, following nature, and harmonizing mind and body. The religion began in the second century A.D. and includes various sects, monasteries, and a complex ritual tradition. Daoism was an important influence on the development of Chinese cuisine, art, medicine, and qigong.

Daoist Canon 道藏 (dao zang)   A collection of approximately 1,120 Daoist texts and commentaries, including scripture, history, poetry, ritual, meditation, philosophy, and qigong, representing many schools of Daoist philosophy and religion. Daoism includes but is not limited to these texts. Although essential for Daoist scholarship, most practicing Daoists have read very little of the *Canon* and base their practices on works not included in it or on oral tradition.

Daoist Sage 仙 (Xian)   Sometimes translated "Immortal." Related etymologically to the word for dance and shaman.

Dao-yin 導引   The most common ancient term for qigong. Means leading and guiding the qi.

De Qi 得氣   "Reaching the qi." An intuitive or energetic sense of contacting the qi, experienced by either healer or healee.

Dong Gong: See Active Qigong.

Embryonic Respiration 胎息 (tai xi)   Also translated "fetal breathing" or "fetal respiration." Sometimes called bi qi, "stopping the breath," the term actually means that the breath is so relaxed, slow, effortless, and quiet that it seems to have stopped. One's breath feels unified with the original breath of the universe.

Entering Tranquillity 入靜 (ru jing)   Means tranquil meditation. Also called Zuo Wang 坐忘 (Sitting and Forgetting) in early Daoist literature; related to Chinese and Japanese Buddhist practice of Zuo Chan 坐禪 (Seated Zen, Zazen in Japanese).

External Qi Healing (EQH) 外氣治療 (Wai Qi Zhi Liao)   Known as 布氣 (bu qi) "spreading the qi" in ancient texts. This is qigong applied to others, rather than for one's own self-healing. Qi is projected, generally through the hands, from the healer to patient. It includes both contact and noncontact treatment and may be applied during acupuncture or massage.

Five Elements 五行 (Wu Xing)   Also translated the Five Activities, Five Phases, Five Energetic Constellations, Five Networks. Five interacting energies that must be balanced for health, consisting of Wood, Fire, Earth, Metal, and Water. The Chinese characters imply movement. Thus, although *wu xing* is most commonly translated Five Elements, "Five Activities or Phases" is more precise. According to the "Creation Cycle," wood creates fire; fire creates earth (ashes); earth yields metal; metal becomes molten, creating water; and water creates (grows) wood. According to the "Destruction Cycle," wood destroys earth; earth destroys (absorbs) water; water destroys fire; fire destroys metal; and metal destroys (chops) wood.

Food Qi or Grain Qi 穀 氣 (gu qi)   The qi derived from food and diet.

Governing Channel 督脈 (du mai)   The yang "superhighway" of qi. Governs all of the yang meridians in the body. Starting at the tip of the coccyx, it follows the spine upward, connecting the kidneys with the brain. From the crown it descends down the front of the face, ending at the upper palate.

Hard Qigong 硬功 (ying gong)   Dynamic or strenuous ways of conditioning the body or demonstrating such conditioning. Including: "rib hitting," "iron shirt," and "iron palm." Often practiced by martial artists.

Intent 意 (yi)   Will or volition. The aspect of the mind that directs the qi.

Jing 精   Sexual energy, essence, germ, a yin form of qi.

Jing Gong: See Passive Qigong.

Lao Gong 勞宮   "Work palace." An important acupuncture point, used to sense or send qi, helps regulate yang, fire energy in the body. The eighth point on the pericardium meridian (anciently on the heart meridian), in the center of the palm. Can be found by bending the fourth finger into the palm.

Lao Zi 老子   The "old" (lao) "child" (zi) or Master (zi) Lao. Originally a court librarian during the Zhou Dynasty, he later wrote one of the great classics of world literature, the *Dao De Jing*. The founder of Daoist philosophy.

Martial Arts   Usually called either wu shu 武術 or gong fu (kungfu) 功夫, although gong fu can also mean "hard work" or any discipline that requires training and practice. In China there are two major schools of martial arts: Inner Martial Arts 內家拳, also called Internal Martial Arts, usually include qigong and may be practiced for health and/or self-defense. The best-known of these are: Taiji Quan 太極拳, Bagua Zhang 八卦掌, and Xing Yi Quan 形意拳. External Martial Arts 外家拳 (wai jia quan) generally place a greater emphasis on strength and stamina conditioning exercises, reserving qigong for later stages of training. There are thousands of schools of External Martial Arts, including Tiger-Crane, Eagle Style, Monkey Boxing, Praying Mantis, Cha Quan, Tan

Tui. Some practitioners call these arts Shao-lin Boxing. There is a venerated but unsubstantiated legend in China that the Buddhist Shao-lin Temple is the birthplace of Chinese martial arts.

Meridians 經絡 (jing luo) or 經脈 (jing mai) The network of channels through which qi is distributed and circulates.

Ming Men 命門 The fourth point on the Governing Channel, approximately opposite the navel, below the second lumbar vertebra. Focusing on the ming men stimulates the qi of the whole body and improves the kidney functions.

Natural Breathing 自然呼吸 or 順呼吸 The preferred method of breathing in qigong. During inhalation, the abdomen expands; during exhalation, it retracts.

Nei Dan: See Alchemy.

Nei Gong 內功 Literally, "Inner Work." Although some teachers believe that this term means a secret dimension of qigong and martial arts, it is actually just another word for qigong. One of the classics of qigong technique is the *Nei Gong Tu Shuo* 內功圖説, "Illustrated Explanation of Nei Gong" by Wang Zu-yuan.

Original Qi 元氣 (yuan qi) The "original qi" inherited from one's ancestors, forming the basis of constitution. Yuan qi is also the creative power of the Dao, the force that gives existence to the cosmos.

Passive or Tranquil Qigong 靜功 (jing gong) Meditative qigong, usually practiced while maintaining one body posture.

Protective Qi 衛氣 (wei qi) Also translated "defensive qi." The energetic immune system, the aspect of qi that prevents external pathogens from invading the body and causing disease.

Qi 氣 Life energy, vital energy, breath of life, force, power, air.

Qigong 氣功 The art and science of regulating internal energy to improve health, calm the mind, and condition the body for martial arts or other sports. Also called dao-yin (leading and guiding), xing qi (moving the qi), tu gu na xin (expelling the old, absorbing the new), nei gong (inner work), and yang sheng (nourishing life).

Qigong Master 老師 (lao shi) or 師父 (shi fu) The former can also mean professor or teacher. The second term is used as a polite address for a qigong master, martial arts master, monk, or nun. Shi Fu can also refer to anyone who has mastered a skill (contrasted with a student or apprentice). A bus driver may be called "Shi Fu."

Qigong Meditation: See Passive Qigong.

Qigong Psychosis 走火入魔 (zou huo ru mo) Delusional or disturbed state of mind induced by excessive or long-term incorrect qigong practice.

Qi Se 氣色   Qi appearance. In Chinese medicine, qi se is the practitioner's energetic impression of the patient's state of health.

Qi Sensation 氣感 (qi gan)   Qi feelings or sensations. The subjective signs that qi is being activated, including warmth, rootedness, vibration, and expansiveness.

Qing Dan 清淡   A pure, light, and delicately flavored qigong diet.

Reverse, Paradoxical, or Oppositional Breathing 逆呼吸 (ni hu xi)   The practice of breathing in the reverse from normal fashion. The stomach contracting on inhalation and expanding on exhalation. Although utilized in some martial arts and breath-control exercises, it may induce hypertension and anxiety and is thus dangerous to practice without supervision.

Shaman or shamanka (female) 巫 (wu)   A practitioner of the world's most ancient religion, shamanism. Shamanism is one of the roots of qigong and Daoism. The shaman enters an altered state of consciousness in order to contact transcendent powers. The role of the shaman is generally to heal, counsel, or perform ritual. In ancient China, shamans who specialized in prayer were known as Prayer Healers or Invokers 祝 (ju).

Shen 神   Spiritual energy, spirit, psyche, the yang form of qi. Sometimes means "the soul," though many texts use the more specialized terms hun 魂, the yang soul, and po 魄, the yin soul. Ancient Chinese believed that each person has three hun and seven po that dissipate during one's life and finally depart at death. In ancient times the same character also meant "spirit medium," "to stretch," or "stretchers," referring to people who used yogalike postures to attract the presence of an ancestral spirit. The character shen 神, should not be confused with shen 腎, a homonym that means kidneys, adrenals, and urogenital system.

Standing Meditation 站樁 (zhan zhuang)   Literally, "standing post" or "standing stake." Cultivating qi while standing perfectly still like a post in the ground. The most important qigong and essential stance training in the Chinese martial arts.

Taiji 太極   A philosophical concept meaning the unity of yin and yang. Yin is the shady slope of the mountain, yang the sunny slope. Taiji is where they meet. It is a state of physical and spiritual harmony. In ancient texts, taiji can also mean "Polestar."

Taiji Quan 太極拳 (spelled T'ai Chi Ch'uan in the Wade–Giles system of romanization)   "Taiji Boxing," a complex choreography of 108 flowing, graceful movements, the most widely practiced whole-body qigong and inner martial art, can be practiced for health, meditation, and self-defense. The major schools of Taiji Quan are Chen Family, Yang Family, and Wu Family. Taiji Quan is often mistranslated "Supreme Ultimate Boxing" or "Chinese Shadow Boxing." Contrary to popular belief, although Taiji Quan cultivates qi, the word qi does not appear in the name Taiji Quan. This misconception may be because in the Wade–Giles method of representing Chinese characters, the word Ch'i (Qi) is confused with Chi in T'ai Chi Ch'uan.

Three Treasures 三寶 (san bao)   The three essential energies of life: jing (sexual essence), qi, and shen (spirit).

Triple Burner, Triple Heater 三焦 (san jiao)   A bodily function that does not correspond to a specific physical substance. Regulates water and energy in three areas of the body—Upper Burner: head and chest, including heart and lungs; Middle Burner: solar plexus to navel, including stomach and spleen; Lower Burner: lower abdomen, including kidneys and liver (because a portion of the liver meridian is in the groin).

Wai Dan: See Alchemy.

Yang 陽   The active, creative, solar, and masculine principle of Chinese philosophy. Originally meant the sunny slope of a mountain. In qigong, yang commonly means warmth, activity (rather than stillness), expansive movements, or a foot that bears all or most of the body's weight.

Yang Organs 腑 (fu)   The hollow organs that transport food or fluids, including bladder, gallbladder, small intestine, stomach, and large intestine. The Triple Burner is also considered one of the fu, though it is not an organ.

Yellow Emperor 黃帝 (Huang Di)   Ca. 2697–2597 B.C. Mythical emperor of China.

Yellow Emperor's Classic of Internal Medicine 黃帝內經 (*Huang Di Nei Jing*)   The classic of Chinese medicine, the earliest portions probably dating to the second century B.C.

Yi Quan 意拳   Mind-Boxing, also called Da Cheng Quan (Great Achievement or Great Success Boxing). The Standing Meditation qigong system and martial art founded by Wang Xiang-zhai (1885–1963).

Yin 陰   The passive, receptive, lunar, and feminine principle of Chinese philosophy. Originally meant the shady slope of a mountain. Stillness or coolness. A part of the body that is passive, retracted, or that is empty of the body's weight.

Yin Organs or Viscera 臟 (zang)   Related to the word "to store, hold." The "solid" organs that store qi: kidneys, liver, heart, spleen, and lungs. The pericardium, the tissue covering the heart, is sometimes considered a yin organ, separate from the heart itself.

Zhuang Zi 莊子   A third-century B.C. Daoist author and the name of the book he wrote or that was attributed to him. Zhuang Zi is traditionally considered a disciple of Lao Zi and one of the founders of philosophical Daoism. His book is filled with wit, wisdom, and paradox. The great sinologist Arthur Waley considered *Zhuang Zi* one of the most profound and entertaining books in the world.

Notes

CHAPTER ONE

1. This means lower costs for patients *and* their doctors. If your doctor is close-minded and unenthusiastic about qigong, teach him or her this "Benefits of Qigong Mantra": "No Malpractice. No Malpractice . . ."

2. Personal communication, the Shenendoah Healing Exploration Meeting, Nov. 5, 1993.

3. Another acceptable term is *complementary and alternative medicine* (CAM), the official phrase adopted by the National Institutes of Health's Office of Complementary and Alternative Medicine (OCAM). In April 1995, Wayne Jonas, M.D., director of OCAM, offered this definition: "Complementary and alternative medicine is defined through a social process as those practices that do not form part of the dominant system for managing health and disease."

4. Kenneth R. Pelletier, *Mind as Healer Mind as Slayer* (New York: Dell Publishing Co., 1977), p. 3.

CHAPTER TWO

1. *Jing Ming Zong Jiao Lu* (Record of the Teachings of Purity and Light).

2. Catherine Despeux, *La Moelle du Phénix Rouge: santé & longue vie dans la Chine du XVI siècle* (The Marrow of the Red Phoenix: Health & Long Life in 16th-century China) (Paris: Guy Tredaniel, 1988), p. 10.

3. Catherine Despeux, "Gymnastics: The Ancient Tradition," in *Taoist Meditation and Longevity Techniques*, ed. by Livia Kohn (Ann Arbor: University of Michigan Press, 1989), p. 238.

4. Richard Wilhelm, trans., *Liä Dsi [Lieh Zi]; Das Wahre Buch vom Quellenden Urgrund; 'Tschung Hü Dschen Ging'; Die Lehren der Philosophen Liä Yü-Kou und Yang Sschu* (Diederichs, Jena, 1921), p. 53. English by Joseph Needham, in *Science and Civilization in China*, vol. 2 (Cambridge: Cambridge University Press, 1975), pp. 143–44.

5. Ilza Veith, trans., *The Yellow Emperor's Classic of Internal Medicine* (Berkeley, CA: University of California Press, 1972), p. 98.

6. Joseph Needham, *Science and Civilization in China*, vol. 2. (Cambridge: Cambridge University Press, 1975), p. 33.

7. Patricia N. H. Leong, *Tao-yin: Art of Healing and Art of Longevity; A Study of the Tao-yin-t'u found in Han Tomb Three at Ma-wang-tui* (manuscript, 1983), p. 16. My understanding of the *Dao-yin Tu* owes much to this groundbreaking manuscript.

8. Wei Bo-yang's work is analyzed in Joseph Needham's *Science and Civilization in China*, vol. 5, pt. 3 (Cambridge: Cambridge University Press: 1976), pp. 50–75. For a translation of the *Can Tong Qi*, see Richard Bertschinger's *The Secret of Everlasting Life* (Rockport, MA: Element Books), 1994.

9. Metal, Water, Wood, Fire, Earth. A theory first developed by the philosopher Zou Yan, circa 350 B.C.

10. Called the "golden elixir" *(jin dan)* by Wei and other alchemists. Gold does not tarnish or lose its brilliance even when placed in the hottest fire. It became a natural symbol of enlightenment and longevity.

11. Kenneth Ch'en, *Buddhism in China* (Princeton, NJ: Princeton University Press), 1964, p. 336.

12. Holmes Welch, *The Practice of Chinese Buddhism 1900–1950* (Cambridge, MA: Harvard University Press, 1967), p. 385.

13. Ibid., p. 386.

14. As well as my own teacher, Dr. Henry K. S. Wong.

15. Garma C. C. Chang, *Teachings of Tibetan Yoga* (Secaucus, NJ: The Citadel Press, 1963), p. 59.

16. Personal communication from Senge Ngawa master L. Shila, visiting Boulder, Colorado, 1982.

17. It should be mentioned that there is also a *Mi Zong Yi* (Labyrinth Style) martial art in China with an associated Mi Zong qigong bearing no relationship to Tibet. This style was made famous by the noted Chinese boxer Huo Yuan-jia (1862–1909). Some practitioners may confuse Tibetan qigong with Huo's art. However, when a system includes Tibetan mantras and Buddhist visualizations, the lineage is clear.

18. According to my teacher, Dr. Wong, there was a tradition of transmitting all techniques in a style to only one disciple. Naturally many lineages were broken or lost. Some masters tried to maintain an economic or martial advantage by following the absurd dictum "Teach your best student forty percent of what you know."

19. The rebellion had originally been directed against the extravagance and oppression of the ruling Manchurians (Qing Dynasty). The governing bureaucracy

believed that their only chance for survival was to ally the Boxers against a common enemy, the foreigners. The battle cry of *Fan Qing, fu Ming* (Overthrow the Qing; return to the Ming [earlier Dynasty]) was changed to *Fu Qing mieh yang* (Support the Qing, exterminate the foreigners).

20. Esherick, Joseph W. *The Origins of the Boxer Uprising* (Berkeley: University of California Press, 1987).

21. Tron McConnell and Zha Leping, "Parapsychology in the People's Republic of China: 1979–1989," *The Journal of the American Society for Psychical Research* 85:2 (April 1991), p. 125. I am indebted to the authors' fine analysis of Qian's role in the acceptance of qigong.

22. Qian Xuesen, "On the Science of Qigong," *Martial Arts of China Magazine* 1:3 (1990), p. 123.

23. Yi Yao, "Somatic science, the wave of the future?" *Liao Wong* (Prospects Weekly), nos. 48 & 49 (1987). Quoted in McConnell and Zha, op. cit.

24. Ibid.

25. "Nature as Last Resort: An Interview with Doctor Pang Heming," *Heaven Earth* 1:3 (January 1992), p. 10.

26. *Internal Arts Magazine* (no longer in print), and *Qi: The Journal of Traditional Eastern Health and Fitness.* Other popular sources of information on qigong include Daoist journals and any of the numerous martial arts magazines.

27. Shaykh Hakim Moinuddin Chishti, *The Book of Sufi Healing* (Rochester, VT: Inner Traditions, 1991), p. 123.

28. Ibid., p. 124.

29. G. S. Kirk and J. E. Raven, *The Presocratic Philosophers* (Cambridge: Cambridge University Press, 1957), p. 158.

30. Ibid., p. 160.

31. Philip Wheelwright, ed., *The Presocratics* (Indianapolis: The Odyssey Press, 1966), p. 268.

32. Ibid., p. 262.

33. Pejoratively called "Bushmen" by some anthropologists.

34. Richard Katz, *Boiling Energy* (Cambridge, MA: Harvard University Press, 1982), p. 42.

35. Ibid.

36. Ibid., p. 56.

37. Robert Lawlor, *Voices of the First Day* (Rochester, VT: Inner Traditions, 1991), p. 372.

38. James Kale McNeley, *Holy Wind in Navajo Philosophy* (Tucson, AZ: University of Arizona Press, 1982).

39. Ibid., p. 48.

40. James R. Walker, *Lakota Belief and Ritual* (Lincoln, Nebraska: University of Nebraska Press, 1980), p. 83.

41. Ibid., pp. 83–84.

42. Needham, Joseph. *Science and Civilization in China*, vol. 5, pt. 5 (Cambridge: Cambridge University Press, 1983), p. 286.

43. Ibid., p. 286.

44. Ibid., p. 284.

45. Zhang He. *Kan Tu Xue Yu Jia* (Illustrated Study of Yoga). Hong Kong: Wu Zhou Publishing Co., 1979.

46. The first Olympic Games were held in 776 B.C. They were discontinued in A.D. 394 due to disapproval by the Church and not reinstated until 1896.

47. P. M. Cibot, *Notice du Cong-fou [Kung-fu] des Bonzes Tao-see [Dao-shi, Daoist priests].* trans. by Joseph Needham in *Science and Civilization in China,* vol. 5, pt. 5 (Cambridge: Cambridge University Press, 1983), p. 173.

48. Mesmer also knew many of the great artists of his day. Mozart immortalized him as a character in his opera *Così Fan Tutte.*

49. N. Dally, *Cinésiologie, ou Science du Movement dans ses Rapports avec l'Éducation, l'Hygiène et la Thérapie; Édudes Historiques, Théoriques et Pratiques* (Paris: Librairie Centrale des Sciences, 1857).

CHAPTER THREE

1. It is also essential that interpretations based on etymology be supported by the actual way in which words were used. Some Westerners have mistakenly assumed that Chinese words are like Rorschach inkblots into which any meaning may be projected. This error has led to many bizarre translations of Chinese terms.

2. Catherine Despeux, trans., *Traité d'Alchimie et de Physiologie Taoïste* by Zhao Bichen. (Paris: Les Deux Océans, 1979), p. 55. My translation.

CHAPTER FOUR

1. I thank the renowned biofeedback researcher Dr. Elmer Green for drawing my attention to this concept.

2. In 1990 a professional organization, the International Society for the Study of Subtle Energy and Energy Medicine (ISSSEEM), was formed to encourage and publish energy medicine research and to help network clinicians and researchers. The first issue of the ISSSEEM newsletter (1:1, spring 1990) included an article by Edgar Wilson, M.D., entitled, "In Search of the Elusive Chi [Qi]: Studies in Energy Medicine Future Directions." The second issue of the newsletter (1:2, fall 1990) focused entirely on qigong theory. Qigong is generally presented at ISSSEEM's annual international conferences.

3. Robert O. Becker, M.D., and Gary Selden, *The Body Electric* (NY: William Morrow and Company, 1985).

4. Such fields were documented more than fifty years ago when Harold Saxton Burr, Ph.D., professor of neuroanatomy at Yale University School of Medicine, coined the term L-Field (Life-Field) for the way the body's bioelectric field fluctuates according to state of health and state of mind. If an individual is anxious or ill, the field is weaker. If an individual is happy and well, the field is stronger. This is remarkably similar to the concept of *wai qi*, External Qi, in qigong.

5. This direct current system of relaying information through the nervous system

complements the more widely understood method of electrochemical transmission, in which electrical impulses are carried along the nerve cells and then jump the gap between cells (the *synapse*) with the help of chemical transmitters. This is how your brain tells your fingers to turn the pages of this book and how the tactile information that the task has been accomplished is relayed back to your brain. Electrochemical messages allow the senses to function and control motor functions. Even such subtle activities as thinking, feeling, and dreaming must be coordinated by billions of precise and almost instantaneous electrochemical changes throughout the body.

Healing, however, takes place through a different mechanism. Becker's research highlights the relationship between flowing electricity and healing, a model that suggests how both qigong and acupuncture work. It is possible that acupuncture points act as booster amplifiers, preventing weak electrical signals (qi) carried along the meridians from losing their charge.

6. Song Kongzhi, Zhi Tingxian, Zhou Liangzhong, and Yan Xiaoxia, "Dynamic Characteristics of Physiological Changes Under the Qigong State" (paper presented at the Second World Conference for Academic Exchange of Medical Qigong, Beijing, 1993), p. 68.

7. George W. Meek, *Healers and the Healing Process* (Wheaton, IL: Theosophical Publishing House, 1977), p. 154.

8. Kenneth M. Sancier, "The Effect of Qigong on Therapeutic Balancing Measured by Electroacupuncture According to Voll (EAV)" (paper presented at the Second World Conference for Academic Exchange of Medical Qigong, Beijing, 1993), pp. 90–91.

9. Glen Rein, Ph.D., and Rollin McCraty, M.A, "Modulation of DNA by Coherent Heart Frequencies" (paper presented at the Third Annual Conference of the International Society for the Study of Subtle Energy & Energy Medicine, Monterey, CA, June 1993), pp. 58–62.

10. Elmer E. Green, Ph.D., Peter A. Parks, M.S., Paul M. Guyer, B.S., Steve L. Fahrion, Ph.D., and Lolafaye Coyne, Ph.D, "Anomalous Electrostatic Phenomena in Exceptional Subjects," *Subtle Energies* 2:3 (1991) pp. 69–94, and "Gender Differences in a Magnetic Field," *Subtle Energies* 3:2 (1992) pp. 65–103.

11. A. T., Barker, ed., *The Mahatma Letters to A. P. Sinnett*, 2nd ed. (London: Rider and Co., 1948), p. 455.

12. Ibid.

13. In reporting the research, the term "regular" was used instead of "normal" to avoid the assumption that a lack of sensitivity to energetic fields is the normal human condition.

14. I was honored to have been chosen as a research subject, one of the "healers of national repute" tested during significant phases of the Copper Wall Project.

15. It is beyond the scope of this book to discuss the influence of the magnets. Interested readers should consult the technical papers cited above. See note 10.

16. According to Dr. Green, my own record was rather unusual in that I was the only healer who generated strong charges on the copper floor. This corresponded to comments I made to Dr. Green immediately after the sessions: *"I felt energy rising*

from my feet." (Interestingly, the qigong classics state that qi "begins at the feet, is controlled by the waist, and manifests in the hands." That is, healing begins with a downward surge of power that immediately rebounds upward, is given impetus by the body's energy pump, the dan tian, and then arrives at the hands. From there, qi can be projected out for healing.) I did not realize then how my impressions paralleled the actual data. I first saw the various graphs a year after the experiment ended, and frankly I was as surprised as the scientists. Not that I had doubted the healing power of qi. I only doubted science's ability to detect it.

17. William Tiller, Ph.D., "Towards Explaining the Anomalous Large Body Potential Surge on Healers" (lecture delivered at the Third Annual Conference of the International Society for the Study of Subtle Energy and Energy Medicine, Monterey, CA, June 1993). Also, with Elmer Green, Peter Parks, and Stacy Anderson, "Towards Explaining Anomalously Large Body Voltage Surges on Exceptional Subjects," *Journal of Scientific Exploration* 9:3 (1995) pp. 331–50.

18. Yang Kongshun et al, "Analgesic Effect of Emitted Qi on White Rats" (paper presented at 1st World Conference for Academic Exchange of Medical Qigong, Beijing, 1988), p. 45.

19. C. Norman Shealy, M.D., Ph.D., and Caroline M. Myss, M.A., Ph.D. (candidate), "DHEA and The Ring of Fire: A Theory for Energetic Restoration of Adrenal Reserves" (unpublished manuscript, 1995). I thank Dr. Shealy for his kind help in providing me with an annotated bibliography on DHEA and the preliminary findings of his research. In a personal communication, May 5, 1995, Dr. Shealy wrote, "I personally believe that DHEA is the basic chemical representation of Qi."

20. The immune-enhancing and anticarcinogenic effects of DHEA seem to be due to the inhibition of an enzyme, glucose-6-phosphate-dehydrogenase. See G. B. Gordon, L. M. Shantz, and P. Talalay, "Modulation of Growth, Differentiation and Carcinogenesis by Dehydroepiandrosterone," *Advances in Enzyme Regulation*, ed. by George Webber (Pergamon Press, 1986), pp. 355–83.

21. 130 nanograms per decaliter in women or below 180 nanograms per decaliter in men.

22. Shealy and Myss, op. cit., p. 8.

23. Men and women who practice Transcendental Meditation have greatly elevated DHEA levels, equivalent to nonmeditators five to ten years younger. J. L. Glaser, et al., "Elevated Serum Dehydroepiandrosterone Sulfate Levels in Practitioners of the Transcendental Meditation (TM) and TM-Siddhi Program," *Journal of Behavioral Medicine* 15:4 (August 1992), pp. 327–41.

24. Dr. Shealy has investigated increasing DHEA levels by artificially stimulating particular acupuncture points with a device that emits the same gigahertz frequency as sunlight at one billionth of a watt/cm^2. He has achieved excellent results treating arthritis, diabetes, back pain, and other problems.

25. Shealy and Myss, op. cit., p. 7.

26. William Regelson, M.D., and Mohammed Y. Kalimi, Ph.D., "DHEA (Dehydroepiandrosterone)—A Pleiotropic Steroid. How Can One Steroid Do So Much?" in *The Superhormone Promise*, ed. by William Regelson, M.D., and Carol

Colman (New York: Simon & Schuster, 1996), p. 302. This essay is an excellent summary of DHEA research.

27. Arthur M. Young, *The Foundations of Science: The Missing Parameter* (San Francisco: Robert Briggs Associates, 1985), p. 9. For more details on the physics and metaphysics of light, see his *The Reflexive Universe* (Robert Briggs, 1976).

28. A. G. Gurvich, and L. D. Gurvich, *Die Mitogenetisch Strahlung* (Jena: Fischer Verlag, 1959).

29. Mae-Wan Ho, *The Rainbow and the Worm* (River Edge, NJ: World Scientific Publishing Co., 1993), p. 130.

30. F. A. Popp, K. H. Li, and Q. Gu, eds., *Recent Advances in Biophoton Research and Its Applications* (River Edge, NJ: World Scientific Press, 1992), p.v. The morphogenetic field is a hypothesis of physiologist and former Harvard University Fellow Dr. Rupert Sheldrake. He hypothesizes that the form, behavior, and characteristics of living organisms (and developing physical systems in general) are a result of form-creating fields. These fields "impose patterned restrictions on the energetically possible outcomes of physical processes." (Rupert Sheldrake, *A New Science of Life* [Los Angeles: Jeremy P. Tarcher, 1981], p. 13.) Like photons, they act beyond space and time. They are like energetic blueprints created by the form and behavior of past members of the same species.

31. F. Musumeci, A. Triglia, and F. Grasso, "Experimental Evidence on Ultra-weak Photon Emission from Normal and Tumour Human Tissues," in Popp, op. cit., p. 322.

32. Barbara W. Chwirot, "Ultraweak Luminescence Studies of Micro-sporogenesis in Larch," in Popp, op. cit., p. 260.

33. Popp, op. cit., preface, p. vi.

34. External Qi Healers believe that they can detect changes in bioluminescence (the aura) during the early stages of disease. It is also likely such energetic changes *precede* physical manifestation. This principle is shared by healers of many traditions. Cyprus's leading healer, Spyros Sathi, says that a healer can see in the aura "where the deficiency in vitality exists. . . . Consequently it becomes possible to foresee and prevent the manifestation of a physical ailment." Kyriacos C. Markides, *The Magus of Strovolos: The Extraordinary World of a Spiritual Healer* (New York: Penguin, 1985), p. 180.

35. "Healing, Energy & Consciousness: Into the Future or a Retreat to the Past?" *Subtle Energies* V:1 (1994) pp. 1–33.

36. Robert G. Jahn, " 'Out of This Aboriginal Sensible Muchness': Consciousness, Information, and Human Health," *The Journal of the American Society for Psychical Research* 89:4 (1995), p. 310. See also Jahn and B. J. Dunne's *Margins of Reality: The Role of Consciousness in the Physical World* (New York: Harcourt Brace Jovanovich, 1987).

CHAPTER FIVE

1. For an excellent overview of this data, see Michael Murphy, *The Future of the Body* (New York: Putnam Publishing Co., 1993), pp. 419–31.

2. Be cautioned, however, that the research is a mixed bag. *Some* of it is good, and I have used this data to support claims and hypotheses presented in this book. Other research is sloppy or poor by Western standards. See Appendix C, "Double-Blind or Double Standard?"

3. Qigong is said to regulate blood pressure, lowering it if it is too high, raising it if it is too low. I have observed this to be true among my own students and have heard similar reports from other qigong instructors. However, I have not seen experimental proof of the ability of qigong to raise blood pressure.

4. Jiao Guorui, *Qigong Essentials for Health Promotion* (Beijing: China Reconstructs Press, 1988), p. 34.

5. Wong Chongxing, Xu Dinghai, Qian Yuesheng, and Shi Wen, "Effects of Qigong on Preventing Stroke and Alleviating the Multiple Cerebro-Cardiovascular Risk Factors—A Follow-up Report on 242 Hypertensive Cases for 30 Years" (paper presented at the Second World Conference for Academic Exchange of Medical Qigong, Beijing, September 1993), p. 123.

6. Xian Biao Huang, "Clinical Observation of 204 Patients with Hypertension Treated with Chinese Qigong" (paper presented at the Fifth International Congress of Chinese Medicine and the First International Congress of Qigong Berkeley, CA, June 1990), p. 101.

7. Though HDL blood levels may not be as significant a risk factor for vegetarians. Dean Ornish, M.D., *Dean Ornish's Program for Reversing Heart Disease* (New York: Ballantine Books, 1990), pp. 269–71.

8. "A Group Observation and Experimental Research on the Prevention and Treatment of Hypertension by Qigong" (paper presented at The First World Conference for Academic Exchange of Medical Qigong, Beijing, China, 1988), p. 113.

9. Qu Mianyu, "Taijiquan—A Medical Assessment," *Martial Arts of China Magazine* 1:5 (1990), pp. 203–204.

10. Cited in Edward Maisel, *Tai Chi For Health* (New York: Dell Publishing Co., 1963), p. 55.

11. Tong Su-Fang and Xe Pei-qi, "Qigong for Increasing Learning Ability" (paper presented at the Fifth International Congress of Chinese Medicine and the First International Congress of Qigong, Berkeley, CA, 1990), p. 124. 170 fourth-grade students, consisting of an equal number of boys and girls, were divided into four groups. For six months two groups did qigong abdominal respiration and quiet sitting for two minutes before each class each day. The control group was not given any qigong instruction. Looking at test results in language, mathematics, and geography, the average test scores in the qigong group increased by 11.9 percent (P<0.01), while those in the control group did not change significantly.

12. See Robert Fried, with Joseph Grimaldi, *The Psychology and Physiology of Breathing: In Behavioral Medicine, Clinical Psychology, and Psychiatry* (New York: Plenum Press, 1993), pp. 138–40, 178–80, 250–52, and Elmer and Alyce Green, *Beyond Biofeedback* (New York: Dell Publishing Co., 1977), pp. 36–41.

13. Wang Binai, Chai Zhaoji, Sheng Xianxiang, and Chai Xiaoming, "The

Influence of Qigong State on the Volume of Human Peripheral Vascular Blood Flow" (paper presented at the Third National Academic Conference on Qigong Science, Guangzhou, November 1990), pp. 11–12.

14. Chai Zhaoji and Wang Binai, "Influence of Qigong State on Blood Perfusion Rate of Human Microcirculation," ibid., p. 116.

15. Jiao Guorui, op. cit., p. 32.

16. Jiao, pp. 30–31.

17. Ibid., p. 25.

18. Ibid., p. 25.

19. Cited in Hu Bing, *A Brief Introduction to the Science of Breathing Exercise* (Hong Kong: Hai Feng Publishing Co., 1982), pp. 9–10.

20. Yu Min, Huo Jiming, Wang Yuain, Zhang Guifang, and Chi Zhenfu, "Experimental Research on Effect of Qigong on the Digestive Tract" (paper presented at Second World Conference for Academic Exchange of Medical Qigong, Beijing, 1993), p. 81.

21. Liu Anxi, Zhao Jing, Zhao Yong, and Du Zhiqin, "Modified Effect of Emitted Qi on Close-Open Kinetic Process of Sodium Channels of Rat Cultured Neuron Cell, ibid., p. 98.

22. Free radicals are formed during ordinary biochemical processes such as the production of energy in all of the body's cells and as a toxic by-product of immune cell activity. Free radicals are also generated from exposure to such external agents as air pollution, sunlight, alcohol, tobacco, aged cheese, and smoked foods. When there are too many free radicals in the blood, one ages more quickly. Free radicals produce wrinkling, the inefficient discharge of internal toxins and waste, and alteration or damage to the body's genetic program—the DNA. For a clear and spirited discussion of the role of free radicals in health and disease, see Hari Sharma, M.D., *Freedom from Disease* (Toronto: Veda Publishing, 1993).

23. Tang Yipeng, Sun Chenglin, Hong Qingtao, and Liu Chunmei, "Protective Effect of the Emitted Qi on the Primary Culture of Neurocytes in Vitro Against Free Radical Damage" (paper presented at Second World Conference for Academic Exchange of Medical Qigong, Beijing, 1993), pp. 100–1.

24. Liu Yuanliang, He Shihai, and Xie Shanling, "Clinical Observation of the Treatment of 158 Cases of Cerebral Arteriosclerosis by Qigong," ibid., p. 125.

25. Xu Dinghai and Wang Chongxing, "Recuperative Function of Qigong on Hypertensive Target Impairment," ibid., p. 124.

26. Elmer and Alyce Green, *Beyond Biofeedback* (Ft. Wayne, IN: Knoll Publishing Co., 1977), p. 122.

27. Personal communication, 1990.

28. Pan Weixing et al, "Changes in EEG Alpha Waves in Concentrative and Non-concentrative Qigong States: A Power Spectrum and Topographic Mapping Study," in *Collected Works of Scientific Research on Qigong*, III (Beijing: Beijing Science and Engineering University Press, 1991), pp. 266–82 (in Chinese).

29. Similar hemispheric asymmetry has been found in qigong theta rhythms. See Pan Weixing, Zhang Lufen, and Xia Yong, "The Difference in Theta Waves

Between Concentrative and Non-concentrative Qigong States," *Journal of Traditional Chinese Medicine* 14:3 (1994), pp. 212–18. Further research is needed on another fascinating asymmetry clinically observed in some meditators: left hemisphere alpha and right hemisphere theta. In a personal communication, the late Ed Wilson, M.D., remarked on the prevalence of this in the EEGs of several healers tested in his laboratory during the 1980s.

30. Yang Sihuan, Yang Qinfei, Shi Jiming, and Cao Yi, "The Influence of Qigong Training on Coherence of EEG During One Year Period" (paper presented at Second World Conference for Academic Exchange of Medical Qigong, Beijing, 1993), p. 72.

31. We must remember that qigong is being contrasted with average, untrained controls. Research suggests that if qigong masters were compared to Yogis, Zen students, or healers from other traditions, they would all demonstrate similar abilities to produce coherent brain waves.

32. Wang Jisheng, "Role of Qigong on Mental Health" (paper presented at Second World Conference for Academic Exchange of Medical Qigong, Beijing, 1993), p. 93.

33. Hayashi, Shigemi. "Qigong and Mental Health: the Positive Effects of the State of Rujing [Tranquillity]" (paper presented at Fourth International Conference on Qigong, Vancouver, B.C., Canada, 1995), pp. 26–27.

34. Jiao Guorui, op. cit., p. 31.

35. Huang Hua, Shen Bin, and Shang Kezhong, "Further Exploration of the Mechanism of Qigong in Treating Bronchial Asthma and Chronic Bronchitis with the Aid of Several New Testing Methods" (paper presented at First World Conference for Academic Exchange of Medical Qigong, Beijing, 1988), pp. 93–95. The specific qigong meditations practiced by the subjects were Fang Song Gong, "Relaxation Qigong," as described in this book in Chapter 8, and Xiao Zhou Tian, "Lesser Heavenly Circulation," directing qi through specific meridians, described in the "Purifying the Meridians" section of Chapter 11.

36. Sun Yinxing et al., "The Role of Qigong and Tiajiquan in Respiratory Rehabilitation," ibid., p. 101.

37. Li Ziran, Liu Fangying, and Zhou Renyang, "An Observation on the Results of Drug and Qigong Therapy for Chronic Respiratory Diseases," ibid., pp. 109–12.

38. Hua Huang, "An Approach to the Treatment of Bronchial Asthma by Qigong" (paper presented at First International Seminar on Qigong, Shanghai, 1986), pp. 92–93.

39. Wang Shouhang, Wang Benrong, Shao Mengyang, and Li Zhenqing, "Clinical Study of the Routine Treatment of Cancer Coordinated by Qigong," (paper presented at Second World Conference for Academic Exchange of Medical Qigong, Beijing, 1993), p. 129.

40. But "the times they are a-changing." Recent surveys indicate an increased willingness for physicians not only to refer patients to alternative providers, but to learn such practices themselves.

41. Sun Quizhi and Zhao Li, "A Clinical Observation of Qigong as a Therapeutic Aid for Advanced Cancer Patients" (paper presented at First World Conference for Academic Exchange of Medical Qigong, Beijing, 1988), pp. 97–98.

42. Jaio Guorui, op. cit., pp. 41–42.

43. R. A. Greenwald and W. W. Moy, *Arthritis Rheumatism* 22 (1979), pp. 251–59.

44. R. A. Greenwald and W. W. Moy, *Arthritis Rheumatism* 23 (1980), pp. 455–63.

45. Xu Hefen, Xue Huining, Bian Meiguang, Zhang Chengming, and Zhou Shuying, "Clinical Study of Anti-Aging Effect of Qigong" (paper presented at Second World Conference for Academic Exchange of Medical Qigong, Beijing, 1993), p. 137.

46. E Mei Nei Gong and Liu Bu Yang Sheng Gong (Six-Step Nourishing Life Qigong).

47. Ye Ming, Zhang Rui-hua, Wu Xiao-hong, Wang Yao, and Shen Jia-qi, "Relationship Among Erythrocyte Superoxide Dismutase (RBC-SOD) Activity, Plasma Sexual Hormones (T, E2), Aging and Qigong Exercise" (paper presented at Third International Symposium on Qigong, Shanghai, 1990), p. 32.

48. Wang Chongxing, Xu Dinghai, Qian Yusheng, and Kuang Ankun, "Research on Anti-aging Effects of Qigong" (paper presented at First World Conference for Academic Exchange of Medical Qigong, Beijing, 1988), p. 85.

49. Jing Yuzhong, Liu Xiude, Wang Zhenmin, Wang Qinglan, and Yao Airong, "Observation on Effects of 31 Cases of Diabetes Treated by *Huichungong* ['Return to Spring, Longevity Qigong']" (paper presented at Proceedings of the Second World Conference for Academic Exchange of Medical Qigong, Beijing, 1993), p. 135.

CHAPTER SIX

1. A researcher in chronobiology, Dr. Franz Halberg, gave potentially lethal doses of radiation to a group of mice for a period of eight days. Half were irradiated in the daytime, half at night. After eight days, those treated during the daytime were still alive. Those treated at night were dead. When he then examined the bone marrow of each group, he found that the mice that had been irradiated during daylight hours had healthier immune cells. Franz Halberg, "Implications of Biological Rhythms for Clinical Practice," in *Neuroendocrinology* (Sunderland, Mass: Sinauer Associates, Inc., 1980).

These cycles have also been found in human subjects. At Nottingham Hospital in England, two hundred nurses and medical students were given injections of a mild antigen and then monitored every three hours for the next twenty-four hours. Researchers found that the immune system was strongest at 7:00 A.M. and weakest at 1:00 A.M. This study was cited in Steven Locke, M.D., and Douglas Colligan's *The Healer Within* (New York: Penguin Books, 1987), p. 43.

2. Harriet Beinfield, L.Ac., and Efrem Korngold, L.Ac., O.M.D., *Between Heaven and Earth* (New York: Ballantine Books, 1991), p. 95.

3. According to Chinese medicine, the term "triple burner" refers to a function rather than a substance, like "blood circulation" rather than "the heart." It refers to the balance of warmth and energy in three regions of the body: the upper burner from the head to the chest, the middle burner around the solar plexus, and the lower burner in the lower abdomen.

4. As with all cases of serious disease, such training should be pursued as *complementary therapy*, with the approval of your physician.

5. Personal communication, July 1993.

6. Early etymological dictionaries state: *"Taiji je beiji ye,"* "Taiji means the Polestar [also called the North Star]."

CHAPTER SEVEN

1. Ruthy Alon, *Mindful Spontaneity* (New York: Avery Publishing Group, 1990), p. 215.

2. Ida P. Rolf, Ph.D., *Rolfing: The Integration of Human Structures* (New York: Harper & Row, 1977), p. 70.

3. Thus, I find it bizarre that many women follow the fashion of wearing blouses with padded shoulders. To anyone familiar with body language, this conveys an impression of physical and emotional distress.

4. A simple experiment can illustrate this principle. Hold an orange in your hand and enjoy the texture of its surface. Now raise your shoulders and notice how this affects the sensitivity of your hands.

5. *The Columbia University College of Physicians and Surgeons Complete Home Medical Guide* (New York: Crown Publishers, 1985), p. 550. Similar advice about the necessity and naturalness of the spinal curves can be found in any text on human anatomy. See the excellent section on the spinal curves in Mabel Elsworth Todd, *The Thinking Body* (New York: Dance Horizons, Inc., 5th printing, 1977), pp. 91–97.

6. The controversy hinges, in part, on the interpretation of a phrase in the Taiji Quan classic *Elucidation of the Thirteen Movements*, "Let no part of the body cave in or push out," sometimes translated as "Have neither hollows nor protuberances." According to qigong instructor Jan Diepersloot, "The main 'hollow' to be filled here is the small of the back, while the protuberances to be flattened are the abdomen and the buttocks. This is the natural, i.e. structurally optimal posture as opposed to the normal or structurally dysfunctional, posture." (Jan Diepersloot, *Warriors of Stillness: Meditative Traditions in the Chinese Martial Arts*, vol. 1 [Walnut Creek, CA: Center for Healing & the Arts, 1995], pp. 8–9.)

Perhaps this posture is "optimal" for the particular style of qigong Mr. Diepersloot is transmitting, but it is certainly not "natural" or structurally sound for everyday activity. I interpret "no hollows or protuberances" to mean that the qigong posture should be even, graceful, and without *exaggerated* curves. In martial arts training, places that are unnaturally concave or convex make one more vulnerable to attack.

7. This expression is often combined with *yuan dang*, "round the crotch," meaning relax the entire groin-genital region. The opposite of yuan dang would be to stand pigeon-toed with the knees collapsed inward. This squeezes and compresses the crotch. Yuan dang is emphasized in Taiji Quan but not in all styles of qigong.

8. Even such commonsense ideas as this are not uniform among qigong practitioners. One of Beijing's most famous qigong instructors tells his students to time their Standing Meditation qigong (see Chapter 10) by watching a one-hour- or two-

hour-long TV program. This is absurd. I would recommend this practice only as a temporary measure for couch potatoes.

9. Adam Hsu, "Matching Kung Fu's DNA," *Qigong Kung Fu* (Winter 1996), p. 21. Hsu, director of the Traditional Wushu Association, is arguably the finest writer on Chinese martial arts in the English language. His articles generally appear in popular American and Taiwanese martial arts magazines. Information about Hsu's work and writings can be found in the journal he publishes, the *Celebrated Mountains Journal*, P.O. Box 1075, Cupertino, CA 95015–1075.

10. I once had the honor of offering qigong instruction to a retired Commanding General of United States Army Intelligence and Security. This gentleman corroborated my opinion when he said, "When I lead a tank battalion, I do not trust a soldier who stands with his knees bent. He is likely to do his own thing."

CHAPTER EIGHT

1. Which may require surgery, medication, or other medical intervention. In some cases, avoidance and lack of awareness may be an essential coping strategy to deal with extreme physical or emotional pain.

2. Moshe Feldenkrais, *The Potent Self* (San Francisco: Harper & Row, 1985), p. 111.

3. Master T. T. Liang, *T'ai Chi Ch'uan for Health and Self-Defense*, ed. Paul Gallagher (New York: Vintage Books, 1977), p. 61.

4. Johannes H. Schultz, *Das Autogene Training* (Stuttgart: Geerg-Theime Verlag), 1953. Translated in Kenneth R. Pelletier's *Mind as Healer Mind as Slayer* (New York: Dell Publishing Co., 1977), p. 230.

5. Feldenkrais, op. cit., p. 184.

CHAPTER NINE

1. Hu Bing, *Qigong Ke Xue Qian Shi* (A Brief Introduction to the Science of Breathing Exercise), text in Chinese and English (Hong Kong: Hai Feng Publishing Co., 1982), p. 17. My translation.

2. Hyperventilation means, literally, "overbreathing," breathing that exceeds the body's metabolic requirements. The hyperventilation syndrome was first described in W. J. Kerr et. al., "Some Physical Phenomena Associated with the Anxiety States and Their Relation to Hyperventilation," *Annals of Internal Medicine* 11 (1937), pp. 961–92. For the clearest explanation of hyperventilation and an insightful discussion of the science of breathing, see Robert Fried, Ph.D., *The Breath Connection* (New York: Plenum Press, 1990). Also see his work with Joseph Grimaldi, *The Psychology and Physiology of Breathing in Behavioral Medicine, Clinical Psychology, and Psychiatry* (New York: Plenum Press, 1993).

3. Fried and Grimaldi, op. cit., p. 44.

4. J. C. Missri and S. Alexander, "Hyperventilation Syndrome: A Brief Review," *Journal of the American Medical Association* 240 (1978), pp. 2093–2096.

5. Fried and Grimaldi, op. cit., p. 69.

6. W. Penfield and H. Jasper, *Epilepsy and the Functional Anatomy of the Brain* (Boston: Little, Brown, 1954), p. 495.

7. Unfortunately, these facts are not very well-known. The authors of *Medical Qigong*, vol. 8 of *The English-Chinese Encyclopedia of Practical Traditional Chinese Medicine* (Beijing: Higher Education Press, 1990) seem unaware of the link between reversed breathing and hyperventilation and imply that abdominal and reversed breathing are equally beneficial. A popular writer on qigong, Dr. Yang Jwing-Ming, mistakenly assumes that reversed breathing is essentially Daoist and the key to success in leading qi to different parts of the body. Of greater concern is his statement "Since you are moving your abdomen, you gain the same health benefits [from reversed abdominal breathing] that you do with the normal abdominal breathing." (Yang Jwing-Ming, *The Root of Chinese Chi Kung* [Jamaica Plain, MA: Yang's Martial Arts Association, 1994], p. 117.) One of the benefits he lists is "greater efficiency in leading chi to the extremities" (p. 118). The evidence of both science and experience leads one to very different conclusions.

I concur with Dr. Yang that natural abdominal respiration was preferred by the Buddhists. Daoists practiced natural *and* reversed breathing. It is impossible to determine which method was more popular among the Daoists at any particular period in Chinese history. Certainly the goal of Daoist meditation, variously expressed as *tai xi*, "embryonic respiration," *lian shen huan xu*, "transform the spirit and return to emptiness," or *neng ying er*, "be like a child" (*Dao De Jing*, Chapter 10), all imply the utmost naturalness in mind and body.

8. Abdominal tension may be symptomatic of psychological problems. For instance, individuals who have been demeaned, sexually abused, or in other ways disempowered may react by deadening sensitivity in the lower abdomen.

9. Moshe Feldenkrais, *Awareness Through Movement* (New York: Harper & Row, 1972), p. 165.

10. One of the best is: B. K. S. Iyengar, *Light on Pranayama* (New York: Crossroad Publishing Co.), 1981.

11. See the translation by Shi Fu Hwang and Cheney Crow, Ph.D., *Tranquil Sitting* (St. Paul, MN: Dragon Door Publications, 1995).

12. Charles Luk, trans., *Taoist Yoga* (New York: Samuel Weiser, Inc., 1973), p. 96.

CHAPTER TEN

1. Felicitas D. Goodman, *Where the Spirits Ride the Wind* (Bloomington: Indiana University Press, 1990). For clear instructions in how to practice these postures, see the work of Dr. Goodman's student: Belinda Gore, *Ecstatic Body Postures* (Santa Fe: Bear & Co., 1995).

2. Goodman, op. cit., p. 20.

3. Goodman, op. cit., p. 106.

4. Unlike qigong practice, Dr. Goodman's experiments are accompanied by rhythmic rattling. Scientific research suggests that percussive music can entrain the brain waves, augmenting or catalyzing the psychological effects of posture.

5. Goodman, op. cit., p. 60.

6. This is detailed in my forthcoming book on Native American healing, to be published by Ballantine Books.

7. With a fine Feldenkrais teacher named Josef Dellagrotte.

8. See Shaykh Hakim Moinuddin Chishti, *The Book of Sufi Healing* (Rochester, VT: Inner Traditions, 1991), pp. 91–109.

9. An army of giant clay figures dating from the third century B.C., guarding the tomb of the Qin Emperor, near the city of Xian, Shanxi Province.

10. Jiang Zhenming, *Timeless History: The Rock Art of China* (Beijing: New World Press, 1991), p. 63.

11. Ibid., p. 109.

12. Ibid., p. 14.

13. Wang did not even have a name for his style. It was difficult to classify his system of teaching since it included Standing Meditation and other qigong exercises, martial arts training, and an emphasis on spiritual enlightenment. Wang did not want to identify his teaching with a particular school, or even with his own lineage of teachers. He was not teaching a *pai* (branch or sect) but rather "a principle that can be applied in daily life." This openness allowed students of many different schools to train with him. Studying a "no-name, no-lineage" style mitigated fears of betraying loyalties to particular clans, families, or other qigong or martial arts schools.

In 1937, a Beijing newspaper editor observed Wang's classes and reported, "Wang has had great success (*da cheng*) in synthesizing the best of Chinese martial arts." As a result, he dubbed Wang's art *Da Cheng Quan*, "Great Success Boxing." Wang, however, could not accept such an egotistical title. He decided to name his style *Yi Quan*, "Mind-Intent Boxing," stressing the primacy of awareness and volition. "If you use your mind correctly, you are using real strength. Awareness *is* power." This power does not depend on outward appearance or strong muscles. "Nowadays, martial artists show off their muscles and think this is a sign of their athletic ability. They do not realize that abnormal development of the muscles is actually useless and an obstacle to good health."

How did Wang develop such an unusual art, one that often ran counter to the practices and philosophy of his day? Wang was a sickly child and often suffered from severe attacks of asthma. At age eight, he began to train under the Xing-Yi Quan grandmaster Kuo Yun-shen, at first just to improve his health and later to develop the combative aspects of the art. Xing-Yi Quan is one of the internal martial arts which, like Taiji, may be practiced as qigong and/or self-defense. (Xing-Yi Quan means "Form-Mind Boxing," implying a balance of body and mind, of form and formlessness. Because Wang was concerned with the way many martial artists obsessively practiced the forms and forgot the spirit, he dropped the word *Xing*, Form, in naming his own art Yi Quan.)

In 1907, Wang began to travel throughout China in order to learn the specialties of other teachers and to refine his own skills. Around 1913, Wang was appointed dean of the Beijing Martial Arts Academy for the Chinese army. This gave Wang an opportunity to meet the great martial arts and qigong instructors in Beijing, many of whom taught under him.

In 1918, Wang journeyed through the provinces of Henan, Hunan, and Hubei. One of the most significant events in those years was a month's sojourn at the famous Shao-lin Temple on Mount Song, Henan Province. There Wang established a close friendship with a monk named Heng-lin, who taught him another version of Xing-Yi boxing and qigong. Next Wang traveled south to Fujian, then north to Tianjin, near Beijing, where he began to teach publicly.

Within a few years, Wang established his reputation as a man of great character and martial arts skill. His students were winning or placing in full-contact tournaments. He was teaching Standing Meditation and martial arts exercises in the parks. Through Standing, students could improve their health, be cured of debilitating diseases (as Wang himself had recovered from asthma), and develop the self-awareness, rootedness, and integrated power necessary for martial arts skill. Naturally, students who wished to perfect the martial arts had to apply their qigong to full-speed sparring. But there were no "forms" or "katas," no choreographed routines that the student had to memorize. Wang's successes perplexed the martial arts community, who couldn't understand the connection between Standing Meditation qigong and self-defense.

Once there was a martial arts demonstration in Beijing, in which all the great luminaries of the period were invited to perform their arts. Wang sat in the audience and observed. After the demonstration was over and the audience had departed, Wang was still speaking with some friends. The other performers noticed the great Yi Quan master and asked him for a private demonstration. Wang tried to decline, but as they persisted, he climbed onto the stage. He assumed a tranquil posture and stood, and stood, and stood. . . . Now the performers were even more confused. Wang apologized, "You, honored masters, are wonderful, the way you remember such complicated movements. I only have this one simple exercise."

Wang disparaged competitiveness and never tried to prove his style better or more orthodox than others. Unlike most teachers of his day, he also never accepted formal disciples. When a student pressed him for a secret "initiation," he laughed. "Do you think this training is a New Year's gift that I can put in your pocket? Just practice the techniques correctly. No need for a special ceremony." (This story was recounted to me by Wang's direct disciple—one of the few living—Tang Ru-kun. His *Yi Quan Qian Shi* [The Essence of Yi Quan] [Hong Kong: Tian Di Tu Shu Co., Ltd., 1986], remains the best work on the subject.) Wang advocated abolishing the traditional Master-disciple system. He felt that such a system discouraged students from questioning their teachers, as their teachers' authority was perceived to be more important than the quest for truth.

14. Quotes from Wang Xiang-zhai are from his *Xi Quan Shu Yao* (A Guide to Martial Arts Training). The complete text can be found in Yao Zong-shun, *Yi Quan* (Hong Kong: Tian Di Tu Shu Co. Ltd., 1986), pp. 151–72.

15. This method of seeing is called *ping shi*, "level gaze." The eyes are relaxed with a soft, wide (peripheral) focus, not trying to see anything in particular. When

we look at specific objects, we tend to think about them. We focus on *this* by exclud-ing *that*. The level gaze, by contrast, encourages intuition. It is interesting that ping shi is almost synonymous with *nei shi*, "inner gazing," the eyes open and seeing, yet not losing awareness of inner bodily sensations. Nei shi combines sight with insight.

Ping shi could also be called "paleolithic vision," as it was the quality of sight re-quired by ancient hunters. (I am indebted to indigenous survival skills expert Richard Dart for alerting me to this important aspect of vision.) With ping shi it be-comes possible to scan a wide area and see the movements of animals or, for parents, to do a task yet maintain awareness of children playing nearby. Martial artists keep a soft focus in order to quickly perceive when the opponent is about to launch an at-tack with any part of the body. If the martial artist looks only at the fists, he is likely to be hit with the feet.

Ping shi also facilitates emotional calm. When we are in emotional distress, the eyes become either glazed—not seeing the outside—or narrowed, a sign of exclusive and imbalanced focus. According to Richard Dart (personal communication), "With a non-focused gaze, it is impossible to maintain extreme emotions such as hate, rage, jealousy or passionate love." Not that there is anything wrong with passionate love, but it is difficult to practice qigong while in this state!

16. When Standing Meditation is practiced as part of martial arts training, it is important to imagine that your body is ready at any moment to defend or attack, like a tiger about to leap on its prey.

17. Kenichi Sawai, *The Essence of Kung-fu Taiki-Ken* (Tokyo: Japan Publications, 1976), p. 14.

18. I am indebted to students of Yi Quan master Jiang Yun-zhong for first sug-gesting the idea of "tests" in Standing practice.

CHAPTER ELEVEN

1. Lancelot Law Whyte, *The Next Development in Man* (New York: Henry Holt & Co., 1948), p. 1.

2. See Jeanne Achterberg, Barbara Dossey, and Leslie Kolkmeier, *Rituals of Healing* (New York: Bantam Books, 1994), p. 46.

3. Readers are directed to three excellent works on this subject: Jeanne Achterberg, *Imagery in Healing* (Boston: Shambala Publications, 1985); Achterberg, Dossey, and Kolkmeier, op. cit.; and Gerald Epstein, M.D., *Healing Visualizations* (New York: Bantam Books, 1989).

4. Liu Gui-zhen, *Shi Yan Qigong Liao Fa* (Hong Kong: Hong Kong Tai Ping Press, 1961). For further English-language descriptions, see Stephen Brown and Marasu Takahashi, *Qigong for Health* (New York: Japan Publications, 1986).

5. Especially, Stephen T. Chang, *The Complete System of Self-Healing Internal Exercises* (San Francisco: Tao Publishing, 1986).

6. I first learned the Six Qi Method in 1978 from a colleague, Daoist adept S. H. Guan. Dr. Ma Li-tang's work was introduced to me a few years later by his first Western student, Taiji Quan Master Patricia Leung. I detailed the healing sounds in an early journal article, "Exercises for Youth and Vitality," *East West Journal* (January

1982). Qigong Master Mantak Chia also described the technique in his *Taoist Ways to Transform Stress into Vitality* (Huntington, NY: Healing Tao Books, 1985).

7. "Exercises for Youth and Vitality," *East West Journal* (January1982.

8. For details on these indigenous methods, see my forthcoming book on Native American healing.

9. Sarah Rossbach and Lin Yun, *Living Color* (New York: Kodansha America, Inc., 1994), p. 140. This is an exceptional work on the Chinese understanding of color in healing the environment, the home, and the body.

10. You will not find this humorous term in the diagnostic manual of the American Psychiatric Association. It was created by personal friends in the Red Cedar Circle, a Native American spiritual group.

11. Some excellent meditations of this type can be found in Huang Runtian, *Treasured Qigong of Traditional Medical School* (Hong Kong: Hai Feng Publishing Co., 1994), p. 53–54.

12. See Wang Peisheng and Chen Guanhua, *Relax and Calming Qigong* (Hong Kong: Peace Book Co. and Beijing: New World Press, 1986). A more accurate translation of the Chinese title on the cover of this book, *Shi Yong Yi Gong*, would be "Practical Training of Intent [in Qigong]."

13. In the cardiac intensive care unit, following a heart attack, "the higher the denial, the lower the mortality." Larry Dossey, M.D., *Meaning and Medicine* (New York: Bantam Books, 1991), p. 220. Also, see Thomas P. Hackett et al., "The Coronary Care Unit: An Appraisal of Its Psychological Hazards," *New England Journal of Medicine* 279 (1968), p. 1365.

CHAPTER TWELVE

1. Wang Huai-qi, *Ba Duan Jin Tu Jie* (Hong Kong: Jin Hua Publishing Co., n.d.).

2. An unrelated system, known as the Bone Marrow Cleansing Gold Classic (*Xi Sui Jin Jing*), is attributed to the Daoists and was first popularized by the late qigong master Ma Li-tang. This style includes self-massage of acupuncture points and various loosening exercises without similarity to the Bone Marrow Cleansing techniques I describe.

3. See Joseph Needham, *Science and Civilization in China*, vol. 5, pt. 5. (Cambridge: Cambridge University Press, 1983), p. 166.

4. The entire set consists of twelve techniques. I have taken some poetic license with the names of these techniques. The original names of the first four exercises are: 1) *Wei Tuo* Posture (meaning "Wisdom"). Wei Tuo is a Chinese transliteration of the Sanskrit *Veda*. It can also mean a God who protects a Buddhist temple. This name is also given to postures two and four. 2) Wei Tuo Posture. 3) Plucking the Stars, Changing the Dipper. 4) Wei Tuo Posture.

5. Translated into English by Yang Shou-zhong, *Master Hua's Classic of the Central Viscera* (Boulder, CO: Blue Poppy Press, 1993). Also, see Dr. Bob Flaws's excellent preface for further information about Hua Tuo.

6. Hou Han Shu, *History of the Later Han Dynasty*. Compiled in the fifth cen-

tury; contains biographies of healers, alchemists, magicians, and recluses. See Kenneth J. DeWoskin, trans., *Doctors, Diviners, and Magicians of Ancient China: Biographies of Fang-shi* (New York: Columbia University Press, 1983).

7. I have to admit that Madame Guo's remission is probably a testament more to the power of placebo than qigong. Her Five Animal Frolics looked like very poorly performed dance—hands and body gesturing in a haphazard manner in stereotyped imitation of the animals. She followed few of the principles of qigong. Those who read the accounts of Madame Guo's cure and widespread influence are often quite shocked when they see what she actually did. Perhaps her belief in qigong is what did the trick. The fact that her Five Animals is so idealized in China may be an indication of the general level of ignorance of the subject.

8. Hu Yao-zhen, *Wu Qin Xi* (Hong Kong: Xin Wen Shu Dian, n.d.).

9. Jiao Guorui, *Qigong Essentials for Health Promotion* (Beijing: China Reconstructs Press, 1988), pp. 190–236.

10. Paul B. Gallagher, *Drawing Silk* (Guilford, VT: Deer Mountain Taoist Academy, 1987), pp. 4–9.

11. An expression of Seneca Indian elder Twylah Nitsch.

12. You may practice this qigong while holding a foot-long "Ruler" between the palms. The Ruler is made of a light, porous wood such as willow and rounded at both ends so it fits comfortably in the hands. The physical ruler encourages the flow of qi.

13. Also known as Chen Bo. *Xi-yi* means "beyond sound and sight" or "unfathomable." It is an honorific conferred upon Chen Bo by his friend Zhao Kuang-yin, the first emperor of the Song Dynasty. Other arts attributed to Chen include a method of harmonizing the qi during seasonal changes, a dreaming qigong which helps create sound sleep and lucid dreams, and a soft martial art, similar to Taiji, known as Liu He Ba Fa (Six Harmonies Eight Methods).

14. Chen Hong-zhen, ed., *Xian Tian Qigong Taiji Chi* (Primordial Qigong: Taiji Ruler) (Taibei, Taiwan: Hua Lian Publishing, 1966), p. 7.

15. Probably the most famous style of hard qigong is one of the variations of the Muscle/Tendon Change Classic *(Yi Jin Jing)*, whose history is similar to the Bone Marrow Cleansing. There is a soft and hard set of Yi Jin Jing. The hard set is a training in progressive tension. Postures are held while one is progressively tensing various body parts more and more tightly in coordination with the breath.

In the martial arts, qigong conditioning methods include "Iron Shirt," "Golden Bell Cover," and "Rib Hitting." These involve particular methods of breathing and concentration while hitting the body (or allowing a training partner to hit one) on specific areas with objects such as bamboo sticks, bags of stones, or fists. Another famed method is the "Iron Palm," in which the hands slap bricks or other objects or are jabbed into heated sand or iron filings, after which the hands must be rubbed with liniments and qi tonics. All of these methods are extremely dangerous if practiced incorrectly or on one's own. Therefore, they will not be detailed here.

Unfortunately, in China and abroad, the very concept of "qigong" is often confused with sensational demonstrations of the alleged abilities of hard qigong masters, for instance bending metal rods on the throat, chopping ice blocks with one's head, catching bullets in the mouth, or breaking stones with the index finger. Some of these demonstrations are real, others are obvious cons. One of China's most famous qigong masters demonstrates his family tradition by breaking boulders over his son's head with a sledgehammer. It seems odd to me that this is called qigong instead of child abuse!

16. There are other very beautiful but rare inner martial arts that resemble Taiji Quan, though their history and lineages are separate. These include Taiyi You Long Gong (The Great Unity Swimming Dragon), Liu He Ba Fa (Six Harmonies Eight Methods), Wuji Quan (Infinity Boxing), and Wudang Quan (Mount Wudang Boxing).

17. An excellent translation of a Xing Yi Quan qigong classic has recently appeared in English. See Dan Miller and Tim Cartmell, *Xing Yi Nei Gong: Xing Yi Health Maintenance and Internal Strength Development* (Pacific Grove, CA: High View Publications, 1994).

18. Stuart Alve Olson, trans., *The Intrinsic Energies of T'ai Chi Ch'uan* (St. Paul, MN: Dragon Door Publications, 1994), p. 27.

CHAPTER THIRTEEN

1. Although still a very important part of traditional Chinese medicine, self-massage seems to be even more popular in Japanese massage therapy traditions, where it is often called either *self-shiatsu* or *do-in*, the Japanese pronunciation of the old Chinese word for qigong, *dao-yin*. Japanese visceral self-massage is an especially powerful method of qi purification and self-healing. See Shizuto Masunaga, with Wataru Ohashi, *Zen Shiatsu* (New York: Japan Publications, 1977).

CHAPTER FOURTEEN

1. A peptide is a string of amino acids, the basic building block of life in the body. A neuropeptide means literally "a peptide produced by a nerve cell," cells which are found throughout the body. We now know that the neuropeptides can also be synthesized from the DNA of other types of cells, such as the immune cells. More than sixty different neuropeptides have been identified, perhaps corresponding to varieties of mood and emotion.

2. Candace Pert, "The Wisdom of the Receptors," *Advances* 3, no. 3: (Summer 1986), p. 16.

3. Ibid., p. 13.

4. Hidemi Ishida, "Body and Mind: The Chinese Perspective," in *Taoist Meditation and Longevity Techniques*, ed. by Livia Kohn (Ann Arbor, MI: University of Michigan Press, 1989), p. 59.

5. At times, these physical problems serve as a *positive* outlet for feeling. Leon Hammer, M.D., notes an incorrect assumption in psychosomatic medicine "that the emergence of physical illness in the presence of a psychological stress is a sign of psychological weakness" (Leon Hammer, M.D., *Dragon Rises, Red Bird Flies* [Northamptonshire, England: Thorsons Publishing Group, 1990], p. 55). He gives a

poignant example: "If a child develops a chronic headache rather than a psychosis in reaction to living with an alcoholic parent, he is in possession of a more than adequate mental-emotional apparatus." The child has probably found an effective, temporary way of coping.

6. Alexander Lowen, M.D., *Bioenergetics* (New York: Coward, McCann & Geoghegan, Inc., 1975), p. 197.

7. Cited in Robert M. Sapolksy, "Lessons of the Serengeti: Why Some of Us Are More Susceptible to Stress," *The Sciences*, New York Academy of Science (May/June 1988), p. 40.

8. Lydia Temoshok, Ph.D., and Henry Dreher, *The Type C Connection* (New York: Penguin Books, 1993).

9. A. Amkraut and George A. Solomon, "Stress and Murine Sarcoma Virus-Induced Tumors," *Cancer Research* 32 (1972), pp. 1428–33.

10. Kiiko Matsumoto and Stephen Birch, *Hara Diagnosis: Reflections on the Sea* (Brookline, MA: Paradigm Publications), 1988, p. 33.

11. The distinction is not clear in Chinese, as the word *bei* is used positively in some texts as "compassion" and negatively in others (such as qigong literature) as "excess empathy."

12. Mark Seem, Ph.D., with Joan Kaplan, *Bodymind Energetics: Toward a Dynamic Model of Health* (Rochester, VT: Healing Arts Press, 1989), p. 72.

13. See Zhang Enqin, *Health Preservation and Rehabilitation* (Shanghai: Shanghai College of Traditional Chinese Medicine, 1990), pp. 232–42. The text recommends that Chinese doctors use words, actions, or objects to arouse particular emotional states to check "morbid mentality." For example, to calm anger, the doctor should persuade the patient to change by using "miserable and sorrowful statements." In my opinion, this is substituting one neurosis for another!

14. See the lucid discussion of somatization in Arthur Kleinman, M.D., *Patients and Healers in the Context of Culture* (Berkeley: University of California Press, 1980), pp. 138–45.

15. Interestingly, in the West, neurasthenia, as a diagnostic label, fell out of use by the 1920s. It was considered vague and imprecise. The term was probably picked up by Chinese intellectuals around that time. After 1949, the term was rejected for many years, as it was assumed that psychological problems were caused by capitalism. Now, shen jing shuai ruo is an accepted complaint.

16. David Eisenberg, M.D., *Encounters with Qi* (New York: W. W. Norton & Co., 1985), p. 172.

17. The same can be said of mystics. There is an increasing incidence in China of what Western transpersonal psychologists call "spiritual emergencies." Individuals who contact the divine either as an external power or a deep and sacred aspect of the self, whether spontaneously or as a result of qigong, prayer, or ritual, may behave strangely not because of the experience, but because of their resistance to it. (See Lee Sannella, "Kundalini: Classical and Clinical," in *Spiritual Emergency*, ed. by Stanislav Grof, M.D., and Christina Groff [Los Angeles: Jeremy P. Tarcher, 1989], p. 106.) Those who have such experiences feel disoriented and confused because of conflict

between their emerging philosophy and majority values. Chinese society disdains mystical experience as "unproductive." Unfortunately, the rare individuals who might be able to guide and provide a map of this dimension of the soul do not have access to psychiatric patients.

18. Arthur Kleinman, M.D., and Joan Kleinman, "Somatization: The Interconnections in Chinese Society among Culture, Depressive Experiences, and the Meanings of Pain," in Arthur Kleinman and Bryon Good, eds. *Culture and Depression* (Berkeley: University of California Press, 1985), p. 440.

19. Kleinman, op. cit., pp. 447–48.

20. Colleagues inform me that Virginia Satir's powerful process of family therapy has been taught and well received in southern China. Several of her works have been translated into Chinese.

CHAPTER FIFTEEN

1. I have been using the concept "Healing Presence" as a core principle of External Qi Healing since the 1970s. Only recently I discovered, to my delight, that this same term has been used in nursing literature since 1976. It is described as "a mode of being available or open in a situation with the wholeness of one's unique individual being: a gift of self which can only be given freely, invoked or evoked." J. G. Paterson and L. T. Zderad, *Humanistic Nursing* (New York: Wiley, 1976), p. 122. For a warm and wise study of the healing presence, see Maggie J. McKivergin, M.S., R.N., and Jean M. Daubenmire, M.S., R.N., "The Healing Process of Presence," *Journal of Holistic Nursing* 12:1 (March 1994), pp. 65–81.

2. Wang Yin, *Qigong Wai Qi Liao Fa* (Qigong External Qi Healing) (Taiyuan: Shanxi Science Education Press, 1986).

3. Ibid., p. 69.

4. Here I differ from Joseph Needham's interpretation of the arrows as acupuncture needles, perhaps made of stone or thorns. See Joseph Needham and Lu Gwei-Djen, *Celestial Lancets* (Cambridge: Cambridge University Press, 1980), p. 78. Evidence from cross-cultural shamanism and medical anthropology suggests that these arrows represent spiritual power.

5. These names were brought to my attention in an unpublished manuscript by Zhou Zi-zong of the University of Wisconsin at Madison: *The Earliest History of Chinese Medicine and the Wu Shamanism*.

6. *Lun Yu* (The Analects of Confucius) XIII: 22.

7. Bi Yongsheng, *Chinese Qigong Outgoing-Qi Therapy*, trans. by Yu Wenping and John Black (Shandong: Shandong Science and Technology Press, 1992), p. 5.

8. Shamanistic performances were banned from the Chinese court around 32–31 B.C. Individuals were disqualified from holding public office if they belonged to "shaman families," and by the Song Dynasty shamans were forbidden to practice their "diabolic ways" (*yao dao*) and "perverse methods" (*xie shu*). "After the establishment of Confucianism as a State religion in the first century B.C. the governing classes tended more and more to look down upon shamans, regarding them at the

best as socially inferior . . . impostors who traded on the credulity of the masses." Arthur Waley, *The Nine Songs* (San Francisco: City Lights Books, 1973), pp. 11–12.

9. Daoists were naturally attracted to healing methods that emphasized spirituality and unity with nature. Ancient Chinese shamans and Daoists shared a common belief in the Universe, the Dao, as the ultimate source of healing power. Indeed, for many Daoists, the Universe *is* healing energy. The Dao is Qi.

10. Called *Zhu You Ke*, the science of healing with prayer, sometimes called "exorcistic prayer," as the ancient Chinese believed that prayer and invocation could expel disease-causing spirits. Today, most Chinese consider prayer unscientific, though they readily accept the validity of intent and external qi. It will be interesting to see what happens as Chinese scientists become aware of the benefits of prayer documented in Western research. The Red Giant would probably fall over in shock if Dr. Larry Dossey's *Healing Words* were translated into Chinese.

11. *Jin Shu: Fang Ji Zhuan*.

12. Ge Hong, *The Master Who Embraces Simplicity (Bao Pu Zi)*, Chapter 8. This is an important notebook of Daoist alchemy, healing, and folklore. For a translation of the key chapters, see James Ware, *Alchemy, Medicine & Religion in the China of* A.D. *320* (New York: Dover Publications, 1981).

13. Daniel J. Benor, M.D., *Healing Research*, vol. I–IV (Southfield, MI: Vision Publications [in press]).

14. Larry Dossey, M.D., *Healing Words* (San Francisco: HarperCollins, 1993).

15. These methods have been taught in the United States by Daoist priest Share K. Lew and his students.

16. Between 701 and 705, Empress Wu helped organize Buddhist monastic hospitals, catering to the poor and destitute. In 744, Emperor Xuan Zong decreed that beggars in the capital could receive treatment, paid by the state, at Buddhist hospitals. In 867, Emperor Yi Zong directly subsidized Buddhist hospitals and charged local authorities to select competent monks as directors. See Mark Tatz, trans., *Buddhism and Healing* (Lanham, MD: University Press of America, 1985), pp. 58–60.

17. As a modern example, a friend recounted an External Qi Healing he witnessed at the Eighteen Lohan Buddhist Monastery outside of Taibei, Taiwan. The Master healed a student of a serious martial arts injury by transmitting qi while massaging his abdomen.

18. Jia Lin and Jia Jinding, "Effects of Emitted Qi on Healing of Experimental Fracture" (paper presented at First World Conference for Academic Exchange of Medical Qigong (Beijing, 1988), pp. 13–14. Chinese institutes of sports medicine have been conducting animal experiments to test the effect of EQH on broken bones and on soft-tissue injuries, such as muscle sprain.

19. Liu Defu, Shen Xiaoheng, and Wang Changan, "Study of the Effect of External Qi on Natural Killer Cell Activity on Mice with Tumors" (paper presented at Third International Symposium on Qigong (Shanghai, 1990), p. 73. See also Xu Hefen et. al., "Effects of Outgoing Qi on Translated Tumor S180 of Rats," ibid., p. 57.

20. The Yi Quan Standing described in Chapter 10 is excellent preparation for qi projection. There are also specialized forms of Standing practiced by some

External Qi Healers, such as Shao-lin Nei Jing Yi Zhi Chan, "Buddhist Internal Strength, One Finger Meditation," a method that combines aligning and stimulating various acupuncture points, tranquil standing postures, and projecting qi between one's own palms or from individual fingers. The method is likely Buddhist in origin, as it begins with the Buddhist mantra OM AH HUNG. This system is presently taught in North America by a very fine qigong master and renowned martial artist, Master Liang Shou-yu. External Qi training postures are described and illustrated in Lin Hou-sheng's *Qigong Shi Ren Jian Kang* (Building Strength with Qigong) (Canton, China: Guangdeng Ke Ji Press, 1981).

21. Personal communication from shiatsu (Japanese acupressure massage) and qi-master and respected colleague Janet Murphy, July 1988.

22. Ambrose A. Worrall and Olga N. Worrall, *The Gift of Healing* (Columbus, Ohio: Ariel Press, 1985), p. 114.

23. Thank you, Kabbalist and mystic Samuel Avital, for this wonderful term. A considerable improvement over "channeling."

24. Worrall, op. cit., p. 165.

25. Kyriacos C. Markides, *The Magus of Strovolos: The Extraordinary World of a Spiritual Healer* (New York: Penguin, 1985). This is a wonderful book. I recently had the honor of meeting Dr. Markides, a university professor who is as committed to personal growth as he is to good scholarship.

26. Lin Hou-sheng, op. cit., p. 130, note 17.

27. A human being lives in a field of physical and social relationships. The health of these relationships can determine the efficacy of any healing therapy. A medication administered in a beautiful environment by a caring nurse will have very different effects than the same medication given by a pessimistic provider in an un-aesthetic clinic. A lonely individual is more likely to suffer side effects from medication than one who has the support of a loving family.

28. It is best to use wild rather than garden sage. Take only as much herbs as you need and will use, always leaving some untouched for reseeding. Out of respect for Native American traditions, these sacred plants should not be bought or sold. For further information, see my forthcoming book on Native American healing.

29. I wish that some creative and courageous colleague would set up an experiment to test improvement or cure in a group of patients treated in a cleansed room compared with a similar group treated in an uncleansed space.

30. Actually, at a high level of practice, the External Qi healer can do almost any kind of massage therapy without any perceptible change in what she is doing. She just reaches in at various depths—skin, muscle, bone.

CHAPTER SIXTEEN

1. For an exceptional video production on high-level Yoga exercises with breath-control techniques, see *Yoga with Richard Freeman* (Boulder, CO: Delphi Productions). Exercises designed to stretch and exercise the meridians are also an excellent complement to qigong practice. These are described in Shizuto Masunaga's *Zen Imagery Exercises* (New York: Japan Publications, 1987).

2. I recommend 10–15 minutes in Chapter 11 only if this exercise is done as an independent qigong or combined only with Crane, Turtle, and Deer. Ten minutes would be excessive here.

CHAPTER SEVENTEEN

1. Michael A. Province, Ph.D., Evan C. Hadley, M.D., et al, "The Effects of Exercise on Falls in Elderly Patients," *Journal of the American Medical Association* (May 3, 1995), pp. 1341–47. See also Shuk-Kuen Tse and Diana Bailey, "T'ai Chi [Taiji] and Postural Control in the Well Elderly," *The American Journal of Occupational Therapy* (April 1992), pp. 295–300. Here again, "there were significant differences between the t'ai chi and the non-t'ai chi groups (p.<05) on three balance tests. . . ." Unfortunately, unlike the rigorous study published in *JAMA*, no conclusions can be drawn from this study because of too few subjects and not controlling for several variables, such as the number of years subjects had practiced, exercise history, occupation, and interests.

2. This may correspond to alopecia areata, an inflammatory and reversible form of patchy baldness, without a clear etiology.

3. The popular, contrasting point of view is expressed by Master Zhao Jin Xiang, originator of Soaring Crane Qigong, one of the most popular styles in China, with an alleged twenty million practitioners. "Some people tend to quit when the diseased parts of the body are being attacked by qi—which can bring unbearable pain. So complete faith in the healing by qigong is required." Zhao Jin Xiang, *Chinese Soaring Crane Qigong*, trans. by Chen Hui Xian et al. (Corvalis, OR: Qigong Association of America, 1993), p. iv. Obviously I disagree with Master Zhao's statement. Nevertheless, the book and style are generally excellent. I do not list it among recommended readings only because of the book's warning not to practice Soaring Crane without a certified teacher.

4. A saying of Rabbi Joseph Gelberman, founder of the New Seminary, an interfaith seminary in New York City.

5. *Diagnostic and Statistical Manual of Mental Disorders*, 4th ed. (Washington, D.C.: The American Psychiatric Association, 1994), p. 847. I cannot claim credit for this definition. It is possible that the term "qigong psychotic reaction" was coined independently by the authors of the DSM IV.

6. Clearly reported by Wallace Sampson and Barry L. Beyerstein in their "Traditional Medicine and Pseudoscience in China: A Report of the Second CSICOP Delegation (Part 2)," *Skeptical Inquirer* 20:5 (September 1996), pp. 27–34.

7. Ibid., p. 29.

8. There are probably more psychotic reactions to the practice of psychiatry than to the practice of qigong. In the United States, psychiatrists have a very high suicide rate.

CHAPTER EIGHTEEN

1. Perhaps this is why, in early Daoist alchemy, the spleen was said to be the source of qi. Daoists manipulated the internal energies according to this formula:

Heart qi + Liver qi = shen (spirit). Lung qi + Kidney qi = jing (sexual essence). Spleen = qi. Jing + qi + shen = dan (the elixir of immortality).

2. Bob Flaws, *Arisal of the Clear* (Boulder, CO: Blue Poppy Press, 1991), p. 10.

3. Ibid.

4. According to a Daoist classic, *Yang Xing Yan Ming Lu* (The Record of Nourishing Nature and Prolonging Life), "If you go to sleep on a full stomach, you lose one day of life." Instead of sleeping, it is best to take a walk after eating. This is reflected in the Chinese saying "After eating take a stroll, and you will live to 99!"

5. "Healthy People 2000: National Health Promotion and Disease Prevention Objectives." Washington, D.C.: U.S. Department of Health and Human Services, Public Health Service, 1990.

6. Eddy, D. M. "Setting Priorities for Cancer Control Programs." *Journal of the National Cancer Institute* 76 (1986), pp. 187–199.

7. *Alternative Medicine: Expanding Medical Horizons; A Report to the National Institutes of Health and Alternative Medical Systems and Practices in the United States*, NIH Publication no. 94–066 (Washington, D.C.: December 1994), p. 210. The information is cited from the World Health Organization Technical Report Series 979 Geneva, 1990.

8. Christopher Bird and Peter Tompkins, *Secrets of the Soil* (New York: Harper & Row, 1989), p. xi.

9. Seaweed is high in nutrients and is a concentrated source of minerals such as calcium, iodine, iron, phosphorus, and zinc. It also has proven detoxifying properties, removing lead and other chemical pollutants from the body. It is important to use various seaweeds because each type (e.g., dulse, nori, kelp, wakame, hiziki) has different nutrients. Seaweed may be used as a food or spice. For example, hiziki is delicious in salads, powdered kelp or crushed nori taste wonderful on rice.

10. See Annemarie Colbin, *Food and Healing* (New York: Ballantine, 1986), pp. 148–160.

11. The effects of these chemicals are painstakingly analyzed in the riveting work of Theo Colborn, Dianne Dumanoski, and John Peterson Myers: *Our Stolen Future* (New York: Dutton, 1996).

12. Jeffrey A. Fisher, M.D., *The Plague Makers* (New York: Simon & Schuster, 1994), p. 90.

13. William M. Welch, "Meat Inspection Plan Faces Delay," *USA Today* (July 11, 1995), p. 6A.

14. Ibid.

15. Ibid. Report by Ron Anderson, legislative aide to Rep. James Walsh, R–N.Y.

16. Although poultry is generally warm, it is hot in terms of its specific effect on the liver. This is why chicken is contraindicated when there is a Chinese diagnosis of liver heat.

17. Here I differ from Henry Lu and other authors who consider beef neutral and lamb only warm. This is not supported by either my personal or my clinical experience.

18. S. Boyd Eaton, "Humans, Lipids and Evolution," *Lipids* 27:10 (1992), p. 817. This article is also the source for my information on the fat content of fried foods.

19. Mary F. Taylor, *New Vegetarian Classics: Entrées* (Freedom, CA: The Crossing Press, 1995), p. 26. This book and her other work, *New Vegetarian Classics: Soups*, are highly recommended for their skillful blend of health-conscious recipes and careful instruction in such cooking basics as food preparation and cooking methods.

20. Bob Flaws, *The Book of Jook* (Boulder, CO: Blue Poppy Press, 1995).

21. Zhang Enqin, ed., *Health Preservation and Rehabilitation* (Shanghai: Shanghai College of Traditional Chinese Medicine, 1990), p. 272. Chinese and English, here my translation.

22. The qing dan diet helps the mind become *ping dan*, "serene, calm and free of artifice." The difference between the qing dan diet and the highly flavored diet is like the difference between tea and wine. Tea is calming, plain yet satisfying. Alcoholic drinks make one excitable; they are strong tasting and can create only temporary feelings of well-being. There is a wise saying that illustrates the mood of qing dan, here applied to friendship rather than cuisine: "The friendship of the small person is sweet as honey. The friendship of the noble person is plain *(dan)* as water." *(Xiao ren zhi jiao tian ru mi. Jun zi zhi jiao dan ru shui.)*

23. See Michael Saso, *A Taoist Cookbook* (Rutland, VT: Tuttle, 1994).

24. Liu Zhengcai, *The Mystery of Longevity* (Beijing: Foreign Languages Press, 1990), pp. 60–68.

25. Roy Walford, *The 120 Year Diet* (New York: Simon & Schuster, 1986).

26. Goodrick et al., cited in ibid., p. 376.

27. R. L. Walford, S. B. Harris, and M. W. Gunion, "The Calorically Restricted, Low-Fat, Nutrient-Dense Diet in Biosphere 2 Significantly Lowers Blood Glucose, Total Leukocyte Count, Cholesterol, and Blood Pressure in Humans," *Proceedings of the National Academy of Science USA* 1992, 89: 11533–11537.

28. For an excellent summary of this data, see "Diet and Nutrition in the Prevention and Treatment of Chronic Disease," in *Alternative Medicine: Expanding Medical Horizons* (Washington, D.C.: U.S. Government Printing Office, 1994), pp. 209–219.

29. Walford, 1986, p. 60.

30. Ibid., p. 61.

31. Also called *jue gu*, "cutting off cereals," or *xiu liang*, "continuing grains."

32. *Da-yu Jing*, in Henri Maspero, *Taoism and Chinese Religion* (Amherst: University of Massachusetts Press, 1981), p. 333.

33. The ancient Heavenly Masters Sect *(Tian Shi Pai)*, dating from the second century, was also called the Five Pecks of Rice Sect *(Wu Dou Mi)*.

34. Perhaps a vestige of Daoism's paleolithic roots.

35. Allergies and/or an inability to digest cereal grains affect both physical and mental health and may be linked with schizophrenia. "Hidden sensitivity to one's daily bread may well be the cause of compulsive and ritualistic behavior, impaired speech development, and mood and behavior changes." Carl C. Pfeiffer, Ph.D., M.D., *Nutrition and Mental Illness* (Rochester, VT: Healing Arts Press, 1987).

36. For reasons explained below, I disagree with those who advise high carbohydrate diets, such as Nathan Pritikin (80 percent) and Dean Ornish, M.D. (75 percent).

37. According to S. Boyd Eaton, M.D., of the Department of Radiology, Emory University School of Medicine, and the Department of Anthropology, Emory University, the percentage of macronutrients in the Late Paleolithic diet (assuming 35 percent meat and 65 percent vegetables) averaged 34 percent protein, 45 percent carbohydrate, and 21 percent fat. S. Boyd Eaton, M.D., and Melvin Konner, Ph.D., "Paleolithic Nutrition," *The New England Journal of Medicine* 312:5 (1985), p. 288. For further details on the nutritional content of preagricultural and post-agricultural foods, see Eaton's "Humans, Lipids and Evolution," *Lipids* 27:10 (1992), pp. 814–820.

38. Eaton and Konner, op. cit., p. 283. Christiane Northrup, M.D., renowned authority on women's health, adds that people with Type A blood (A–1 and A–2) need to be especially careful about overconsumption of grains, "which are a relative newcomer to human diets and can lead to carbohydrate addiction, gluten intolerance, bloating and PMS and chronic yeast infections." *Health Wisdom for Women* 2:7 (July 1996).

39. See Rachael F. Heller and Richard F. Heller, *The Carbohydrate Addict's Diet* (New York: Penguin, 1993).

40. What the Daoists did not realize is that not all carbohydrates are created equal. Scientists have discovered that the real culprits are those which enter the bloodstream more quickly (a high *glycemic index*), causing rapidly elevated blood sugar and a stronger insulin response. These include rice (white and brown), pasta, bread (including whole grain), potatoes, carrots, and millet. More favorable carbohydrates, with a slower rate of entry (lower glycemic index) and less dramatic insulin response, include barely, oatmeal, rye, lentils, soybeans, kidney beans, apples. This does not mean that you must avoid rice. Sufficient dietary fiber (nondigestible carbohydrate) and fat slows down the rate of entry of carbohydrates into the bloodstream. So if you are going to have bread, it might be a good idea to add a little tomato sauce and mozzarella, but limit yourself to one slice!

41. Barry Sears, Ph.D., with Bill Lawren, *The Zone* (New York: HarperCollins, 1995). Sears adds an important chapter to macronutrient research. He writes about a powerful class of hormones known as *eicosanoids* that control major functions such as blood pressure, inflammation, immune response, and pain transmission. There are healthy and unhealthy eicosanoids. The healthy eicosanoids help to prevent heart disease, cancer, diabetes, and all kinds of pain. Unhealthy eicosanoids promote these same conditions. Sears found that a ratio of 30 percent protein:40 percent carbohydrate: 30 percent fat encourages the production of healthy eicosanoids. Overconsumption of carbohydrates with the ensuing high insulin levels enhances the activity of delta 5 desaturase, an enzyme that leads to the production of unhealthy eicosanoids. Your body also creates harmful eicosanoids when you consume unhealthy fats, particularly fatty red meat, organ meats, and egg yolks. The safest fats are monounsaturated fats as found in canola oil, olive oil, avocados, almonds, peanuts and peanut oil, and tahini (sesame butter).

42. Liu Jilin, ed., *Chinese Dietary Therapy* (New York: Churchill Livingstone, 1995), p. 103.

43. Flaws, *Arisal of the Clear*, p. 62.

44. W. J. Blot, J.-Y. Li, P. R. Taylor, et al., "Nutritional Intervention Trials in Linxian, China: Supplementation with Specific Vitamin/Mineral Combinations, Cancer Incidence, and Disease-Specific Mortality in the General Population," *Journal of the National Cancer Institute* 85 (1993), pp. 1483–1492.

45. D. C. Cook, "Subsistence Base and Health in Prehistoric Illinois Valley: Evidence from the Human Skeleton," *Medical Anthropology* 3 (1979), pp. 109–24; C. S. Larsen, "Skeletal and Dental Adaptations to the Shift to Agriculture on the Georgia Coast," *Current Anthropology* 22 (1981), pp. 422–423; C. M. Cassidy, "Nutrition and Health in Agriculturalists and Hunter-Gatherers: A Case Study of Two Prehistoric Populations," in *Nutritional Anthropology: Contemporary Approaches to Diet and Culture*, ed. by R. F. Jerome and G. H. Pelto (Pleasantville, N.Y.: Redgrave, 1980), pp. 117–145.

46. About six inches taller than their post-agricultural descendants. Eaton and Konner point out that "we are now nearly as tall as were the first biologically modern human beings." Eaton and Konner, op. cit., p. 284. See P. R. Nickens, "Stature Reduction as an Adaptive Response to Food Production in Mesoamerica," *Journal of Archaeological Science* 3 (1976), pp. 31–41; J. L. Angel, "Paleoecology, Paleodemography and Health," in S. Polgar, ed., *Population, Ecology and Social Evolution* (The Hague: Mouton, 1975), pp. 167–90.

47. See Eaton and Konner, op. cit.

48. Linus Pauling, *How to Live Longer and Feel Better* (New York: W. H. Freeman & Co.), 1986.

49. Similarly, fish eyes are said to benefit the eyes; duck feet send qi to the feet. It seems to me that this principle is sometimes carried to extremes. For instance, a tincture of herbs mixed with gekko genitalia allegedly increases sexual potency.

50. Personal communication, August 21, 1995. For insight into the spirit, ecology, and story of water, see Tom Heidlebaugh's inspiring text *One with the Watershed: A Story-Based Curriculum for Primary Environmental Education* (1994). Available through the Northwest Indian Fisheries Commission, Olympia, WA.

51. *Bi Yan Lu* (The Blue Cliff Record), Case 50. The Blue Cliff Record, a classic of Zen Buddhism, is a collection of one hundred anecdotes compiled during the Song Dynasty. See Thomas and J. C. Cleary, trans., *The Blue Cliff Record*. 3 vols. (Boulder, Co.: Shambala, 1977).

CHAPTER NINETEEN

1. The English and French get the word "tea" or *thé* from the pronunciation in China's Fajian Province. Other countries borrow the word from the Cantonese or Mandarin dialects, where it is pronounced "cha."

2. Ma Shou-chun, *Chinese Nutrition Reference Material* (Seattle: Northwest Institute of Acupuncture and Oriental Medicine, 1995, unpublished manuscript).

3. W. Young, "Tea and Atherosclerosis," *Nature* 216 (1967), pp. 1015–16.

4. Jean Carper, *Food—Your Miracle Medicine* (New York: HarperCollins, 1994), p. 78.

5. Kit Chow and Ione Kramer, *All the Tea in China* (San Francisco: China Books and Periodicals, 1990), p. 105.

6. Ibid.

7. Carper, op. cit., p. 78.

8. Ibid.

9. M. Hertog, "Dietary Antioxidant Flavonoids and Risk of Coronary Heart Disease: the Zutphen Elderly Study," *The Lancet* 342 (1993), pp. 1007–11.

10. Y. T. Gao, J. K. McLaughlin, W. J. Blot, et al. "Reduced Risk of Esophageal Cancer Associated with Green Tea Consumption." *Journal of the National Cancer Institute* 86 (1994), pp. 855–58.

11. *The Seattle Tea Times* 1:2 (1991). Publication of Teahouse Kuan-yin.

12. Carper, op. cit., p. 213.

13. Tsuneo Koda et al., "Detection and Chemical Identification of Natural Bio-Antimutagens: A Case of the Green Tea Factor," *Mutation Research* (Amsterdam) (February 15, 1985).

14. Mauro Serafini, "Red Wine, Tea and Antioxidants," *The Lancet* 344 (1994), p. 626.

15. Information obtained from Kida Taichi. "Science of Tea—Part III," *Chanoyu Quarterly* (Winter 1970), pp. 61-66, and Kit Chow, op. cit., p. 90.

16. "Coffee and Health," *Consumer Reports* (October, 1994), pp. 650–51.

17. Kida Taiichi, "Science of Tea—Part I," *Chanoyu Quarterly* (Summer, 1970), p. 53.

18. Unfortunately, China does not officially certify any teas as organic. "The closest to commercial organic farming is what they call *San-wu: the three nos*—1. no chemical fertilizer, 2. no pesticides, 3. no pollution." David Lee Hoffman, "The Hunt for Jade Spring," *Tea: A Magazine* 4 (September 1995), p. 22.

19. David Lee Hoffman, "Leaf & Water" brochure (Lagunitas, CA: Silk Road Teas, n.d.).

20. Soshitsu Sen XV, *Tea Life, Tea Mind* (New York: Weatherhill, 1979).

CHAPTER TWENTY

1. *Su Nü Jing* (Classic of the Pure Maiden), a Han Dynasty text. *Su* also denotes "unbleached silk," thus rendering the name Su Nü as "Silken Maiden."

2. From Daoist alchemist Tao Hong-jing's eleventh-century classic, *Yang Xing Yan Ming Lu* (Record of Nourishing Nature and Lengthening Life), trans. by Joseph Needham, in *Science and Civilization in China* vol. 5, pt. 5 (Cambridge: Cambridge University Press, 1983), p. 190.

3. Judaism being the other. Thus, there are no Jewish monasteries nor a celibate priesthood. In fact, unmarried rabbis are considered an oddity. Readers might object that Indian Tantra also includes techniques of sexual union. True enough, but consider the following. In India, sexual yoga has generally been considered an inferior path, revealed by Lord Siva as appropriate for this Kali Yuga, the final age of decline before world conflagration. Sexual yoga is not practiced as a sacred, healing act in and of itself, but is rather taken as a symbol of the interplay of cosmic forces, the God

and Goddess. It is also interesting to note that techniques of coitus reservatus are described in Chinese literature long before their first appearance in India. In the journals of Buddhist pilgrims Fa Xian (A.D. 317) and Xuan Zhuang (A.D. 612) there is no mention of Indian sexual practices, whereas sexual rites had been practiced in China since the second century.

4. From Chapter 6 of the *Yang Xing Yan Ming Lu* (Record of Nourishing Nature and Lengthening Life), trans. by Douglas Wile, in *Art of the Bedchamber: The Chinese Sexual Yoga Classics Including Women's Solo Meditation Texts* (Albany: State University of New York Press, 1992), pp. 121–22. Professor Wile is one of the few scholars of Chinese language and literature who also have an avid interest in Taiji Quan and Qigong. His book is a treasure and highly recommended.

5. The liturgy for this choreographed orgy is preserved in the Daoist *Huang Shu* (Yellow Book). I will never forget the crack made by one of my professors of Daoist history, after a lecture on the Yellow Book: "If you are wondering about a class laboratory, please see me during my orifice hours."

6. For a scholarly yet poetic account of the "Divine Woman" in Chinese literature, see Edward H. Schafer, *The Divine Woman: Dragon Ladies and Rain Maidens in T'ang Literature* (Berkeley: University of California Press, 1973). There is a masterful study of Daoism and feminine alchemical-qigong practices in Catherine Despeux, *Immortelles de la Chine Ancienne: Taoïsme et alchimie féminine* (Puiseaux, France: Éditions Pardès, 1990). As Despeux states, we should not ignore the ambiguity of Daoist feminism: the presence of a philosophy extolling the feminine does not necessarily suggest that women had an elevated status in society. "One notes, to the contrary, that an exaltation of the feminine image frequently corresponds to a period of social oppression of women" (p. 12).

7. Since the fourth century, some Daoist sects have allowed marriage, while others required celibacy. Daoist priests became known as *Dao-shi*, "practitioners of the Way," a term that had originally been applied to celibate Buddhist monks. Instead of seeking yin-yang balance, many Daoists began to advocate cultivating a state of "pure yang," purging the body of the mundane, putrefying, and evil elements, now labeled "yin." I suspect that many Daoists were as guilty as Confucians of contributing to patriarchy.

8. Li Yu-ning, "Historical Roots of Changes in Women's Status in Modern China," in Li Yu-ning, ed., *Chinese Women Through Chinese Eyes* (Armonk, NY: M.E. Sharpe, 1992), p. 117.

9. Repression and frustration probably contribute to the dramatic increase in prostitution in the P.R.C. in recent years.

10. Stress inhibits the production of testosterone in men and both estrogen and progesterone in women, shutting down many aspects of the reproductive system. Stress can also weaken the health of a fetus by interfering with the flow of blood.

11. Robert M. Sapolsky, *Why Zebras Don't Get Ulcers* (New York: W. H. Freeman, 1994), p. 124.

12. *Shun zi si, ni zi xian.*

13. According to Chinese medicine, "one drop of jing makes ten drops of blood." If jing supply drops, red blood cell count can drop dramatically.

14. Personal communication, April 1996.

15. Carl C. Pfeiffer, M.D., *Mental and Elemental Nutrients* (New Canaan, CT: Keats Publishing, 1975), p. 449.

16. A question begging for research! Perhaps the Deer raises spermine levels by increasing the assimilation of certain trace elements on which spermine production depends—particularly manganese and zinc.

17. There are unconfirmed reports of postmenopausal women beginning to ovulate and have menses again as a result of practicing the Deer.

18. For example, see Dr. Stephen T. Chang, *The Tao of Sexology* (San Francisco: Tao Publishing, 1986), p. 109.

19. Sapolsky, op. cit., p. 119.

20. Personal communication, Dr. Bob Flaws, November 10, 1995.

21. Ibid. Dr. Flaws's comment brings up another issue. What was the lifestyle of women practicing cutting the dragon? Who were they? Hu Yao-zhen, well-known qigong scholar and teacher, believes that the technique was developed for Buddhist nuns (in *Qigong Jing Xuan,* "Selected Articles on Qigong," edited by Yan Hai, cited in Wile, op. cit., p. 55). One of the most famous Daoist proponents of the technique was the twelfth-century Daoist female master Sun Bu-er. However, she began the practice at age fifty-one, after she had already had three children. See Thomas Cleary, *Immortal Sisters: Secrets of Taoist Women* (Boston: Shambala, 1989).

22. Admittedly the *frequency* of menstruation in modern societies may be unnatural and contribute toward women's reproductive problems. In hunter-gatherer societies, past and present, infants are kept near the breast and allowed to feed for a minute or two about every fifteen minutes. This keeps prolactin levels high and acts as a natural contraceptive for the next three years. A year later, when the first child is four, another child is born. During the course of her lifetime, a woman might have about twenty periods, compared with about five hundred for a modern Western woman. See Sapolsky, op. cit., pp. 116–22.

23. Mantak and his wife Maneewan Chia recommend an interesting vaginal-strengthening exercise in their *Healing Love Through the Tao: Cultivating Female Sexual Energy* (Huntington, NY: Healing Tao Books, 1986). They describe a method of inserting a small obsidian ball into the vagina. The ball is squeezed and moved about. The Chias also describe a variation, in which a weight is attached to the ball. This seems somewhat extreme. I am not convinced of its safety, or of similar practices where the man lifts and swings a weight suspended from his penis.

Many years ago, when I was first searching for a good qigong teacher, I interviewed a Chinese gentleman who, to convince me of the authenticity and power of his system, exclaimed, "If you learn from me, you will be able to lift fifty pounds with your erect penis." (No, I did not ask for a demonstration.) I fail to understand the fascination with genital weight lifting. I would have been much more impressed if the master had claimed, "You will, at age fifty, be able to maintain an erection for three hours."

24. Robert Ornstein, Ph.D., and David Sobel, M.D., *Healthy Pleasures* (Redding, MA: Addison–Wesley, 1995).

25. Ibid., p. 74.

26. See Wile, op. cit., p. 119.

27. Some feminists incorrectly assume that the separation of men and women during menstruation is a demeaning custom created by men. It is interesting to note that in American Indian culture, the custom of avoiding intimacy during "the moon-time" was established by women. Men who transgress this rule are severely chastised for their disrespect (personal communication, 1984, Grace Spotted Eagle, Lakota-Sioux, respected spiritual teacher). This subject will be explored in greater detail in my forthcoming book on Native American healing.

28. Wile, op. cit., pp. 142–43.

29. Ibid., p. 141.

30. *Precious Prescriptions* (Qian Jin Yao Fang), significant portions of which are translated in ibid., pp. 114–19.

31. Mantak Chia and Michael Winn, *Taoist Secrets of Love: Cultivating Male Sexual Energy* (New York: Aurora Press, 1984).

32. Wile, op. cit., p. 44.

33. Sexual vampires, past and present, practice what some call *zuo dao*, "left hand dao." They *cai yin bu yang*, "take the yin to nourish the yang," or *cai yang bu yin*, "take the yang to nourish the yin." Sex is treated as a battle, where either or both individuals are trying to win a prize from the other. The proper attitude is *give* the yin to nourish the yang; give the yang to nourish the yin.

CHAPTER TWENTY-ONE

1. There is, however, a truly reprehensible class of great experts: the know-it-all teachers. In surveying the available English and Chinese literature on qigong, I found that, with very few exceptions, these works contain no footnotes, no bibliography, no sources. This leads me to the awesome conclusion that these books were written by an all-knowing authority: that is, by God.

I am not trying to belittle poetic and creative writing, in which footnotes and bibliographies are extraneous. However, in works that attempt to convey the richness of an ancient medical tradition with thousands of years of literature behind it, footnotes are necessary to both establish the author's credibility and to guide further research.

Unfortunately, some students buy into their teachers' delusions of grandeur and will imitate or follow their teachers even when common sense tells them it is a blind alley. Here Great Experts produce more Great Experts. I have seen some rather humorous examples of this phenomenon. For example, a whole school of qigong students trembling uncontrollably while practicing Standing Meditation. Their instructor also trembles, only in his case it is a side effect of medication for a neurological disorder. He never revealed this fact to his students, lest his frailty cause him to lose face. Another example, a master who tells his students never to urinate before qigong. "Your body will re-absorb the water, so you won't be thirsty all day." I don't know how following this advice affected thirst; however, it did affect the students' kidneys. Several developed nephritis.

2. Pushing people or objects from a distance is known as *kong jing*, "empty force." This can actually be a valid and useful qi-sensitivity exercise. The student senses qi from either his teacher or a classmate. When the teacher makes an expansive motion, the student deliberately plays along, moving with the energy field. With practice, he can sense the field from farther away. Eventually, the "receiver" agrees to respond to the "sender's" intent. From the outside this looks like magic. The master seems to be pushing the student or students without touching them. Or the master might simply look at the student, and the student suddenly bounces back as though hit by an invisible force. Is it real? Depends on how you define real. He *is* pushing them. A very sensitive voltmeter could probably detect changes around the master, the student, and in the field between them. But this does not translate into obvious physical movement unless the student agrees to do so. If the master tried to push an untrained individual or a chair, I doubt if anything would happen.

Unfortunately, this exercise is often demonstrated as an example of qigong's supernatural power. The audience is never made aware of the hidden "agreement" between teacher and student. I believe that this is unethical. The gullible are convinced that qigong is mystical and supernatural. The skeptics lose interest in qigong, incorrectly assuming that it is all trickery.

I was delighted to find corroboration of my opinion in Jan Diepersloot, *Warriors of Stillness* (Walnut Creek, CA: Center for Healing & the Arts, 1995), pp. 208–14. Diepersloot's "interacting fields of awareness" (p. 209) is an excellent description of what actually occurs during the practice of kong jing.

3. Personal communication, 1979.

APPENDIX C

1. Robert Shellenberger, Ph.D., and Judith Alyce Green, Ph.D. *From the Ghost in the Box to Successful Biofeedback Training* (Greeley, CO: Health Psychology Publications, 1986), p. 7.

2. For a review of methodological problems in Chinese medicine research see Cristina de la Torre, "The Choice of Control Groups in Invasive Clinical Trials Such as Acupuncture," in *Frontier Perspectives* 3:2 (Fall 1993).

3. "Assessing the Efficacy and Safety of Medical Technologies," Congressional Office of Technology Assessment, 1978, p. 7.

4. Richard Smith, "Where is the wisdom . . . ?" *British Medical Journal* 303 (1991), pp. 798–99.

5. Alan H. Roberts, et al., "The Power of Nonspecific Effects in Healing: Implications for Psychosocial and Biological Treatments," *Clinical Psychology Review* 13 (1993), pp. 1–17.

6. Herbert Benson, M.D., and David P. McCallie, Jr., "Angina Pectoris and the Placebo Effect," *The New England Journal of Medicine* (July 21, 1979), pp. 1424–29.

7. Herbert Benson, M.D., "Commentary: Placebo Effect and Remembered Wellness," *Mind/Body Medicine* 1:1 (March 1995), p. 44.

8. Carol J. Schneider, Ph.D., and Wayne B. Jonas, M.D., "Are Alternative Treatments Effective? Issues and Methods Involved in Measuring Effectiveness of Alternative Treatments," *Subtle Energies* 5:1 (1994), pp. 69–92.

9. See Kevin Corcoran, and Joel Fischer, *Measures for Clinical Practice: A Sourcebook*, 2 vols., (New York: Macmillan, 1994).

10. Ed Gracely, Ph.D., letter to the editor, *Alternative Therapies in Health and Medicine* 1:5 (November 1995), p. 16.

11. Li Hongqui and Huang Jianzhong, "Glaucoma . . ." (paper presented at Fourth Annual Conference of the International Society for the Study of Subtle Energy and Energy Medicine, Boulder, CO, 1991), p. 53.

12. Wan Sujian, He Yuzhu, Hao Shuping, Liu Yuding, Yu Chuan. "Repeated Experiments Using Emitted Qi in Treatment of Spinal Cord Injury." (paper presented at Second World Conference for Academic Exchange of Medical Qigong, Beijing, 1993), pp. 97–98.

Bibliography: Selected and Recommended

CHINESE MEDICINE

Beinfield, Harriet, and Efrem Korngold. *Between Heaven and Earth: A Guide to Chinese Medicine*. New York: Ballantine Books, 1991.

Flaws, Bob, and Anna Lin. *The Dao of Increasing Longevity and Conserving One's Life: A Handbook of Traditional Chinese Geriatrics and Chinese Herbal Patent Medicines*. Boulder, CO: Blue Poppy Press, 1991.

Hammer, Leon, M.D. *Dragon Rises, Red Bird Flies: Psychology and Chinese Medicine*. Barrytown, NY: Station Hill Press, 1990.

Kaptchuk, Ted J., O.M.D. *The Web That Has No Weaver: Understanding Chinese Medicine*. New York: Congdon & Weed, Inc., 1983.

Larre, Claude, S.J., and Elisabeth Rochat de la Vallée. *Rooted in Spirit: The Heart of Chinese Medicine*. Barrytown, NY: Station Hill Press, 1995.

Seem, Mark, Ph.D., with Joan Kaplan. *BodyMind Energetics: Toward a Dynamic Model of Health*. Rochester, VT: Healing Arts Press, 1989.

Unschuld, Paul U. *Medicine in China: A History of Ideas*. Berkeley: University of California Press, 1985.

Veith, Ilza. *The Yellow Emperor's Classic of Internal Medicine*. Berkeley: University of California Press, 1966.

Wiseman, Nigel, Andrew Ellis, and Paul Zmiewski. *Fundamentals of Chinese Medicine*. Brookline, MA: Paradigm Publications, 1985.

Wu Jing-Nuan, trans. *Ling Shu or The Spiritual Pivot*. Honolulu: University of
    Hawaii Press, 1993.
Zhang Enqin, ed. *Health Preservation and Rehabilitation*. Shanghai: Shanghai
College of Traditional Chinese Medicine, 1990.

DAOIST PHILOSOPHY, RELIGION, AND CULTURE

Blofeld, John. *The Secret and Sublime: Taoist Mysteries and Magic*. NY: E. P.
    Dutton & Co., 1973.
———*Taoism: The Road to Immortality*. Boulder, CO: Shambala Pub-
    lications, 1978.
Chan, Wing-Tsit, trans. *The Way of Lao Tzu*. New York: The Bobbs-Merrill
    Co., 1963.
———*A Source Book in Chinese Philosophy*. Princeton, NJ: Princeton
    University Press, 1963.
Chang Chung-yuan. *Creativity and Taoism: A Study of Chinese Philosophy,
    Art, and Poetry*. New York: Harper & Row, 1970.
Cleary, Thomas, trans. and ed. *Immortal Sisters: Secrets of Taoist Women*.
    Boston: Shambala, 1989.
Fung Yu-Lan. *The Spirit of Chinese Philosophy*. Trans. by E. R. Hughes.
    Boston: Beacon Press, 1962.
Goullart, Peter. *The Monastery of Jade Mountain*. London: The Travel Book
    Club, 1961.
Graham, A. C. *Chuang Tzu: The Inner Chapters*. Boston: George Allen &
    Unwin, 1981.
Kaltenmark, Max. *Lao Tzu and Taoism*. Stanford, CA: Stanford University
    Press, 1969.
Kohn, Livia, ed. *The Taoist Experience: An Anthology*. Albany: State
    University of New York Press, 1993.
Lin Yutang. *The Importance of Living*. New York: John Day, 1937.
Needham, Joseph. *Science and Civilization in China*. Vol. 2. Cambridge:
    Cambridge University Press, 1975.
Paper, Jordan. *The Spirits Are Drunk: Comparative Approaches to Chinese
    Religion*. Albany: State University of New York Press, 1995.
Porter, Bill. *Road to Heaven: Encounters with Chinese Hermits*. San Francisco:
    Mercury House, 1993.
Schipper, Kristofer. *The Taoist Body*. Berkeley: University of California Press,
    1993.
Waley, Arthur. *The Way and Its Power: A Study of the Tao Te Ching*

and Its Place in Chinese Thought. London: George Allen & Unwin Ltd., 1968.

Watts, Alan. *Tao: The Watercourse Way*. New York: Pantheon Books, 1975.

Watson, Burton, trans. *Chuang Tzu: Basic Writings*. New York: Columbia University Press, 1964.

Welch, Holmes. *Taoism: The Parting of the Way*. Boston: Beacon Press, 1966.

DIET AND NUTRITION: EAST AND WEST

Anderson, E. N. *The Food of China*. New Haven: Yale University Press, 1988.

Carper, Jean. *Food—Your Miracle Medicine: How Food Can Prevent and Cure Over 100 Symptoms and Problems*. New York: HarperCollins, 1994.

Colbin, Annemarie. *Food and Healing*. New York: Ballantine, 1986.

Flaws, Bob. *Arisal of the Clear: A Simple Guide to Healthy Eating According to Traditional Chinese Medicine*. Boulder, CO: Blue Poppy Press, 1991.

———*The Book of Jook: Chinese Medicinal Porridges, a Healthy Alternative to the Typical Western Breakfast*. Boulder, CO: Blue Poppy Press, 1995.

Flaws, Bob, and Hanora Wolfe. *Prince Wen Hui's Cook: Chinese Dietary Therapy*. Brookline, MA: Paradigm Publications, 1983.

Lin, Hsiang Ju, and Tsuifeng Lin. *Chinese Gastronomy*. New York: Hastings House, 1969.

Liu Jilin, ed. *Chinese Dietary Therapy*. New York: Churchill Livingstone, 1995.

Lu, Henry C. *Chinese System of Food Cures: Prevention and Remedies*. New York: Sterling Publishing, 1986.

———*Chinese Foods for Longevity*. New York: Sterling Publishing, 1990.

Pauling, Linus. *How to Live Longer and Feel Better*. New York: W. H. Freeman & Co., 1986.

Pitchford, Paul. *Healing with Whole Foods: Oriental Traditions and Modern Nutrition*. Berkeley: North Atlantic Books, 1993.

Pfeiffer, Carl C., Ph.D., M.D. *Mental and Elemental Nutrients: A Physician's Guide to Nutrition and Health Care*. New Canaan, CT: Keats Publishing, 1975.

———*Nutrition and Mental Illness: An Orthomolecular Approach to Balancing Body Chemistry*. Rochester, VT: Healing Arts Press, 1987.

Saso, Michael. *A Taoist Cookbook: With Meditations Taken from the Laozi Daode Jing*. Rutland, VT: Tuttle, 1994.

Sears, Barry, Ph.D. *The Zone: A Dietary Road Map*. New York: HarperCollins, 1995.

Walford, Roy, L., M.D. *The 120-Year Diet: How to Double Your Vital Years.* New York: Simon & Schuster, 1986.

Williams, Dr. Roger J. *Nutrition Against Disease.* New York: Bantam Books, 1981.

MIND-BODY MEDICINE

Achterberg, Jeanne. *Imagery in Healing: Shamanism and Modern Medicine.* Boston: Shambala, 1985.

Achterberg, Jeanne, Ph.D.; Barbara Dossey, R.N., M.S., F.A.A.N.; and Leslie Kolkmeier, R.N., M.Ed. *Rituals of Healing: Using Imagery for Health and Wellness.* New York: Bantam Books, 1994.

Alon, Ruthy. *Mindful Spontaneity: Moving in Tune with Nature: Lessons in the Feldenkrais Method.* Garden City Park, New York: Avery Publishing Group, 1990.

Alternative Medicine: Expanding Medical Horizons. Washington, D.C.: NIH Publication No. 94-066, 1992.

Barasch, Marc Ian. *The Healing Path: A Soul Approach to Illness.* New York: Penguin Books, 1993.

Becker, Robert O., M.D., and Gary Selden. *The Body Electric: Electromagnetism and the Foundation of Life.* New York: William Morrow & Co, Inc., 1985.

Benor, Daniel J., M.D. *Healing Research.* Vols. 1 & 2. Deddington, Oxfordshire, U.K.: Helix Editions, Ltd., 1992.

Bird, Christopher, and Peter Tompkins. *Secrets of the Soil.* New York: Harper & Row, 1989.

Borysenko, Joan, Ph.D. *Minding the Body, Mending the Mind.* New York: Bantam, 1988.

Brooks, Charles V. W. *Sensory Awareness: The Rediscovery of Experiencing.* New York: Viking Press, 1974.

Chopra, Deepak, M.D. *Ageless Body, Timeless Mind: The Quantum Alternative to Growing Old.* New York: Crown Publishers, 1993.

———*Quantum Healing.* New York: Bantam Books. 1989.

Colborn, Theo, Dianne Dumanaski, and John Peterson Myers. *Our Stolen Future: Are We Threatening Our Fertility, Intelligence, and Survival?—A Scientific Detective Story.* New York: Dutton, 1996.

Cousins, Norman. *Anatomy of an Illness as Perceived by the Patient: Reflections on Healing and Regeneration.* New York: W. W. Norton & Company, 1979.

Dossey, Larry, M.D. *Healing Words: The Power of Prayer and the Practice of Medicine.* San Francisco: HarperCollins, 1993.

————*Meaning and Medicine: Lessons from a Doctor's Tales of Breakthrough and Healing.* New York: Bantam Books, 1991.

Epstein, Gerald, M.D. *Healing Visualizations: Creating Health Through Imagery.* New York: Bantam Books, 1989.

Feldenkrais, Moshe. *The Potent Self: A Guide to Spontaneity.* San Francisco: Harper & Row, 1985.

————*Awareness Through Movement: Health Exercises for Personal Growth.* New York: Harper & Row, 1972.

Fisher, Jeffrey A., M.D. *The Plague Makers: How We Are Creating Catastrophic New Epidemics—and What We Must Do to Avert Them.* New York: Simon & Schuster, 1994.

Frank, Jerome D., Ph.D., M.D., and Julia B. Frank, M.D. *Persuasion and Healing: A Comparative Study of Psychotherapy,* 3rd ed. Baltimore, MD: The Johns Hopkins University Press, 1991.

Fried, Robert, with Joseph Grimaldi. *The Psychology and Physiology of Breathing: In Behavioral Medicine, Clinical Psychology, and Psychiatry.* New York: Plenum Press, 1993.

Fried, Robert, Ph.D. *The Breath Connection: How to Reduce Psychosomatic and Stress-Related Disorders with Easy-to-Do Breathing Exercises.* New York: Plenum Press, 1990.

Goleman, Daniel, Ph.D., and Joel Gurin, eds. *Mind Body Medicine.* Yonkers, New York: Consumer Reports Books, 1993.

Green, Elmer, and Alyce Green. *Beyond Biofeedback.* New York: Dell Publishing Co., 1978.

Grof, Stanislav, M.D., and Christina Grof. *Spiritual Emergency.* Los Angeles: Jeremy P. Tarcher, 1989.

Keleman, Stanley. *Somatic Reality.* Berkeley: Center Press, 1979.

Kabat-Zinn, Jon, Ph.D. *Full Catastrophe Living: Using the Wisdom of Your Body and Mind to Face Stress, Pain, and Illness.* New York: Dell, 1990.

Krieger, Dolores, Ph.D., R.N. *Accepting Your Power to Heal: The Personal Practice of Therapeutic Touch.* Santa Fe: Bear & Co., 1993.

Liberman, Jacob, O.D., Ph.D. *Light: Medicine of the Future; How We Can Use It to Heal Ourselves Now.* Santa Fe: Bear & Company, 1991.

Locke, Steven, M.D., and Douglas Colligan. *The Healer Within: The New Medicine of Mind and Body.* New York: Penguin Books, 1986.

Lowen, Alexander, M.D. *Bioenergetics.* New York: Coward, McCann & Geoghegan, 1975.

Macrae, Janet. *Therapeutic Touch: A Practical Guide.* New York: Knopf, 1988.

Mann, John. *Secrets of Life Extension.* Berkeley: And/Or Press, 1980.

Meek, George W., ed. *Healers and the Healing Process.* Wheaton, IL: Theosophical Publishing House, 1977.

Murphy, Michael. *The Future of the Body: Explorations into the Further Evolution of Human Nature*. Los Angeles: Jeremy P. Tarcher, 1993.

Northrup, Christiane, M.D. *Women's Bodies, Women's Wisdom: Creating Physical and Emotional Health and Healing*. New York: Bantam, 1994.

Ornish, Dean, M.D. *Dr. Dean Ornish's Program for Reversing Heart Disease*. New York: Ballantine Books, 1990.

Ornstein, Robert, Ph.D., and David Sobel, M.D. *The Healing Brain: Breakthrough Discoveries About How the Brain Keeps Us Healthy*. New York: Simon & Schuster, 1988.

Pelletier, Kenneth R. *Mind as Healer Mind as Slayer*. New York: Dell Publishing Co., 1977.

———*Sound Mind, Sound Body: A New Model for Lifelong Health*. New York: Simon & Schuster, 1994.

Rolf, Ida P., Ph.D. *Rolfing: The Integration of Human Structures*. New York: Harper & Row, 1977.

Sapolsky, Robert M. *Why Zebras Don't Get Ulcers: A Guide to Stress, Stress-Related Diseases, and Coping*. New York: W. H. Freeman and Company, 1994.

Shealy, C. Norman, M.D., Ph.D. *Miracles Do Happen: A Physician's Experience with Alternative Medicine*. Rockport, MA: Element Books, 1995.

Shealy, C. Norman, M.D., Ph.D., and Caroline M. Myss, M.A. *The Creation of Health: The Emotional, Psychological, and Spiritual Responses That Promote Health and Healing*. Walpole, NH: Stillpoint Publishing, 1993.

Tart, Charles T., ed. *Altered States of Consciousness*. New York: HarperCollins, 1990.

Timmons, Beverly H., and Ronald Ley, eds. *Behavioral and Psychological Approaches to Breathing Disorders*. New York: Plenum Press, 1994.

Todd, Mabel Elsworth. *The Thinking Body: A Study of the Balancing Forces of Dynamic Man*. New York: Dance Horizons, Inc., 1977.

Walford, Roy L., M.D. *Maximum Life Span*. New York: W. W. Norton, 1983.

Weil, Andrew, M.D. *Health and Healing: Understanding Conventional and Alternative Medicine*. Boston: Houghton Mifflin, 1983.

———*Spontaneous Healing: How to Discover and Enhance Your Body's Natural Ability to Maintain and Heal Itself*. New York: Knopf, 1995.

Whitehead, Alfred North. *Science and the Modern World*. New York: Macmillan, 1967.

QIGONG PRACTICES:
HEALING AND MEDITATION

Bi Yongsheng and Yu Wenping, trans. *Chinese Qigong Outgoing-Qi Therapy.* Jinan, P.R.C.: Shandong Science and Technology Press, 1992.

Bi Yongsheng and Yu Wenping, eds. *Medical Qigong.* Vol. 8 of *The English-Chinese Encyclopedia of Practical Traditional Chinese Medicine.* Beijing: Higher Education Press, 1990.

Brown, Stephen, and Masaru Takahashi. *Qigong for Health: Chinese Traditional Exercises for Cure and Prevention.* Tokyo: Japan Publications, 1986.

Chan, Luke. *101 Miracles of Natural Healing.* Cincinnati, OH: Benefactor Press, 1996.

Chang, Dr. Stephen T. *The Complete System of Self-Healing: Internal Exercises.* San Francisco: Tao Publishing, 1986.

Chia, Mantak. *Awaken Healing Energy Through the Tao.* New York: Aurora Press, 1983.

———*Chi Self-Massage: The Taoist Way of Rejuvenation.* Huntington, NY: Healing Tao Books, 1986.

Cleary, Thomas, trans. *The Secret of the Golden Flower.* San Francisco: Harper Collins, 1991.

Diepersloot, Jan. *Warriors of Stillness: Meditative Traditions in the Chinese Martial Arts.* Vol. 1. Walnut Creek, CA: Center for Healing & the Arts, 1995.

Dong, Paul, and Aristide H. Esser. *Chi Gong: The Ancient Chinese Way to Health.* New York: Paragon House, 1990.

Dong, Paul, and Thomas Raffill. *Empty Force: The Ultimate Martial Art.* Rockport, MA: Element Books, 1996.

Eisenberg, David, M.D. *Encounters with Qi: Exploring Chinese Medicine.* New York: W. W. Norton & Co., 1985.

Flaws, Bob. *Imperial Secrets of Health and Longevity.* Boulder, CO: Blue Poppy Press, 1994.

Gallagher, Paul B. *Drawing Silk: A Training Manual for T'ai Chi.* Guilford, VT: Deer Mountain Taoist Academy, 1988.

Hu Bing. *A Brief Introduction to the Science of Breathing Exercise.* Hong Kong: Hai Feng Publishing Co., 1982.

Hu Zhaoyun, ed. *Chinese Qigong.* Shanghai: Publishing House of Shanghai College of Traditional Chinese Medicine, 1988.

Huard, Dr. Pierre, and Ming Wong. *Oriental Methods of Mental and Physical Fitness: The Complete Book of Meditation, Kinesitherapy & Martial Arts in China, India & Japan.* New York: Funk & Wagnalls, 1977.

Huai-Chin Nan. *Tao & Longevity: Mind-Body Transformation*. Translated by Wen Kuan Chu, Ph.D. York Beach, ME: Samuel Weiser, Inc., 1984.

Hwang, Shi Fu, and Cheney Crow, Ph.D., trans. Yin Shih Tzu's *Tranquil Sitting*. St. Paul: Dragon Door Publications, 1994.

Jiao Guorui. *Qigong Essentials for Health Promotion*. Beijing: China Reconstructs Press, 1988.

Kohn, Livia, ed. *Taoist Meditation and Longevity Techniques*. Ann Arbor: University of Michigan Press, 1989.

Lam Kam Chuen, Master. *The Way of Energy: Mastering the Chinese Art of Internal Strength with Chi Kung Exercise*. New York: Simon & Schuster, 1991.

Lin Housheng and Luo Peiyu. *300 Questions on Qigong Exercises*. Guangzhou, China: Guangdong Science and Technology Press, 1994.

Lin Yun and Sarah Rossbach. *Living Color: Master Lin Yun's Guide to Feng Shui and the Art of Color*. New York: Kodansha America, 1994.

Liu Zhengcai. *The Mystery of Longevity*. Beijing: Foreign Languages Press, 1990.

Maspero, Henri. *Taoism and Chinese Religion*. Amherst: University of Massachusetts Press, 1981.

Masunaga, Shizuto, with Stephen Brown. *Zen Imagery Exercises: Meridian Exercises for Wholesome Living*. New York: Japan Publications, 1987.

Needham, Joseph. *Science and Civilization in China*. Vol. 5, Pt 5. Cambridge: Cambridge University Press, 1983.

Robinet, Isabelle. *Taoist Meditation: The Mao-shan Tradition of Great Purity*. Translated by Julian F. Pas and Norman J. Girardot. Albany: State University of New York Press, 1993.

Saso, Michael. *The Gold Pavilion: Taoist Ways to Peace, Healing, and Long Life*. Rutland, VT: Tuttle, 1995.

Shih, T. K. *The Swimming Dragon: A Chinese Way to Fitness, Beautiful Skin, Weight Loss & High Energy*. Barrytown, NY: Station Hill Press, 1989.

Tohei, Koichi. *Book of Ki: Co-ordinating Mind and Body in Daily Life*. New York: Japan Publications, 1976.

Tung, Timothy, trans. *Wushu!: The Chinese Way to Family Health & Fitness*. New York: Simon & Schuster, 1981.

Wang, Simon, M.D., Ph.D., and Julius L. Liu, M.D. *Qi Gong for Health & Longevity: The Ancient Chinese Art of Relaxation/Meditation/Physical Fitness*. Tustin, CA: The East Health Development Group, 1994.

QIGONG PRACTICES:
INNER MARTIAL ARTS

Chen, William C. C. *Body Mechanics of Tai Chi Chuan*. New York: William C.C. Chen, 1985.

Cheng Man Ch'ing. *Cheng Tzu's Thirteen Treatises on T'ai Chi Ch'uan*. Translated by Benjamin Pang Jeng Lo and Martin Inn. Berkeley: North Atlantic Books, 1985.

Delza, Sophia. *T'ai-Chi Ch'üan: Body and Mind in Harmony: The Integration of Meaning and Method*. Albany: State University of New York Press, 1985.

Jou, Tsung Hwa. *The Tao of Tai-Chi Chuan*. Rutland, VT: Charles E. Tuttle, 1980.

Liang, Master T. T. *T'ai Chi Ch'uan for Health and Self-Defense: Philosophy and Practice*. Edited by Paul B. Gallagher. New York: Vintage Books, 1977.

Liang Shou-yu, Master, and Dr. Yang Jwing-Ming. *Chinese Internal Martial Art: Hsing Yi Chuan; Theory and Applications*. Jamaica Plain, MA: Yang's Martial Arts Association, 1990.

Liang Shou-yu, Master, Dr. Yang Jwing Ming, and Mr. Wu Wen-Ching. *Chinese Internal Martial Art: Baguazhang (Emei Baguazhang): Theory and Applications*. Jamaica Plain, MA: Yang's Martial Arts Association, 1994.

Liang Shou-yu, Master, and Wu Wen-Ching. *A Guide to Taijiquan: 24 and 48 Postures with Applications*. Jamaica Plain, MA: Yang's Martial Arts Association, 1993.

Liao, Waysun. *T'ai Chi Classics*. Boston: Shambala Publications, 1990.

McNeil, Master James W. *Hsing-I*. Burbank, CA: Unique Publications, 1991.

Miller, Dan, and Tim Cartmell. *Xing Yi Nei Gong: Xing Yi Health Maintenance and Internal Strength Development*. Pacific Grove, CA: High View Publications, 1994.

Olson, Stuart Alve, trans. *The Intrinsic Energies of T'ai Chi Ch'uan*. Chen Kung Series, vol. 2. St. Paul, MN: Dragon Door Publications, 1995.

Pang, T. Y. *On Tai Chi Chuan*. Bellingham, WA: Azalea Press, 1987.

Park Bok Nam and Dan Miller. *The Fundamentals of Pa Kua Chang: The Method of Lu Shui-T'ien as Taught by Park Bok Nam*. Pacific Grove, CA: High View Publications, 1993.

Smith, Robert W. *Chinese Boxing: Masters and Methods*. New York: Kodansha International, Ltd., 1974.

Stevens, John. *Abundant Peace: The Biography of Morihei Ueshiba, Founder of Aikido*. Boston: Shambala Publications, 1987.

Suzuki, D. T. *Zen and Japanese Culture*. Princeton, NJ: Princeton University Press, 1970.

Wile, Douglas, trans. *T'ai-chi Touchstones: Yang Family Secret Transmissions.* Brooklyn, NY: Sweet Ch'i Press, 1983.

QIGONG PRACTICES: SEXUAL

Chang, Jolan. *The Tao of Love and Sex: The Ancient Chinese Way to Ecstasy.* New York: E. P. Dutton, 1977.

Chang, Dr. Stephen T. *The Tao of Sexology: The Book of Infinite Wisdom.* San Francisco: Tao Publishing, 1986.

Chia, Mantak, and Maneewan Chia. *Healing Love Through the Tao: Cultivating Female Sexual Energy.* Huntington, NY: Healing Tao Books, 1986.

Chia, Mantak, and Michael Winn. *Taoist Secrets of Love: Cultivating Male Sexual Energy.* New York: Aurora Press, 1984.

Van Gulik, R. H. *Sexual Life in Ancient China.* Leiden: E. J. Brill, 1974.

Watts, Alan. *Nature, Man and Woman.* New York: Vintage Books, 1970.

Wile, Douglas. *Art of the Bedchamber: The Chinese Sexual Yoga Classics Including Women's Solo Meditation Texts.* Albany: State University of New York Press, 1992.

QIGONG HUMOR

Does such a thing exist? It should! A healthy dose of humor is a good way to keep your qigong enthusiasm in balance and an antidote to early cases of qigong fanaticism. "Mom, I need a quarter for the gummy ball machine." Mom: "Sorry, wrong protein to carbohydrate ratio."

If you are willing to dedicate your life to a daily regimen of qigong, meditation, Chinese language study, perfect nutrition, and espresso denial, while living in a pristine natural environment without electricity (to avoid electromagnetic fields), refrigeration (so food must always be either fresh or rotten), or TV, with only skunk, mice, and health nerds for neighbors, then do not read these books:

Adams, Patch, M.D., with Maureen Mylander. *Gesundheit! Bringing Good Health to You, the Medical System, and Society Through Physician Service, Complementary Therapies, Humor, and Joy.* Rochester, VT: Healing Arts Press, 1993.

Barry, Dave. *Dave Barry Turns 40.* New York: Ballantine Books, 1990.

———*Stay Fit & Healthy Until You're Dead.* Emmaus, PA: Rodale Press, 1985.

Hyers, Conrad. *Zen and the Comic Spirit.* Philadelphia: The Westminster Press, 1973.

Klein, Allen. *The Healing Power of Humor*. Los Angeles: Jeremy P. Tarcher, Inc., 1989.

Wooten, Patty, R.N. *Compassionate Laughter: Jest for Your Health*. Salt Lake City, UT: Commune-A-Key Publishing, 1996.

TEA

Blofeld, John. *The Chinese Art of Tea*. Boston: Shambala Publications, 1985.

Chow, Kit, and Ione Kramer. *All the Tea in China*. San Francisco: China Books and Periodicals, 1990.

Lu Yu. *The Classic of Tea*. Translated by Francis Ross Carpenter. Boston: Little, Brown and Company, 1974.

Okakura, Kakuzo. *The Book of Tea*. New York: Kodansha International, 1989.

Sen, Soshitsu XV. *Tea Life, Tea Mind*. New York: Weatherhill, Inc., 1979.

OTHER HEALING TRADITIONS

Beck, Peggy V., and Anna L. Walters. *The Sacred: Ways of Knowledge, Sources of Life*. Tsaile (Navajo Nation), AZ: Navajo Community College, 1977.

Chishti, Shaykh Hakim Moinuddin. *The Book of Sufi Healing*. Rochester, VT: Inner Traditions, 1991.

Goodman, Felicitas D. *Where Spirits Ride the Wind: Trance Journeys and Other Ecstatic Experiences*. Bloomington: Indiana University Press, 1990.

Iyengar, B. K. S. *Light on Pranayama*. New York: Crossroad Publishing Co., 1981.

———*Light on Yoga*. New York: Schocken Books, 1974.

Katz, Richard. *Boiling Energy: Community Healing among the Kalahari Kung*. Cambridge: Harvard University Press, 1982.

Kleinman, Arthur. *Patients and Healers in the Context of Culture: An Exploration of the Borderland Between Anthropology, Medicine, and Psychiatry*. Berkeley: University of California Press, 1980.

Krippner, Stanley, and Patrick Welch. *Spiritual Dimensions of Healing: From Native Shamanism to Contemporary Health Care*. New York: Irvington Publishers, 1992.

Lad, Vasant. *Ayurveda: The Science of Self-Healing*. Santa Fe: Lotus Press, 1985.

Lawlor, Robert. *Voices of the First Day: Awakening in the Aboriginal Dreamtime*. Rochester, VT: Inner Traditions, 1991.

Long, Max Freedom. *Mana or Vital Force (Selections from Huna Research Bulletins)*. Cape Girardeau, MO: Huna Research, Inc., 1981.

Markides, Kyriacos C. *The Magus of Strovolos: The Extraordinary World of a Spiritual Healer.* New York: Penguin Books, 1985.

Pukui, Mary Kawena, E. W. Haertig, M.D., and Catherine A. Lee. *Nana I Ke Kumu (Look to the Source).* Vol. 2. Honolulu: Queen Lili'uokalani Children's Center, 1979.

Svoboda, Robert E. *Ayurveda: Life, Health and Longevity.* New York: Penguin Books, 1992.

Worrall, Ambrose A., and Olga N. Worrall. *The Gift of Healing: A Personal Story of Spiritual Therapy.* Columbus, OH: Ariel Press, 1985.

JOURNALS

Advances: The Journal of Mind-Body Health. Kalamazoo, MI: The John E. Fetzer Institute, Inc. (800) 875-2997.

Alternative & Complementary Therapies. Larchmont, NY: Mary Ann Liebert, Inc. (914) 834-3100, (800) M-LIEBERT.

Alternative Therapies in Health and Medicine. Aliso Viejo, CA: Inno Vision Communications. (800) 345-8112.

The Journal of Alternative and Complementary Medicine: Research on Paradigm, Practice, and Policy. Larchmont, NY: Mary Ann Liebert, Inc. (914) 834-3100, (800) M-LIEBERT.

Journal of Asian Martial Arts. Erie, PA: Via Media Publishing. (800) 455-9517.

Journal of Holistic Nursing. Thousand Oaks, CA: Sage Publications, Inc. (805) 499-0721.

Natural Health. Brookline Village, MA: Natural Health Limited Partnership. (800) 526-8440.

New Age Journal. Watertown, MA: New Age Publishing. (815) 734-5808, (800) 755-1178.

Noetic Sciences Review. Sausalito, CA: The Institute of Noetic Sciences. (415) 331-5650.

Qi: The Journal of Traditional Eastern Health and Fitness. Anaheim Hills, CA: Insight Graphics, Inc. (800) 787-2600.

Subtle Energies. Golden, CO: The International Society for the Study of Subtle Energy and Energy Medicine. (303) 278-2228.

T'ai Chi Magazine. Los Angles: Wayfarer Publications. (213) 665-7773, (800) 888-9119.

Yoga Journal. Berkeley, CA: California Yoga Teachers Association. (800) 334-8152.

DISTRIBUTORS OF QIGONG BOOKS

Blue Poppy Press. (800) 487-9296
Dragon Door Publications. (800) 247-6553, (612) 645-0517
Redwing Book Company. (800) 873-3946, (617) 738-4664
Wayfarer Publications. (800) 888-9119, (213) 665-7773

COMPUTER DATABASE

The Qigong Database™ for Macintosh and IBM/DOS compatible computers has bibliographic references for more than 1,000 qigong science abstracts from journals and conference proceedings, including more than 600 complete abstracts. Not all studies follow strict scientific (or grammatical) standards; nevertheless, there are many gems here. Hard copies of conference proceedings are also available. Write: The Qigong Institute, East West Academy of Healing Arts, attn. Dr. Sancier, 450 Sutter Street, Suite 916, San Francisco, CA 94108.

Fine Tea

Blue Willow Tea Company™
(800) 328-0353

The Republic of Tea®
(800) 298-4832

Grace Tea Company Ltd.
(212) 255-2935

Silk Road Teas
(415) 488-9017

Imperial Tea Court
(800) 567-5898

Ten Ren Tea Company®
(800) 292-2049

Further information about tea and tea suppliers can be found in the pages of *Tea: A Magazine*. P.O. Box 348, Scotland, CT 06264. (860) 456-1145.

Audio-Video Training With Kenneth S. Cohen

Published and distributed by Sounds True®, Boulder, Colorado.
(800) 333-9185

AUDIO COURSES

Chi Kung Meditations.
Taoist Healing Imagery.

The Way of Chi Kung.
Healthy Breathing.

VIDEO

Qigong: Traditional Chinese Exercises for Healing the Body, Mind, and Spirit.

Index

ABOUT THE AUTHOR

Kenneth S. Cohen, M.A., is a renowned qigong master, China scholar, and health educator. He is one of the pioneers introducing qigong to the West and establishing a bridge between qigong and medical science. He was one of nine exceptional healers studied in the Menninger Clinic's Copper Wall Project. Ken began his qigong training in 1968. He is a graduate of the William C. C. Chen School of T'ai Chi Ch'uan and also studied with Masters B. P. Chan, Madame Gao Fu, and others. He was an apprentice to Daoist Master Rev. K. S. Wong, C.A., Ph.D., and collaborated with Alan Watts in the 1970s. Academically, Ken pursued Chinese language and Daoist studies at Queens College, the New School for Social Research, and the University of California at Berkeley. Ken is an Adjunct Professor at Union Graduate School and a popular conference speaker. He has previously written more than 150 journal articles and is the author of the bestselling "Way of Chi Kung" audio course (Sounds True).

In addition to his training in qigong, Ken has devoted more than twenty years to the study of indigenous medicine, working closely with Native American and African healers. In 1994, he was asked to represent both Chinese and Indigenous Medicine at the World Congress on Energy Medicine in Switzerland.

Ken lives with his wife and daughter at 9,000 ft. elevation where, as he puts it, "just breathing is qigong!"